TRAPPED BY SUCCESS

CONTEMPORARY AMERICAN HISTORY SERIES

William E. Leuchtenburg, General Editor

CONTEMPORARY AMERICAN HISTORY SERIES

WILLIAM E. LEUCHTENBURG, GENERAL EDITOR

TRAPPED BY SUCCESS

The Eisenhower Administration and Vietnam, 1953–1961

David L. Anderson

Columbia University Press
New York

HOUSTON PUBLIC LIBRARY

Columbia University Press
New York   Oxford
Copyright © 1991 Columbia University Press
All rights reserved

Library of Congress Cataloging-in-Publication Data

Anderson, David L., 1946–
Trapped by success : the Eisenhower administration and Vietnam, 1953–1961 / David L. Anderson.
p.   cm. — (Contemporary American history series)
Includes bibliographical references and index.
ISBN: 0-231-07374-7
1. United States—Foreign relations—1953–1961.   2. United States—Foreign relations—Vietnam.   3. Vietnam—Foreign relations—United States.   4. Eisenhower, Dwight D. (Dwight David), 1890–1969.
I. Title.   II. Series.
E835.A72   1991
327.730597—dc20   90-19794
                                                   CIP

Casebound editions of Columbia University Press books are Smyth-sewn and printed on permanent and durable acid-free paper

Printed in the United States of America

c 10 9 8 7 6 5 4 3 2 1
p 10 9 8 7 6 5 4 3 2 1

To my parents and in-laws
Lucille and Benjamin Anderson
Eleanor and Herbert Fleischer

CONTENTS

Contents

PREFACE

All you need in life is ignorance and confidence, and then success is sure.

—MARK TWAIN

Irony pervades the history of American involvement in Vietnam. Not the least of many incongruities is the striking contrast between the early self-assurance and the eventual self-doubt that characterized American thought about the Indochina conflict. In the 1950s, the Eisenhower administration proclaimed the fate of Vietnam to be of vital strategic importance to the United States and initiated a determined effort to deny control of that country to America's perceived enemies. Limited accomplishments during the decade deluded American leaders into taking on steadily increasing risks, costs, and commitments in Southeast Asia. To borrow from Mark Twain's wry observation, ignorance and confidence bred an illusion of success that trapped Eisenhower and subsequent U.S. presidents in a frustrating and futile effort to define and defend U.S. interests in Vietnam.

This book is an examination of the role of the Eisenhower administration in the origins of what became a massive U.S. war in Vietnam in the 1960s. Numerous other studies have probed for explanations of the American military intervention. As time has passed since the end of the Vietnam War, as more sources have become available to historians, and as the public debate over Vietnam has become less acrimonious, there has been a discernible evolution in the historiography on the origins of the war. Unlike the pattern of scholarship on other twentieth-century wars, initial studies of the Indochina conflict were highly critical of American policy. They employed concepts such as quagmire, stalemate, and flawed containment to describe U.S. actions. About the time of Ronald Reagan's election as president, however, a new interpretation, which characterized the war as a noble effort, gained some acceptance. This hawkish revisionism is now being answered by postrevisionist works, but these latest studies do not simply revive the earlier critiques.[1]

The various theories of causation address the official U.S. government rationale for intervention, an explanation that endured throughout the years of the American involvement in Vietnam. Beginning with President Harry Truman and his advisers, many U.S. officials decreed that Vietnam was a target of Soviet and Chinese communist aggression. In a conscious application of the so-called Munich analogy, these American leaders believed that communist dictatorship, like fascist dictatorship in the 1930s, had to be confronted forcefully and not appeased. Eisenhower agreed and declared that Vietnam and the nations of Southeast Asia were joined together with the United States and its allies "in the never-ending struggle to stem the tide of Communist expansion."[2] Despite increasing costs and risks, American strategists persisted in this effort through the 1950s and 1960s and into the 1970s.

Two of the earliest critiques of the seeming inability of U.S. policy makers to abandon an ever more perilous course in Vietnam are the quagmire thesis and the stalemate argument. According to the first of these interpretations, a sequence of small steps, each believed to be the last needed (or at least a move away from a larger problem), led deeper and deeper into a major U.S. commitment in Vietnam. Because of misunderstandings and miscalculations, the United States found itself inadvertently entangled in a course of action in which withdrawal posed as difficult an option as continuation. This unanticipated dilemma led historian Arthur M. Schlesinger, Jr., to write in 1967 that the American war in Vietnam was "a tragedy without villains."[3]

Like the quagmire thesis, the stalemate argument focuses on the process of gradually deepening involvement, but it challenges the notion that America's political leaders were innocent victims of their own naiveté. Advanced initially by bureaucrats who had an insider's perspective on government decisions, the stalemate theory contends that expert advisers made American leaders well aware that there were no good solutions for the United States in Vietnam and that the prospect of

American success was not promising. This cynical interpretation alleges that, from Truman through Richard Nixon, presidents waged a limited war designed primarily to avoid a military defeat and, hence, a political disaster during the incumbent's term.[4]

Despite the apparent differences between the stalemate and quagmire interpretations, the actual process of involvement may have included both elements. Each may have characterized different officials or the same officials at different times. Secretary of State John Foster Dulles, for example, starting from a stalemate position of wanting merely to stave off disaster in Indochina, eventually came to a belief, like that suggested by the quagmire concept, that a little more time and effort would bring victory.

Underlying the official rationale for involvement, and most of the criticisms of it, is the presumption that America's basic cold war strategy of containment shaped policy in Vietnam. Consequently, many historians have long accepted an analysis of U.S. intervention in Vietnam known as flawed containment. This argument holds that a policy developed for Europe was not directly applicable to Asia, that it overextended U.S. power around the globe, and that it was too narrow and inflexible to respond effectively to complex social revolutions. George F. Kennan, the architect of the containment strategy, later complained about the globalization and militarization of the doctrine.[5] His original formulation addressed a specific threat, namely the Soviet military and political presence in Eastern Europe, and it advocated precise economic, political, and military countermeasures based on the capabilities of the well-established nations of Western Europe. These same preconditions did not exist in Southeast Asia. The Soviet Army was not poised on the borders of Indochina. Furthermore, the states of the region—just emerging from years of colonial exploitation—generally lacked even the rudimentary structures necessary for conducting government, business, and war.

Regardless of the inherent differences in the sociopolitical environments of Europe and Asia, the revisionist historians revive the Truman-Eisenhower emphasis on Soviet-American confrontation and defend the decision to draw the containment line at the seventeenth parallel that divided North and South Vietnam. They contend that the U.S. war effort in Vietnam was a justifiable, indeed moral, stand in defense of freedom against tyranny and that the war could have and should have been won.

Preface

The unrelenting negativism of Vietnam War critics, in their view, continues a pattern of self-doubt and self-defeat that can endanger American security.[6]

Postrevisionists question whether greater American willpower or firepower was the answer to the Vietnam challenge, but they are more sympathetic to U.S. decision makers as victims of ignorance or circumstance than were some earlier critics. These historians are searching for more pervasive pathologies in American society to explain the origins of the Vietnam War. Some of the themes that they examine include cultural ignorance or prejudice, economic imperatives or neocolonialism, and domestic political pressures. As historian Robert A. Divine has written, scholars are moving beyond "condemnation of a wicked policy to search for an understanding of how a great nation could go wrong."[7]

Not only the origins but also the policy implications of the war divide scholars. Retrospective assessments present a range of four interpretations. At one extreme is the isolationist "no more Vietnams" school that finds problems indigenous to other peoples beyond the capability of the United States and hence to be avoided. In the middle are two deterministic interpretations. The more radical of these is the "inevitability" school, which holds that the war demonstrated America's compulsion to be number one in the world. Eisenhower detected evidence of such arrogance in the attitude of some Americans and condemned the notion as befitting Genghis Khan.[8] More moderate is the "diplomatic intervention" school, which maintains that great power brings global responsibilities that the United States cannot avoid whether it takes or shuns action in a specific case. The fourth interpretation, at the opposite extreme from the "no more Vietnams" view, is the "win" school. It complements the revisionist explanation of the origins of the war and maintains that Vietnam was not and need not remain a lost cause. Assuming the war should have been fought, this view asserts that, with proper methods, the war could have been won.[9]

This last argument is particularly disquieting for Americans accustomed to thinking of their nation as invincible. Proponents of the "win" thesis contend that the United States did not exert enough force in Indochina from America's vast military arsenal. The statistics on American deaths, casualties, bombs, and dollars are staggering, however, and place Vietnam among America's largest military efforts, surpassing even World War II in total bombing tonnage. This massive destruction fell short of achieving victory, the "win" advocates counter, because the United States suffered a failure of will and because defeatists (perhaps even traitors) in the media or antiwar movement undermined the war effort. Conversely, measurements of public opinion reveal that most Americans supported the U.S. role in Vietnam from the 1950s through the late 1960s. For over a decade, the media and public gave the U.S. government virtually a free hand, but no victory was gained over that period. Even after the public began to waver and doubt at the time of the 1968 Tet Offensive, many Americans continued to support the war well into the 1970s.[10]

Rather than concentrating on the means, including the power and determination of the United States, analysis of the American debacle in Vietnam must consider the ends. What was America's goal in Vietnam? Inherent in the argument that the United States could have "won" in Vietnam is the assumption that it had an obtainable objective in the conflict. From the termination of France's Indochina War in 1954 to the end of America's Indochina War in 1975, the U.S. goal was the survival of an independent, noncommunist, pro-Western government in Vietnam south of the seventeenth parallel to provide a Vietnamese nationalist alternative to the communist Democratic Republic of Vietnam in the North. In the global defense against international communism, known as the containment policy, South Vietnam was to join the list of other fragmented nations—West Germany, South Korea, and Taiwan—as cold war bastions in the moral, economic, and strategic fight against the spread of godless, totalitarian, and aggressive communism emanating from Moscow in Europe and Beijing in Asia.

This book analyzes the Eisenhower administration's decision to pursue that goal, and it assesses Washington's efforts over Eisenhower's eight years in office to achieve America's purposes in Vietnam. The Eisenhower administration simply postponed the day of reckoning in Vietnam. Contrary to the stalemate theory that American leaders were putting up a bold but purposefully bogus front of success in Vietnam, Eisenhower and his advisers believed that time was on their side. As the quagmire thesis suggests, Washington deceived itself about progress in Vietnam, while in fact the stakes were getting higher and a tough problem was getting even more difficult. The Eisenhower policies were also an example of flawed containment. U.S. strategy was negative. It sought to hold off defeat and wait for a better day with little regard for the internal dynamics of Vietnamese society. Indeed, the administration's wholehearted support of South Vietnamese president Ngo Dinh Diem obstructed political reform.

Other historical studies of Eisenhower's Vietnam policies, many of which are less critical, have concentrated largely on U.S. reaction to the climactic French battle at Dienbienphu and the Geneva Conference of 1954 that ended France's Indochina War. Scholars have chosen these subjects because of both their inherent significance in the chronicle of U.S. involvement in Southeast Asia and the availability of archival sources to document U.S. government activity through 1954. This present study benefits from the release in 1987 of a large block of previously classified State Department records for the period 1955–59. These records combined with White House files, collections of personal papers, and published government documents detail much more of the Eisenhower team's management of the Vietnam issue than has been known. Some individual documents and other files, especially those containing information about intelligence operations and agencies, still remain classified.

The recent accessibility of government records from the 1950s helped me make the decision to write this book now, but the origins of the project were more personal. I served in the U.S. Army in Vietnam during most of 1970. Like many Vietnam veterans and others of the Vietnam generation that reached adulthood in the late 1960s and early 1970s, I have had a need to know how and why this national trauma occurred. When some of the events described in this book took place, I was still a child playing army, and, when I grew up, those same events lay behind the very real combat that I witnessed. The Vietnam War was part of my own passage from innocence to maturity, and, with the benefit of historical perspective, hopefully it can be a growth experience for the American nation.

Many individuals provided me invaluable assistance with the research and preparation of this monograph. I am grateful to Robert Ferrell, who was of great help in initiating and facilitating the research. Nancy and Michael Rubino made it possible for me to talk with her father, J. Lawton Collins, and in other ways generously aided and encouraged my work. I am thankful for their permission to read General Collins' Vietnam office files before the documents' transfer to the Eisenhower Library. Numerous archivists and librarians guided and expedited the search for further materials. Especially deserving of thanks are Sally

Marks and John Taylor, National Archives; Kathy Struss, Eisenhower Library; Nancy Bressler, Princeton University Library; Ron Bulatoff, Hoover Institution Archives; Fred Honhart, Michigan State University Archives; and Christine Guyonneau, University of Indianapolis Library. Deep gratitude goes to those people who consented to be interviewed or provided personal papers: Leland Barrows, Bui Diem, J. Lawton Collins, James Cooley, Thomas J. Corcoran, John Hannah, Walter Judd, Randolph A. Kidder, Edward G. Lansdale, Mike Mansfield, Ralph Smuckler, and Ralph Turner. Grants from the National Endowment for the Humanities, the Indiana Humanities Council, and the University of Indianapolis supported portions of the research. George Herring, William Leuchtenburg, Leland Barrows, William Pickett, and others reviewed all or parts of the manuscript, and their comments were most constructive. Any errors that remain are solely the author's responsibility. A final note of appreciation goes to my wife Helen and my daughter Hope, who shared in virtually every aspect of this project.

TRAPPED BY SUCCESS

I

Vietnam, Colonialism, and Cold War (1941–January 1953)

AFTER FIVE nights of trying negotiations in the elegant Hotel Matignon in Paris, French premier Edgar Faure surrendered to an American diplomatic tour de force on Indochina. Following daily sessions of the North Atlantic Council in early May 1955, U.S. Secretary of State John Foster Dulles met late into the evening with Faure. Dulles convinced the weary and wary premier to acquiesce in Washington's determination to sustain a noncommunist, pro-Western government in Saigon under South Vietnamese prime minister Ngo Dinh Diem. This French diplomatic capitulation came exactly one year after the final remnants of France's military garrison at Dienbienphu fell in May 1954 to the overwhelming charge of the communist-led Vietminh Army. The year between May 1954 and May 1955 was one of the most momentous in the troubled saga of the Vietnam War. The French defeat at Dienbienphu that began the year set the stage for the Geneva Conference and the termination of France's eight-year war against the Vietminh. The American-French negotiations in Paris that ended the year started the Americanization of the ongoing struggle against the Vietnamese communists —a struggle that ended two decades later with a communist victory.

What went wrong in Vietnam? This question has haunted Americans since that chaotic day—April 29, 1975—when helicopters lifted the final evacuees off the roof of the U.S. embassy in Saigon. The United States has seldom suffered such humiliation at the hands of a foreign foe. The British burning of Washington in 1814 and the Japanese devastation of Pearl Harbor were similarly dark moments. From those two reverses the United States eventually rebounded, and the nation has also survived its defeat in Vietnam. Still, many Americans remain confused and troubled about the origins and lessons of the Vietnam War, which cost the United States over 58,000 lives, billions of dollars, and untold social and political trauma.

Where to begin searching for an explanation is difficult to determine because the flow of past events seldom reveals clearly delineated points of departure. The origins of the massive American involvement in Vietnam in the 1960s are no exception to this rule. There are numerous antecedents to President Lyndon B. Johnson's decisions to deploy U.S. combat divisions in South Vietnam and to initiate U.S. bombing raids over North Vietnam. Tracing events backward through the Kennedy, Eisenhower, Truman, and Roosevelt administrations, one could conceivably make a case for several turning points in U.S. policy toward Vietnam.

The argument for concentrating on Eisenhower's presidency is that, during his administration from 1953 to 1961, the French military left Vietnam, the Republic of Vietnam (RVN) came into existence in South Vietnam, and the United States became the principal patron of the new southern regime. These notable developments raise a number of basic interpretive questions. Was American assistance to the RVN the product of innocence and ignorance? Were Eisenhower and his foreign policy bureaucracy not resolving the Vietnam issue but simply managing it for domestic political purposes? Was aid to Saigon a misplaced application of containment strategy? Was help to the South an effort worth attempting?

The actions of the Eisenhower administration did not make the eventually massive U.S. military intervention in Vietnam inevitable. John F. Kennedy's expansion of military assistance and his resolve to make Vietnam a test of U.S. cold war credibility as well as Johnson's escalation of U.S. involvement were the responsibility of those presidents. There were alternative courses that Kennedy and Johnson could have taken. Still, the eight years of the Eisenhower administration laid the foundation for the subsequent decisions to intervene, conditioned American public opinion to accept intervention, and greatly expanded the U.S. commitment to South Vietnam.

The Eisenhower administration was somewhat of an interregnum. Its eight years of moderate Republicanism came between the Democrats' activist New Deal–Fair Deal before and New Frontier–Great Society afterward. The period brought relative peace to America compared to the hostilities and casualties endured in Korea earlier and Vietnam later. It was a time of pause between the First and Second Indochina Wars. Harry S. Truman made the decision to aid France in Vietnam; Johnson sent American bombers and combat divisions. The Eisenhower years, however, were not a lapse but rather a link between these events. His administration decided to hold the line in Vietnam by bolstering the South to deny the Vietminh the full fruits of their victory over the French and thereby to buy time for strengthening an alternative to the communists. The negative goal of holding the communists at bay was successful, but the positive aspect of building a new nation in the South was not. By 1961, the RVN was a government but not a nation.

In the 1950s, when the United States first articulated the concept of South Vietnam as an important ally in a strategically valuable area, the idea seemed consistent with other features of American foreign policy. Communist movements aided and largely controlled by the Soviet Union had swept to power in Eastern Europe after World War II, and the United States had countered these developments with the Truman Doctrine, the Marshall Plan, and the North Atlantic Treaty Organization. There would be no appeasement of communist totalitarianism as there had been of fascist dictatorship in the 1930s. In 1949, the vast population of China—inhabiting an area the size of all of Europe—had fallen under the sway of the Chinese Communist Party. The outbreak of war in Korea in 1950 raised the threat of another communist success in Asia. The United States responded with military force in Korea and with aid and reassurance to the remaining nationalist Chinese redoubt on Taiwan. By 1953, the year Dwight D. Eisenhower became president of the United States, the Korean War had come to a stalemate and the containment policy in Europe was in a momentary crisis over the issue of rearming West Germany, but the basic pattern had been established. Since total war meant nuclear war, the policy of choice was not assault on Moscow or Beijing, but rather to shore up the weak spots—areas like Vietnam, Guatemala, or the Philippines where revolutionary or radical movements posed the possibility of further communist gains in the global cat-and-mouse game.

The United States had managed this standoff with some success in Korea and elsewhere, but no two of these troubled areas were identical. The history, culture, leadership, institutions, and other specific factors that determined the outcome of political and military contests varied greatly from one cold war battleground to the next. Viewed through the smoky haze created by years of fighting, the Vietnam of 1954–55 appears to have been a very poor choice of a place for America to stand and fight.

As the French prepared to withdraw after more than a half-century of colonial rule, the United States assumed the stupendous task of not only aiding but in fact creating a sovereign state in South Vietnam. Meanwhile, in North Vietnam, the Vietminh could lay a strong claim to legitimacy through their role in the defeat of the French overlords. The Vietminh leader Ho Chi Minh and his lieutenants were not unchallengeable; they did not possess an undeniable mandate. But, forged on the field of battle, their claim was powerful. By contrast, alternative Vietnamese leaders had weak claims. The former emperor Bao Dai was tainted by collaboration with the French and by the appearance of corruption and decadence. Various other political and religious groups were too small and often too mutually antagonistic to form workable coalitions.

In some ways, Vietnam in 1954 was like the United States in 1783 at the moment of its victory over England. The patriot faction represented by George Washington had defeated the British and was about to embark on an effort to launch a nation. The future course and even success of that effort was not readily apparent, but there was little doubt as to who would lead it. Conversely, the tory faction that had favored remaining part of the British Empire and that disliked the patriots' republican ideology, was largely discredited and in disarray. If European monarchists, who also feared the patriots' ideology, had decided to intervene and assist a small group of tories in forming an alternative regime to the patriots, the effort would almost certainly have failed. For the United States to step into Vietnam in 1954–55 and attempt to fashion a counterbalance to the Vietminh was almost equally doomed. What went wrong in Vietnam was not so much a failure of means as of ends. The

United States set out to accomplish a virtually impossible task. The effort failed, and the lesson of that failure was the need to understand and acknowledge the costs and limitations inherent in external manipulation of internal revolutions.[1]

Such a revolution was clearly under way in Vietnam long before Eisenhower became president. World War II was the catalyst that unleashed the pent-up forces of nationalism in Southeast Asia. In French Indochina, decades of colonial dominance crumbled under the twin blows of the Japanese occupation of France's prized imperial possession and the Nazis' humbling of the home government in Paris. Furthermore, the success of Japanese power eclipsed the white man's prestige in Asia, and, despite Tokyo's eventual capitulation to Western forces, the political status quo ante bellum was no longer possible.[2]

During the war against Japan, the Indochinese Communist Party became the vehicle for the expression of Vietnamese nationalist sentiment. Under the leadership of Ho Chi Minh in 1941, the Party established the Vietnam Doc Lap Dong Minh Hoi (Vietnamese Independence League) or Vietminh as it was called. This communist front organization led the anti-Japanese resistance throughout the war. French colonial officials in Vietnam, meanwhile, followed the lead of the collaborationist Vichy regime in France and cooperated with the Japanese. By early 1945, however, France had been liberated, and agents of General Charles de Gaulle appeared among the old colonial masters intent on restoring French authority in Indochina. Facing imminent defeat from the Allies, Japan attacked French troops and civil servants in Indochina on March 9, 1945 and, within two days, had complete control of the political administration of Vietnam. The Japanese quickly recognized an independent Vietnam with Emperor Bao Dai as head of state. Bao Dai installed a cabinet of politically inexperienced intellectuals at the old imperial capital of Hue. Challenged by the well-organized and politically astute Vietminh, this government had little chance of survival without Japanese support. Shortly after Japan's surrender to the Allies, Bao Dai abdicated his throne. On September 2, 1945, in an emotion-filled ceremony in Hanoi before thousands of Vietnamese, Ho Chi Minh formally proclaimed the independence of the Democratic Republic of Vietnam (DRV).[3]

In the spirit of national unity, Ho initially welcomed Bao Dai into the Vietminh-dominated government as a "supreme political adviser," but the two men remained separated by a vast chasm of ideological and historical differences. Bao Dai was then thirty-one years old. As a teenager in 1932, he had inherited the throne of the Nguyen dynasty that had ruled Vietnam at the time of the French conquest in the 1880s. The French had stripped the imperial court in Hue of any real power but had allowed it to remain in a largely ceremonial role. Upon assuming the throne, the earnest and intelligent Bao Dai had upset the French by restructuring his royal cabinet. He selected some young, energetic mandarins in an attempt to strengthen the monarchy's influence with the colonial administration. He appointed a thirty-two-year-old mandarin named Ngo Dinh Diem as minister of the interior and secretary of a "commission on reform." This modest effort to assert some Vietnamese nationalism quickly came to naught in the face of French recalcitrance, and Diem resigned from the cabinet in protest in 1933. Recognizing the futility of his efforts, Bao Dai lapsed into an indolent life of hunting, gambling, and womanizing. When the Japanese handed him an unencumbered sovereignty upon their departure from Vietnam, Bao Dai accepted it gravely, but he had virtually no personal basis for political power except whatever ephemeral legitimacy his ancestry gave him.[4]

In contrast to the effete emperor, Ho was a shrewd, ruthless, masterful politician. By 1945, he had dedicated most of his fifty-five years to the single goal of Vietnamese independence. In his twenties, he had journeyed from Vietnam to France in search of adventure and answers for his patriotic longings. In Paris he became one of the founding members of the French Communist Party, and, in Marxism-Leninism, he believed he had found the ideology around which to fashion a successful revolution. For twenty years he worked in the Soviet Union, China, and elsewhere gaining valuable experience as a party organizer. Although he helped create the Indochinese Communist Party in 1930, he did not return to live in his native Vietnam until after the Nazi conquest of France in 1940. From a remote base in the mountains along the China-Vietnam border, Ho and other Vietnamese communists created the Vietminh organization and a strategy for revolution. In a uniquely Vietnamese variation of the Chinese communist model, they fashioned an appeal to the Vietnamese people based on nationalism and social revolution. Stressing independence and democracy and muting the harsher Marxist-Leninist rhetoric of class warfare, the Vietminh worked to recruit adherents in northern Vietnam. The Japanese occupation and the history of French exploitation made some Vietnamese willing converts. By 1945, the Vietminh formed the core of a well-organized, highly disciplined, nationalist movement. Its charismatic leader, known by his followers as Uncle Ho, was "part Gandhi, part Lenin, all Vietnamese."[5]

The contrast between Ho and Bao Dai was striking, but Vietnamese society was much too complex to be represented simply by an anachronistic monarch on the one hand or a radical revolutionary on the other. Many peasants in the villages that constituted the basic units of Vietnamese society adopted the traditional wait-and-see attitude with which the masses of East Asia had always reacted to a change in power. From their Confucian heritage, they were aware that the mandate of heaven ebbs and flows over time and that 1945 was one of those times. The half-century of French colonial rule had penetrated into the villages and permanently shattered the peasants' traditional isolation from centralized authority. Now that French power was broken, however, the peasants believed that heaven would eventually sanction a new authority. But who would inherit the mandate?[6]

While the peasants waited to assume their role in a new order, much of Vietnam's intellectual elite grew impatient. Many teachers, physicians, civil servants, and other educated persons were neither Vietminh nor, despite their French educations, French collaborators. Among them were ardent nationalists, who were members of small clandestine political parties, such as the Vietnam Quoc Dan Dang (VNQDD), Dong Minh Hoi, or Dai Viet. Under French colonial rule, such organizations were illegal, and the sûreté constantly searched for their followers. Recruitment and internal communication were very difficult. The members of these parties, often university students, were courageous and resourceful but lacked the discipline of the similarly outlawed Vietminh. The noncommunist groups had little opportunity to mobilize as an effective political force. Their ideologies were shallow, consisting primarily of simple patriotism and abstract notions of democracy. Yet, despite their weaknesses, they did exist as a potential alternative to the Vietminh and to Bao Dai.[7]

Much of Vietnam in 1945 was a political vacuum. Ho Chi Minh had boldly proclaimed the founding of the DRV, but his own Communist Party had only about five thousand members. Ho and his comrades were keenly aware that, if they were to rule 24 million Vietnamese, they had to enhance their own legitimacy and following among the people. Their advantages over other parties and leaders included a clearly articulated revolutionary ideology, strict party discipline, and an established network of operatives. Through their leadership of the Vietminh, they also had strong claim as the voice of anti-Japanese and anti-French nationalism. Any attempt by other parties or leaders to supplant or even coexist with the Vietminh would depend on the ability of these rivals to create their own nationalist legitimacy and popular following.[8]

In September 1945, the Vietminh set to work to strengthen its tenuous hold on Vietnam's fledgling government. Ho's lieutenants made deals with the VNQDD and Dong Minh Hoi that allowed these two small parties token participation in the government. These parties were very weak compared with the Vietminh, but they had ties with the Chinese government of Chiang Kai-shek. Under arrangements made at the Potsdam Conference in July 1945, units of Chiang's army entered Vietnam in September. They were to accept the surrender of Japanese troops north of the sixteenth parallel but did more pillaging than repatriating. The Vietnamese communists bought temporary cooperation from the Chinese nationalist forces by giving some seats in the DRV national assembly to the VNQDD and Dong Minh Hoi. When the Chinese troops departed in 1946, the Vietminh suppressed the two parties. In January 1946 the Vietminh also staged a "national" election, which, in fact, occurred only in localities under its control. Over 90 percent of the votes cast went to the Vietminh. Besides political deals and rigged elections, the Vietminh added the insurance of carefully targeted assassinations of rival nationalist leaders. Many political activists outside the ranks of the Vietminh died or disappeared mysteriously during 1945–46. The precise number is unknown, but two victims were Trung Tu Anh, leader of the Dai Viet party, and Ngo Dinh Khoi, eldest brother of Ngo Dinh Diem.[9]

The Vietminh made these moves against the backdrop of a reemerging French presence in southern Vietnam. By the same arrangement that placed Chinese troops in northern Vietnam, British troops entered south of the sixteenth parallel to repatriate Japanese forces. Although the Vietminh organization was considerably weaker in the South than in the North, thousands of armed Vietminh partisans attempted to seize control of Saigon. Some mass rallies in support of the DRV resulted in attacks on French citizens. As casualties mounted, especially among civilians, the small British force of 1500 rearmed both Japanese and French troops to help restore order. The British commander ignored local Vietnamese leaders who appealed for his support. He assumed that

France had a legitimate claim of authority, and he welcomed new arrivals of French soldiers that by December 1945 numbered 50,000.[10]

Throughout 1946, the French and Vietminh attempted to negotiate an agreement on the future of Vietnam. In March, Ho Chi Minh and French envoy Jean Sainteny signed an accord recognizing "the Republic of Viet-Nam as a Free State having its own government, parliament, army, and treasury, and belonging to the Indochina Federation of the French Union."[11] This brief document represented concessions by both sides. It seemed a good start toward a peaceful settlement, but it was never carried out largely due to the precipitate action of Admiral Thierry d'Argenlieu, the French high commissioner in Saigon. On May 30, 1946, d'Argenlieu recognized, without authorization from Paris, a "free" Republic of Cochinchina around Saigon under terms identical to Sainteny's agreement with Ho. On his way to Paris at that moment to arrange a final modus vivendi, Ho continued negotiations for a time. D'Argenlieu's bold move to erect a separate French-backed regime in Saigon to rival the DRV in Hanoi, however, inflamed passions in Vietnam. Violent incidents increased between the Vietnamese and French, and, in December, a carefully planned Vietminh assault on French civilians in Hanoi was answered by a heavy French counterattack. The Indochina War had begun.[12]

Vietnam at war quickly became a nation divided not North and South but urban and rural. French forces controlled the cities and towns, and the Vietminh retreated into the villages and mountains and undertook a guerrilla-style war. Despite major military campaigns in 1947, the French were frustrated by their elusive enemy's irregular tactics. Furthermore, France's attempt to extinguish the Vietminh by brute force was not only ineffective but enhanced the popularity and credibility of Ho and his party as nationalist leaders.

In order to challenge the Vietminh's appeal as guardians of the Vietnamese nation, the French reached an agreement with Bao Dai in June 1948 for an independent Vietnam within the French Union. This vague convention did not specify how the changes would be implemented. After more talks, the so-called Elysée agreements of March 8, 1949 between Bao Dai and French president Vincent Auriol dissolved the Republic of Cochinchina and further clarified the legal status of what was to be called the State of Vietnam.[13]

The reappearance of Bao Dai as head of a new Vietnamese regime had long-term historical significance. The new government and its successor regime, the Republic of Vietnam, became the rallying point not only of the French but also of Vietnamese and later Americans who hoped to foster a Vietnamese nationalist alternative to the communist DRV. The "Bao Dai solution" was controversial at the time of its inception, and it has remained the subject of debate. For those observers and historians who have believed that Ho's claim to nationalist leadership was unassailable, Bao Dai was simply a French puppet, and the Elysée agreements were mere camouflage for continued French colonial dominance. Bao Dai's well-earned reputation as a playboy and "nightclub emperor" underscored this view.[14] Other interpreters of the Indochina War, however, who have noted that Ho's communism was not representative of most Vietnamese in 1948, have characterized Bao Dai as a hard bargainer who achieved real political concessions from Paris. The most debauched of his nightclub life, some claim, came after 1949.[15] Regardless of what Bao Dai was, though, all accounts agree that he did not achieve real independence from France.

The failure of the Bao Dai solution rested primarily with the French, not Bao Dai. The former emperor wanted independence for his homeland, but he had little leverage with the French, except for their need for a symbol of political legitimacy. To his credit, he exploited that need as far as he could. In the Elysée agreements, he got the French to include the hallowed word "independence"—"doc lap" in Vietnamese—something Ho had not obtained in his 1946 negotiations. He secured the end of the Republic of Cochinchina and recognition of the principle of a unified Vietnam. On key issues such as defense arrangements and economic coordination, Bao Dai obtained terms from the French not very different from the U.S. grant of independence to the Philippines in 1946.[16] After 1949, Bao Dai's diplomats continued to gain concessions from the French in a process of "perfecting" independence that went on until 1954. Yet, without an unqualified French guarantee of full autonomy for the State of Vietnam, these gains rang hollow. The French absolutely refused to take the last step to total independence, and that French stubbornness broke the back of the Bao Dai solution.[17]

Bao Dai's diplomatic successes generated no popular enthusiasm and proved no match for the Vietminh's appeal garnered from its heroic armed resistance. On July 1, 1949, Bao Dai issued Ordinance Number One, the basic constitution of his new state. In Saigon, the new capital, there was no fanfare—no parades, no banners, no speeches—such as had greeted Ho Chi Minh's declaration of Vietnamese independence in Hanoi in 1945. The official birth of the State of Vietnam was a political and psychological nonevent. Despite diplomatic recognition from France, the United States, Great Britain, and eventually other nations, Bao Dai's regime never had the loyalty of the Vietnamese themselves. Whether the test of legitimacy was the ancient concept of the mandate of heaven or the modern notion of national sovereignty, the proof was effective leadership. Until the Saigon government could begin to meet the political, social, and economic needs of Vietnamese from the peasantry to the professoriat, it remained only an aspirant to power and to public acceptance.[18]

In 1949, the State of Vietnam was not on a par with the DRV in either power or popularity, but some Vietnamese chose to hope that the politicians in Saigon might eventually mount an effective challenge to the communists concentrated in the North. Vietnamese opponents of the Vietminh were in an impossible position once the Franco-Vietminh War began. If they continued to oppose or refused to cooperate with the Vietminh, they appeared to be traitors to the cause of national independence. If they supported the Vietminh, they were aiding an organization that had already revealed its plans for their political and physical liquidation. Many non-Vietminh nationalists tried to remain neutral between the Vietminh and Bao Dai. Others decided to grasp the thin reed of the Bao Dai solution as their only apparent opportunity to escape their dilemma. They had no future with the Vietminh, but, by joining the Bao Dai government, they could hope to play some role in determining their own and their country's future. They believed it was their only option, although they knew many Vietnamese would immediately label them as collaborators with the Western imperialists. This collaborationist cloud was a critical handicap and would hang over Saigon until the demise of the government there in 1975.

While many anti-Vietminh nationalists became fence-sitters and others resignedly identified with the Bao Dai solution, there was one especially crucial rejection of the emperor's appeal for supporters. Ngo Dinh Diem remained aloof. As he had done when he left the imperial cabinet in 1933, Diem concluded that the French would never yield genuine concessions to Bao Dai. Diem was not averse to seeking political deals with foreign powers. In 1945 he had unsuccessfully solicited the Japanese for appointment as prime minister after their move to crush the French colonial establishment. In 1949, however, he rejected an offer of the same post from Bao Dai because he perceived it to be a political dead end. Thus, he remained unsullied by the charge of collaboration with the French and would later parlay this advantage into an appointment as prime minister of the State of Vietnam in 1954 with the French on their way out. Despite this eventual result, Diem's disdain for the Bao Dai solution in 1949 created a debilitating problem for the anti-Vietminh nationalists. Diem and his supporters, who were primarily his own large family, harbored genuine contempt for those Vietnamese who initially supported the tainted Bao Dai regime. Conversely, those politicians who had endured great personal risks to try to make the State of Vietnam a viable alternative to the DRV distrusted the sanctimonious Diem and the clannish and ambitious Ngo family. The absence of political unity in Saigon made the already difficult task of competing with the Vietminh even more formidable.[19]

The particular political alignments within Vietnam, which eventually would preoccupy and confound U.S. officials, attracted little interest in the United States before 1950. For decades, Southeast Asia had been so clearly identified as a British, French, and Dutch sphere of interest that Washington had developed little bureaucratic expertise on the area. When American policy makers gave any thought to Indochina, it was almost always in the context of American-French relations with virtually no attention to specific issues, groups, or individuals within Vietnam, Laos, and Cambodia. With Germany's conquest of France and Japan's occupation of Indochina during World War II, President Franklin D. Roosevelt assumed that France's Asian empire was finished. The United States itself was intent on granting independence to the Philippines as quickly as possible after the defeat of Japan, and both Roosevelt and his successor Harry S. Truman made the end of Western colonialism a postwar objective. Even before World War II ended, however, mounting U.S. suspicions of the Soviet Union's hostile intentions toward Western Europe led both Roosevelt and Truman to soften America's anticolonialism for the sake of unity with Britain and France.[20]

To aid or even condone a French colonial war in Indochina was repugnant to most U.S. officials, but Soviet machinations in Europe were even more troubling and much more critical to American interests. The touchstone of all U.S. foreign policies in the late 1940s was the contain-

ment of Soviet power and ambitions. From 1947 to 1949, the Truman administration began to construct this containment policy with the Truman Doctrine, Marshall Plan, and North Atlantic Treaty Organization. Although often global in rhetoric, these specific initiatives were designed to bolster Western Europe against the Soviets, and, for this American-led effort to work, France would have to be a full participant.

The Truman administration initially struck a neutral pose between the French and the Vietminh, although Ho attempted to incur America's favor by quoting from the U.S. Declaration of Independence in his declaration of Vietnamese independence. To secure French cooperation in Europe, Washington's neutrality in Indochina became increasingly pro-French. When Paris made use of Marshall Plan aid to free resources for use in Indochina, the United States made no objection. Similarly, the administration secretly allowed France to equip its army in Vietnam with unused American Lend-Lease matériel stockpiled in the Pacific during World War II.[21]

The Truman administration's identification of Soviet communism as the principal danger to America and the world gave Ho's communist background enormous significance. Ho was indisputably a communist. Not only was his ideology Marxist-Leninist, but his entire career had been as a party organizer closely connected with the Communist Party of the Soviet Union. U.S. State Department officials were aware of Ho's appeal within Vietnam as a nationalist leader, and they were unable to discover any evidence of Soviet management of the Vietminh front. These considerations could not obviate the belief in Washington, however, that a Vietminh victory over France would be a victory for the Soviet Union. From the beginning of the Indochina War, it was an article of faith in Washington that a communist-led Democratic Republic of Vietnam was an enemy of the United States and a threat to American security. There was little acknowledgment that the United States was opposing a nationalist revolution.[22]

Events across Vietnam's northern frontier in 1948–49 added to the specter of a spreading communist menace in Asia. Mao Zedong's Chinese communist insurgents pushed into South China and sent Chiang Kai-shek's nationalist Chinese government and army in flight to Taiwan. The "Red Tide" sweeping China troubled American and French strategists and raised the hopes of Ho's followers. Although history taught the Vietnamese to distrust their powerful northern neighbors, the Vietminh leaders decided to declare publicly their affinity with international communism in order to court Chinese communist aid.

Long before Mao formally proclaimed the founding of the People's Republic of China in October 1949, French leaders confronted the immediate threat of a logistical and manpower link between the communist forces in China and Indochina. Indeed, this danger, coupled with growing French frustration in countering the Vietminh militarily and politically, motivated Paris to make its arrangements with Bao Dai that led to the Elysée agreements of March 1949. It took the French National Assembly almost a year to ratify the Elysée agreements, but, during the final debate in January 1950, those deputies who supported ratification argued that the war with the Vietminh was a war with international communism. Furthermore, U.S. aid to France could be expected in such a war. With the arrival of the Chinese communists on Vietnam's northern border, Deputy Edouard Frédéric-Dupont declared, "Indochina has become the frontier of Western civilization and the war in Indochina is integrated into the cold war."[23]

The prediction that Washington could not remain indifferent to a potential communist success in Southeast Asia proved correct, and the United States entered the Indochina War in 1950. On February 7, five days after French ratification of the Elysée agreements, the United States extended diplomatic recognition to the State of Vietnam. In May the Truman administration committed $10 million in military assistance to the new regime, and by summer there was a U.S. Military Assistance Advisory Group in Saigon to oversee American aid to the French war effort. A complex of factors, most of them external to Vietnam, had brought the U.S. to this commitment. The American-Soviet confrontation in Europe required good U.S. relations with France and a moderating of U.S. criticism of French colonialism. Similarly, in another compromise with colonialism, Washington agreed to help Britain and Japan preserve their trade areas in Southeast Asia to ensure access to the markets and raw materials they needed for industrial growth. Mao's triumph in China in 1949 further convinced many Americans that the Soviet menace in the form of international communism now threatened Asia as well as Europe. Some members of Congress and the media, dubbed the "China Lobby," mounted sharp criticisms of the Truman administration for its alleged "loss of China."[24]

For American leaders, developments in Asia contributed to a global crisis. By the fall of 1949, the Soviets had the atomic bomb. Highly publicized spy-trials of Julius and Ethel Rosenberg and Alger Hiss created anxiety about Russian infiltration of the U.S. government. The demagogic Senator Joseph McCarthy began trumpeting such charges in February 1950. Far from the newspaper headlines, in the highly guarded secrecy of the National Security Council (NSC), an April 1950 report, known in bureaucratic shorthand as NSC 68, concluded that the time had come for the United States to assume unilateral defense of the entire noncommunist world. This finding seemed to be confirmed when the communist North Korean Army invaded South Korea in June and ignited the Korean War. All of Asia was a cold war battleground. In the highly charged atmosphere of 1950, a strong American stand in Southeast Asia against communism seemed not only logical but imperative.[25]

The Truman administration's plunge into Indochina in 1950 was a momentous step, but it was far from an Americanization of the war against the Vietnamese communists. With U.S. forces engaged in combat with North Korean and, after November 1950, Chinese troops, Washington had no desire for a major military role in Vietnam. This preference suited the French, who welcomed U.S. matériel and moral support but who considered the Indochina conflict still to be their war. French pride and self-interest had helped precipitate the fighting, and they impelled French politicians and generals to resist stubbornly American advice or criticism. The French remained especially sensitive and obdurate in response to America's continuing insistence that Bao Dai's regime be made more truly independent. Meanwhile, victory still eluded France, and, in fact, its army suffered heavy losses of men and supplies in some large-scale battles in 1950–52. To shore up the French effort, U.S. assistance edged steadily upward. In fiscal year 1953, the United States paid a third of the French war costs in Indochina.[26]

Although many U.S. officials considered the French militarily inept and diplomatically pigheaded, Washington could see no alternative but to stand by them and the Bao Dai solution. American leaders faced much the same dilemma as the Vietnamese opponents of the Vietminh. To side with France and the State of Vietnam was to support contemptible colonialism and what, so far, had been a failing effort. To withhold support was deemed more dangerous, however, because that would jeopardize U.S. containment strategy in both Europe and Asia. To strengthen European defenses against the Soviet Army, the United States wanted France to accept the rearmament and integration of West Germany into a European Defense Community. For officials in Paris, dealing with Germans was personally and politically abhorrent, and they extorted more aid for the Indochina War as their price for even considering the plan. Furthermore, without U.S. aid, there was the possibility that France might withdraw entirely from Indochina. With U.S. forces committed to Korea and the defense of Europe, Washington would have been overextended if it tried to take up the fight in Indochina directly. The Truman administration was already under political attack for not securing greater allied participation in Korea and for excessive foreign and domestic spending.[27]

By the time Truman left office in January 1953, the risks and complexity of the Indochina War were much greater than they had been in 1950. Despite the resilience of the Vietminh and the difficulties for and with the French, though, Washington gave virtually no thought to doing nothing in Vietnam. The cold war in Europe, the "loss of China," and the stalemate in Korea made a communist success in Vietnam unacceptable. American officials were already characterizing the effort against the Vietminh as vital to the defense of all of Southeast Asia against communism.[28] Truman's successor, Dwight D. Eisenhower, would give this explanation a name—the domino theory.

II

Eisenhower, Dulles, Dominoes, and Dienbienphu (January 1953–May 1954)

DWIGHT D. EISENHOWER entered the presidency convinced that the Indochina War was of global strategic importance to the United States. In his first State of the Union Address to Congress on February 2, 1953, he described France as holding "the line of freedom" in Indochina against the "calculated assault" of "Communist aggression throughout the world."[1] A few days earlier, the new secretary of state, John Foster Dulles, had itemized the danger more explicitly. He declared that the Soviet Union was intent on controlling Japan and India through the possession not only of Korea but also of Indonesia, Siam, Burma, and Malaya. Even beyond this threat to Asia, the large French effort there subtracted, in the secretary's calculations, from France's capacity to contribute to the defense of Europe against the same Soviet menace.[2] After a March meeting with the president to discuss U.S.–French relations, Dulles recorded that the Indochina situation "had probably the top priority in foreign policy, being in some ways more important than Korea, because the consequences of loss there could not be localized, but would spread throughout Asia and Europe."[3]

At the time that Eisenhower and Dulles made these assessments, hostilities still continued in Korea. With the Korean cease-fire in July 1953, however, both the United States and its most dangerous Asian communist antagonist, the People's Republic of China, turned greater attention to Indochina. By 1954, the French war with the Vietminh had assumed a central role in America's cold war struggle for freedom over dictatorship. The Vietnamese communists had dropped the name Vietminh in 1951 and adopted the new designation Dong Lao Dong Vietnam or Vietnamese Workers Party to broaden their appeal within Vietnam.[4] Their opponents continued throughout most of the 1950s, though, to refer to Vietnamese communists as Vietminh. Thinking in terms of a global communist threat, U.S. officials paid no more heed to the nuances of the name change than they did to Vietminh claims of anticolonialist legitimacy.

In an April 1954 news conference, Eisenhower enunciated the "falling domino" principle that became the rationale for U.S. policy in Southeast Asia for twenty years. This domino theory was not new, but the president now expanded the list of dominoes beyond mainland Southeast Asia to include Taiwan, the Philippines, Australia, and New Zealand. He explained that, if the communists knocked over the first domino, "you could have the beginning of a disintegration that would have the most profound influence." Valuable resources of tin, tungsten, and rubber would be lost and so too would a strategically valuable geographical position. Most serious of all, though, was that Asia had "already lost 450 million of its people to *the* Communist dictatorship," and the collapse of the dominoes would place "millions and millions and millions of people" under communist "enslavement."[5]

There was no question that the Eisenhower administration considered defeat of the Vietminh to be an urgent national security goal. It was much less clear, however, how and to what extent the United States should risk employing its own power in an area so remote from the United States and so far from the more vital strategic area of Europe. This uncertainty was part of a larger reassessment of U.S. foreign policy that had begun with the presidential campaign in 1952 and continued with the change in administrations in 1953.

In 1952, the Republican Party was on the attack against Truman's containment policy. In 1944 and 1948, the GOP had taken a bipartisan approach to foreign affairs, but many Republican leaders, especially conservatives of the so-called Old Guard, had since become angry and frustrated with the nation's course in the postwar world. Soviet-American tension had continued to mount, especially with Russian acquisition of nuclear weapons. The North Atlantic Treaty Organization (NATO) was off to a slow start with the seemingly interminable wrangling among Europeans over the role of a rearmed West Germany in the proposed European Defense Community (EDC). In Asia, the communist victory in China and the stalemated war in Korea were bitter pills to swallow. Old Guard spokesmen argued that the time had come to move beyond containment to retaliation and even to liberation of those areas that had fallen under communism. The Republican platform of 1952, which John Foster Dulles helped draft, labeled containment as "negative, futile, and immoral" because it abandoned "countless human beings to a despotism and Godless terrorism." It specifically called for the liberation of "captive peoples."[6]

This Republican rhetoric was bold and shrill, but the party's candidate in 1952 had a reputation for pragmatism and caution. A newcomer to partisan politics, Dwight Eisenhower had won the nomination largely on the basis of his enormous popularity as the supreme commander of the victorious allied armies in Europe in World War II. He personified the belief of many Americans in the goodness and moral ascendancy of their nation in the wake of the war. He also possessed an infectious grin that could disarm even the most cynical critics. Throughout the previous decade, this congenial general had been at or near the highest levels of international relations, and his tact and managerial skill had been mainstays of allied unity during the war and of NATO after the war. Appointed as the first supreme commander of NATO forces by President Truman, Eisenhower had not been part of the Republican chorus condemning containment, and, in fact, he had won the nomination away from Senator Robert Taft, leader of the Old Guard. Both as candidate and as president, Eisenhower relied on his well-practiced skills for coalition politics to coexist with both the conservatives in his party who favored liberation and the moderates who tended more toward containment.[7]

As the man in the middle, the president's own views were often obscured by the commotion generated by advisers vying for his endorsement of their views. During his presidency, in fact, his public image was that of an amiable but bumbling and listless figurehead dominated by his cabinet and staff. After he left office and the internal records of the Eisenhower White House became more available to scholars, this unflattering portrait was almost completely reversed. Under the label of Eisenhower revisionism, many writers have rejected the old characterization and have argued that Eisenhower energetically directed the work of his lieutenants, especially in foreign affairs.[8] These historians and political scientists have tended also to view Eisenhower's diplomacy as carefully crafted and generally successful, although that thesis, especially as it is applied to the Third World, has been challenged.[9]

Regardless of the revisionists' findings, any analysis of Eisenhower's foreign policies must weigh the influence of Secretary of State Dulles and assess the Eisenhower-Dulles relationship. The scion of a family of diplomats and clergymen, the austere secretary was a formidable personality. Years of successful experience as an international lawyer, world churchman, and diplomatic envoy lay behind his air of self-confidence and self-righteousness. His moral abhorrence for atheistic communism was deeply rooted in his own personal values, and it ennobled him in the eyes of conservative Republicans. As the Eisenhower administration's principal and forceful spokesman on world affairs, he gave a clear public impression that he was the architect of Eisenhower's foreign policies.

The Eisenhower revisionists have dispelled much of this overemphasis on Dulles. The president assumed office possessing his own wealth of experience during World War II in both diplomacy and the management of talented and energetic subordinates. Through the orderly structure of weekly National Security Council (NSC) meetings and almost daily conferences or communications with Dulles, Eisenhower was constantly and substantively part of the policy process. He shared privately in the drafting of most of Dulles' major public statements, but he preferred that the secretary of state be the one to run the public gauntlet of praise and criticism. This "hidden-hand" allowed the president political and diplomatic flexibility. The Eisenhower–Dulles relationship was a partnership based on mutual respect in which the president exercised final authority while allowing Dulles extensive freedom. This arrangement generally produced a foreign policy that was a joint product of the White House and Department of State.[10]

When the Eisenhower–Dulles team replaced the team of Truman and Secretary of State Dean Acheson, there was no perceptible change in the goals of American foreign policy. Despite the liberation rhetoric of the campaign, the new administration's objective remained the containment, not the roll-back, of world communism. When conservative Republican senators attempted to repudiate the Yalta and Potsdam agreements, which they maintained had allowed Soviet control of Eastern Europe, Eisenhower and Dulles opposed this symbolic gesture as too extreme and diplomatically destabilizing. Similarly, in 1953, the administration prudently chose to take no positive action to support anti-Soviet rioters in East Berlin or to vanquish North Korea. This caution was an acknowledgment that liberation in practice meant the risk of World War III.[11]

Having no more desire for war with Russia or China than the voters who elected them, the Eisenhower–Dulles team sought to improve the effectiveness of America's global resistance to communist expansion in other ways.[12] After weeks of study, they adopted a top-secret report, NSC 162/2, on October 30, 1953 that outlined a new strategy. Generally known as the New Look, it was an amalgam of various doctrines of containment, liberation, deterrence, and negotiation; hence, it incorporated a complex range of methods. These means were knitted together by two common threads: cost reduction and regaining the initiative in the cold war. The Korean War and Truman's entire global policeman effort undertaken under NSC 68 were deemed too burdensome on the American economy. Simultaneously, though, the New Look assumed that the Democrats' containment policy had been too passive and reactive. This new plan promised to fulfill Eisenhower's campaign pledges to be both aggressively anticommunist and fiscally conservative.[13]

In a bellicose public address in January 1954, Secretary Dulles seemed to equate the New Look with massive retaliation, but that nuclear deterrent concept was only part of the Eisenhower–Dulles strategy. In veiled but unmistakable language, the administration let the world know that the United States was willing to use its nuclear arsenal in localized as well as general military confrontations. This threat was not a bluff, and it allowed for cost-saving reductions in U.S. conventional forces worldwide. Beyond massive retaliation, however, the New Look meant greater reliance on military alliances and the use of other nations' ground forces supported by American air power. It also included more emphasis on "psychological warfare," such as propaganda campaigns and ominously ambiguous public statements to keep adversaries off balance. Covert operations by the Central Intelligence Agency (CIA) were expanded and used successfully to topple allegedly radical governments in Iran and Guatemala. These were relatively inexpensive actions and also easy to coordinate with administration policies, since the secretary of state's brother, Allen W. Dulles, headed the agency. Finally, there were some limited direct diplomatic contacts with the Soviets and the Chinese communists.[14]

Eisenhower and Dulles employed all the various elements of the New Look in Indochina. Like containment, the New Look's basic premise was that a bipolar U.S.–Soviet conflict shaped world affairs. This concept allowed little room for nationalism, finite limitations on the power of the two major antagonists, global economic interdependence, or popular desire for social justice and human rights. Geopolitical strategy was a simple we–they equation. Such an approach to the problems of revolutionary upheaval in an underdeveloped region like Indochina was akin to putting the square peg in the round hole.

Dulles was aware of some of the inherent contradictions. He candidly informed the Senate Foreign Relations Committee in secret testimony in April 1953 that the stakes were high in Indochina and that the choices for the United States were not good. He laid out the domino scenario and placed special emphasis on the extreme threat to the development of Japan as a U.S. ally, if it lost access to the food, raw materials, and markets of Southeast Asia. He assured the senators that the new administration contemplated no direct U.S. military intervention to defend the area, but he noted that the remaining options were distasteful. It would take time, Dulles explained, for the long-colonized inhabitants of Indochina to build a strong enough system of government to resist Soviet and Chinese infiltration. The communists, he asserted, were masters of exploiting such vulnerable situations, and, thus, a continuing French presence would be necessary to help secure the area. Besides having to tolerate the colonialists a while longer, the United States also faced the problem of whom among the native leaders to support. Mentioning Korea's Syngman Rhee and China's Chiang Kai-shek as specific examples elsewhere, Dulles declared that "they are not the people, under normal circumstances, that we would want to support. We would be trying to get someone else, but in times like these, in the unrest of the world today, and the divided spirit, we know that we cannot make a transition without losing control of the situation."[15]

At first the administration attempted to follow the Truman approach of aiding and encouraging France to pursue aggressively the war against the Vietminh. It threatened to withdraw needed U.S. military and financial aid unless Paris developed and executed a sound strategic plan in

Indochina. In May 1953, Eisenhower wrote directly to Ambassador C. Douglas Dillon in Paris and named specific French generals that he wanted the embassy to recommend for command in Vietnam. The same letter also renewed the appeal to French officials for a public declaration of greater self-rule for Indochina. France could also play diplomatic hardball, though, since it still had its own leverage in the U.S. need for French cooperation in the establishment of the EDC. In addition, the French could choose at any time to leave the anticommunist fight in Southeast Asia to the United States alone.

Paris did select a new commander for Vietnam, Lieutenant General Henri Navarre. He was not a favorite of Washington, but Navarre developed a plan for concentrating his forces and going on the offensive. In part because of optimistic reports after an inspection visit by Lieutenant General John W. O'Daniel and from a lack of other alternatives, Washington granted $385 million to finance the Navarre plan. With this allocation, U.S. aid reached almost 80 percent of France's total military costs in Indochina for fiscal year 1954. Also to appease Paris, American diplomats in Saigon asked Bao Dai's representatives to moderate their campaign for immediate political concessions from the French. Eisenhower was finding the French as difficult to influence as had Truman, but he insisted that aid to France was not "a giveaway program." It was "the cheapest way" to protect the United States from a "most terrible" threat, Eisenhower grimly reassured an audience of state governors.[16]

During the last weeks of 1953, as Washington initiated the New Look strategy, Navarre began to man and fortify a large outpost near the isolated mountain village of Dienbienphu. Why the general chose this location on the floor of a valley and far from his main force in the Red River delta has never been fully explained. It may have been a move to block Vietminh access to resupply through northern Laos or to cut them off from the lucrative opium trade in the area. It may also have been a lure to entice the elusive Vietminh Army into a set-piece battle in which French planes and artillery could smash the enemy. Whatever the purpose, Dienbienphu was a target that Vo Nguyen Giap, the Vietminh military commander, could not resist. Contrary to French expectations, he was able to place artillery on the ridges above the garrison, and he surrounded the valley with a force that outnumbered the French two to one.[17]

While war clouds gathered over Dienbienphu, the Eisenhower administration continued to search for a more effective approach to Indochina. The activity at Dienbienphu created concern but no sense of immediate crisis in Washington. The NSC discussed the topic at its meeting of January 8, 1954 and weighed several options. The president himself was ambivalent. At first he "bitterly opposed" the notion of putting U.S. forces in Vietnam, but, later in the meeting, he appeared willing to consider the possibility. Eisenhower responded positively to an estimation by Admiral Arthur W. Radford, chairman of the Joint Chiefs of Staff (JCS), that "if we put one squadron of U.S. planes over Dien Bien Phu for as little as one afternoon, it might save the situation." The council's deliberations produced no conclusions. The president expressed the prevailing indecision when he remarked that "while no one was more anxious than himself to keep our men out of these jungles, we could nevertheless not forget our vital interests in Indochina."[18]

Following this meeting, Eisenhower created a high-level, ad hoc committee representing the Departments of State and Defense, the CIA, and the NSC staff to try again to devise a precise plan for making better use of U.S. aid to influence and invigorate the French. Their charge included consideration of committing U.S. ground or air forces to Indochina. The group first met at the Pentagon on January 29, and eventually produced some specific recommendations in February and March. Its proposals for leverage with the French still suffered under the old limits imposed by U.S. need for French cooperation in Europe. The committee believed, however, that Indochina was of sufficient military and political value to the United States to keep open the option of committing U.S. forces there, even if France failed to achieve a military victory.[19]

One of the most notable aspects of this Indochina working group was the presence in the CIA contingent of a then little-known Air Force colonel, Edward G. Lansdale. Lansdale was an "unconventional warfare" officer working with the CIA who had impressed American intelligence officials with his help to Philippine President Ramon Magsaysay's successful efforts to quell the communist-led Huk rebels. CIA Director Dulles suggested at the January 29 meeting that Lansdale be sent to Vietnam. Admiral Radford agreed but wanted the colonel to remain in Washington for a while as part of the working group. In subsequent months and years, Lansdale was to become a key figure in U.S.-Vietnam relations.[20]

While the president's ad hoc advisory group started to work, Secretary of State Dulles was in Berlin meeting with the foreign ministers of France, the United Kingdom, and the Soviet Union to discuss European and East Asian security issues. Since the death of Soviet leader Joseph Stalin in March 1953, the Kremlin had adopted a conciliatory pose in the cold war, and, at Berlin, the Soviets proposed to convene an international conference on Far Eastern questions including the Indochina War. French Premier Joseph Laniel and his foreign minister George Bidault saw the conference idea as a promising diplomatic opening. The Laniel government was under mounting pressure at home to extricate France from the seven-year-old war. The idea of a compromise settlement with Asian communists, especially since the Soviets suggested inviting a delegation from Beijing to the meeting, deeply distressed Dulles. Ultimately the secretary of state acquiesced, though, to a conference at Geneva, Switzerland, to begin on April 26. In his opinion, a U.S. veto of negotiations would have been tantamount to a "moral obligation" to continue military support of the French war. If French efforts did not improve, however, he feared that Congress and the Pentagon might "lose interest" in sustaining the aid. Furthermore, the secretary's hopes for French ratification of the EDC rested on Bidault, who favored the concept. Dulles was "on guard lest Indochina also carry [the] European Defense Community down the drain."[21]

The decision at Berlin to open negotiations at Geneva started the military clock ticking at Dienbienphu. Vietminh leaders recognized immediately that a resounding battlefield success before April 26 would pay big diplomatic dividends at the conference table. Holding the high ground, possessing numerical superiority, and having access to Chinese supplies through Laos, General Giap decided for the first time in the war to launch a large unit attack on a fortified camp. On the night of March 13, Vietminh infantry with heavy artillery support overran some of the outer perimeter defenses at Dienbienphu. This assault began eight weeks of agony and death for the French garrison and for the idea of a French military reconquest of Indochina.[22]

At the weekly meeting of the NSC on March 18, Eisenhower did not exhibit any particular sense of urgency over the outbreak of fighting at Dienbienphu. Although U.S. intelligence sources rated the French chances of holding out as about 50–50, the soldier-president expressed doubt that the military situation was that bad. Since the French had planes, napalm, and heavily fortified positions, he reasoned, the two-to-one numerical advantage of the Vietminh was not very significant. Moreover, even if Dienbienphu fell, it would cost Giap heavy casualties, and Navarre had large forces in more strategically valuable areas, such as the Red River delta, that remained unimpaired. The French were in a tight spot, but at this meeting and at subsequent sessions, Eisenhower gave every indication that militarily the situation was manageable.[23]

Scarcely forty-eight hours after this NSC meeting, the pressure increased for direct U.S. action in Indochina. On March 20, General Paul Ely, chairman of the French Chiefs of Staff, arrived in Washington and confronted Eisenhower and his advisers with an ominous reality. Ely did not request immediate U.S. intervention nor divulge any startling military information. Rather, the general bluntly warned that "a major defeat would have serious adverse effects" on French public opinion. Ely consciously avoided a defeatist tone, but his words galvanized the administration into action. Although the possibility of a complete French withdrawal from Indochina had concerned Washington for months, such a decision now appeared imminent.[24]

As Eisenhower considered how to pull the French "chestnuts out of the fire," as he later put it, he received the recommendations of his advisers. After lengthy conversations with Ely, JCS Chairman Radford urged the president to "be prepared to act promptly and in force possibly to a frantic and belated request by the French for U.S. intervention."[25] Although the use of American ground troops was, in Eisenhower's words, an "ever-present, persistent, gnawing possibility," Radford did not favor it, and Army Chief of Staff General Matthew Ridgway actively opposed it.[26] If the United States decided to take military action, the most likely form was a massive, conventional air strike on the Vietminh positions at Dienbienphu.

Admiral Radford was a naval aviator with absolute confidence that air power could break the siege without U.S. ground combat forces. He informed Ely that 350 planes from aircraft carriers in the Gulf of Tonkin could be in the battle on two days' notice, and, with a little more time, heavier bombers from Okinawa and the Philippines could be used. Although the *Pentagon Papers* and other sources have referred to this plan as Operation Vulture, Radford was unaware of that French code name until late April. Radford later insisted that, during Ely's visit, he gave the French general no personal promise of support, but Ely returned to Paris on March 24 believing that Washington would respond favorably to an appeal for armed intervention.[27]

The secretary of state's position during the early days of the Dienbienphu siege was more cautious than Radford's. In January, Dulles had publicly brandished the New Look and the massive retaliation doctrine in a seemingly militant, inflexible reliance on America's nuclear deterrent capabilities. His tough rhetoric had, in fact, been intended in part as a warning to Moscow and Beijing not to interfere in Indochina. Neither he nor any other top administration official seriously advocated the use of nuclear weapons at Dienbienphu, despite Bidault's claim in later years that Dulles raised the possibility. There were staff discussions and contingency plans involving nuclear weapons, but the only high-level consideration of their use came in regard to the unlikely possibility of large-scale Chinese intervention as had occurred during the Korean War. The use of American naval and air power as Radford had proposed did fit into the "more bang for the buck" philosophy of the New Look, however, provided that one attack proved sufficient. The risk that immediate, unilateral U.S. action might be unsuccessful troubled Dulles. Although not rejecting intervention, he warned Ely and advised Eisenhower that "if the United States sent its flag and its own military establishment— land, sea, and air—into the Indochina war, then the prestige of the United States would be engaged to a point where we would want to have a success." Defeat, Dulles believed, "would have worldwide repercussions."[28]

As for the president, he was keeping several options open in a fluid situation. Although in later years Eisenhower scoffed at the usefulness of bombing at Dienbienphu, his initial reaction to Radford's proposal was not so negative. He agreed with Dulles that "political preconditions [were] necessary for a successful outcome," but he did not "wholly exclude the possibility of a single strike, if it were almost certain this would produce decisive results."[29] At the NSC meeting on March 25, Dulles posed the central question: "Who should fill the void left by the collapse of French power. . . . Would it be the Communists, or must it be the U.S.?" French difficulties with guerrillas around Dienbienphu "seemed sufficient indication," the president admitted, "that the population of Vietnam did not wish to be free from Communist domination." Despite that provocative observation, Eisenhower was not proposing that the Vietnamese determine their own future. He wanted more study of the "extent to which we would go in employing ground forces to save Indochina from the Communists." Hastening to add that Congress had to be "in on" any U.S. intervention, he also wondered what other nations "might be induced to join us in a broadened effort to save Indochina." Evoking the domino analogy, the president declared that Indochina's collapse "would produce a chain reaction which would result in the fall of all of Southeast Asia to the Communists." The meeting concluded with a directive to the NSC staff to study the "circumstances and conditions" of intervention "in concert with the French or in concert with others or, if necessary, unilaterally."[30]

It is apparent that, in late March, Eisenhower was considering strong action in Indochina including the possibility of an air strike or even ground combat forces. Yet, in May, Dienbienphu fell, and, in July, the Geneva Conference implicitly recognized the existence of a communist government in North Vietnam—both without the United States firing a shot. What restrained the president? Numerous theories have been proposed and include: (1) congressional opposition; (2) allied, especially British, reluctance; and (3) General Ridgway's warnings about pursuing land wars in Asia. Historian Townsend Hoopes has even concluded that the president simply had "a feeling in his bones."[31] Remarks at the March 25 NSC meeting suggest that the need for allies and need to satisfy Congress were critical considerations, but these mutually reinforcing constraints did not mean that Eisenhower let others make this decision. They were more indicative of a hope to avoid Truman's political error in Korea of committing U.S. forces without first securing adequate congressional and allied support.

During the closing days of March, the French position at Dienbienphu deteriorated rapidly and presented the administration with the need to act quickly, if at all. As late as March 26, Washington believed that the approaching rainy season in northern Vietnam would end the fighting before the Vietminh assault could achieve success. Since the French were almost totally dependent on parachute drops for resupply and reinforcement, however, the worsening weather was hurting Dienbienphu's defenders more than the attackers. If an air raid was to have any chance of success, Radford concluded, the time to act had arrived. His conviction was so strong that, on March 31, he recommended an immediate U.S. offer of air support to the French despite the unanimous dissent of the other service chiefs. Ridgway argued that air power alone would not win any war and that any U.S. involvement in Indochina would ultimately lead to the use of ground troops under extremely unfavorable battlefield conditions. The result would be "a dangerous strategic diversion of limited United States military capabilities . . . in a non-decisive theatre to the attainment of non-decisive local objectives."[32]

Meanwhile, Dulles was declaring, like Radford, that it was time for resolute action in Southeast Asia. On the evening of March 29, in a highly publicized address that Eisenhower had read carefully and approved, Dulles asserted that Indochina was of "great strategic value" and that the Vietminh were Soviet puppets. He termed a Vietminh victory "a grave threat to the whole free community" that "should not be passively accepted but should be met by united action."[33] Dulles' intent was to convey U.S. determination to other nations, prepare the American public for possible U.S. involvement in the fighting, and promote the idea of multilateral intervention.

"United action" was only a vague formula, however, unsupported by any specific arrangements with other nations. The rapidly changing battlefield situation at Dienbienphu meant that there might not be time to secure even an ad hoc alliance. On the morning of March 29, at a regular weekly briefing of Republican congressional leaders, the president bluntly announced that "at any time within the space of forty-eight hours, it might be necessary to move into the battle of Dien Bien Phu." The reference to forty-eight hours was notable, since that was the amount of time Radford had estimated would be necessary to launch an air strike. If this contingency should arise, the president asserted, "I will be calling in the Democrats as well as our Republican leaders to inform them of the action we're taking."[34] His use of the word "inform" rather than "consult" revealed no inclination to defer to Capitol Hill on this matter.

When he met with the NSC on the morning of April 1, Eisenhower was rapidly coming to a decision. In the meeting, he toyed with Radford's air strike plan. He specifically brought up the disagreement between Radford and the service chiefs over the air attack. He termed this question one for "statesmen," and even though he could "see a thousand variants in the equation and terrible risks," he declared that the intervention decision had to be confronted. When Dulles then tried to turn the discussion to specifics, however, Eisenhower abruptly dropped the issue.

He would not delegate the decision to the NSC but announced that he would pursue it after the meeting with a small group in the Oval Office.[35]

Although there are no records of this meeting nor even a list of participants in the Eisenhower Library or the Department of State files, it must have been a dramatic session. Dulles was present, and, from his telephone conversations later in the day, it is clear that (1) "something fairly serious had come up," (2) "time was a factor," and (3) there was need for an urgent meeting of the bipartisan congressional leadership.[36] The tenor of these conversations following on the heels of the NSC meeting implied the imminent possibility of implementing Radford's plan. In fact, shortly after the private session in his office, the president confided to two luncheon guests that the United States "might have to make decision to send in squadron from 2 aircraft carriers off coast to bomb Reds at Dien Bien Phu." He immediately added that "of course, if we did, we'd have to deny it forever."[37]

That last comment raises several questions about the president's decision to bring the congressional leadership "in on" the Vietnam deliberations at this point. Did Eisenhower want a formal authorization from Congress to use armed force in Vietnam? If so, why would legislatively sanctioned action have to be denied forever? Did he want something from Congress other than a joint resolution? The confusion over the president's motives derives from the ambiguous nature of his relationship with Capitol Hill. He later wrote that "we have a constitutional government and only when there is a sudden, unforseen emergency should the President put us into war without congressional action."[38] Dienbienphu was not a sudden development, and there is no reason to doubt Eisenhower's sincere respect for the constitutional role of Congress in decisions for war. On the other hand, he had little respect for the legislature's wisdom on international affairs. In February, the administration had managed to abort the Bricker Amendment that would have nullified executive authority in foreign policy. Privately, Eisenhower complained of the lack of congressional support, especially among Republicans, for his foreign policies. He had called the Dienbienphu decision one for "statesmen," and he did not include the leaders of Capitol Hill under that label.[39]

The meeting between administration representatives and congressional leaders was set for Saturday, April 3. In preparation, Eisenhower conferred on Friday with Dulles, Radford, and Secretary of Defense Charles Wilson. Dulles arrived at this session with a draft congressional resolution authorizing the president, at his discretion, "to employ the Naval and Air Forces of the United States to assist the forces which are resisting aggression in Southeast Asia."[40] Eisenhower agreed with the content of the draft but did not want it submitted to the congressmen. The Saturday briefing was only for Dulles and Radford "to develop" congressional thinking, and, in fact, the president would not even be present. Before confronting the legislators, however, the administration's own position needed to be clarified. Dulles' proposal for united action, which would require time for international consultations, conflicted with Radford's recommendation for an immediate strike. The admiral resolved this difference by making a significant concession. He declared that it was now too late for an air attack to save Dienbienphu itself. He maintained that armed intervention might still be needed in Indochina, but its use no longer depended on the Dienbienphu timetable. The meeting then adjourned with Wilson's suggestion that congressional support would "fill our hand" in negotiations with other nations on joint action.[41]

The eight congressional leaders present Saturday morning at the State Department accepted the premise that Indochina was of vital strategic importance but declared that "we want no more Koreas with the United States furnishing 90% of the manpower."[42] They insisted on commitments of allied support before Congress endorsed the use of U.S. forces in Southeast Asia. Concerned about the possible use of American land forces, they seemed satisfied by Radford's reassurance that no such action was contemplated. Afterward Dulles telephoned the president, who had gone to Camp David, Maryland, for the weekend. The secretary reported that the session had gone "pretty well—although it raised some serious problems."[43] The difficulty for the administration was not the insistence on allied support but that Congress wanted such support guaranteed before approving armed intervention. Dulles had hoped to be able to approach European leaders with the assurance of congressional sanction already secured. Despite this diplomatic complication, it would be an exaggeration to argue, as did journalist Chalmers Roberts in an account based on information leaked by Congressman John McCormack (D–Mass.), that April 3 was "the day we didn't go to war."[44]

Upon his return from Camp David on Sunday evening, Eisenhower made his basic policy known in a private White House gathering with Dulles, Radford, and a few others. According to his assistant Sherman Adams, the president agreed "to send American forces to Indo-China under certain strict conditions." There were three provisions—none of which included any reference to a congressional resolution. Eisenhower specified that (1) any intervention must be multinational and include Asians, (2) France must agree to stay in the war, and (3) the future independence of Vietnam, Laos, and Cambodia must be guaranteed to avoid any hint of colonialism.[45]

By coincidence, about an hour after this White House meeting, an urgent telegram arrived from Ambassador Dillon in Paris relaying an informal request by Premier Laniel for "immediate armed intervention of US carrier aircraft at Dien Bien Phu."[46] At about the same moment, a personal message from Eisenhower to British Prime Minister Winston Churchill was being prepared to begin the quest for allied intervention. The following morning, April 5, Dulles wired Dillon with the president's approval that "it is not possible for US to commit belligerent acts in Indochina without full political understanding with France and other countries." This message also declared that "Congressional action would be required" for U.S. military involvement.[47] Eisenhower, however, never pressed Congress for any specific authorization. In his memoirs, he credited Congress with the three preconditions for involvement, and Dulles claimed at the time that they "emerged" from the meeting on the third of April with congressional leaders.[48] These criteria had been developed by the administration, however, long before April 3. Also, neither Dulles' minutes of the meeting nor Roberts' account mentions such criteria. Congress received more retrospective credit for shaping U.S. policy in Indochina than it deserved.

Eisenhower was trying in late March and early April to finesse Congress into approving armed American intervention in Indochina without running the gauntlet of a formal vote. His weekly White House briefings of Republican leaders, Dulles' united action speech, and the April 3 meeting were all moves in a effort to bring key congressional leaders into the decision making without really giving them a voice. The president had just fought a battle with powerful members of his own party over executive authority in foreign affairs, and he was trying to circumvent another clash. What he wanted was "some kind of arrangement" with Congress but not a formal resolution supporting intervention for which the administration would have to fight "like dogs" on Capitol Hill.[49]

Eisenhower was not necessarily intent on U.S. military intervention in Indochina, but he wanted an unfettered hand if he decided that the situation required direct American action.[50] Since January, when the NSC first confronted the challenge of Dienbienphu, the president had been constantly improvising, and the final direction of U.S. policy remained unclear to him. Doubtlessly he recognized that his three requirements for U.S. intervention made the immediate use of American forces unlikely, but they did not foreclose that option. Eisenhower had affirmed, albeit torturously, that a rationale existed for the insertion of U.S. armed might. His search for a prudent but decisive American contribution to the struggle against communism in Southeast Asia was just beginning.

For three weeks after the dispatch of Eisenhower's letter to Churchill on April 4, the administration sought unsuccessfully to arrange an immediate, allied military intervention in Indochina. On April 6, the president stated emphatically that "there is no possibility whatever of unilateral intervention in Indochina." Instead, he enthusiastically called for a political organization for the "defense of Southeast Asia even if Indochina is lost."[51] Collective defense was not a new idea, but here the president planted the seeds of what in September 1954 blossomed into the Southeast Asia Collective Defense Treaty, also known as SEATO or the Manila Pact.[52]

Despite the eventual commitment to a formal treaty structure, in early April the concept was improvisational and not carefully conceived. The American diplomatic initiative sought primarily to satisfy the president's three preconditions for intervention. If the proposed alliance could include the Associated States of Vietnam, Laos, and Cambodia as well as France, the United Kingdom, and regional nations such as Thailand, the Philippines, Australia, and New Zealand, then all three criteria could be met and joint military intervention against the Vietminh could proceed. The long-term implications of a regional arrangement were less clear and, in fact, quite confused. In arguing for the concept, Eisenhower used the domino theory to justify it, but he simultaneously suggested that with this structure the loss of Indochina would not necessarily mean the loss of all of Southeast Asia. Another contradiction, noted by Vice President Richard M. Nixon, was whether a NATO-like defense against overt aggression could combat internal communist subversion by a guerrilla movement. Secretary of the Treasury George Humphrey was also concerned that the United States might be embarking on a "policy of policing all the governments of the world." Eisenhower, however, could not be dissuaded. With a regional grouping "the battle is two-thirds won," he believed optimistically, because with domestic and allied support "we might thereafter not be required to contemplate a unilateral American intervention in Indochina."[53]

During April, though, no regional defense group materialized. Both Britain and France promptly rejected the notion of taking any provocative action that might undermine the approaching Geneva negotiations. Both nations expressed concern that a Western-backed alliance might precipitate direct Chinese communist intervention in Vietnam and even run the risk of World War III. For Premier Laniel, any appearance of evading a reasonable diplomatic solution at Geneva risked the fall of his government. Also, some French politicians seemed to prefer the loss of Indochina over the ignominy of rescue by an international posse, because such humiliation could encourage greater unrest in France's African colonies. The responses of other nations varied from Australian caution to Philippine enthusiasm, but European intransigence was the major obstacle to the American plan. Britain's reaction especially disappointed Eisenhower and Dulles, who already had differences with London over hydrogen-bomb testing and East-West trade. The British indicated support for the regional defense concept in Southeast Asia but disagreed that it had to be accomplished prior to Geneva. Furthermore, Churchill simply did not view Vietnam as Armageddon: "I have suffered Singapore, Hong Kong, Tobruk," he remarked; "the French will have Dien Bien Phu."[54]

Despite the diplomatic frustration, the United States remained prepared for immediate military intervention. Radford continually updated contingency plans, and the White House staff was "on an hour's call to return to Washington because of Indochina" even while the president took time for a brief escape to his golf retreat at Augusta, Georgia. As late as April 24, Eisenhower's press secretary James Hagerty noted in his diary that the option of using two aircraft carriers "to support French troops at Dien Bien Phu" was still in place. Eisenhower remained committed, however, to his decision that there would be no unilateral U.S. intervention. Nixon observed that the president "seemed resigned to doing nothing at all unless we could get the allies and the country to go along." When newspapers published a supposedly off-the-record remark by the vice president on April 16 about U.S. forces possibly replacing French troops in Indochina, the White House quickly announced that the quote did not reflect the administration's position and reaffirmed Dulles' united action speech of March 29 as the authoritative statement on U.S. policy. Nixon assumed individual responsibility for his statement but claimed later that Dulles personally agreed with him.[55]

By the time the Geneva Conference opened on April 26, the option of immediate, allied military intervention was, in effect, dead. Although remnants of the French garrison at Dienbienphu still held out, their final collapse was imminent. On April 23, Laniel informed Dulles that the only remaining alternatives were a massive U.S. air strike or a cease-fire. In other discussions, the French admitted that bombing could no longer save Dienbienphu but argued that it might strengthen collapsing morale in France and enable the government to continue the war. France might withdraw in any case, though, and Eisenhower reaffirmed his position that "concerted action is the only acceptable formula." After personal meetings in Paris and London with French and British leaders, Dulles reported on April 25 that there was simply no time left to arrange the political understandings necessary for joint action.[56]

Although the real likelihood of immediate U.S. military intervention had passed, the possibility of such action did reappear during the Geneva Conference. After the final fall of Dienbienphu on May 7 and with negotiations at Geneva showing little prospect of quick progress, Laniel reopened the subject of U.S. intervention, perhaps without Britain. After conferring with Dulles, Radford, Wilson, and others, Eisenhower renewed the offer of American military involvement in Indochina, but his conditions were as firm as ever. He did not make British participation a prerequisite, but the president insisted that the war be "internationalized." He declared that the Philippines and Thailand must join and that Australia and New Zealand had to be willing to enter soon. Further, France would have to guarantee the full independence of the Associated States. There was no apparent reason to doubt that, if these conditions were met, the United States would have been willing to use armed force. Dulles speculated, however, that France was seeking to keep open the option of U.S. intervention only as a bargaining ploy with the Vietminh. When France failed to satisfy Washington's conditions, Dulles observed that "probably the French did not really want intervention but wanted to have the possibility of a card to play at Geneva."[57]

Eisenhower's insistence on internationalizing the war and refusal to rush to France's rescue at the eleventh hour reflected a shift in his thinking toward a long-term, allied, military defense of Southeast Asia. The regional defense group proposal had been under consideration since Dulles' united action speech of March 29, but, until the start of the Geneva Conference, the plan was contemplated primarily as a means of reinvigorating the French effort. During the last week of April and first week of May, the regional alliance concept increasingly took on a rationale of its own without reference to France. Anticipating the surrender of Dienbienphu, the president wanted to draw lessons from the French debacle and move on to broader concerns.

In Eisenhower's estimation, Dienbienphu raised two fundamental issues: imperialism and collective security. At his weekly conference with Republican congressional leaders on April 26, he argued that Dienbienphu dramatized the importance of avoiding "any implication of colonialism as well as any implication that the United States would carry alone the burden of defense of the free world."[58] A regional military coalition that included Asians solved both problems. "To contemplate anything else," Eisenhower wrote in a personal letter on the same day, "is to lay ourselves open to the charge of imperialism and colonialism or —at the very least—of objectionable paternalism."[59] In his opinion, France had failed largely because it never gave the vast majority of Vietnamese, who were not Vietminh, anything for which to fight. By unequivocally promising independence, Eisenhower envisioned a Western-Asian partnership that would put the struggle in the proper perspective, namely "the free world against the forces of enslavement."[60]

Eisenhower's cold war rhetoric articulated his sincere faith in collective security forged in his World War II experiences. In 1948, he had concluded his wartime memoirs, *Crusade in Europe,* with the prediction that "the areas in which freedom flourishes will continue to shrink unless the supporters of democracy . . . meet Communist-regimented unity with the voluntary unity of common purpose."[61] In 1954, Eisenhower warned that "we must have collective security or we'll fall." With an alliance, he asserted confidently, "our determination to lead the free world into a voluntary association . . . would make further Communist encroachment impossible."[62]

By early May, the president could not even conceive of some of his earlier policy considerations. On May 5, he declared with apparent conviction that "the US had *never* considered unilateral intervention solely to help the French," although on March 25 the NSC, chaired by the president, had directed its staff to study unilateral intervention among other alternatives.[63] Eisenhower now denounced unilateral intervention. One disadvantage, especially if France withdrew from the fight, was that "in the eyes of many Asian people [the United States would] merely replace French colonialism with American colonialism." In language similar to that of General Ridgway, he also argued that the United States would exhaust its global power if it were drawn unilaterally into "brush-fire wars" that "frittered away our resources in local engagements." He told the NSC that the prospect of U.S. combat divisions scattered over the world as a police force frightened him to death, and that he would ask Congress for a general mobilization for war before sending divisions to Indochina. Furthermore, Eisenhower contended that allies were essential to prevent America itself from becoming an isolated outpost much like Dienbienphu with no choice but "to surrender or die." He decried the "damn fool fortress America idea" of some Old Guard Republicans that left no alternative but "an attack with everything we have. What a terrible decision that would be." To Eisenhower, then, a policy of unilateral intervention invited charges of imperialism, a weakening of U.S. global power, and the risk of total war.[64]

Conversely, a regional defense alliance in Southeast Asia had a number of positive attractions for the president. It would demonstrate determination "to oppose chipping away of any part of the free world" and would "get what we wanted at the least cost" in money and men. If the proposed coalition materialized, he said, "I don't see any reason for American ground troops to be committed to Indo China." Eisenhower reasoned that "there are plenty of people in Asia, and we can train them to fight well." In this 1954 version of what became known as Vietnamization in the late 1960s, Eisenhower envisioned the use of "some of our planes or aircraft carriers off the coast and some of our fighting craft we have in the area for support." In the president's view, an alliance was a tough stand acceptable to the American public as long as the administration did "not talk of intervention with U.S. ground forces."[65]

In May 1954, Americans were not fighting and dying in Vietnam. For that result Eisenhower deserved credit. Consistent with the revisionist historians' image, the president actively directed the policy-making process during the Dienbienphu crisis.[66] Contrary to the revisionists' emphasis on his restraint, however, the old soldier had not beaten his sword into a plowshare. Throughout the Indochina discussions, he focused consistently on a military deterrent to communist expansion in Southeast Asia. As he confided privately to his longtime friend Swede Hazlett, the president wanted to see the communists "take a good smacking in Indochina."[67] Eisenhower never decided not to intervene militarily in Vietnam. Rather he chose to define very specific criteria for intervention that simply allowed a momentary escape from what historian Bernard Fall called "the cul-de-sac of military intervention," which Eisenhower's own administration had constructed.[68] Eisenhower charted the course that President Lyndon Johnson followed to the fateful decisions of 1964 and 1965 to drop the bombs and land the Marines.

Eisenhower's emphasis on allies, air power, anticolonial appeals, cost-cutting, and tough rhetoric was impeccably consistent with New Look strategy. He sought to avoid the criticism of "no more Koreas," but simultaneously he was laying the groundwork for future involvement. U.S. military intervention in Vietnam in the spring of 1954, with or without allies, would have been part of France's war and its controversial legacy. Dulles later called Dienbienphu "a blessing in disguise" because "we have a clear base there now, without a taint of colonialism."[69] When the Laniel government fell in mid-June and the new premier Pierre Mendès-France decided to compromise with the Vietminh at Geneva, two of Eisenhower's three criteria for intervention—French pledges to stay in the war and to speed Indochinese independence—became largely moot. Eisenhower's third precondition—a Southeast Asian defense coalition—was finally obtained in September with the Manila Pact.

Eisenhower's interest in Radford's air strike plan suggests that the president was prepared to commit U.S. air power to Indochina, provided that his preconditions were met. It could be argued that congressional opposition intimidated the administration, but the more likely scenario is that the administration was trying to circumvent Congress. The initial moves did not work before the battlefield conditions at Dienbienphu collapsed. As of early April, however, the French war in Indochina was not over, and there was still time for more gambits. The April quest for united action was one of these, and there would be others. The SEATO treaty would be the master political stroke, for with it Eisenhower and Dulles would largely neutralize congressional concerns about the unilateral burden of America's last war.[70] In their jockeying with Congress, however, they were creating a legal rationale for America's next war. The dictum of "no more Koreas" had Congress and the president looking back over their shoulders instead of forward toward where they were headed.

III

The Geneva Conference and the "Diem Card" (May–June 1954)

As HAD been true in the past, policy considerations external to Southeast Asia played a greater role in U.S. decisions during the Geneva Conference than did the internal realities of Vietnamese politics. Yet, during the meeting, the question of who among the Vietnamese would lead the opposition to the Vietminh assumed increasing importance. Both the Truman and Eisenhower administrations had often demanded that France grant full independence to Bao Dai's State of Vietnam. With the French delegation at Geneva surrendering much of French power in Indochina, the creation of an autonomous anticommunist regime in Saigon became more critical to U.S. hopes of holding the line against communist expansion in the region. Throughout the Indochina portion of the Geneva Conference from May 8 to July 21, 1954, Washington pursued a two-track approach. Seeking to preserve harmony within the Western alliance, the Eisenhower administration stood aside while French diplomats bargained with the communist delegations. At the same time, American officials began looking beyond Geneva for ways to help Vietnamese nationalists prevent "Communist colonialism" from replacing French colonialism.[1]

Like the Versailles Conference after World War I, the Geneva Conference marked the end of one war but sowed the seeds for a second and more devastating conflict. Also similar to 1919 was the olympian and even sanctimonious U.S. attitude toward the proceedings. In both cases, American officials believed that the misguided ideologies and selfish ambitions of those who initiated the fighting had produced an unnecessary tragedy. To U.S. leaders, the situation was still salvageable. Although the United States chose to observe at Geneva, not lead as it had at Versailles, ultimately America refused to sanction the results of either conference in calculated displays of disgust with imperfect compromises.

The Eisenhower administration had not liked the implications of negotiations from the inception of the idea at Berlin in February 1954. Any compromise with communists was at best more of the old containment strategy, and at worst was a loss of ground to communist expansion. Either way, compromise was not consistent with the New Look strategy of regaining the initiative against world communism. According to New Look theory, some limited diplomatic contact with adversaries might be advantageous, but John Foster Dulles worried about British and French eagerness to negotiate with the communists. He shuddered at comparisons to Locarno, Munich, and Yalta as precedents of diplomatic weakness in the face of dictatorial, ambitious, and ruthless regimes. His fears of appeasement grew when Pierre Mendès-France replaced Joseph Laniel as French premier on June 18, and pledged to reach an agreement at Geneva by July 20. Although the Eisenhower-Dulles team had hoped that the conference might deadlock and end with no agreement, it made no active attempt to prevent a settlement. Rather, the U.S. tactic was to make every effort to keep the door ajar for an Americanization of the anticommunist effort after Geneva.[2]

Largely to avoid a political firestorm from right-wing Republicans, the Eisenhower administration decided to maintain a low profile at Geneva. Secretary of State Dulles headed the U.S. delegation at the opening of the conference on April 26, but had returned to Washington before the Indochina talks began on May 8. He left Under Secretary Walter Bedell Smith in charge. A close confidant of both Eisenhower and Dulles, Smith kept the administration intimately but less publicly in touch with the negotiations. He also had served as U.S. ambassador in Moscow and as CIA director and could provide Washington expert assessments of Soviet conduct during the talks.[3]

The most prominent Western leader at the meeting, aside from the French diplomats, was Britain's foreign secretary Anthony Eden. He served as cochairman of the conference with Soviet foreign minister Vyacheslav M. Molotov. Somewhat to the dismay of his aides, Eden sought to cultivate a personal rapport with the Russian. He believed that the Soviets shared his desire to act as a moderating influence on the more bellicose Americans and Chinese. Eden's attitude and the previous British resistance to Washington's proposals for united action in Indochina made Washington reluctant to remain entirely passive at Geneva.[4]

With the approval of Washington, Smith engaged in some exploratory contacts with the Soviet and Chinese delegations. The New Look strategy included the idea that talks with the enemy could be manipulated to U.S. advantage, and the Geneva venue offered an opportunity to test that approach. Despite official American rhetoric condemning the international communist monolith, some U.S. analysts believed that it might be possible to split the Russians and Chinese through careful diplomacy. Smith probed for signs of an opening that the United States might exploit but found none. The abstract benefits of negotiations fell victim to the real distrust that had long pervaded U.S.–Soviet dialogue. The administration then turned its efforts away from its adversaries to its allies.[5]

With regard to Britain and France, U.S. policy continued to emphasize the idea, which had emerged from the Dienbienphu deliberations, of a collective defense system for Southeast Asia. For this plan to succeed, the United States needed good relations with its Western allies and, optimally, a military foothold in Indochina. A frequently mentioned scenario that would achieve these objectives was to partition Vietnam between the Democratic Republic of Vietnam (DRV) in the North and the State of Vietnam in the South. Such a plan would leave the French an area of influence in their former colony, satisfy the British desire for peaceful compromise, and provide the United States a base for building up anticommunist strength in the region.[6]

Regardless of its merits, partition had some serious limitations. To espouse it publicly would expose the Eisenhower administration to damaging political attacks. Some members of Congress and some journalists were already censuring the mere presence of U.S. diplomats at Geneva, and they would likely label it a sellout if the United States accepted a settlement that left communists in possession of part of Vietnam.[7] Furthermore, all Vietnamese factions claimed to reject totally the idea of partition. If they adhered to that position, any attempt to force partition on the Vietnamese could break up the conference and lead to a resumption of hostilities. In the wake of the Vietminh victory at Dienbienphu, the return to battle risked the conquest of Vietnam by DRV forces.

When the Geneva Conference convened, the Democratic Republic of Vietnam's bargaining position appeared strong. It had military and political strength in large areas of rural Vietnam; the French clearly wanted out of *la guerre sale* ("the dirty war"); and U.S. bombers remained in their bases and on their aircraft carriers. These were positive factors for the Vietminh, but they were far from decisive and were, in fact, misleading. Chaotic efforts at land reform in Vietminh-dominated areas had unleashed turmoil between peasants and communist cadres that severely weakened the DRV's economic and political base. Although the French wanted a military disengagement, they were not ready to surrender any more political influence or economic interests in Indochina than necessary. As for American intervention, the use of U.S. armed forces against the Vietminh was only in abeyance and not absolutely proscribed. The uncertainty of Washington's future course weighed heavily in the considerations of all the parties at Geneva.

Since Geneva was a "big power" conference, the DRV also found itself in the role of pawn, not king, in a cold war chess game. While not surprised that the capitalist nations—the United States, the United Kingdom, and France—sought to thwart them, the Vietnamese communists discovered that their proletarian allies—the Soviet Union and the People's Republic of China (PRC)—placed their own interests over those of their Vietminh comrades. Neither Moscow nor Beijing wanted a showdown with Washington over Indochina. A failure to achieve an armistice at Geneva could prolong the war and increase the possibility of U.S. military intervention—either unilaterally or as part of a "united action." By being flexible on Southeast Asia, the Soviets hoped to encourage Paris to resist American arguments for the creation of an anti-Russian European Defense Community (EDC). A reasonable compromise also conformed to Chinese objectives. The Beijing regime needed a period of "peaceful coexistence" to allow it time to struggle with its enormous internal task of converting China's hundreds of millions of people—mostly peasants—into socialists obedient to the Chinese Communist Party. That effort had been interrupted by the Korean War, and the PRC's leaders wanted "no more Koreas" for a while. Hence, the Chinese and Soviet delegations joined with the British and French to fashion a settlement that fell far short of the DRV's initial expectations.[8]

The proceedings at Geneva disappointed the DRV, but they threatened the French-installed State of Vietnam with possible extinction. That demise would mean the end of U.S. hopes to salvage an alternative to the Vietminh. At the time of the Geneva Conference, the practically moribund regime in Saigon appeared to be Washington's last best hope to keep at least part of Vietnam out of the clutches of communism. Some American officials expressed a desire for a "third force" that was neither communist nor colonialist, but no such organized group existed. Although acutely aware of Bao Dai's "known deficiencies," Dulles instructed the U.S. delegation at Geneva "not to attempt [to] find [a] substitute for Bao Dai but to avail ourselves of what he has to offer."[9]

The Bao Dai solution was as problem-plagued in 1954 as it had been when the French initiated it in 1949–50. Although the emperor was head of state, he avoided almost completely his capital city of Saigon. When in Vietnam, he stayed at his hunting lodge near the mountain resort of Dalat. When in France, he preferred Cannes, on the French Riviera, where he went to live in the spring of 1954, never to return to Vietnam. It is difficult to measure precisely the extent of Bao Dai's personal involvement in the affairs of his government. He had a steady stream of official visitors, but his contact with his administrators was often through Nguyen De, his "cabinet director." De was a mysterious and secretive figure whom some observers believed was or had been a French secret agent. His tasks supposedly were to see that Bao Dai's notorious appetite for the pleasures of the flesh was satisfied, to keep him politically impotent, and to maintain the façade of Bao Dai's authority as the source of legitimacy for the State of Vietnam.[10]

When the Geneva Conference began, Prince Buu Loc was Bao Dai's prime minister and the fifth man to hold that post. Bao Dai had begun as his own prime minister when Ngo Dinh Diem turned down the office in 1949. Nguyen Phan Long, a journalist, held the position for a few weeks in early 1950, but his desire for more direct U.S. participation in the Indochina War angered France. To satisfy Paris, Bao Dai replaced Long with Tran Van Huu, a rich landowner and French citizen. Under Huu and his successor Nguyen Van Tam, a bureaucrat who had long been notorious for his collaboration with the colonialists, the State of

Vietnam was unquestionably a French puppet regime. This thriving neocolonialism had outraged so many Vietnamese by late 1953 that Bao Dai had no choice but to restructure his cabinet. Buu Loc, the emperor's thirty-nine-year-old cousin, faced the challenge to initiate some nationalist reforms or preside over the collapse of the Bao Dai experiment.[11]

Historian Bernard Fall has noted that Britain granted independence to Burma in 1948 in a four-page document but that France followed the Elysée agreements with a 258–page convention covering every detail of Vietnam's internal administration.[12] Despite talks between Saigon and Paris from 1950 to 1953, the French refused to yield on Vietnam's membership in the French Union, currency regulations, protection of French property, and dozens of other restrictions of Vietnamese sovereignty. One of the biggest criticisms of the Saigon regime, beyond its inability to gain concessions from Paris, was its failure to provide some form of popular assembly to give the many religious and political factions, especially in the South, a sense of participation in the regime. Another major problem was the nondevelopment of the Vietnamese National Army (VNA). Although there were over two hundred thousand Vietnamese in the VNA by December 1953 and this army was part of the French Union forces battling the DRV's People's Army of Vietnam, the French allowed these troops no autonomy or sense of national service. In March 1954, Buu Loc traveled to Paris to seek an agreement on "independence and association" that would give the State of Vietnam the political integrity it needed for survival but that would maintain an alliance with France to counter the continuing military threat from the communists.[13]

While Buu Loc negotiated in Paris and Bao Dai brooded in Cannes, other Vietnamese leaders maneuvered for advantage or influence within the incredibly fractionalized politics of southern Vietnam. Principal among these alternative leaders were Nguyen Van Hinh, Phan Huy Quat, and Ngo Dinh Diem. In addition, three so-called sects—the Hoa Hao, Cao Dai, and Binh Xuyen—possessed their own political ambitions and sources of power.

Hinh and Quat both held office in the Bao Dai government, but the two represented very different elements of Vietnamese society. General Hinh was chief of staff of the VNA and the son of former prime minister Nguyen Van Tam. Like his father, Hinh was a French citizen and generally viewed as a French stooge. He typified that thin strata of

Vietnamese who blatantly embraced the colonialists for personal advantage. His military ability and personal support within the VNA were minimal, but his ambition was excessive. With more swagger than good sense, he envisioned himself becoming a military dictator, who, with the help of some of his pals from the French officer corps, would lead the State of Vietnam to triumph over the communists.[14]

As minister of national defense, Phan Huy Quat was supposedly Hinh's superior, although such distinctions were meaningless in Bao Dai's fragile regime. A forty-five-year-old Hanoi physician, Dr. Quat had served as defense minister under Long and Tam and was the senior member of Buu Loc's cabinet. He became acting prime minister when Buu Loc traveled to Paris in March 1954. This lean, energetic intellectual with piercing eyes was one of the most able of the anti-Vietminh politicians who had cast their lot with Bao Dai after the Elysée agreements. An ardent nationalist, Quat had worked hard from within the limitations of the Bao Dai solution for greater independence for the State of Vietnam and for the development and autonomy of the VNA. As a leading figure in the Dai Viet party, he had a meaningful political base. His party was small but larger and better organized than most Vietnamese political groups. Within Vietnam, Quat had an excellent reputation for intelligence, political experience, and integrity.[15]

Outside Bao Dai's government stood Ngo Dinh Diem with his own reputation for nationalist and anticommunist integrity. Facing a threat of Vietminh assassination, Diem had left Vietnam in 1950 shortly after his rejection of Bao Dai's offer of the prime ministership. He did some traveling in Japan, Europe, and the United States but for two years lived an essentially secluded life in a Roman Catholic seminary in Lakewood, New Jersey. While in America, he met some lower-level State Department bureaucrats, some Catholic leaders including Francis Cardinal Spellman, and some members of Congress such as Senator Mike Mansfield (D-Mont.) and Congressman John Kennedy (D-Mass.). Although usually critical of Bao Dai's subservience to the French when talking with Americans, he kept the door open for a possible role in a Bao Dai government. He wanted to be prime minister, and, through family members in Vietnam and France, he maintained contact with the emperor.

In many respects Diem was an unlikely candidate for national leadership. In 1954 he was fifty-three years old and had not held any government office for over twenty years—a virtual millennium in view of the revolutionary upheaval in his country since 1945. Although respected for his honesty and courage, he was also quite eccentric. From his youth, he had been a loner and had developed an ascetic and reclusive life-style. He avoided and even feared women and spent many hours alone reading and meditating. He was no conversationalist and often exhausted visitors with long monologues on Vietnamese history. He had a wide face and usually dressed in white suits, which, on his short, round body made him look like a "porcelain Buddha."[16]

Diem and his five brothers and three sisters were the children of an aristocratic but not wealthy Catholic family from the old imperial capital of Hue. Their family heritage automatically set them apart from the Vietnamese masses, who were primarily peasants, Buddhists, and concentrated in the Red River delta in the North and the Mekong delta in the South. The oldest brother, Ngo Dinh Khoi, was a provincial governor before his murder in 1945. Ngo Dinh Thuc, the next oldest, was bishop of Vinh Long in 1954 and one of his country's leading Catholic churchmen. Diem was next in age followed by Ngo Dinh Nhu. "Brother Nhu," as American officials later came to call him, was variously a librarian, journalist, and labor organizer, but his primary job was promoting and protecting the political future of his brother Diem. Ngo Dinh Can, the second-youngest brother, lived in the ancestral home in Hue from where he wielded extensive power as the virtual political boss of central Vietnam. The youngest brother was Ngo Dinh Luyen, who was educated as a mechanical engineer but who served primarily as the family's agent in Europe. Little is known of the three Ngo sisters, but Ngo Dinh Nhu's attractive, impulsive, and clever wife Tran Le Xuan — known to Westerners as Madame Nhu — was a forceful figure within the family. Although Nhu had established a network of political contacts, the Ngo family operated essentially as its own political group separate from other organized parties. It benefited from the natural affinity of the 10 percent of Vietnamese who were Catholics, but there was no organized Catholic political party.[17]

Although there was neither a Catholic nor a Buddhist party in South Vietnam, locally powerful political-religious sects exercised actual political, economic, and military control over sizable areas. The largest and best organized of these was the Cao Dai, which claimed over a million adherents and had an army of 10,000 to 20,000 troops. From its "Holy See" and administrative center at Tay Ninh, it taxed and governed much of the population immediately north and northwest of Saigon. The Cao Dai religion was an eclectic blend of Buddhism, Catholicism, and peasant beliefs in spirits and mediums. Many observers considered its leader or "pope," Pham Cong Tac, the shrewdest politician in Vietnam. He had often demonstrated his ability to join with the Vietminh, the French, or neither in order to protect and expand his sect's power. Southwest of Saigon, the Hoa Hao sect exercised a role similar to the Cao Dai north of the city. Its religious doctrine was a simplistic variant of Buddhism that had strong appeal to poor peasants unable to afford elaborate rituals. Its leadership was more fractionalized and oppressive than that of the Cao Dai, and its total following was smaller. Still, Hoa Hao armed forces totaled several thousand.[18]

A third sect, the Binh Xuyen, was not religious in any way but possessed some of the same quasi-feudal characteristics as the Cao Dai and Hoa Hao. The Binh Xuyen was a criminal gang of 2500 well-armed thugs, and its fief was the vice establishments of Cholon, Saigon's sprawling suburban slum. There it operated the huge Grande Monde gambling complex, the largest brothel in Asia (known as the Hall of Mirrors), an opium factory, scores of opium dens, and other illicit as well as legitimate businesses that produced millions of dollars in revenues. The leader of this mob was an illiterate former river pirate known as Bay Vien. His real name was Le Van Vien. In his heavily fortified headquarters in Cholon, he kept a tiger and crocodiles to whom, reputedly, he fed those who displeased him. The French had given him the rank of colonel and later brigadier general and with it a token of respectability in order to gain his cooperation against the Vietminh.[19]

Despite the political fragmentation of the State of Vietnam, Bao Dai boldly asserted in January 1954 that many of the factions were loyal to him or at least had a "nostalgic" attachment to the monarchy. In a conversation with Donald R. Heath, the U.S. ambassador in Saigon, the emperor declared that he could count on support from Quat, the Catholics, the Ngo family, and the peasants. He admitted that many members of Vietnam's elite were "fence-sitting" and that the sects were an "uncertain" element. He blamed the French for encouraging the sects to sell their loyalty to the highest bidder. To gain the aid of the large Cao Dai and Hoa Hao armies against the Vietminh, the French were giving their commanders large cash subsidies.[20]

With the announcement at Berlin in February that the negotiations scheduled for Geneva would include Indochina, the loosely woven fabric of Bao Dai's regime began to show definite signs of unraveling. Saigon filled with confusion and rumors. Fearing that a Geneva agreement might include the communists in a coalition government, the Cao Dai, Hoa Hao, and Dai Viet began in advance of the conference to demand a greater role in the present government. Bao Dai himself complained that Buu Loc had not done enough to placate the sects with cabinet posts and the granting of lucrative rice export licenses. General Hinh began making ominous warnings that, unless the State of Vietnam acted quickly against the Vietminh before the Geneva meeting, "you might as well wipe Vietnam off the map." He recommended that the VNA "assume a political role" in place of Buu Loc's cabinet of "school boys from Paris." Meanwhile, some Catholic leaders, including Ngo Dinh Nhu, were meeting with representatives of the Binh Xuyen and Cao Dai in a purported effort to form a new nationalist coalition—the Movement of National Union. All of this activity prompted Bao Dai to reshuffle the cabinet in mid-April and to integrate Cao Dai, Hoa Hao, and Binh Xuyen forces into the VNA. He stopped short of removing Buu Loc in the midst of his talks with the increasingly shaky Laniel government, which was in the throes of the Dienbienphu crisis.[21]

In Washington, Eisenhower and Dulles were working to arrange allied support for joint military action in Indochina and not giving much thought to the composition of Bao Dai's cabinet. The president's ad hoc advisory committee on Indochina recommended in March, however, that the United States establish a psychological warfare program for the "development of indigenous leadership which will be truly representative and symbolic of Indo-Chinese national aspirations and win the loyalty and support of the people."[22] This program was to be a joint State-Defense-CIA effort, and CIA Director Allen Dulles selected Air Force Colonel Edward G. Lansdale to lead it.[23] In April, as the leadership question in Saigon grew increasingly urgent, Lansdale was in Manila working on a similar program for the Philippine government of Ramon Magsaysay. Lieutenant General John W. O'Daniel, the chief of the U.S. Military Assistance Advisory Group (MAAG) in Indochina, brought Lansdale to Saigon for consultations on April 24, and sent a message to Washington requesting the colonel's reassignment to Vietnam "under guise Assistant Air Attache" effective May 15. Lansdale returned briefly to Manila, but by the first of June he was setting up shop in Saigon.[24]

At about the same moment that O'Daniel was starting the wheels in motion for clandestine American efforts to influence and strengthen Vietnam's leadership, Bao Dai made a major move of his own to protect his interests. Over the protests of Buu Loc, the emperor officially transferred control of the Vietnamese Sûreté or national police to the Binh Xuyen effective May 1, and prepared to place the local Saigon-Cholon police under the control of the vice lords. By this incredibly mercenary move, Bao Dai gained millions of dollars of income in bribes and kickbacks and a forceful political ally in Bay Vien. He also greatly exacerbated the internal problems of his country. The other sects and political groups were quick to oppose the Binh Xuyen's new authority, and the way was open to total lawlessness in Saigon, Cholon, and throughout southern Vietnam.[25]

During the first two weeks of May, the future prospects of the State of Vietnam could not have been bleaker. Dienbienphu fell as the Indochina phase of the Geneva Conference opened. The DRV seemed on the verge of victory in the Indochina War, and the State of Vietnam was in shambles. The Cao Dai pope issued a public appeal to Ho Chi Minh for cooperation. Quat labeled Buu Loc as "spineless," and Bao Dai demonstrated no interest in returning to Vietnam to take personal charge of his government. Robert McClintock, the U.S. chargé d'affaires in Saigon while Ambassador Heath served on the U.S. delegation in Geneva, described the situation as an "instance of how governance of an oriental kingdom by remote control can prove unfortunate." An incredible message from Bao Dai to Acting Prime Minister Quat prompted McClintock's comment. The emperor instructed his officials to "compose their differences" or prepare for the "arrival of foreign troops on Vietnamese soil and even possible use of atom bomb."[26]

The atom-bomb reference indicated to the American chargé that Bao Dai considered U.S. intervention the last hope of the State of Vietnam. Although Washington was not planning a nuclear strike, State Department bureaucrats were discussing who might assume leadership in Saigon if the present government fell. Analysts in the Division of Philippine and Southeast Asian Affairs produced a list of sixteen people whom they considered both anticommunist and pro-American. Ngo Dinh Diem headed the list, which also included Nhu, Thuc, and Quat. This report described Diem as "perhaps the most popular personality in the country after Ho Chi Minh" and claimed further that Diem had "strong backing in Vietnam."[27] Robert E. Hoey, the officer in charge of Indochinese affairs, and Everett F. Drumright, deputy assistant secretary of state for Far Eastern affairs, reacted warily that "the national following of the listed personalities is pretty much unknown."[28] In fact, in early May, Diem and Nhu appeared powerless and far removed from any political prospects. According to a French friend of the Ngos, Nhu made "his living by running a very minor publication and lives with his wife in a tiny hut in an out-of-the-way part of Saigon." Diem was in France and reportedly had "no more than three shirts to his name" and was "supported by friends."[29]

By mid-June, the down-and-out Diem was the new prime minister of the State of Vietnam. How this appointment came about has long intrigued journalists, scholars, and other observers of Vietnamese politics. Its details were obscure at the time and have remained largely hidden. One theory holds that American officials picked Diem and either forced or urged Bao Dai to accept their choice. While true that Cardinal Spellman, Senator Mansfield, and some other prominent Americans knew Diem, there is no evidence that the White House or State Department promoted him or that Eisenhower or Secretary Dulles were any more than vaguely aware of him. According to confidential reports from the U.S. embassy in Saigon, the identification of Diem as the American candidate was simply a rumor. Since CIA records for the period remain classified, it is impossible to assess to what extent the agency may have clandestinely orchestrated or encouraged the selection of Diem. A National Intelligence Estimate issued by the CIA and military intelligence branches on May 21 made no mention of Diem or even of an anticipated change in prime ministers. Similarly, there was no discussion of any political changes in Saigon recorded in the National Security Council minutes for May and June.[30]

Rejecting the thesis that American pressure produced the Diem government, other writers have argued that Bao Dai turned to Diem because he was the only available choice. This theory maintains that all other prominent nationalist leaders had lost credibility by past collaboration with the French or rejected the seemingly impossible task of resuscitating the Saigon regime. Diem won his post without competition, in this view, and may have been a scapegoat to preside over the final demise of the State of Vietnam. Some authors theorize that the French, who disliked Diem and expected him to fail, arranged his appointment as a way to discredit him and to make way for someone less hostile to French interests.[31] These are facile explanations, however, in view of the number of individuals and factions in Saigon who stood ready to seize what power and influence they could.

The most likely scenario was that Bao Dai chose Diem not as the last act of the Bao Dai solution but rather as the first step in a new strategy for the beleaguered State of Vietnam. The fall of Dienbienphu on May 7 and the likelihood of a negotiated settlement at Geneva signaled the beginning of the end for the French in Indochina. After years of forced dependence on the French for his personal and political welfare, Bao Dai had to look elsewhere for a patron for his endangered state. The emperor was a "true Asian monarch, with a subtle grasp of politics and an instinctive ability to manipulate men," according to Bui Diem, an aide to Phan Huy Quat. Bui Diem was in France in the spring of 1954 to work for his boss' selection as prime minister, belying the notion that Ngo Dinh Diem had no competition. From his close vantage point, Quat's representative observed that Bao Dai had always shifted prime ministers as appropriate for the moment and that, in the monarch's estimation, "the time for the Americans had arrived."[32] Ngo Dinh Diem knew the Americans, and, regardless of what Bao Dai otherwise may have thought of Diem, he was the most likely channel to American aid. To ensure that the emperor did not overlook this fact, Ngo Dinh Luyen actively lobbied Bao Dai for his brother's appointment. Diem himself later recalled Luyen's efforts as being the reason for his appointment.[33] Luyen had been a classmate of Bao Dai and had good rapport with him. The Ngos were also close to Bao Dai's cabinet director Nguyen De, a fellow Catholic. With the importuning of Luyen and De, Bao Dai chose to play his "Diem card."[34]

Although vague on some key details, Bao Dai's own account of the decision sustains this interpretation. In his memoirs, he declares that, during the Geneva Conference, he could no longer count on France, that "the Americans remained our only allies," and that, moreover, the United States "had the ability to help us continue the fight against communism." He met at Cannes with Vietnamese of varying political and religious views and gained, he claims, their enthusiastic approval for his plan to replace Buu Loc with Diem. Maintaining that he was well aware of Diem's "difficult temperament," he explains:

> I also knew about his fanaticism and messianic tendencies. But, in the present situation, there was no better choice. Indeed, for several years, [Diem] had known some Americans who admired his intransigence. In their eyes, he was especially suited for this particular juncture; also, Washington would not spare him its support. From his past and from the presence of his brother [Nhu] at the head of the Movement of National Union, it appeared that he would have the cooperation of the fiercest nationalists, those who had been behind the defeat of Tam and Buu Loc. Finally, because of his stubbornness and fanaticism, he was the surest guarantee against communism. Yes, truly, he was the man for the job.[35]

On May 13, less than a week after the opening of the Indochina phase of the Geneva Conference, Bao Dai addressed a letter to the head of the U.S. delegation at Geneva. It charged that France and the Vietminh were conniving "against the interest of Vietnam and world peace," and it appealed to the nations who were "friends of peace and of Vietnam," that is, the United States, to take "concerted action aiming, through a noncommunist Vietnam, to consolidate world peace diplomatically or by any other means."[36] The letter also empowered Ngo Dinh Luyen to represent the emperor in discussions of such actions. On May 18, Luyen handed the message to Bedell Smith and Philip Bonsal, the director of the State Department's Office of Philippine and Southeast Asian Affairs, who was in Geneva as a special adviser. At the same time, Luyen, claiming to speak for Bao Dai, complained that the French had "thwarted" Bao Dai's efforts to form a truly national government and army. In an indirect fashion, the Vietnamese emissary inquired if the United States was willing to replace France in Indochina. Luyen further hinted that, with assurance of U.S. support, Bao Dai would ignore French objections to Diem and name him prime minister. Although not certain how much credence to give everything Luyen said, Bonsal, after conferring with Heath, recommended that the United States establish direct contact with Diem in Paris.[37]

Luyen made two additional calls on Bonsal on the nineteenth and twentieth. He pressed for some indication of continued U.S. support for the State of Vietnam regardless of what course France might take. He added the information that, if his brother became prime minister, the new government's first priority would be strengthening the VNA, for which it would need assistance directly from the United States rather than having supplies and funds channeled through the French. Bonsal favored delaying an American response to Luyen's questions and proposals, but Assistant Secretary of State for Far Eastern Affairs Walter S. Robertson, who was in Geneva as Smith's deputy, believed Washington should not wait to give its nod to Bao Dai.[38]

Bao Dai's letter and Luyen's lobbying efforts revealed that the initiative for Diem's appointment as prime minister came from within Vietnamese circles and not from the Americans, who, in fact, were not quite sure how to respond. In his memoirs, Bao Dai claims that he told Dulles of his plan to appoint Diem before he spoke to Diem, but the publicly available U.S. memorandum of Dulles' meeting with Bao Dai in Paris on April 24 reveals no discussion of Diem. It records only that Bao Dai and the Vietnamese that he had consulted desired U.S. support to continue the fight against the communists. There may have been other contacts between Dulles and Bao Dai through clandestine or unofficial channels, but the first mention of Diem's appointment in normal diplomatic discussions was the Smith and Bonsal meeting with Luyen on May 18. On May 22, Secretary Dulles authorized the U.S. delegation in Geneva to exploit discreetly the offer of direct contact with Bao Dai, but the instruction made no mention of Diem. The cable noted the emperor's liabilities as a leader but concluded that there was no current substitute for whatever legitimacy he provided the State of Vietnam. The State Department was also concerned, as were Smith and Bonsal, that any contacts with Bao Dai be handled delicately in order not to appear to be subverting the negotiating efforts of the politically vulnerable Laniel government.[39]

There was to be no Smith–Bao Dai meeting, however, because of the quick movement of events culminating in Diem's designation as prime minister. Diem had met with the emperor on May 14, even before Luyen delivered Bao Dai's letter to Smith. According to Bao Dai, Diem at first declined the post and indicated that he planned to enter a religious order. He quickly yielded, though, to the emperor's appeal to his patriotic duty. Bao Dai then produced a crucifix and had Diem swear before his God to defend Vietnam against the communists and, if necessary, the French. By the time the U.S. embassy in Paris made its first direct contact with Diem on May 24, Nguyen De had informed Buu Loc of his dismissal, and Diem was preparing to travel to Vietnam to explore the possibility of forming a cabinet. The outgoing prime minister stalled for a few days, seeking perhaps to reverse the irresolute monarch's decision or to gain time to transfer assets out of Vietnam. On the evening of June 15, Buu Loc resigned, and, on June 18, without having yet returned to his country, Ngo Dinh Diem formally agreed to head a new government. In Paris, Pierre Mendès-France took office as premier the same day.[40]

Initial assessments of Diem were predictable. His vehemently anti-French sentiments made him anathema to French officials. Maurice Dejean, former French commissioner general in Indochina, characterized Diem as "too narrow, too rigid, too unworldly, and too pure" to create an effective government.[41] Mendès-France considered Diem to be a "fanatic" and took the precaution of requesting U.S. assistance in gaining Diem's acquiescence to any French-Vietminh agreements reached at Geneva. Within Vietnam, only the Ngos' hometown of Hue exhibited any elation with the selection of the new prime minister, who was heralded for his honesty. Elsewhere, Vietnamese observers, including Catholics who said that they would support him, noted his arrogance, inexperience, and lack of recognition and contacts within the country. The U.S. embassy in Saigon reported that the announcement of Diem's appointment aroused no enthusiasm and that there was little movement toward him by the religious and political groups or the *attentistes* (fence-sitting intellectuals). The members of his first cabinet were so "relatively obscure and undistinguished," according to reports in Vietnam, that Diem himself was said to be " '*completement dégonflé*' (completely deflated)."[42]

With a refrain that was to be repeated often over the ensuing months, the State Department labeled the Saigon embassy's reports of little support for Diem as "somewhat premature" and claimed that there was evidence to the contrary.[43] Most American officials took a wait-and-see approach. For example, the embassy staff in Paris concluded that, for the moment, Bao Dai represented the only source of traditional authority on "our side of the Bamboo Curtain in Vietnam" and his selection of Diem was at least a "diametric change from [the] prototype of [the] suave Europeanized money-seeking dilettante," such as former prime ministers Buu Loc and Tran Van Huu.[44] After embassy officers had talked with Diem in Paris, Ambassador Dillon reported: "On balance we were favorably impressed but only in the realization that we are prepared to accept the seemingly ridiculous prospect that this Yogi-like mystic could assume the charge he is apparently about to undertake only because the standard set by his predecessors is so low." [45]

Arriving at Tan Son Nhut Airport outside Saigon on June 25, Diem sped quickly into the capital city in a closed limousine. The crowd that had gathered along the route to greet him received no wave of the hand or even a glimpse of their new leader. Security may have been a concern, but Diem's entry also reflected his attitude toward the public. With the background of a traditional mandarin, he took for granted the obligation of the people on the street to accept authority. He did not need them. All the mandate that he required he carried with him in a document published the following day in the *Vietnam Presse*. It was an ordinance signed by the emperor on June 19 giving him "full civil and military powers." [46]

Bao Dai had never granted full authority to any of his other prime ministers, and why he gave it to Diem is not clear. There were reports that Diem obtained the power by enticing the emperor with a claim that he had a "secret understanding" with the Americans for full support. [47] Bao Dai may have been placing the full burden of responsibility for the fate of the Saigon regime on Diem in the event of failure. Or, more positively, he may have recognized that the leadership vacuum in South Vietnam required such powers, if Diem were to have any chance of success. Many Vietnamese, French, and American officials had long been of the opinion that Bao Dai himself should return to Vietnam to provide a rallying point for his collapsing state. To the disgust of most of his critics, the emperor chose to remain in the comfort of Cannes as a symbolic rather than active leader. Of course, his role since his youth had been symbolic, and there was no evidence that his return to Saigon would have produced significant results. Furthermore, Bao Dai probably did not believe that he was taking a great risk in his grant of full powers to Diem, although Diem made clear that he did not want his chief in Vietnam. If the prime minister did manage to revive the government and then began to assert too much personal power, the emperor thought that he could count on General Hinh to force Diem out. Perhaps aware of this contingency, Diem planned to remove Hinh from command of the VNA at the first opportunity. [48]

Aside from a deep distrust of all Vietnamese outside his own family circle and an outright hatred for the French and Vietminh, Diem entered office with only one clearly defined policy. The full extent of his program was to obtain "greater and more direct US assistance."[49] From the time of Luyen's initial conversations with Smith and Bonsal, the Ngos had identified direct U.S. supply and training of the VNA as the specific form of aid. Once in Saigon, Diem and Nhu, whom McClintock tagged the "informal co-Prime Minister," continued to press this request. The impulsive Nhu complained bitterly to Randolph A. Kidder, first secretary of the Saigon embassy, about the vagueness of U.S. policy toward Indochina. After a call on Bao Dai in Cannes, Heath reported that the emperor "personally has 'capitulated' unless we intervene militarily to pull his chestnuts out of the fire." Like his prime minister, Bao Dai asserted that "with American intervention, the National Army could be strengthened decisively to defeat the Viet Minh."[50]

Aware of these appeals, virtually all American officials believed that the United States could do a far superior job to that of France in militarily strengthening the State of Vietnam. Eisenhower declared to a friend that he was "weary" of French ingratitude for U.S. help. He believed that France's "seemingly hysterical desire to be thought such a 'great power' " was the reason for its rebuffs of U.S. offers to assume "the burden of training native troops, and numerous offers of help in the logistics field."[51] Only two days after the president's private comments, the new French high-commissioner and commander of French forces in Indochina, General Paul Ely, made an informal request to General O'Daniel for the U.S. MAAG to begin training the VNA. Two weeks later, on the eve of Diem's arrival in Saigon, a comprehensive status report prepared with the concurrence of all American civil and military agencies in Vietnam advised that "development of a Vietnamese national army constitutes, in our judgment, the number one military objective toward which U.S. policy must be oriented."[52] Yet, despite Vietnamese, American, and even some French interest in bolstering the VNA, the Departments of State and Defense chose to delay any specific U.S. training program. In mid-June, Mendès-France had just replaced Laniel in Paris, Diem had yet to form a cabinet in Saigon, and the final outcome in Geneva was unpredictable. If the United States expanded its military role in Indochina without a detailed and comprehensive agreement with France, American forces could be left "holding the bag." Prudence dictated that Washington wait and watch developments.[53]

Recognizing the paramount importance of the Geneva talks, Diem restructured the State of Vietnam's representation there on July 2, even before installing his cabinet. With the exception of one holdover from Buu Loc's group, the five-man delegation had a definite Ngo family complexion. It included brother Luyen, Tran Van Chuong, who was the father of Madame Nhu, and Nguyen Huu Chau, who was the husband of another of Chuong's daughters. Tran Van Do, Chuong's brother, headed the delegation. Do also became Diem's minister of foreign affairs, and, after the Geneva Conference, Chuong became ambassador to the United States. A highly respected physician, Do was a prominent *attentiste*, who, despite his family connection to the Ngos, was also very close to Quat and leading members of the Dai Viet.[54]

In Geneva, Do and his colleagues possessed almost no influence and very little knowledge of what was being decided. Every other delegation, including that of the DRV, participated in private discussions of details such as partitioning and elections, to which the State of Vietnam's representatives were neither invited nor informed. According to Do, American and French diplomats came running to him with sketchy briefings only after he held a short, private meeting with Pham Van Dong, head of the DRV's delegation. Some Americans in Geneva complained that Saigon's representatives clung to unrealistic and, by implication, bothersome hopes to prevent partition of the country. On the other hand, Do deeply resented the callous disregard that the American, French, and British negotiators manifested toward the envoys of a government that they recognized and professed to support.[55]

After Mendès-France became premier and as he prepared to negotiate directly with the PRC and DRV, Eden and Prime Minister Winston Churchill traveled to Washington during a recess of the conference to discuss issues relating to France. Eisenhower and Dulles pressed their visitors to stand firm for the EDC, toward which Mendès-France was much less receptive than his predecessor. These talks also produced a seven-point plan that Washington and London considered an acceptable outcome at Geneva. It included independence for Laos and Cambodia and a partitioning of Vietnam. The provisions were entirely acceptable to Mendès-France, and the final terms arranged at Geneva essentially adhered to these seven points.[56]

As the conference proceeded toward its conclusion, Do performed with courage, integrity, and skill, despite his lack of any real leverage. Neither Diem nor Bao Dai gave him any detailed guidance, and he perceived more keenly than did his chief in Saigon the extreme limitations under which he worked. Recognizing the inevitability of partition and the weakness of his government, he still boldly and publicly refused to approve any agreement that divided Vietnam, failed to confirm the independence of the State of Vietnam, or left French troops in Vietnam. American observers considered his statements futile and possibly dangerous. Ambassador U. Alexis Johnson, who headed the U.S. delegation in early July, cautioned Do to seek cooperation with Mendès-France, whose government the weak Saigon regime could not risk alienating completely. Do insisted, however, that he was seeking to provide unimpeachable evidence of his government's nationalist credentials in preparation for the political struggle with the Vietminh that would follow Geneva. As the conference drew to a close, he accomplished one additional patriotic ploy beyond the passive protest of refusing to associate his government with the final agreements. Threatening to remove his delegation from Geneva and thereby deprive France of any claim to a continued political link with Vietnam, Do convinced Mendès-France to give him a letter recognizing Vietnam's independence and pledging to withdraw French troops from the country. Although the conference's International Secretariat did not publish this document, its wording was, in the opinion of Nguyen Huu Chau, who helped draft it, "a recognition of true independence." It put the South "on the same footing as the North," Chau later argued, and with it "France recognized simultaneously the existence of two sovereign states in the territory of Vietnam."[57]

As Do and his aides labored to prepare for life after Geneva, American officials too searched for how to make the best of a bad situation. During a brief visit to Washington over the Fourth of July holiday, Heath recorded that "in the high levels the attitude was one of pessimism and not knowing what to do." He found Eisenhower wondering what more could have been done to get the French to internationalize the war. Dulles and Robertson were complaining about the British attitude of peace at any price. Among State Department officers below the undersecretary level, Heath discerned a virtual consensus for some form of direct U.S. intervention in Indochina. The need was especially urgent because of the apparent lack of leadership in Saigon. There was no excuse, in Heath's judgment, for Bao Dai's cowardly refusal to return to Vietnam. Chargé McClintock in Saigon deemed any reliance on Bao Dai as "foolish" and "immoral" and described Diem as "a messiah without a message." As Heath prepared to return to his post as ambassador in Saigon, he recommended that "we need to keep up at least a façade of Government [there] until we find someone to take over."[58]

For the moment and for whatever it was worth, the government in Saigon was Ngo Dinh Diem alone with little visible support, except from his family. Deciding that he needed a signal from Washington to strengthen his resolve, the State Department prepared a message from the secretary for Heath to convey orally to the prime minister. With bold rhetoric, it proclaimed that the United States stood ready to "support countries everywhere seeking [to] maintain their freedom against [the] godless Communist menace." More specifically, the message pledged America's "best efforts to assist patriotic Vietnamese in building up strength in that part of Vietnam remaining outside Communist occupation."[59] Beyond these assurances, however, Dulles would not go until the Geneva Conference concluded. To do more, he feared, could damage U.S.–French relations and his hopes for French ratification of the EDC. The danger was the possibility of misunderstandings or recriminations that might flow from the United States either getting into the "Yalta business" of guaranteeing a settlement with communists or, conversely, making an unsustainable unilateral commitment of U.S. power in Southeast Asia. The secretary met with Mendès-France in Paris on July 13 and 14 to make the U.S. position clear. Despite the caution of his approach, he returned to Washington believing that his trip demonstrated to all parties at Geneva that ultimately the United States was the "key nation" in this and in all important world issues.[60]

In his report to the NSC on his trip to Paris, Dulles asserted that the U.S., French, and British governments were now in accord that the final Geneva agreements should provide for "the independence and integrity of the southern half of Vietnam."[61] This concept of a post-Geneva state of South Vietnam paralleled the secretary's promise to Diem to sustain "that part of Vietnam remaining outside Communist occupation." Washington had begun to envision the South as the place from where to continue the war against communism in Vietnam, but the precise objective in this struggle remained undefined. American officials in Saigon and Geneva assured Diem and Do that Washington viewed partition as temporary and that it recognized the justice of the State of Vietnam's claims to sovereignty over all Vietnamese territory. Such talk implied reuniting Vietnam under Saigon's authority, but how was unclear, since the United States pledged not to use force to upset the Geneva agreements and talked instead of the weaker and less promising reliance on reunification through nationwide elections.[62]

On July 20, French, DRV, and Cambodian officials signed armistice agreements covering Vietnam, Laos, and Cambodia, and, on July 21, the British, French, Chinese, Soviet, and DRV representatives at Geneva agreed orally to an unsigned Final Declaration on Indochina.[63] In a carefully prepared statement, Smith announced at the final session that the United States "takes note of the agreements" and would "refrain from the threat or use of force to disturb them."[64] The fundamental feature of the agreements was the temporary partitioning of Vietnam into two regroupment zones divided at approximately the seventeenth parallel. Within three hundred days, all DRV forces were to be north of the demarcation line and all French Union forces were to be south. There was to be free movement of refugees between zones during the regroupment period; there were to be no military reinforcements or establishments of foreign military bases or alliances within either zone; and a supervisory commission composed of Indian, Polish, and Canadian members would monitor compliance. The Final Declaration stipulated further that, after regroupment, "the competent representative authorities of the two zones" would consult on arranging a "free general election" throughout Vietnam in July 1956. Although this election provision was obviously linked to the issue of Vietnamese reunification, the Geneva conferees created only the vaguest of guidelines. Unable to devise any formula for the distribution of political power in Vietnam, the diplomats simply dumped "the settlement of political problems" into an undefined "free expression of the national will." In a further attempt to duck responsibility for a political settlement, the delegates asserted that "the military demarcation line is provisional and should not in any way be interpreted as constituting a political or territorial boundary."[65] Regardless of this caveat, DRV signatures on the armistice agreements and DRV participation in the Final Declaration were tantamount to recognition of the DRV as "the competent representative authority" north of seventeen degrees.

The critical unanswered question was what constituted "the competent representative authority" south of seventeen degrees. Article fourteen of the Vietnam armistice agreement decreed that "the conduct of civil administration in each regrouping zone shall be in the hands of the party whose forces are to be regrouped there in virtue of the present Agreement."[66] That statement meant the DRV in the North; it meant France in the South. In a separate declaration, however, the French government pledged to respect "the independence and sovereignty, the unity and territorial integrity of Cambodia, Laos, and Viet-Nam."[67] If this promise was sincere, the French would not speak for the Vietnamese in the South. Furthermore, on June 4, in one of its last acts in Indochina, the Laniel government had signed a new treaty of "independence and association" with the State of Vietnam. The Mendès-France government gave no indication, however, of being bound by that convention. French diplomats kept Bao Dai's representatives at Geneva completely out of their final negotiations with the DRV. The State of Vietnam was not a signatory to any Geneva agreement, and like the United States, refused to endorse the Final Declaration. The Geneva Conference adjourned leaving South Vietnam virtually a political vacuum.[68]

This open historical situation was about the best for which the Eisenhower administration could have hoped. It left room to maneuver against communist expansionism in Southeast Asia. Conservative critics labeled Geneva a "Far Eastern Munich" and, reviving the "loss of China" indictment leveled at the Truman administration, declared that "the Communists have gained another smaller China."[69] Liberal Senator Mansfield charged that "the dominoes are falling" because French and American policy had failed to foster independence of the Indochinese states.[70] Dulles, however, chose to think positively. He claimed that the communist gains at Geneva were "relatively moderate" and that the goal now was to "salvage what the Communists had ostensibly left out of their grasp in Indochina." Britain and other nations, he thought, would now be amenable to the formation of a coalition to defend the rest of Southeast Asia. One problem for the administration, he cautioned the NSC, was Congress, where economy-minded legislators might try to reduce funds available for use in Indochina. Even more problematical was France, whose future course was unpredictable. Dulles was inclined to favor a complete French withdrawal from Indochina that would "permit the United States to work directly with the native leadership in these states."[71]

As official Washington went to work the day after the closing session at Geneva, South Vietnam's political prospects appeared dismal. CIA Director Dulles reported to the NSC on the morning of July 22 that Do had resigned and that Diem might resign. Although Diem refused Do's resignation and stayed on himself, the specter of political paralysis in Saigon seemed real. Admiral Arthur W. Radford, chairman of the Joint Chiefs of Staff, worried that the armistice agreement required withdrawal of the U.S. MAAG but offered that Ely wanted somehow for American forces to "get around" the Geneva restrictions and help train the VNA. Secretary of State Dulles acknowledged these problems but tried to be upbeat and talked of salvaging what was left in Indochina. The council took no action except to instruct its staff to make a policy review of the situation in terms of the results at Geneva.[72]

Later the same day, Allen Dulles telephoned his brother to continue the morning discussion. "We should act soon," he warned, because "Diem is wondering what to do and may resign." The CIA chief said that he was "sending in a couple of new people" and that he could handle "the covert side of it." He believed, though, that "we should be coordinating" and that a working group from State, Defense, CIA, and Foreign Operations (which administered aid programs) "should really get going on practical problems." The secretary agreed and asked his brother what he wanted him to do. It was decided to convene as high-level a group as possible on the twenty-fourth.[73]

As the Dulles brothers swung into action, the goal of the Eisenhower administration in Southeast Asia stayed the same as it had been since the United States recognized the State of Vietnam in February 1950. "The remaining free areas of Indochina," Foster Dulles stated simply, "must be built up if the dike against Communism is to be held."[74] The task itself, though, was formidable. If South Vietnam was to become an effective counterweight to the DRV, a nation would have to be built south of the seventeenth parallel where none currently existed. In its infancy, this state would require a security shield, presumably from a Southeast Asian collective security arrangement. Congress would have to ratify American participation in a collective defense pact, and congressional cooperation would also be essential for the appropriation of the necessary economic and military aid. Furthermore, the French, who were down but not out in Indochina, would likely resist any heavy-handed American effort to dictate Western policy in Vietnam. Finally, and most troubling, was the absence of political unity and promising native leadership in Saigon. From Washington's perspective, the "Diem card" was not an ace, but, hopefully, it was not a deuce either.

IV

SEATO and Other Stopgaps to Shore-up South Vietnam
(June–November 1954)

ALTHOUGH THE military and diplomatic drama of Dienbienphu and Geneva has attracted considerable historical attention, the Eisenhower administration's most crucial Vietnam decisions came in the weeks and months following the Geneva Conference. In what ultimately became a long and painful American involvement in Indochina, the unwillingness to risk a unilateral, armed rescue of the French garrison at Dienbienphu was an exceptional moment of restraint. Despite Washington's refusal to endorse them, the Geneva agreements proved to be an important milestone in Vietnam's three decades of conflict. They provided the initial parameters of what the United States eventually characterized as a war between two Vietnams—North and South. In terms of an affirmative commitment of American power and prestige to the defense of South Vietnam, however, the Eisenhower-Dulles team's post-Geneva answers to several key policy questions were pivotal. Could an independent, nationalist regime survive in Saigon? Was Ngo Dinh Diem the best and perhaps only available leader for that government? Would the French support Diem or even a separate South Vietnamese state? Were French and American policies in Indochina compatible? How and to what extent should the United States, either alone or with France, gamble on the success of Diem or of any other opponent of Ho Chi Minh and the communists? It required almost a year of difficult deliberations both among American leaders and between U.S. and French officials to fashion answers to these queries.[1]

The choices facing the United States in Vietnam were not good. Diem's limitations and liabilities were known, and the Eisenhower administration might simply have washed its hands of him and Vietnam. It could have left the South to the possible annexation of the Democratic Republic of Vietnam and let any Western blame for failure fall on France. It would be unrealistic and ahistorical, however, to contend that abandoning South Vietnam to the communists was a true option. The "loss of China," the stalemate in Korea, the global cold war, and assumptions of French ineptitude combined to prevent the United States from walking away. Furthermore, American officials presumed that successful covert operations in Iran in August 1953 and in Guatemala in June 1954 had established that the United States could counter communism and the allies, or potential allies, of the Soviet Union and the People's Republic of China (PRC) in the Third World.[2] The question was where and how to take a stand. If the United States was going to draw a line, would it be the seventeenth parallel, Cambodia, Laos, Thailand, Burma, India, or elsewhere? Such considerations were not new and recalled Secretary of State Dean Acheson's declaration of a "defense perimeter" in the Pacific before the Korean War.

As the Geneva Conference closed, the search began for a way to keep southern Vietnam out of communist hands. "The important thing from now on is not to mourn the past," Secretary of State John Foster Dulles told news reporters on July 23, 1954, "but to seize the future opportunity to prevent the loss of northern Viet-Nam from leading to the extension of communism throughout Southeast Asia and the Southwest Pacific."[3] Despite this bold assertion of an "opportunity," the administration's private assessment was bleak. Its analysts found that the United States had failed to realize the objectives enumerated by the National Security Council (NSC) in its January 16 statement of U.S. policy in Southeast Asia (NSC 5405): elimination of the Vietminh threat, retention of the strategically valuable Tonkin delta, and obstruction of communist expansion. An interdepartmental review of the post-Geneva situation, initiated by Dulles and his brother, Central Intelligence Agency (CIA) Director Allen W. Dulles, characterized the Final Declaration of the Geneva Conference as "a drastic defeat of key policies in NSC 5405 and a serious loss for the free world." The communists had seized "an advance salient," and the need now was for the United States to establish a new defense line.[4]

In terms of Washington's prevailing New Look strategy, the events of the spring and summer of 1954 had eliminated two components of that approach. The decision against even a conventional bombardment at Dienbienphu made the likelihood of massive retaliation extremely remote, and U.S. nonparticipation in the Geneva agreements revealed no inclination to negotiate directly with the enemy. The rejection of both conflagration and compromise, though, still left the New Look options of a regional alliance, psychological warfare, and covert operations. The administration had great confidence in such programs, but their successful implementation would require some intricate, perhaps even impossible, balancing of U.S. policy toward the French and the Vietnamese nationalists in Saigon.

This problem was keenly apparent to the Dulles brothers as they worked in tandem to devise a Southeast Asian strategy. Historically, Foster Dulles believed, the French had not allowed the development of native leadership in Vietnam, and he doubted that "this leadership could be developed unless the French get out completely."[5] Allen Dulles agreed that the South needed a "pretty good strong nationalist government" but reminded his brother that, until one was in place, the French Expeditionary Corps (FEC) was the only insurance of order and security in South Vietnam.[6] Consequently, the United States was in the anomalous position of seeking French cooperation in Vietnam while simultaneously trying to reduce French influence. The impossibility of such a course should have been inherently obvious.

While the joint working group representing the Departments of State and Defense, the CIA, the Foreign Operations Administration, and the United States Information Agency labored to craft a precise policy formula, various individual assessments and recommendations came forward. A National Intelligence Estimate dated August 3 gave the South Vietnamese regime's chances of survival a "poor" rating and added that there was no evidence to indicate a radical change in France's past reluctance to grant Saigon full independence. Lieutenant General John W. "Iron Mike" O'Daniel, the combat-hardened chief of the U.S. Military Assistance Advisory Group (MAAG) in Vietnam, complained of the lack of "intestinal fortitude" among France's military and political leaders. He refused to be pessimistic and urged a strong American presence to "assist in pointing Vietnam [in the] right direction." "This is war in every sense," O'Daniel declared, and it is a "testing ground to combat . . . the warfare Communists would hope [to] employ everywhere including US."[7]

Although less dramatic than the general, Ambassador Donald R. Heath in Saigon joined him in endorsing direct U.S. aid and advice to Diem's government. He also cautioned that "we will have to watch [the] French pretty carefully." Like Secretary Dulles, Heath believed that there was little chance of a politically strong Vietnam as long as the French held dominant positions in the country. Even worse, the ambassador interpreted the current and vaguely defined mission to Hanoi by French diplomat Jean Sainteny, who had negotiated an aborted compromise with Ho Chi Minh in 1946, as a sign of a possible rapprochement with the communists to protect French interests. Equally disturbing, Heath reported, was that Diem might ultimately prove to lack the "political sagacity or executive ability" to form or conduct a viable government regardless of U.S. and French actions.[8]

Against this discouraging background, the NSC met on August 12, 1954 and approved a new policy statement for Southeast Asia (NSC 5429). According to this paper, past U.S. support for France in Indochina meant that the recent French reverses there had damaged American prestige and raised "doubts in Asia concerning U.S. leadership and the ability of the U.S. to check the further expansion of Communism in Asia." It was imperative, the council declared, that the United States "protect its position and restore its prestige in the Far East by a new initiative in Southeast Asia, where the situation must be stabilized as soon as possible to prevent further losses to Communism through (1) creeping expansion and subversion, or (2) overt aggression." One critical component of this initiative was to be the creation of a Southeast Asia Treaty Organization (SEATO), which would allow the president to fashion a military response to communist-armed attacks in the region. Specifically within South Vietnam, NSC 5429 indicated that the United States would seek to strengthen South Vietnam's military forces, improve its economic condition, and promote democratic reforms, and would do so by cooperating with the French "only insofar as necessary."[9]

Although the SEATO proposal and aid to South Vietnam were the central issues of the moment in Indochina, the most revealing feature of the NSC's August 12 meeting was the group's inability to agree on the wording of paragraph eight of NSC 5429. Entitled "Action in the Event of Local Subversion," this paragraph attempted to set guidelines for U.S. policy "to defeat local Communist subversion or rebellion which does not constitute external armed attack."[10] After some inconclusive discussion, Eisenhower professed to be "frankly puzzled" by the problem of local subversion, and the council decided to carry the topic over to its next meeting.[11] At the August 18 meeting, Dulles introduced a revised paragraph eight that provided for a broad range of possible U.S. actions but avoided "a fixed or automatic commitment" to any specific course. The president had now decided that the United States would not intervene in "strictly local" subversion unless it were "the result of Chinese Communist motivation." Vice President Richard Nixon quickly pointed out the opinion of many that Ho Chi Minh was a Soviet agent rather than a Chinese puppet. Eisenhower rejoined that "of course if the Soviet Union were the motivating source of the subversion, it would mean general war." With that understanding, the council approved Dulles' revised paragraph.[12]

Scholars have noted a lack of appreciation of Third World nationalism in the Eisenhower-Dulles foreign policy and the painful legacy of that lapse in Vietnam, Latin America, the Middle East, and elsewhere.[13] The problem, though, was larger than simply an arrogant disregard for nationalist aspirations. Eisenhower and Dulles were aware of Vietnamese nationalism and frequently raised the issue with the French. More fundamental was the profound absence of a positive U.S. response not only to nationalism but to the full spectrum of social, cultural, economic, and historical factors in the Third World. As the NSC's discussions revealed, America's top policy makers were at a loss to deal with any situation outside of overt Soviet or Chinese action. Trapped between the distasteful options of risking war or accepting local successes by "godless communists," stopgap measures emerged with little relevance to the historical upheaval in Asia and throughout the Third World.

A major element obscuring Washington's view of Asia was the cloud of European concerns that always hung over any policy discussion. During the NSC's August 12 meeting, the Dulles brothers raised the sensitive problem of the need for French troops in Indochina for temporary security despite the damaging effect of that military presence on Saigon's independence. Eisenhower wondered if the United States could pressure the French for a firm statement of their intention to withdraw as soon as possible, but Foster Dulles cautioned that Washington should not be too tough on its NATO ally. A few days later, while welcoming Saigon's new ambassador, Tran Van Chuong, to Washington, the president complained again that, in the past, the United States "had been compelled to use the French channel" to do something for Vietnam and "in a sense our hands had been tied." [14] Two days after this conversation, Secretary Dulles sent a personal message to Pierre Mendès-France advising the premier that the United States planned to initiate direct aid to South Vietnam and that the president would be sending a personal letter of support to Diem. Paris' immediate acknowledgment of Dulles' message proved the secretary's wariness of French sensibilities to be well founded. Although Mendès-France ultimately sent a temperate reply, the Foreign Office's initial response revealed, in the words of Ambassador Douglas Dillon, that the "French consider we have [an] almost psychotic attachment to 'independence.' " [15]

Besides French sniping at American policies, Eisenhower and Dulles also faced opposition from within the administration. Secretary of Defense Charles E. Wilson and the Joint Chiefs of Staff (JCS) had grave doubts about the wisdom of beginning a U.S. military training and assistance program in South Vietnam without "a reasonably strong, stable civil government in control." Not only would such a program likely violate the limits set at Geneva on foreign military aid, in the Defense Department's opinion, but it would also prove to be a "hopeless" effort without a regime that could provide adequate pay, recruitment, and other forms of self-support. In a letter to Wilson drafted by Robert McClintock, the foreign service officer who headed the interdepartmental working group on Indochina, Dulles contended that the question of which comes first—military strength or effective civil government—was a "hen and egg argument." Both were needed in Vietnam, he acknowledged, but insisted both could be developed simultaneously. As for the Geneva armistice agreements, the secretary of state maintained that his department could find no limitations on U.S. MAAG assuming a training function. [16]

This exchange of letters between Dulles and Wilson occurred during the week that the administration approved NSC 5429, and their two arguments began a debate that was to rage among U.S. policy makers until the demise of the Saigon regime in 1975. In view of South Vietnam's internal political weakness, could American military assistance ever be successfully utilized by Saigon, and, conversely, could Saigon's political weakness ever be overcome without first achieving some military success? During the deliberations over Dienbienphu, Pentagon leaders, with the notable exception of JCS Chairman Admiral Arthur W. Radford, had noted the limits and risks of American military involvement in Indochina. During the August NSC meetings, Wilson was again the voice of caution. When he was president of General Motors, the secretary of defense was known for his tenacity and his engineer's aversion to playing a hunch. He now warned the council that "we should not trap ourselves into going to war in Southeast Asia to save South Vietnam."[17] Neither Dulles nor Eisenhower agreed with Wilson's implication that the United States should simply give up on Saigon. Because of Eisenhower's military background and his unhappiness with Wilson's inability to limit defense spending, the president often acted as his own secretary of defense.[18] In this discussion, he backed his secretary of state. When Dulles described the proposed Southeast Asian treaty as intended "to draw the line [against aggression] to include Laos, Cambodia, and South Vietnam on our side," Wilson objected. He retorted that the loss of the three states "would not be a loss to us, inasmuch as they had never belonged to us." Thinking undoubtedly of the decision at Geneva to partition Vietnam, the president terminated the discussion by declaring that "some time we must face up to it: we can't go on losing areas of the free world forever."[19]

As Eisenhower's determined tone revealed, the Southeast Asia Collective Defense Treaty signed in Manila on September 8, 1954 was a central component of the administration's post-Geneva policy in Indochina. Dulles viewed it as a "no trespassing" sign warning Russia and China to keep hands off the region. "Communists will stop where we stand and not before," he warned, and this pact would give them reason to pause.[20] Unlike NATO, the SEATO treaty did not require an automatic response from all its members if one were attacked. Also, the convention did not include such influential Asian nations as India, Burma, and Indonesia, although Washington and London made an effort to enlist them. Britain, France, Australia, New Zealand, the Philippines, Thailand, and Pakistan joined the United States in agreeing that each would regard an armed attack "in the treaty area" as a danger to "its own peace and safety" and would "act to meet the common danger in accordance with its constitutional processes." Although the Geneva agreements prohibited the Indochinese states from joining military alliances, a separate protocol declared Laos, Cambodia, and South Vietnam within the treaty area. In the event of subversion, rather than overt aggression, the signatories were to consult on measures for their common defense, and, in any case, no actions would be taken except with the invitation and consent of the threatened government. As a further safeguard against involvement in regional frictions such as existed between India and Pakistan, the United States appended an understanding that its involvement would be against "Communist aggression."[21]

The secretary of state was extremely pleased with the loosely knit alliance. He traveled personally to Manila with Senators Mike Mansfield (D-Mont.) and H. Alexander Smith (R–N.J.) to conclude the treaty, which he preferred to call the Manila Pact. The SEATO acronym suggested another NATO, but Dulles argued that the new treaty was more like the Monroe Doctrine—a "moral offensive" with no standing military commitment such as the United States had in Europe. It was a caution to aggressors and an affirmation—in an addendum entitled the Pacific Charter—of U.S. support for the self-determination and independence of the Southeast Asian states. To do more, Dulles conceded, would expose American prestige to great risks in an area where the United States had little control and saw little promise, but to do less would abandon the area without a struggle. He had posed this dilemma to Eisenhower before finalizing the pact, and the two men agreed the risks inherent in the Southeast Asia treaty were worth taking.[22]

For the administration, the Manila Pact struck not only a psychological blow in the cold war, it also marked the realization of "united action" in Indochina and thereby largely neutralized congressional objections to U.S. military intervention in Southeast Asia. In the closing session of the Manila Conference, Dulles explicitly traced the treaty back to his March 1954 speech calling for united action. According to Richard M. Bissell, Jr., who worked closely with Allen Dulles at the CIA, the secretary believed that "the lack of a position in international law" and "domestic constitutional problems" had "tied our hands on the occasion of Dien Bien Phu." A Southeast Asia treaty, Bissell later recalled Foster Dulles saying, "would have in effect made possible the overcoming of these obstacles to military intervention in the area." Such a treaty alone would not empower the president to initiate a major war, Dulles continued, "but it clearly would grant him the power to react quickly in situations on the pattern of, for instance, the Truman response in Korea."[23]

The Senate, with two of its members as signers of the treaty, held essentially perfunctory hearings and debate before ratifying the pact overwhelmingly. At no point was Dulles asked to define precisely the vague reference in the treaty to "constitutional processes." In the 1960s, despite its cautious language, the SEATO treaty became a cornerstone of U.S. military intervention in Vietnam. In a 1965 interview, former Vice President Richard Nixon argued that SEATO "gave an aura of an interest bigger than just the big selfish United States now going in there and knocking over the little Vietnamese."[24] In 1966, after President Lyndon B. Johnson had sent 200,000 American troops to Indochina, Senator J. William Fulbright (D–Ark.) asked Secretary of State Dean Rusk: "Does the . . . Southeast Asia Treaty Organization commit us to do what we are now doing in Vietnam?" "Yes sir," Rusk replied, "I have no doubt that it does."[25]

Beyond shoring up congressional support for the administration's policies, SEATO was a stopgap with other, long-lasting implications. The inclusion of South Vietnam in the treaty area was a major step toward converting the seventeenth parallel into another thirty-eighth parallel. In accordance with the fundamental tenets of New Look strategy, the frontier between North and South Vietnam became an integral element in the "ring of alliances" that the administration forged around the Soviet Union and the People's Republic of China. Dubbed "pactomania" by critics, mutual defense arrangements extended beyond the NATO, ANZUS (Australia, New Zealand, United States), and Philippine treaties of the Truman years. The New Look alliances included an enlarged NATO, SEATO, CENTO (the Central Treaty Organization covering the Middle East, which the United States supported but did not join), and new bilateral pacts with Japan, South Korea, and Taiwan. Although some of these conventions provided for use of U.S. ground troops, most relied, as did SEATO, on America's "mobile striking power" to provide the deterrent to aggression. If the United States was prepared to use its retaliatory power, Dulles told reporters, "to such an extent that an aggressor would lose more by his aggression than he would gain by it, we don't think he will do it." A correspondent asked if this striking power would be used in the event of an attack against South Vietnam.

"Yes," the secretary affirmed; "it does not mean that we are going to drop atomic bombs on Peking or Moscow, but it does mean in retaliation or in relation to the area which would be signified and not particularly confined to the particular segment that the enemy picked for the attack."[26]

Such menacing, "brinkmanship" rhetoric and the vagaries of Dulles' comparison of SEATO to the Monroe Doctrine had little relevance to the crisis in leadership facing South Vietnam and threatening to terminate Ngo Dinh Diem's regime at any moment. Eisenhower and Dulles believed that pacts like SEATO improved the morale of leaders like Diem and provided them tangible support with the promise to deploy U.S. armed might in an emergency. But, if Diem's collapse came not with a bang but a whimper, as was the most likely scenario, Moscow or Beijing would have little to fear from Washington. SEATO could provide South Vietnam with a worst-case backup and could provide a rationale to limit the size of the Vietnamese armed forces (which would save money) or to eliminate the FEC (which would reduce French influence). Since it was primarily a ploy in the global cold war, though, it could do little to enhance immediately the viability of the Diem government within Vietnam.

Although NSC 5429 placed a priority on strengthening the Saigon regime, after the Manila Conference, the president and secretary of state devoted less of their personal attention to the inscrutable politics of Vietnam. West Germany and Taiwan, perennial cold war trouble spots, crowded Indochina aside. On August 30, 1954, the French National Assembly finally rejected the long-standing proposal for a European Defense Community (EDC) that would have integrated a rearmed West Germany into Western Europe's military defenses. It was a dark moment for the Western alliance system, in Eisenhower's view, and he and Dulles placed the search for an alternative to EDC at the top of their foreign policy agenda. In late September, the secretary of state traveled to London for a nine-power conference to hammer out a new European defense plan. In Paris on October 23, the nine nations concluded agreements to provide for the entry of a sovereign and armed West Germany into NATO. While Europe was Eisenhower's first concern, he and his advisers simultaneously confronted a Chinese crisis. On September 3, the president received word that Chinese communist forces were shelling the islands of Quemoy and Matsu, which were occupied by the nationalist

Chinese. If this artillery action proved to be prelude to an invasion of Taiwan, pressure for a U.S. counterattack against the mainland would become enormous. Although the shelling and a communist military buildup continued throughout the fall, no invasion occurred. Still, as it had done at Manila, the administration decided to erect another of its "no trespassing" signs—a mutual defense treaty with the Republic of China on Taiwan signed December 2, 1954.[27]

While the top level of the nation's foreign policy command wrestled with the European and Chinese questions, other Americans set to work to buttress the South Vietnamese regime. In addition to the diplomatic and military officers in Washington, Saigon, and Paris who routinely dealt with Indochinese affairs, help in this effort came also from two irregular operatives. One was Colonel Edward G. Lansdale, who headed the so-called Saigon Military Mission (SMM). The other was a "bouncy little professor" of political science from Michigan State College named Wesley R. Fishel. Fishel had met Diem in Japan in 1950, and the professor and the politician began to correspond.[28] In 1951, Diem came to Michigan State to reside for a time as a consultant to the Government Research Bureau, of which Fishel was assistant director. By 1954, Fishel was, in the words of one State Department officer, "a sort of press agent and advisor" for Diem in America.[29] When Diem became prime minister, he immediately asked Fishel to join him in Saigon as an adviser and expressed interest in an entire team of experts from Michigan State. Fishel hurried to his friend's assistance and eventually even moved into the prime minister's palace. At this time, the professor wrote: "If Diem fails, there is no one else to whom we can turn. Diem is the only possible counterbalance to Communist domination. The 'Third Force' is the West's last chance in Indochina."[30]

Contrary to implications in some accounts, Fishel probably did not work for the CIA.[31] He would be more accurately described as a freelance secret agent. He had a World War II background in military intelligence and had conducted a study for the U.S. Army in Korea in 1953 for which he held a top-secret security clearance. American diplomatic and intelligence officials recognized his close association with Diem as an asset and utilized it. When Fishel went to Vietnam in August 1954 to aid Diem, the State Department made him a consultant on government reorganization attached to the U.S. Operations Mission (USOM) in Saigon that supervised American nonmilitary aid programs.

In 1955, other Michigan State faculty members followed under USOM auspices as instructors in public and police administration.[32]

Fishel and Lansdale were what the CIA called "coopted" agents, but the Air Force colonel was more of a true clandestine operative (a "spook" in American GI jargon). He was Allen Dulles' "own representative" in Vietnam.[33] He invented the name Saigon Military Mission as a cover designation for his specially recruited team of Philippine and American agents. "I was backed by CIA myself," he acknowledged many years later and added that "I had CIA people."[34] The SMM operated with virtually total independence from the regular CIA station in Saigon, and its members engaged in special operations ranging from espionage to propaganda to free medical aid for peasants. Lansdale himself developed a close relationship with Diem. Watching the prime minister's inauspicious arrival in Saigon on June 25, the colonel thought that "perhaps he needed help" establishing his political leadership. That night, Lansdale wrote out some suggestions for military, political, economic, agrarian, and other reforms. After obtaining permission from Heath and O'Daniel the next day, he personally and unofficially delivered the paper to Diem, whom he found working alone in his office. From this first meeting, Lansdale later recorded, "our association gradually developed into a friendship of considerable depth, trust, and candor."[35]

Much has been written and speculated about Lansdale's activities. His clandestine cavortings were the real-life inspirations for Graham Greene's *The Quiet American* and the character Colonel Hillandale in William J. Lederer and Eugene Burdick's *The Ugly American*. Historians, journalists, and Lansdale himself in a memoir have chronicled his remarkable and controversial career as an unconventional warrior, but the full scope and significance of his role remain hidden behind a veil of classified government documents. The French were among his harshest critics. They considered him the organizer of what they called "American special services" in Southeast Asia whose motto was "to defeat the brigands, you must become brigands."[36] Lansdale himself believed that his mission was "to help the Vietnamese help themselves."[37]

Diem needed a lot of help. He installed his first cabinet on July 7. Most of its members were almost totally lacking in political experience, virtually unknown in Vietnam, and related in some way to the Ngo family. The group was not necessarily worse than Bao Dai's earlier cabinets, but the absence of any representatives of the Cao Dai, Hoa

Hao, Binh Xuyen, Dai Viet, or any other organized party starkly revealed the narrowness of Diem's political base. Furthermore, many Vietnamese Catholics, his most likely constituency, were trapped in Vietminh-occupied areas of the North. Between Diem's taking office and naming his cabinet, came the devastating news that French forces were evacuating the southern Red River delta and pulling back to the so-called Hanoi-Haiphong corridor. This prudent military decision "broke Diem's back" politically because it meant that the Geneva armistice would place hundreds of thousands of Catholics living in the southern delta in the Vietminh's regroupment zone. As he announced his cabinet and declared his commitment to Vietnamese independence, the vulnerable prime minister also had to make a public appeal to France and the United States for support.[38]

The plight of the northern Catholics set the stage for a dramatic U.S. and French air- and sealift of refugees in the summer and fall of 1954. Code-named "Passage to Freedom" by the U.S. Navy, this operation did much to establish in the minds of Americans that the United States goal in Vietnam was to assist a freedom-loving people in their struggle to break from the yoke of communist tyranny. As permitted by the Geneva agreements, over one million people—80 percent of them Catholic—left their northern ancestral homes to relocate in southern refugee camps. Many of them had a history of resistance to the Vietminh and unquestionably were voting with their feet, either from political conviction or fear of reprisals. Because these voters would be vital in the 1956 elections mandated by the Geneva conference to decide reunification of Vietnam, their exodus was not left entirely to chance. Lansdale's SMM, along with French and South Vietnamese agents, spread the word that "Christ has gone to the South" and that five acres and a water buffalo awaited those who moved. Black propaganda also circulated, including descriptions of Vietminh forced labor camps and even a scenario attributed to the French that a U.S. nuclear barrage would exterminate whomever remained in the North.[39]

Whatever the motivation, the influx of Catholics into South Vietnam was both a boon and a burden for Diem. Even with the refugees, Catholics only accounted for 10 percent of the South's population, but they, along with the national army and French-educated bureaucracy, were potential political supporters for the Saigon government. Meanwhile, though, the total inadequacy—virtual nonexistence—of facilities

77

for the thousands of newcomers arriving daily threatened to drown the regime in the sea of mud that was supposed to be refugee camps. There was almost no food, housing, medical facilities, sanitation, or local transportation in the reception areas. The wretched conditions provided fuel not only for communist propaganda assaults on Diem but also for French attacks on his ineptitude. Ambassador Dillon provided a graphic description of Paris' paternalistic disdain by using an analogy to a child's toy. The French believed, he reported, "that if the Vietnamese are given, without restriction, an erector set with all the parts for a ten story building they will end up with a one story cabin and the remaining parts will either be sold or end up in the pockets of the builders." With careful supervision and much difficulty, however, they could build a five-story building. The French further maintained, according to Dillon, that their own sacrifices for Vietnam and obligations to the French Union "dictate that they should be the construction supervisor."[40]

Although most American officials were inclined to take a wait-and-see approach to Diem's performance, many Frenchmen and Vietnamese were busily at work to remove him. There were several separate and overlapping schemes involving Bao Dai; former prime ministers Phan Van Huu, Nguyen Van Tam, and Buu Loc; Bao Dai's left-leaning cousin Buu Hoi (a scientist living in Paris); and the leaders of the various sects. The most dangerous of these intrigues revolved around General Nguyen Van Hinh, chief of staff of the Vietnamese National Army (VNA). Although Hinh had long bragged that he could seize control of the government any time that he chose, the first serious threat of an imminent coup attempt surfaced at a Saigon cocktail party on August 26. Heath attended this reception hosted by Jacques Raphael-Leygues, a French diplomat closely associated with Buu Hoi. There he found an obviously staged show of unity among several conspirators including Hinh, the Cao Dai pope, General Tran Van Soai (the Hoa Hao military chief), the political adviser to General Nguyen Thanh Phuong (the Cao Dai military chief), and a Binh Xuyen representative. The ambassador learned that the group had a plan to unite the sects and the VNA officer corps in a demarche to Bao Dai to remove Diem unless the prime minister dismissed his brothers from the government, broadened his regime, offered to protect sect interests, and launched a firm anticommunist program. This threat and these demands were to become standard political fare in Saigon over the coming weeks and months.[41]

Heath immediately began efforts to mend the tear in the thin fabric of the Saigon government. He warned Hinh that a coup could destroy the chance for direct American aid to the VNA. At the same time, he urged Diem to meet personally with sect leaders to negotiate for their cooperation, and he cautioned the prime minister not to force Hinh's hand by a peremptory dismissal. Foreign Minister Tran Van Do, the one member of Diem's cabinet who enjoyed genuine public respect, made his own attempt to build support for the regime among the sects, but he threatened to resign if Diem did not prove willing to offer them some concessions. Heath's efforts helped ease momentarily the danger of a coup, but he was not convinced that Diem could meet the challenge. He suggested to Washington that "we must keep our eyes open for another leader."[42]

Other maneuvering against Diem reached far beyond Saigon and further darkened his prospects. Bay Vien, the Binh Xuyen chief, flew to Cannes to persuade Bao Dai to replace Diem, and Ngo Dinh Luyen rushed to the Riviera to defend his brother's interests. At the same time, Guy La Chambre, the French minister in charge of relations with the Associated States, sought to oust Diem or at least push him aside in a coalition with the sects. At the Manila Conference, where he served as his nation's representative, La Chambre made a forceful presentation to Dulles. Since Diem took office, he declared, there had been no political progress in South Vietnam while the clock ticked inexorably closer to the 1956 elections. Meanwhile, the Vietminh were organizing and intimidating the population in the South to support them. Only the sects had the capacity to counter this Vietminh propaganda and intimidation campaign. Turning to specific Vietnamese personalities, La Chambre expressed a preference for Tam as minister of the interior and Buu Hoi as a prime minister who could form a broad-based government. Dulles responded that "he had no particular fondness for Diem" but reiterated that the U.S. view was to try to broaden the Saigon government while retaining Diem. He added that Senator Mansfield, his fellow delegate at Manila, had just come from Vietnam and believed that Diem might be the "last chance" for an effective prime minister.[43]

As the Manila Conference concluded and Vien and Luyen lobbied Bao Dai, Diem provoked a showdown with Hinh on September 10. After some "verbal fencing," Diem relieved Hinh as chief of staff, ordered him to France on a six-month "study" mission, and named General Nguyen Van Vy as his replacement. When Vy refused the post, Diem turned to a colonel on the general staff who also declined. The prime minister then designated the civilian secretary of state for defense, Le Ngoc Chan, as chief of staff. Diem himself already held the portfolio as defense minister. Hinh then arranged a public show of resistance to Chan's efforts to force him out of the country and countered with a threat to "take action." Diem began making hurried efforts to strengthen his small palace guard.[44]

Hinh's successful defiance of Diem, at least for the moment, generated a dangerous civil-military crisis. VNA officers felt compelled to side with Hinh, and the burden fell to the prime minister to prove that he could exercise his authority.[45] The confrontation brought the vitally important process of constructing an effective government in Saigon to a virtual standstill for weeks while a number of Vietnamese, American, and French individuals and groups intrigued and inveighed with and against each other. The basic plot of the melodrama centered on whether Diem was the best or worst hope for organizing a viable regime to counter the communists, but there were many subplots arising from differences within the various factions.

The inner dynamics of the Ngo family itself were the most difficult to decipher. In a culture where kinship ties are transcendent, the clan would certainly defend itself against all others, but it was unclear who led within the family and with whom, if anyone, the Ngos would ally. The worldly and conniving Nhu and Luyen worked so closely with their monkish brother that the Hinh plotters had demanded the brothers' removal as a needed reform. From Lansdale's and Fishel's inside observations, however, Diem did not appear to be a simple yes-man for his siblings. An example of Ngo family fidelity was the case of Phan Huy Quat, the former defense minister who had long labored for a strong national army. As soon as the Hinh impasse developed, Diem talked with Quat about entering the cabinet. The logical post for Quat was defense minister, but Diem and his brothers were wary of giving a political rival such prominence. The interior ministry and a special reform ministry charged with organizing a popular assembly were also discussed. After a few weeks, the talks collapsed, and the inability to bring a strong leader like Quat on board became a symbol of the Ngos' insecurity and inflexibility.[46]

Diem's stubbornness especially infuriated the French. Under the terms of the Geneva armistice, General Paul Ely, who was both the French military and diplomatic chief in Vietnam, possessed paramount civil and military authority south of seventeen degrees. Fully aware of Diem's liabilities, he was still inclined to give Diem a chance to broaden the government, but Ely's superiors in Paris were impatient. La Chambre, possibly under pressure from "old colonial hands" accustomed to wire-pulling in Indochina, instructed Ely to pressure Diem to make Tam minister of the interior. Since Tam was Hinh's father and a notorious Francophile, the prime minister adamantly refused, and Washington objected strongly to Paris over this "virtual ultimatum" to Diem. Dulles believed that "the French were about to 'pull the rug out' from under Diem because he was not French-minded enough."[47] Tension between American and French officials became so great over how to proceed in Indochina that La Chambre and Ely traveled to Washington for consultations in late September. Dulles also discussed the issue with Mendès-France while the secretary was in Europe to deal with the future of West Germany. These high-level Franco-American talks produced a French pledge to "give Diem a good try."[48] As the Democratic Republic of Vietnam took possession of Hanoi on October 9 in accord with the Geneva timetable and Hinh continued to defy Diem in Saigon, however, La Chambre visited Vietnam and avoided any public show of cooperation with the prime minister. Despite Ely's warnings to Hinh against a coup, Dulles characterized French support for Diem as "half-hearted." A State Department analysis, in fact, forecast a possible French attempt to use Tam and Hinh (both French citizens) to resurrect the old colonial-type Republic of Cochinchina that had existed from 1946 to 1949.[49]

Meanwhile, though, another French creation, the State of Vietnam, still existed, and its debauched monarch Bao Dai seemingly possessed the constitutional authority to resolve the Diem-Hinh dispute one way or another with the stroke of his pen. Both Washington and Paris considered him "played out" and largely ineffectual as a leader, but the absentee emperor could provide a cloak of legitimacy for Diem or Hinh or whomever he chose to sanction. Most observers believed that his endorsement was for sale. In the spring of 1954 he had in effect sold control of the South Vietnamese police to the Binh Xuyen to maintain his millionaire's lifestyle, and he chose Diem as prime minister primarily as a bid to gain access to American aid. These two inducements—Binh Xuyen bribes and American largess—still remained the keys to Bao

Dai's role. After Binh Xuyen leader Bay Vien trekked to Cannes with "bags of gold," the emperor telegraphed a polite invitation to Diem to resign. The prime minister, through his brother Luyen, protested that he remained the avenue to U.S. support. Heath urged Washington to reenforce this argument with a direct American approach to Bao Dai. From Paris, Dillon contended that, for the sake of U.S.-French harmony, the French should deal with the emperor. Over Heath's objections, Washington agreed to allow Maurice Dejean, a longtime French liaison to Bao Dai and known critic of Diem, to visit Cannes.[50]

This initiative changed nothing, and, indeed, Diem's prospects worsened on two different fronts. On the one hand, Bao Dai sent more telegrams to Saigon urging the inclusion of Hinh and Vien in Diem's cabinet and the appointment of well-known French collaborator General Nguyen Van Xuan as a vice premier. Simultaneously, a number of French officials began to urge Mendès-France to give up entirely on the State of Vietnam and seek a rapprochement with Ho Chi Minh. These dire developments led Washington to ask Heath pointedly if he thought that the United States could "make a synthetic strongman" of Diem. The ambassador responded in the affirmative but with two cautions. Because of Diem's "intrinsic faults," prudence dictated that American officials look "for a relief pitcher and get him warming up in the bullpen."[51] Also, Bao Dai's interference had to be prevented, and to do that, Heath offered to go himself to Cannes. The State Department agreed, and, on October 3, Heath talked with Bao Dai in the wake of a similar visit by Ely. Confronted by the two chief Western diplomats posted in Saigon, the emperor professed his faith in Diem's loyalty. On October 7, he cabled instructions to Hinh, Vien, and Xuan to cooperate with Diem. Although intrigues continued to swirl around the monarch, he increasingly began to distance himself from Hinh and the other anti-Diem plotters.[52]

The disagreement among American officials in Saigon, Paris, and Washington over when and how to approach Bao Dai was only one of several debates within U.S. circles. Despite a general consensus that Diem should be given a chance to prove himself, American assessments varied widely about his prospects. Greatest pessimism came from the secretary of defense. The Diem-Hinh stalemate only reenforced the Pentagon's existing reservations about U.S. aid to South Vietnam. At an NSC meeting on September 24, Secretary Wilson argued against CIA

Director Dulles' recommendation that the French and Americans "unite firmly in support of one local leader." It would be better "for the United States to get completely out of the area," Wilson countered, because he saw no chance "of saving any part of Southeast Asia."[53] Despite continued State Department arguments to the contrary, the JCS stood firmly by the judgment that U.S. aid to Vietnamese armed forces, including a MAAG training program, was unwise under the current unstable political conditions. Foster Dulles and Wilson pointedly disagreed on this issue in an October 18 meeting with Eisenhower, but, two days later, the Defense Department yielded slightly by agreeing to a MAAG training mission "if it is considered that political considerations are overriding."[54]

Although not as pessimistic as Wilson, Secretary Dulles and his chief lieutenants at the State Department approached the Indochina problem cautiously and with a grim sense of almost desperate determination. The assistant secretary of state for Far Eastern affairs was Walter S. Robertson, who had obtained his appointment with the backing of conservative Republican Congressman Walter H. Judd. Like Judd, Robertson was a staunch advocate of a tough line in support of Chiang Kai-shek and other nationalist foes of Asian communism. In mid-September, Kenneth T. Young assumed charge of the Office of Philippine and Southeast Asian Affairs, and he and Robertson regularly consulted the Senate's expert on Indochina, Mike Mansfield. Although acknowledging that the United States was not "wedded" to Diem and admitting his weaknesses, these three men became forceful advocates of wholehearted support for him. In their view, which was seconded by a National Intelligence Estimate dated September 15, Diem was the only "visible" South Vietnamese leader with sufficient honesty and genuine nationalism to thwart the Vietminh. On October 15, Mansfield issued publicly a personal report to the Senate Foreign Relations Committee that immediately became the cornerstone of this pro-Diem position. In it, he expressed doubt "that under the pressure of time a more satisfactory substitute" for Diem could be found. If Diem were forced out, he concluded, "the United States should consider an immediate suspension of all aid to Vietnam and the French Union forces, except that of a humanitarian nature, preliminary to a complete reappraisal of our present policies in Vietnam."[55] From Mansfield's perspective, in other words, it was Diem or failure.

As advocacy for Diem increased in Washington, Ambassador Heath in Saigon marched to a different drummer. He believed, unlike Wilson, that a government and army could be built in South Vietnam, but he disagreed with the view that Diem was the only hope. A week after the release of Mansfield's report, Heath sent Dulles a long, musing telegram on the internal situation in Saigon. He recalled that Hinh had initiated the clash with Diem but insisted that the prime minister's stubborn refusal to compromise had dangerously prolonged the crisis. Forty days had been lost that could have been better used establishing the regime's authority in the provinces, fighting Vietminh infiltration, and working to win over the rural population. According to the diplomat, Diem was incapable of sharing or delegating power, the Vietnamese people never saw him, and most French officials, except Ely and Mendès-France, were working to get rid of him. "Everyone in the embassy," he wrote, "is convinced that Diem cannot organize and administer strong government."[56] A few days after the secretary received this negative assessment, Heath was on his way out as ambassador.

The transfer of Heath from Saigon had been rumored for weeks. On September 1, a Washington newspaper headlined a story "US Will Can Top Diplomat in Major Indochina Shake-up." Claiming that "there has been a clamor for Mr. Heath's scalp" in the State Department, the article labeled him as "the American most closely identified with French record of blunder and failure in Indochina." The State Department issued a public affirmation of confidence in the ambassador, but did not deny that, after four years in Saigon, a routine rotation of assignment was overdue and would be normal within the next few months. Behind the scenes, Secretary Dulles thought that Heath "was too close to the French," but he commended him for "standing up to them" on the Hinh issue and placed no blame on him for "the deterioration in South Vietnam."[57] Still, Heath's hesitancy about how far the United States should commit itself to Diem combined with another factor—a strained relationship with O'Daniel and Lansdale—to hazard his tenure in Saigon.

Although the ambassador maintained a correct and even cooperative association with the MAAG chief and the head of SMM, the personal style of the two military officers clashed with that of the diplomat. O'Daniel, the hard-charging infantryman, and Lansdale, the master of intrigue, were different personalities, but both possessed great faith in their own and their country's ability. While Heath approached the Diem-

Hinh clash with the circumspection of an experienced diplomat, they often plunged ahead with their own initiatives without the knowledge or approval of the embassy. On more than one occasion, Heath complained to Washington of how O'Daniel's "impetuous temperament" nearly wrecked delicate negotiations.[58] O'Daniel and Lansdale both liked Hinh and tried to reconcile him with the prime minister, while Heath was trying to get the VNA commander out of the country under some face-saving formula. Since the three Americans all sought to sustain the Diem regime, though, their efforts overall were complementary. In late September, for example, Diem gave Cao Dai General Phuong and Hoa Hao General Soai honorary offices as ministers of state in an effort to divide these sects from the Binh Xuyen. At the same time Cao Dai dissident General Trinh Minh The agreed to support the government. These developments were the fruits of Heath's diplomatic initiatives supplemented by Lansdale's arrangement of financing for the sect troops.[59]

More disturbing for the future course of American policy in Vietnam than differences in style among the embassy, MAAG, and SMM was the separate management and operation of U.S. overt and covert activities. Heath did not always know what O'Daniel and Lansdale were doing, because they had support and communications channels through the CIA separate from the embassy. Moreover, Lansdale had powerful patrons in Washington—the Dulles brothers. With instructions from Foster Dulles to "do what you did in the Philippines," Lansdale set out to mold Diem into an effective leader like Ramon Magsaysay. After fewer months in Vietnam than Heath had years, the colonel decided that Diem had the potential to be "a highly popular person." In later years, he acknowledged that his estimate differed from "the foreign service professionals, who were out there observing the thing."[60] Whether optimistic, back-channel reports from Lansdale undercut Heath's credibility with the State Department is unknowable without greater access to CIA message files.

Finally, at a meeting of the NSC on October 22, and after weeks of political crisis and stalemate in Saigon, President Eisenhower ordered the immediate implementation of "a crash program to sustain the Diem government and establish security in Free Vietnam." His decision sought to end quickly the wrangling among American, French, and Vietnamese before Diem went "down the drain with no replacement in sight." Declaring that "he knew something from personal experience about doing this kind of job in this kind of area," Eisenhower overruled the Defense Department's objections and demanded that O'Daniel "get busy" with a MAAG training program. Specifically, he wanted to give the general a modest appropriation of five to seven million dollars "to produce the maximum number of Vietnamese military units on which Prime Minister Diem could depend to sustain himself in power." As part of the plan, the French would be expected to help "get Hinh out of the picture." The president believed that the French would go along, but, if not, it would be necessary to "get tough" with them. "We ought to lay down the law to the French," he decreed. "It is true that we have to cajole the French with regard to the European area, but we certainly didn't have to in Indochina."[61]

In Paris for the signing of the new agreement on West Germany on October 23, Secretary Dulles informed Mendès-France and British foreign secretary Anthony Eden that the United States planned an initiative to bolster Diem. Eden welcomed greater American involvement in South Vietnam but was pessimistic about Diem's future. Mendès-France responded that his government supported the prime minister at the moment but reiterated the desire to identify some alternatives to Diem. The next day, however, French officials were up in arms upon receipt of an advance copy of a letter from Eisenhower to Diem. Drafted weeks earlier, this letter was now being sent as an integral part of the crash program. It was a carefully worded pledge to provide U.S. aid directly to Diem's government—rather than indirectly through the French—if his administration made progress in urgently needed military, political, and economic reforms within South Vietnam. Heath handed the letter to Diem on October 25, and it was also released to the press. Although Dulles had notified Mendès-France back in August that the United States contemplated direct aid to Saigon, the French were angry and for good reason. Despite its being addressed to Diem, the letter was blunt notification to Paris that the United States would be using its aid leverage to pursue the policies that it desired in Vietnam.[62]

When Acting Secretary of State Herbert Hoover, Jr., reported to the NSC on October 26 about France's "very violent adverse reaction," Eisenhower was more determined than ever to get tough. Hearing speculation that the French response might be evidence of a secret understanding reached at Geneva with the Vietminh and known to Eden, the president demanded the "lowdown" even if he had to ask Winston

Churchill himself. When Allen Dulles interjected that the French hoped to maintain a colony in Cochinchina, Eisenhower snapped that the United States had not spent large amounts in Indochina "to enable them to carry out a colonization project." Picking up on the president's obvious disgust, Wilson seized the opportunity to renew his plea that the United States get completely out of Indochina. "The situation there was utterly hopeless," he asserted, "and these people should be left to stew in their own juices." Eisenhower disagreed. American interests dictated American policy, he argued, and a U.S. retreat in the area would endanger U.S. security. A better approach was to "try to get the French out." Wilson knew that he was beaten, but he added with chilling prescience that "he could see nothing but grief in store for us if we remained in this area."[63]

Despite the president's resolute rhetoric, the crash program, including the letter to Diem, did not represent a firm commitment to Diem himself. It was, in fact, another stopgap like SEATO to prevent a complete breach in the line containing Asian communism before an effective regime could be formed in Saigon. To ensure the success of the crash program and to begin to get the confused situation in Vietnam "straightened out," Dulles proposed that the administration send to Saigon a high-ranking official—preferably an Army officer with considerable prestige and proven political judgment in whom the president and the cabinet had great confidence. He suggested Army Deputy Chief of Staff Lyman L. Lemnitzer or either of the Army's two principal commanders in Korea, John E. Hull or Maxwell D. Taylor. The president approved the secretary's idea, but his choice as "the best qualified U.S. Army Officer that he could think of" was General J. Lawton Collins.[64]

"Lightning Joe" Collins was a soldier-statesman in whose judgment and ability Eisenhower had had great confidence for years. Collins had been one of General Eisenhower's most successful corps commanders during World War II, and, in 1947, Army Chief of Staff Eisenhower personally had selected Collins to be his deputy chief. Collins subsequently had served a distinguished term as Army chief of staff during the Korean War, and, in 1954, he was the U.S. representative on the NATO Military Committee and Standing Group. Although not intimates, Eisenhower and Collins were warm and loyal friends. In March 1952, for example, Eisenhower privately had sought Collins' advice on how to arrange his military status for a possible presidential candidacy. The president's staff secretary, Colonel Andrew J. Goodpaster, suggested Collins for the Vietnam assignment, but unquestionably "Lightning Joe" was the man Eisenhower himself wanted in Saigon at this critical juncture.[65]

On November 3, the president handed Collins a letter of appointment as "Special United States Representative" with "broad authority to direct, utilize and control all the agencies and resources of the United States Government in Viet-Nam."[66] These sweeping powers served several purposes. One was to provide a rationale for easing out Heath. Eisenhower's letter gave the general the "personal rank of Ambassador," and, indeed, he was to function as the chief U.S. envoy in Vietnam. In part, the public characterization of Collins as a diplomat was to avoid the appearance of a violation of the Geneva restrictions on military missions to Indochina. Since federal law prohibited active-duty military officers from holding civil appointments, though, a bit of legal legerdemain was required to define his assignment as a temporary (sixty to ninety days) military mission while the embassy counselor, Randolph A. Kidder, officially became chargé d'affaires ad interim.[67]

More important than the replacement of Heath, the grant of full authority to Collins enabled him to deal directly and expeditiously with the Vietnamese and French in Saigon without constant reference to Washington for instructions. His joint civil-military powers were similar to those that Paris had given Ely, and hopefully the two generals, who were already acquainted through overlapping assignments to the NATO Standing Group, could work well together. With the Vietnamese, the administration expected Collins to proceed in emergency fashion to organize and build an effective military force and to promote internal political stability and control. In a predeparture briefing, the secretary of state admitted to Collins that his chances of success were about one in ten, but, Dulles added, "the importance of checking the spread of communism in Southeast Asia is worth the effort."[68] Current policy was to support Diem, Collins' instructions emphasized, but the president also invited his friend to exercise his own judgment. "As this immediate program progresses," Eisenhower's November 3 letter stated, "I will expect to receive your recommendations."[69]

With the dispatch of Collins to assist and assess the Diem regime, Eisenhower and Dulles dropped the wait-and-see approach in favor of direct American involvement in the internal politics of South Vietnam. From the time of Ngo Dinh Luyen's initial meeting with Walter Bedell Smith in Geneva in May 1954, direct U.S. aid and advice to the VNA had been identified as the fastest and most promising help that Washington could provide Saigon. France's continued possessiveness toward South Vietnam, as revealed by French complicity in the Hinh plots, meant, however, that overt American action would have political implications far beyond simply strengthening the South against the North. Eisenhower, Dulles, and other Americans decried France's old-fashioned colonialism. This attitude was partly a manifestation of America's long-standing defense of self-determination as found in the Declaration of Independence, the Fourteen Points of World War I, the Atlantic Charter of World War II, and the Pacific Charter signed at Manila. Partly, it was disdain for France's self-promotion as a world power despite its humiliation at the hands of the Nazis in Europe and the Vietminh in Indochina. In addition, and less candidly, it was a product of America's own self-assurance, ambition, and self-interests.

Despite its anti-imperialist protestations, the United States in the 1950s was the world's most powerful nation and was preparing to move into an economically underdeveloped and politically weak region. This imbalance by its very nature placed the United States in a position to manipulate the politics of Vietnam with the actual or potential use of economic and military force. When the administration spoke of "Free Vietnam," which was the initial designation many U.S. officials employed for South Vietnam after Geneva, it used the label "free" in two deeply felt and genuine ways. "Free" meant "not communist" in the cold war jargon of the time, and "free" meant "not colonial" in the Fourth-of-July tradition of American ideals. Yet, despite the assertion that South Vietnam was free from communist or colonialist domination, it was not free in two important respects: (1) Bao Dai's vacuous State of Vietnam was so anarchic, plagued by factionalism, and devoid of basic government services that individual freedom in South Vietnam was easy prey for guerrillas, renegade generals, bandits, or other self-seekers with guns and ambition; (2) The United States and France chose to manipulate the "free" Vietnamese for Western purposes. With France's military power waning in Indochina, some French officials and businessmen resorted to intrigue to manipulate Vietnam's internal politics for French advantage. The U.S. approach too was indirect in that it rejected any appearance of an outright effort to make South Vietnam an American dominion.

The United States chose as its weapons the promise of giving and the threat of withholding economic and military assistance. This technique gave Washington real and effective leverage that the French and the Vietnamese found impossible to resist. In one of Heath's last efforts to use the aid ploy with Hinh, the Vietnamese general responded with a pointed comment. Although recognizing that U.S. aid was essential to containing the communist threat in Southeast Asia, "he said with [a] wry smile that [the] 'political influence' of this aid is becoming 'assommant' (overwhelming)."[70] Americans complained that Bao Dai was wire-pulling from Cannes by giving or withholding legitimacy to various Vietnamese leaders or factions, but the supreme wire-puller was the United States, using dollars for wires. This dollar diplomacy was so effective and relatively inexpensive (compared with a political and military occupation of Vietnam) that its limits were obscured. Among Vietnamese, this American manipulation generated resentment. American pressure, as well as French interference and Vietminh intimidation, frustrated the nationalist aspirations of Saigon's pro-Western elite, which was acutely aware of its own dependence. There were also long-term political conditions that the U.S.-aid weapon could not address: U.S. dollars could force or entice leaders to make certain choices, but they could not convert autocrats into democrats, mandarins into peasants, or urban bureaucrats into rural reformers. The historical, social, and economic mosaic of Vietnam's village-based culture was resistant to American outside manipulation and much too complex and imbedded to be changed quickly by American wealth and good intentions.

V

The Collins Mission and Washington's "Point of No Return" (November 1954–May 1955)

W HEN GENERAL J. Lawton Collins arrived in Saigon on November 8, 1954, the Eisenhower administration hoped that he could somehow revive the practically moribund State of Vietnam. Faced with Vietminh intimidation, French recalcitrance, Bao Dai's corruption, sect scheming, American caution, and its own ineptitude, Prime Minister Ngo Dinh Diem's government appeared on the verge of complete collapse. When Collins left Vietnam six months later, Diem's prospects seemed much more promising. Although he still had to be concerned with Bao Dai and the communists, the prime minister had demonstrated enough leadership to stand up to the sects and to gain Paris' reluctant acceptance and Washington's wholehearted endorsement. Ironically, the dramatic transformation in Diem's fortunes came about despite Collins' recommendation that the United States withdraw support from the prime minister. In the spring of 1955, the general disagreed emphatically with officials in Washington who argued that Diem was indispensable to the creation of a successful, noncommunist regime in South Vietnam. Collins came very close to prevailing, but at virtually the last possible moment, the State Department decided to support the ill-fated prime minister as the best hope for a Vietnamese nationalist alternative to Ho Chi Minh and for the containment of communism in Southeast Asia. By the middle of May 1955, the Eisenhower administration had bound the American government to a futile and tragic partnership with Diem.

Accustomed to the military chain of command, General Collins assumed that his broad grant of authority as the president's special representative made him solely responsible for the implementation and evaluation of U.S. policy in Vietnam. In reality, American activity was much more fragmented and complex. Lightning Joe kept General O'Daniel and Colonel Lansdale under tighter reign than had Ambassador Heath, but they still operated independently. Lansdale claimed in his memoirs that he walked out during Collins' first Country Team meeting in Saigon because he disagreed with the general's ordering of priorities in South Vietnam. In a later interview, Collins said he "didn't recall that incident, because, if he had walked out on me, he wouldn't have come back again. That's all there was to it."[1]

Besides Lansdale, O'Daniel, and their cohorts, another informal network, which journalists later dubbed the Vietnam Lobby, maintained a flow of information and recommendations from Saigon directly into influential Washington circles. Professor Wesley Fishel was a key member of this group, as were prominent American Catholics such as Francis Cardinal Spellman and the Joseph Kennedy family of Massachusetts. Fishel served as a valuable link for Collins with the Ngo family and other Vietnamese in Saigon, but he also maintained his own channel of communication to Ngo Dinh Luyen in Paris. Luyen, in turn, kept in touch with Senator Mike Mansfield, Senator Hubert H. Humphrey (D–Minn.), and others in the United States. Although this Fishel-Luyen-Mansfield channel was known to the State Department, its activities were not shared with the Vietnamese embassy in Washington, because Luyen did not fully trust Ambassador Tran Van Chuong's loyalty to Diem. The precise impact of the Vietnam Lobby is difficult to measure, but it was significant. On occasion, the State Department specifically requested Mansfield's views on developments in Saigon. On the day Collins was selected for his special mission, a State Department cable conveyed a personal message from Fishel (temporarily in the United States) to Diem that urged the prime minister to trust U.S. assurances of backing against General Nguyen Van Hinh.[2]

The Diem-Hinh impasse, which had brought about Washington's "crash program" and the dispatch of Collins, was on its way toward resolution even before Collins arrived at his new post. A deal was struck whereby Bao Dai ordered Hinh to come to France and Binh Xuyen leader Bay Vien to cease opposition to Diem in return for assurances from the Ngos that the emperor's "crown and purse" would be guaranteed. Soon after reaching Saigon, Collins met with Hinh as well as Diem. As did O'Daniel and Lansdale, the new ambassador liked the young Vietnamese general and thought that he had leadership potential despite his immature judgment. Collins warned Hinh against further scheming and urged him to heed Bao Dai's summons. On November 17, Collins held a press conference to announce his support for Diem and for the Vietnamese National Army (VNA), as long as it backed Diem. On November 19, the commander of the VNA flew out of Saigon, and the emperor formally relieved Hinh as chief of staff ten days later. At the same time, Collins turned to the task of trying to create an effective VNA loyal to the prime minister.[3]

Eisenhower's explicit instructions to Collins were "to assist in stabilizing and strengthening" the Diem government through military and other reforms.[4] With American training and advice, Washington believed, the VNA officer corps could assume independent command over their French-created and -led army. An autonomous Vietnamese force with native leadership would presumably develop the esprit de corps and national loyalty essential to the establishment of a viable regime in Saigon. Although plausible, the objective given to Collins was fraught with formidable obstacles. No officer in the VNA had ever commanded more than a regiment in combat, for example, nor had the French allowed the Vietnamese to direct technical or staff services.[5]

Not only had the French left the VNA in shambles, but Collins could expect resistance to his efforts from French military and political leaders and from Diem. As Heath left to make way for Collins, the outgoing ambassador warned against the inclination of some Americans to "try to ride roughshod" over the French. "Obtaining loyal French cooperation" was as essential as Hinh's removal, in Heath's opinion, if "Free Vietnam" was to be preserved. Even with a joint Franco-American effort, he cautioned, Diem's stubbornness, narrowness, and other liabilities "may be greater than all support and guidance we give him and a possible successor must be sought." Heath noted especially the prime minister's lack of interest in rapid or radical agrarian reform. Rural land ownership was not only a central theme of Vietminh propaganda, Heath noted, but it was also the "single most important thing [Diem] could do to capture [the] loyalty of officers and men of [the] National Army."[6]

Before attempting to reform Diem and his policies, Collins set to work on the problem of French cooperation. Upon learning of Collins' appointment, General Paul Ely had objected to this special mission. While professing the highest personal regard for the American general, the French high commissioner contended that the much publicized posting of such a senior American official in Saigon would give the impression that the United States was taking over Vietnam. Ely arranged to be absent from the capital when Collins arrived, but the new envoy traveled immediately to the resort city of Dalat to call upon his French counterpart. Although the initial formalities were strained, the two generals quickly stood at ease with each other. Despite some occasionally sharp policy differences in the weeks and months that followed, they developed a good working relationship based on mutual respect and a shared sense of duty and honor. As Ely had feared, however, Vietminh propaganda and the French press often chose to label the Collins mission as American usurpation of Vietnamese and French interests. Many Frenchmen in Vietnam referred to the new American ambassador as "the Governor General."[7]

Working with Ely, Collins made significant advances on military issues. In mid-December, the generals signed a joint memorandum that the Vietnamese armed forces would be gradually reduced about 50 percent to approximately 88,000 men. These forces would have full autonomy under Vietnamese unit commanders by July 1, 1955; and, in January 1955, the U.S. Military Assistance Advisory Group (MAAG) would assume full responsibility for the organization and training of these forces, although Ely would remain the commander-in-chief in South Vietnam. The State Department immediately approved the agreement, but Premier Pierre Mendès-France and his colleagues stalled. French politicians expressed concern about possible violations of the Geneva agreements and the demoralizing effect within South Vietnam of a large military demobilization. They also questioned the U.S. contention that the Manila Pact made possible a smaller and hence less costly native army. Washington agreed to raise the Vietnamese force level to 100,000, but the major French objection still remained—the surrender of French influence over the Vietnamese military. Right-wing deputies in the assembly considered it an insult to French honor, and left-wing politicians viewed it as an obstacle to their desire for a rapprochement with the Vietminh as the best protection of French interests in Indochina. Finally, after Dulles assured Mendès-France that the United States would continue to consult France on policy alternatives in Vietnam and would continue some financial support for the French Expeditionary Corps (FEC), Paris approved the military arrangement. In February 1955, O'Daniel's MAAG officers began their long-desired training program.[8]

Even more sensitive and intractable than military reform was the question of Diem's continued leadership. French officials, including Ely, regretted that Eisenhower's instructions to Collins and October letter to Diem made the prime minister the explicit recipient of U.S. support. As they had since the Geneva Conference, the French preferred to seek a Saigon alternative to Ho Chi Minh other than Diem. They also maintained a hedge against a complete collapse in Saigon by posting Jean Sainteny in Hanoi as an unofficial French consul. Notwithstanding assertions to the contrary by Mendès-France and Ely, Paris was playing a "double game." With practically each day that passed, some French official proclaimed the Diem experiment a failure and called for a new leader in the South or for further negotiations with the North. In response, Washington held firm to the proposition that Diem be given more time and elicited reassurances of French acceptance of Diem "for the moment." Collins was acutely aware that the prime minister's performance would determine future U.S. as well as French support of Diem's government or of any regime in the South. Consequently, he outlined an ambitious, seven-point reform program for (1) the Vietnamese armed forces, (2) strengthening and stabilizing the Diem government, (3) refugee resettlement, (4) land reform, (5) creation of a national assembly, (6) financial and economic aid, and (7) improving Vietnamese administrative personnel. All of these problem areas demanded urgent attention. The Collins-Ely military memorandum addressed the first, but the second was the one upon which all others hinged.[9]

A week after Collins reached Saigon, he informed Dulles that he doubted Diem's capacity to manage the country. After a month, he still rated Diem's prospects as "only fair at best."[10] The prime minister's best hope, Collins believed, was to bring some strong leaders into his cabinet to provide the practical executive skills Diem lacked. Collins soon fastened upon Phan Huy Quat as precisely the type of "first rate" official he had in mind. Quat had a forceful advocate in Paul J. Sturm, whom the State Department had sent with Collins to Saigon as the general's personal adviser on Vietnamese politics. Sturm was the former U.S. consul in Hanoi and had long known and liked Quat. Collins repeatedly urged Diem to name Quat minister of defense. The ambassador's persistence prompted Ely to remark that "the desire on the part of the Americans to get Quat into the Cabinet was a sort of 'hobby horse' the Americans are riding at the moment" to give the appearance of government reorganization in order to gain congressional appropriations for Indochina.[11]

Ely, Lansdale, Mansfield, and Kenneth T. Young, the State Department officer in charge of Southeast Asian affairs, shared Sturm's and Collins' high regard for Quat's abilities, but his appointment was not their decision. Advised by his brothers Luyen and Nhu, Diem resisted the ambassador's pleadings. As they had done in the early days of the Hinh crisis, the Ngos claimed that Quat would antagonize the sects, which considered him hostile to their private armies. Yet, Diem too opposed the existence of the sect forces, which should have made Quat an ally. In reality, the Ngo regime was unwilling to risk allowing a highly respected nationalist rival to assume charge of the vital reform of the armed forces. Aware of these fears, Collins considered Diem's decision a "grave mistake," and he cabled Dulles that it was convincing proof of the lack of unity and decisive leadership in South Vietnam. He recommended avoiding any new personal pledges to Diem while investigating the possibilities of either a return of Bao Dai to Vietnam or even the gradual withdrawal of U.S. strategic commitments back to a Laos-Cambodia-Thailand-Burma-India line.[12]

Collins' assessment produced a flurry of consultations in the State Department. Secretary Dulles was in Paris with Counselor Douglas MacArthur II for a meeting of the North Atlantic Council. Young and Assistant Secretary of State Walter S. Robertson conferred with Mansfield and forwarded an analysis, dictated by the senator, to Paris for MacArthur and to Saigon for Collins. Ambassador Dillon in Paris and Ambassador Robert McClintock in Phnom Penh, Cambodia, who was Young's predecessor as head of the interdepartmental working group on Indochina, provided estimates of current French attitudes and the implications of the Saigon situation for other parts of Southeast Asia. Heath, back in Washington and assigned to Young's office, also prepared a memorandum on Collins' recommendation. From these studies, a consensus emerged that brought Washington's Vietnam policy into sharp focus.

"The Secretary has analyzed the situation as one in which we are conducting a time buying operation," Heath wrote.[13] The consistent advice of all those consulted was that the United States had no choice but to support Diem and the southern regime for as long as it was at all feasible. Acting Secretary of State Herbert Hoover, Jr., instructed Collins to continue working with Diem but to insert "escape provisions" into any agreements or understandings in case of the Saigon government's "unwillingness or inability to carry out undertakings."[14] The department had serious doubts that Bao Dai could salvage the situation but did not foreclose entirely the possibility of turning to him. As for an American withdrawal, the department's prediction was that the French would then seek a modus vivendi with the Vietminh that would allow Hanoi, probably through elections in 1956, to gain control of the whole country. With enough time, however, the French might be persuaded to resist compromise with the communists, and the states neighboring Vietnam might be stronger and better able to combat the subversive tactics employed by the communists worldwide. Upon his return to Washington, Dulles sent Collins both formal instructions and a personal message complimenting the progress made, acknowledging the difficulties faced, and stressing how important it was that he was "gaining the time which is so essential for us to strengthen the adjacent free area."[15]

Like the loyal soldier that he was, Collins continued to work on his seven-point reform program. On paper, at least, agreements were soon reached with Diem for a national assembly, land reform, and other needed changes in addition to the military proposals already developed. As with the armed forces program, Collins gained Ely's cooperation in shaping most of these plans. Although Diem had appointed a new defense minister, Ho Thong Minh, who was competent but undistinguished, the American ambassador continued to ask without success that the prime minister find some office for Quat. By mid-January, though, Collins could report to Washington that real progress had been made on all of the seven-point program except broadening the government. In fact, he concluded that "prospects are brighter" in Saigon and that Diem should be allowed more time to prove himself.[16]

On January 27, 1955, Collins met in Washington with the National

Security Council (NSC) to examine what had been accomplished and what remained to be done. He summarized his recent reports of Diem's strengthening position and asserted that the regime had "a reasonable prospect of success" with firm U.S. support and, at least, French acquiescence if not cooperation. Collins was careful to point out, however, that Diem had yet "to establish broad popular confidence in, and support for, his Government."[17] Owing his position to the tenuous legitimacy of Bao Dai and having no political party of his own, Diem had to develop an indigenous political base if he was going to maintain his authority. If the entire reform program could be accomplished, though, Collins concluded that "there was at least a 50–50 chance of saving South Vietnam from the Communists."[18] His Washington audience was encouraged by Collins' seeming success and hoped that his assessment was accurate, but, as Young observed, prudence suggested that South Vietnam's odds for survival might now be one in five rather than the original one in ten. The general declined an offer from Dulles to become the permanent ambassador, but Eisenhower sent Collins back to Saigon to work toward implementation of the seven-point program and also to evaluate further the long-term prospects of Diem's leadership.[19]

In his report to the NSC, Collins identified the hostility of the armed sects as a more immediate danger to Diem's rule than the Vietminh. The Cao Dai, Hoa Hao, and Binh Xuyen were separate forces united in nothing except their opposition to any centralized authority that even potentially menaced their proprietary interests. They threatened, harassed, and effectively blocked government programs. Meanwhile, according to Collins, the communists faced serious economic problems in the North and had chosen "to lie low in Free Vietnam and observe strictly the rules of the game agreed upon at the Geneva Conference" pending the outcome of the nationwide elections proposed for 1956.[20]

The question for the Diem government was whether to attempt to coexist with the sects at considerable expense to the government's authority and integrity, or to try to eliminate these powerful rivals at the risk of a violent civil war that the fledgling regime might not survive. The Binh Xuyen vice lords were especially dangerous because of their control of the national police, purchased with large bribes to Bao Dai. As long as the Hinh challenge denied him the support of the VNA, Diem had little choice but to conciliate the sects. In September he had brought some Cao Dai and Hoa Hao representatives into his cabinet. Collins and

Ely encouraged this move as part of their effort to broaden support for Diem's government among all South Vietnamese factions in anticipation of the 1956 elections. The French had long tolerated and, in fact, subsidized the sects as allies against the Vietminh. Despite French and American advice and his initial caution, however, Diem had always maintained that the sects eventually would have to be eliminated. As Chargé d'Affaires Randolph A. Kidder wryly observed: "Hornets' nests seem to have an irresistible fascination for Diem."[21]

In February 1955, Diem began to put the squeeze on his southern opponents. He refused to renew the Binh Xuyen's license for its huge and profitable Grande Monde casino in Cholon and discontinued the former French practice of subsidizing the Cao Dai and Hoa Hao forces. Supported by Collins' recommendation for a smaller VNA, he revealed plans to integrate only a few sect soldiers into the national army. Utilizing various clandestine contacts, including those of Lansdale, Diem used bribes and other inducements to gain the assurance of support from Cao Dai generals Trinh Minh The and Nguyen Thanh Phuong and some other individual commanders. All these moves had been accomplished by the end of February, when Secretary Dulles stopped briefly in Saigon after a conference in Bangkok of the Southeast Asia Treaty Organization.[22]

Meeting Diem for the first time, Dulles praised the prime minister's leadership of "Free Vietnam" and assured him of the "solid support" of the United States, which "had [a] great stake in him and in Vietnam." Assuming that the recent moves against the sects had strengthened Diem's personal authority, Dulles suggested that now he could "afford to bring into his government other men who might otherwise be his political opponents."[23] Diem protested that his security, especially relative to the sects, was still a problem. Separately, Collins advised the secretary that, aside from the continued narrowness of its political base, "the Diem Government has developed a sound and progressive program" and "to replace Diem at any time between the present and July 1956 would seriously retard those essential programs, if not fatally obstruct them."[24] Dulles left Saigon "favorably impressed by Diem who is much more of a personality than I had anticipated." Upon his return to Washington, he declared that he was "convinced that his Government deserves the support which the United States is giving."[25]

Despite Dulles' and Collins' positive outlooks, the real test between

Diem and the sects was just beginning as the secretary departed from Saigon. On March 4, the sect pot began to boil. The Cao Dai pope, Phan Cong Tac, proclaimed a united front of the Cao Dai, Hoa Hao, and Binh Xuyen in opposition to government "dictatorship." Among those joining with Tac in this statement were Hoa Hao General Tran Van Soai and Binh Xuyen boss Bay Vien. Privately, Soai inquired about the U.S. attitude toward a change in government. With Collins temporarily absent in Manila, embassy officers told him that the United States supported Diem "at this time" and opposed a coup. These ominous rumblings prompted Dulles to label Saigon "about the most critical spot in the whole international scene."[26]

Collins hurried back from Manila and met with Diem, Ely, and others. He ascertained that there was no immediate threat of sect military action but discovered several other troublesome factors. Diem charged that the French were aiding and encouraging the sects against the government to create a pretext for keeping the FEC in Vietnam and thereby preserving French colonial influence. Although Ely denied this accusation, some individual French officers were in league with the sects. Another difficulty was the Bao Dai–Bay Vien connection. Collins thought that the emperor should remove the police from Binh Xuyen control, but Ely doubted that Bao Dai would undercut Vien, the emperor's staunchest nonfamily supporter within Vietnam. The sinister implications of the emperor-gangster relationship led Collins to warn Bao Dai's agent in Saigon that any effort to unseat Diem as prime minister could mean the end of all U.S. aid to Vietnam. To reinforce this threat, the ambassador cited Mansfield's October recommendation to the Senate Foreign Relations Committee that the United States not risk its funds on anyone in Vietnam except Diem.[27]

More disturbing to Collins than the machinations of French provocateurs or Bao Dai's dalliance with Vien were Diem's actions. From Lansdale, Collins learned that Diem was prepared to order the VNA to crush the sects militarily. Minister of Defense Ho Thong Minh believed that such a move would result in a civil war that Diem would lose and that the Vietminh would ultimately win. Collins did not accept Minh's dire prediction at face value, but the ambassador did seek to restrain the prime minister. Collins' own intelligence adviser, James Cooley, estimated that, as time passed, Diem's military support from the national army would increase and simultaneously the sects would grow weaker.

Collins' greatest fear was that the head-strong Diem would act prematurely and upset the apple cart.[28]

Getting Diem to be patient became increasingly difficult, though, as the cat-and-mouse game between the sects and government escalated. On March 21, the sect front, now joined by Generals The and Phuong, gave Diem five days to restructure his cabinet to meet its approval. The front ultimatum stopped short of demanding Diem's resignation, but clearly the sects were attempting to establish a veto power over government policies. There was little indication that the sects would take military action, but the French high command in Saigon—Ely was absent in Paris for consultations with new French Premier Edgar Faure—panicked momentarily and sent a request to Paris for Bao Dai to intervene. They also urged Diem to make concessions to the sects. Angry and exasperated with all the parties, Collins spoke sharply to the French officials about acting without consulting him and not trying to restrain the sects. He declared that The and Phuong were acting like "two stubborn four year old children" and warned them to behave. To Diem, the general gave a two-sided message: (1) be firm and do not let the government's integrity be compromised by yielding to intimidation, and (2) broaden the government and initiate immediate reforms or face termination of U.S. support.[29]

When the internally divided front allowed its five-day deadline to pass with no concessions from the government, it was Diem's turn to put on the pressure. Ignoring suggestions from Collins and Lansdale to put the front on the defensive psychologically by initiating new reform programs, the now "cocky" prime minister wanted to go for a coup de grâce. Singling out the Binh Xuyen and its police power as the backbone of the front and his greatest nemesis, Diem decided to name his own chief of the national police and to order the national army to take over the police headquarters and the Binh Xuyen command post in Cholon. Defense Minister Minh refused to carry out the orders and resigned. With the strong support of Ely, who had just returned from Paris, the VNA's chief of staff General Le Van Ty also resisted Diem's orders. The prime minister backed down momentarily but continued to insist that he was correct.[30]

Diem's conduct brought Collins to a personal crossroads with the prime minister. The general had always maintained that American hopes for a successful Diem-led government in South Vietnam would be realized only if Diem was ultimately willing to share and delegate authority in a broadly representative cabinet. In the present crisis, Collins was less concerned with the prime minister's eagerness to battle the sects than he was with the way Diem was planning to carry out his desire. Abetted by Nhu and Luyen, Diem was trying to by-pass his cabinet and senior military commanders to launch what could easily become an army mutiny and civil war, which would benefit only the Vietminh. Collins had already asked Diem's older brother, Bishop Ngo Dinh Thuc, to try to get Nhu and the other Ngo brother, Ngo Dinh Can, the political boss of central Vietnam, to leave the country for a while to remove the growing concern within Vietnam that a family dictatorship was forming. Collins now gave it to Diem straight: if the prime minister wanted continued U.S. backing, he should make every effort to keep Minh in the government, immediately give his cabinet a representative composition acceptable to Ely and Collins, and take no further steps without consulting them. The insistence that Diem's conduct be acceptable to the French and American representatives was a blatant affront to Vietnamese independence, but Collins wanted Diem to understand that he faced a critical test of whether the two generals could continue to recommend that their governments support him.[31]

As Collins threw down the gauntlet to Diem, open warfare erupted briefly in Saigon and Cholon between the VNA and the Binh Xuyen police and commandos. The fight lasted only a couple of hours after midnight on March 29–30 and included a few mortar rounds aimed at Diem's government palace. The hostilities were short-lived, in large part because French armored units blocked the streets. With information provided by Lansdale and Cooley, Collins believed that the Binh Xuyen was responsible for the outbreak, but Ely was inclined to think that Diem provoked the clash. General Fernand Gambiez of Ely's staff mediated an uneasy truce while all sides pondered their next move.[32]

Collins found himself aligned with neither Diem nor Ely. Diem complained that the French military had prevented him from striking a crushing retaliatory blow against the Binh Xuyen, but the American agreed with Ely that the fighting had to be contained. Collins protested to Ely, though, that French mediation treated the gangsters as equals with the government. Collins argued that, to maintain the regime's authority, Diem had no alternative now but to remove Lai Van Sang, the Binh Xuyen lieutenant who was chief of police, and place the police under government command. Ely responded that such an act would only reignite the fighting. Despite this difference, Ely and Collins agreed that Diem needed quickly to add men of national stature to his government if he was going to maintain any public support. Yet, almost as they spoke, the two generals received word that Foreign Minister Tran Van Do was resigning. Do had ably represented the State of Vietnam at Geneva and was precisely the kind of distinguished public official that Diem needed in his government. On the heels of Minh's resignation, Do's defection left Diem with only the support of his relatives and a few obscure bureaucrats.[33]

Declaring that Diem now was "operating practically one-man government," Collins predicted that Diem could not last much longer. He recommended to Washington on March 31 that the United States begin active consideration of alternatives to Diem, and he suggested either Do or Quat.[34] Neither Dulles nor Eisenhower was prepared for such a radical proposal. They assumed that U.S. support for Diem had been settled during Dulles' February visit to Saigon. Furthermore, the president and secretary of state were preoccupied by delicate negotiations with Chiang Kai-shek over the defense of Quemoy and Matsu and by controversy surrounding the resumption of nuclear testing in Nevada. Upon receipt of Collins' evaluation, Dulles immediately telephoned Eisenhower. The secretary expressed surprise at the ambassador's views and thought that it was impossible to know from Washington what to advise. The president admitted that he did "not know what we should do" but wanted Dulles to instruct Collins "not to give up on Diem until it is quite certain because we bet so heavily on him." He thought that the French and Mansfield could be queried for their current assessments of Diem but that basically Collins would "have to play it by ear."[35]

While Eisenhower and Dulles waited in suspense, Collins and Ely engaged in lengthy deliberations on how best to maintain order. Throughout Saigon and Cholon, weapons bristled from behind sand-bagged fortifications and out of armored vehicles. The two generals agreed that the core of the crisis was who would control the police, but they differed sharply on what to do next. Collins argued that Diem should proceed with the immediate removal of Police Chief Sang, but Ely countered that this move would only renew the fighting. The French high commissioner also declared that Diem was on the verge of megalomania and needed to be restrained, not encouraged to take provocative action. Reasoning that something had to be done quickly, Collins finally agreed to Ely's suggestion that they seek a truce extension while they asked Washington and Paris to consider an invitation to Bao Dai to arbitrate. The plan called for Diem, Vien, and various sect leaders to travel to France and consult with the emperor.[36]

Washington vetoed the Ely proposal. Young drafted the reply, which had the concurrence of Dulles, MacArthur, Chairman of the Joint Chiefs of Staff Admiral Arthur W. Radford, Deputy CIA Director Frank G. Wisner, and other high-level officials. Their concern was that Bao Dai's direct involvement and Diem's departure from Vietnam at this critical juncture would greatly hazard the prime minister's authority. Also, they were convinced that Ely and his superiors had already written off Diem. Collins accepted Ely's explanation that he sought only to be a peacemaker, but Washington believed Ely and his staff were helping the Binh Xuyen against the government. Meanwhile, Paris proposed a coalition government as an alternative to Diem and suggested that, if "Free Vietnam" collapsed under Diem, the responsibility would be solely American. In rebuttal, Young's cable not only rejected Bao Dai's arbitration but insisted that France recognize Diem's authority, essential to any magistrate, to deal with gangsters.[37]

The president agreed fully with the decision to "press" the French to bolster Diem against the Binh Xuyen. "It would be too bad," if Diem failed, Eisenhower told Dulles, "but it would be better to find out now rather than later whether the National Army on which we were spending so much money was loyal."[38] Armed with this support, Dulles dispatched a "Dear Joe" letter to Collins declaring that the time had come for Diem to prove his staying power. "I thought we felt when I was in Saigon," the secretary admonished the ambassador, "that the decision to back Diem had gone to the point of no return and that either he had to succeed or the whole business would be a failure." He added that the opinion in Washington was that Diem could prevail with U.S. and French moral and logistical support. Dulles reasserted his confidence in Collins' judgment but informed the general that the president's "mind runs along with mine in the foregoing respects." He also pointedly reminded Collins that congressional backing for Diem would impede a shift to anyone else.[39]

The secretary's concern about Capitol Hill was not just routine political caution. The Democrats had recaptured Congress in the midterm

elections of 1954, and the administration's high-priority legislative programs, such as an interstate highway system and school construction,
were stalled. Furthermore, Dulles was making a concerted effort to
maintain bipartisan congressional agreement to give the administration
a free hand in dealing with issues arising in the Taiwan Straits. The
timing was not good for the White House to confront Congress on
Indochina. Democratic Senators Mansfield, Humphrey, and John F.
Kennedy favored continued U.S. support for Diem. On the Republican
side, Congressman Walter Judd of Minnesota and Congresswoman Edna
Kelly of New York, among others, stood ready to argue for Diem. From
the domestic political perspective, the status quo in Saigon had great
appeal to the administration.[40]

Dulles' cable confronted Collins with the need to make the critical
decision that he had been edging toward for several days. In his opinion,
the White House, State Department, and Congress were making a dangerously inflexible commitment to Diem. As the French were incessantly
repeating, there were many more problems with Diem's government
than the fact that a Binh Xuyen henchman was the chief of the national
police. On April 7, the president's special representative advised Dulles
that in his judgment "Diem does not have the capacity to achieve the
necessary unity of purpose and action from his people which is essential
to prevent his country from falling under communist control." Collins
genuinely regretted that he could not endorse Diem, whom he considered
to be a patriot, but he just as sincerely believed that Diem lacked the
personal qualities of leadership, executive ability, and creative thinking
to manage successfully the complex forces within Vietnam. In his opinion, Diem was not indispensable to the successful creation of a noncommunist Vietnam, as many in Washington asserted. Collins maintained
that either Do or Quat could lead a progressive government. By coincidence, Ely arrived at the same conclusion at the same time, and for the
same reasons. He informed Collins of his intention to recommend to
Paris that France support a change of government in Vietnam, but there
can be no doubt that Collins' decision was his own. In fact, he never at
the time or in the days that followed revealed to Ely his own recommendation against Diem, and, in his dealings with Ely, he always presented
a united front with Washington.[41]

Collins' cable set off a beehive of activity in the State Department.
Aware of the general's broad grant of presidential authority, Young and

his staff feared that he might be about to act abruptly against Diem. They telegraphed an urgent request for details on how Collins envisioned the implementation of Diem's removal. His reply was an impressive, twelve-page cable of probable scenarios and contingencies that doubtless did little to ease the concern of those in Washington determined to support the prime minister. With the help of his staff, Collins provided not only specific facts but pointed rebuttals to criticisms of his position implicit in the department's questions. For example, one of the queries was for an estimate of the "grass-roots" support for Diem. One could almost hear the embassy officers chuckling at Washington's naiveté when they wrote in response that "there is no proper grass roots support of any leader in Viet Nam, leaving aside Ho Chi Minh."[42]

With Collins' forthright challenge to the proposition that Diem was the best and only hope for a successful nationalist government in Saigon, a virtual impasse gripped the inner circle of the policy process. After talking with Eisenhower, Dulles informed Collins that "we are disposed to back whatever your final decision is but before you actually finalize we want to be sure you have weighed all the factors which concern us here." A list followed of cautions and questions that would have shaken even the firmest resolve of most people. If Diem was removed, Dulles warned for example, the known opposition of the French to Diem would make it appear that the United States had forsaken a "true nationalist leader" under the pressure of "colonial interests." Would not the ouster of Diem mean, Dulles asked, "that from now on we will be merely paying the bill and the French will be calling the tune?" Despite this attempt to put Collins on the defensive by making continued support of Diem a test of American foreign policy independence, Lightning Joe was unbowed. He simply jotted down "not so" in the margin of the cable next to the secretary's question.[43] Collins provided counterarguments for each of Dulles' concerns. He insisted that he had no desire to be "contentious" and that he was thinking only of American interests and the "good of Vietnam, rather than in terms of a single man."[44]

It was clear to Dulles that the effort to shake Collins' stand was not working. On his way to a midday meeting with the president on April 11, the secretary confided to his brother Allen that "it looks like the rug is coming out from under the fellow in Southeast Asia [Diem]." Although both brothers wanted "to hold on to him a bit longer," the president was inclined to go along with Collins.[45] At the White House,

Eisenhower and the secretary of state revised a draft telegram to Collins "to acquiesce in plans for Diem's replacement." The president wanted the instructions to specify that the new premier not be "a tool of French colonialism" and that the new government control the Vietnamese police. Dulles returned to the department to incorporate these changes into the telegram, but, at the same time, Young was handing Robertson an alternate draft. Willing to go along with Collins "in principle," Young thought that "we should not discard Diem so abruptly or completely." He wanted to explore "several intermediary combinations" and, moreover, to avoid any procedure that put an obvious "French and American label on the new prescription and the new injection."[46] At a 5:00 P.M. meeting, of which there is no known record of its substance or participants, the Young draft apparently was substituted for the earlier Dulles–Eisenhower draft. The cable dispatched finally to Collins on the evening of April 11 contained no authorization to replace Diem, raised new procedural questions, and effectively delayed a decision on the prime minister.[47]

Eisenhower had great confidence in Collins' judgment, but he also had great respect for the advice of Secretary Dulles. The president acted as referee between the two and allowed both to advance their arguments. Although ready to back his special representative, he gave the State Department extra time to try to get Collins to reconsider his position. In response to the April 11 instructions, the ambassador assured Washington that he would not accept a French "pig in a poke" and that he sought an evolutionary rather than abrupt change in the Saigon government.[48] Believing that there was still time to devise a policy formula that retained Diem in some capacity, Dulles requested permission from Eisenhower on April 16 to have Collins return to Washington for consultations. There was a risk that the ambassador's absence in the midst of the uneasy truce in Saigon could tempt the French, the sects, or Bao Dai to move against Diem. On the other hand, in Washington, Collins could perhaps be persuaded to modify his position. The president was receptive to Dulles' warning that the United States should not be too hasty "to shift horses until we had another one to shift to."[49] Also, since Eisenhower had long maintained that Southeast Asia was a critical front in the containment of world communism, he was concerned about congressional threats of cutting off aid to Vietnam if Diem fell. Consequently, without giving any indication of overruling Collins, the president agreed that the ambassador be summoned to Washington to seek a resolution of the conflict between the general and the secretary of state.[50]

In anticipation of a policy confrontation in Washington, Collins and Dulles began to prepare their positions. After lengthy final discussions with Ely, Diem, Do, Quat, and others, the general wired Washington that he still saw "no alternative to the early replacement of Diem."[51] In Washington, Dulles was marshalling his arguments in rebuttal to Collins. Although the secretary was resigned to the possibility of a change in the Saigon government, he had Young's recommendation to stand behind Diem and a strong warning from Mansfield that an overthrow of Diem could generate a civil war in the South that would allow Ho Chi Minh to "walk in and take the country without any difficulty."[52] In a "Dear Joe" letter to Collins on April 20, Dulles took up the Young-Mansfield arguments. The secretary expressed doubt that there was a clear-cut alternative to Diem and repeated the warning of congressional opposition to an abrupt change in Vietnam's government. Dulles also blamed the French authorities in Saigon for preventing Diem from solving the Binh Xuyen problem militarily during the brief fighting on March 30 and for treating the Saigon gangsters as the equal of the government. Dulles pointedly contended that no Vietnamese leader "can survive without *wholehearted* backing."[53]

In addition to the secretary's direct efforts to persuade Collins to modify his stand, someone within the State Department apparently made an indirect attempt to discredit Collins' recommendation. On April 18, C. L. Sulzberger alleged in the *New York Times* that Collins had given in to French pressure and had joined Ely in advising that Diem be replaced. Actually, Collins was very careful not to reveal his specific conclusions to Ely. Some of the phrasing of the newspaper article followed almost exactly the wording of Dulles' top-secret cable to Collins on April 4 that had described U.S. policy as having already "gone to the point of no return" in support of Diem. Sulzberger's account also identified specific Vietnamese—Quat, Do, and others—that Collins had mentioned to replace Diem. The list was remarkably accurate, considering how carefully the U.S. government guarded the secrecy of obviously sensitive discussions of Vietnamese political personalities. After attempting to saddle Collins and Ely with primary responsibility for undercutting the policy of strong support for Diem, the journalist asserted that "such a substitute" would mean "humiliation for the United States."[54]

General Collins won the first round when he finally squared off face-to-face with the Washington bureaucracy, but ultimately he lost the fight. In a day-long debriefing by Young's State Department working group on Friday, April 22, Collins seized the initiative by vigorously declaring continued U.S. support of Diem to be a "major error." He reiterated the arguments that he had been sending Washington for the past month and forthrightly stated a preference for Quat as Diem's successor. In fact, Collins endorsed a plan put forth by Bao Dai on April 21, in which the emperor had offered to name Quat prime minister. Young tried unsuccessfully to change Collins' view. As a Defense Department account of the meeting noted, the general held his ground while the representatives of the State Department were "reluctant to face the fact that they must admit a failure in U.S. policy."[55]

Also on Friday, in the midst of this debriefing, Collins met with Eisenhower over lunch. Collins earnestly advised the president that "the continuation of the present government under Diem was no longer supportable" and again recommended Quat as the best alternative. To Eisenhower's surprise, the general did not attribute Diem's weakness to his being undermined by the French. Collins argued that Diem's ineptitude long predated the current French opposition to him. The meeting concluded without any decisions being made other than for further study by the State Department and "that Mansfield would be asked in."[56] The day before, Mansfield had complained to an officer of the French embassy in Washington that the administration was putting "major responsibility on me" for the retention of Diem, but the senator had insisted that any decisions were the responsibility of the president and the secretary of state.[57] Although Eisenhower was involved in these discussions, he avoided an active role in the decision. Demonstrating his trust in both Dulles and Collins, the president waited for them to reconcile their differences.

In what appeared at the time to be decisive meetings on Monday, April 25, Collins prevailed. In the morning, Young and his colleagues reluctantly acquiesced to Collins' recommendation. Paul Sturm had accompanied the general to Washington and strongly supported him throughout these sessions. At lunch that day, Collins and Dulles finally conferred directly. Faced with essentially a fait accompli, the secretary accepted a shift in U.S. policy but tried to hold out for at least the interim retention of Diem until a Vietnamese-inspired solution appeared.

Collins and Sturm deemed that an impossible expectation. Over the next two days, Secretary Dulles, Collins, Sturm, Young, Mansfield, and CIA Director Dulles worked out two very complicated telegrams to be dispatched to Paris with simultaneous copies of each to Saigon. Their purpose was to initiate a very careful, step-by-step process toward "some change in political arrangements in Viet-Nam." Despite the extreme caution of the initiative, the Collins recommendation had now brought the State Department to the point of actually naming Phan Huy Quat and Tran Van Do as the anticipated successors of Ngo Dinh Diem. The two cables, numbered 3828 and 3829, were sent from Washington at 6:10 P.M. on April 27. They were never to be implemented.[58]

At 11:56 the same evening, Dulles sent urgent cables instructing the Paris and Saigon embassies to take no action on telegrams 3828 and 3829 until further advised. These "blocking" cables were prompted by reports, which were received in Washington soon after the dispatch of the first cables, that fighting had erupted in Saigon between the Vietnamese National Army and the Binh Xuyen forces. For the next several hours, Washington waited for an indication of how the battle was going. By mid-morning reports were arriving that the VNA was responding effectively and gaining the upper hand. With this news, the State Department began to press the French for a commitment to support the legal government of Vietnam (without specific reference to Diem) in its efforts to uphold law and order.[59]

The propitious timing of the battle in Saigon and the Vietnamese army's apparent success against the Binh Xuyen enabled Diem's advocates in Washington to prevent the implementation of Collins' recommendation. Rather than a phased transition to a Quat government, the United States reverted to wholehearted support of Diem and insisted that the French government and Bao Dai follow the same course. Most officials in Washington believed that the Binh Xuyen had attacked the government and that Diem axiomatically deserved support as the established head of the duly constituted government under attack from gangsters and would-be usurpers. Conversely, French observers and Bao Dai's partisans generally thought that Diem was a "self-seeking War Lord" who had initiated a "premeditated" crisis that would rally the wavering Americans back to his side but that would not alter the reality of his incompetence. Either way, the battle of Saigon was no "chronological accident."[60]

Having nothing to lose and everything to gain, Diem almost certainly began the battle. With rumors rampant in Saigon that Collins was in Washington to recommend against Diem and that Quat was to become prime minister, Diem had issued a decree on April 26 removing Lai Van Sang as chief of the national police and placing restrictions on the movements of Binh Xuyen forces. Sang immediately announced that he would not obey Diem, but both French and American sources in Saigon believed that Sang's Binh Xuyen bosses would appeal to Bao Dai to overrule Diem before taking any retaliatory action themselves. It made little sense for the Binh Xuyen to attack Diem if, as it definitely appeared, the prime minister was on the way out anyway. Also, open warfare was not the Binh Xuyen's style of operation. Unlike the Hoa Hao and Cao Dai, both of which had armies numbering in the thousands, the Binh Xuyen was a mob of armed thugs numbering in the hundreds that wielded power through bluff, bluster, bribery, and brutality. Communist provocateurs or disgruntled Frenchmen who wanted an excuse to keep French forces in Vietnam could have been behind the violence, but Diem himself was the most likely suspect.[61]

Diem's own official explanation of the outbreak claimed that the Binh Xuyen started the fight by lobbing mortar rounds into the grounds of the prime minister's palace at 1:15 P.M., Saigon time, April 28 (which was 12:15 A.M. in Washington).[62] This shelling did occur, but to single it out as the cause of the battle was disingenuous, since it began after Secretary Dulles had sent his blocking telegrams at 11:56 P.M., Washington time, April 27. According to both Ely and Lansdale, a major gun-battle was under way in Cholon on rue Petrus Ky one or two hours before the mortar attack.[63] Neither Ely nor Lansdale indicated who started the fire-fight, but the fact that it was between VNA paratroopers transported to Cholon in trucks and Binh Xuyen soldiers in fortified positions suggested that the government forces were the aggressors. There was also fighting at Bay Vien's Cholon headquarters well before the mortar attack on the palace. These hostilities around the Binh Xuyen strongholds in Cholon began about four hours after Dulles dispatched cables 3828 and 3829 that signaled a U.S. shift away from support of Diem. The timing gave every indication of being a now-or-never act of political survival by the Diem government.[64]

One of the most intriguing questions about the events of April 27–28 is what role, if any, Lansdale played in initiating or encouraging Diem's move. Many of the U.S. government documents that might provide the necessary evidence to establish Lansdale's role remain classified. According to Lansdale's memoirs, Diem summoned him to the government palace at about noon on April 28 (11:00 P.M., April 27 in Washington) and told him that word had just arrived from Washington that a decision had been made at the highest levels in the U.S. capital to "dump" Diem. Lansdale recounts that Diem refused to reveal his source of information, and Lansdale claims that he told Diem he was personally in the dark about any high-level U.S. policy change in regard to Vietnam but would "check with Washington by radio." This conversation supposedly concluded at almost the exact moment the State Department's blocking telegrams were leaving Washington and about fifteen minutes before the mortar attack on the palace.[65]

Other available sources challenge Lansdale's account. Young later told journalist Robert Shaplen that Dulles learned about the Saigon fighting and sent the blocking telegrams, which Young drafted, because of a cable from Lansdale. Robertson recalled that Lansdale's "reporting was of inestimable value here in Washington" during the battle against the sects.[66] An April 28 memorandum by Fisher Howe, the secretary of state's deputy special assistant for intelligence, reveals that a "flood" of messages received from Lansdale on the evening of April 27 in Washington prompted hurried discussion in the capital that resulted in the dispatch of the blocking telegrams. Only one such message, sent at 7:48 P.M., Washington time, is included in the Department of State's *Foreign Relations of the United States,* but these published documents do include three cables from Lansdale to Washington after the blocking telegrams. In his memoirs, Lansdale mentions only one telegram on the twenty-eighth, which he says he sent late in the afternoon (Saigon time) to counter what he perceived as the American embassy's pessimistic assessment of Diem's prospects.[67]

Lansdale had a separate channel of communication to Washington, according to Collins, that was "completely independent" of the ambassador. "The big mistake made frankly with respect to Lansdale and me," the general later reflected, "was that there were two people supposedly representing the United States government. I [was] getting instructions from the president of the United States, and this guy Lansdale, who had no authority so far as I was concerned, [was] getting instructions from the CIA. It was a mistake. That's all there was to it."[68] Conceivably, someone in Washington used Lansdale's secret channel to send immediate word to Saigon about the 6:10 P.M. telegrams, and information about the Saigon-Cholon fighting could have been sent back to Secretary Dulles by the same means. Bao Dai has charged that MAAG officers under Lansdale's direction "prepared the operation" against the Binh Xuyen. It is unproved whether Lansdale, whom the French called the "Boy Scout" and "Lawrence of Indochina," was the agent provocateur, but Americans in Saigon heard rumors that "Diem precipitated the conflict" and "that Lansdale told him if you don't start it today you won't be in a position to next week." [69]

With the results of Diem's gambit still unknown, the NSC met on April 28. Collins and Sturm attended and thus had one final opportunity to argue their case before hurrying back to Saigon. Allen Dulles began the discussion with an intelligence summary that identified the 1:15 P.M. shelling of the palace as the start of hostilities. He made no mention of the clashes that had occurred in the morning, but he acknowledged the difficulty of determining who actually initiated the battle. Foster Dulles added that the situation was now one of waiting to see if Diem would be overthrown or if he would emerge as a "hero." In regard to the discussions that had been under way with Collins, the secretary of state asserted that Washington now had to look for alternatives to Diem because the French did not support the Vietnamese leader. The secretary complained, however, that France had no specific recommendation except that Bao Dai be urged to mediate the conflict in Saigon. In Dulles' opinion, Bao Dai was totally unacceptable in such a role because of his close connection with the Binh Xuyen. [70]

As before, Collins disagreed with much of Secretary Dulles' assessment. The problem was Diem's ineptitude, he declared, not French attitudes. Although the general favored continuing American assistance to South Vietnam, he insisted that "Diem's number was up" and that the prime minister was not "the indispensable man." Obviously thinking of the current crisis, Eisenhower interjected that the destruction of Binh Xuyen power was a "sine qua non" for any government in Saigon. Collins agreed but maintained that to seek a military solution to the problem would only transform the Binh Xuyen into an antigovernment guerrilla force. Collins preferred a political solution in the form of a coalition government, which he doubted Diem would ever accept. Without objection, the NSC then agreed that the United States should "continue its support of South Vietnam, while recognizing that the composition of the government might have to be changed and keeping the situation under constant review." [71]

Before new instructions could be transmitted to Saigon, Ely subjected U.S. Chargé d'Affaires Kidder to a withering personal attack. With much of Cholon in flames and civilian and military casualties streaming into hospitals, the French high commissioner felt duty bound to restore order immediately. Since he believed Diem to be responsible for the violent outbreak, he pointedly asked Kidder if the United States would support a French removal of the prime minister. Having received no specific guidance since receipt of the blocking telegram, the American had no idea what direction U.S. policy would take, but, as he later recalled, "I would be damned if I was going to say I didn't know. With my legs shaking in my trousers, as they did the day I was married, I told Ely 'No.' " The general was "flabbergasted" and launched into a "violent tirade." In a manner reminiscent of his misunderstanding of the administration's commitment to Radford's proposals during the Dienbienphu crisis, Ely protested that he thought he had Collins' agreement that Diem must go. Kidder respected Ely and recognized the pressure that he was under, but the chargé held his ground. As patiently as possible, he pointed out that, despite Collins' serious concerns about Diem, the U.S. envoy had never indicated any change in U.S. policy to Ely, and Kidder repeated previous American arguments for support of the prime minister. Acutely aware that this was the first time in his career that he had made a policy decision entirely on his own responsibility, Kidder's "relief was literally boundless" when the department telegraphed to endorse his position and to commend his "wise and cool" performance. Collins, too, made clear to Ely later that he approved the chargé's conduct. [72]

On April 29 and 30, while Collins traveled back to Saigon, Washington's officialdom began to swing rapidly behind Diem in his hour of trial. Mansfield issued a long statement (quickly supported by Humphrey and others in Congress) reiterating that there was no satisfactory alternative to Diem and equating Diem in this crisis with "the forces standing for decency and honesty and genuine national independence." If Diem fell, Mansfield warned, "the cause of human freedom in Asia [would] not gain." [73] O'Daniel cabled from Saigon that "any change in leadership or command at this time could result in chaos," and Young insisted that more than ever "we should stick with Diem now." [74] Fishel came to Washington and joined an agent sent from Paris by Luyen to promote Diem and to undercut Collins' views with U.S. officials and the press. The mounting defense of Diem enabled Dulles to notify the embassies in Paris and Saigon on April 30 that "American opinion is increasingly opposed to removal of Diem particularly at this juncture."[75]

After heavy fighting, the national army routed the Binh Xuyen forces, and Diem seemingly met the test of strength that Collins and Ely had previously doubted he could survive. When Collins arrived back in Saigon on May 2, he found a message from Dulles that characterized the prime minister as a "popular hero." Drafted by Young, who confided to Robertson that he and his working group never believed in the plan to ease Diem out, the secretary's cable declared that "Diem rightly or wrongly is a living symbol of Vietnamese nationalism struggling against French colonialism and corrupt backward elements." Consequently, the State Department deemed American participation in the removal of Diem to be "domestically impractical" and "highly detrimental [to] our prestige in Asia." Collins' instructions were to support Diem's efforts to maintain his authority and to urge Ely not to "prejudice" Diem's position.[76]

In Saigon the political situation rapidly evolved in Diem's favor as Vietnamese factions maneuvered frantically for power. Diem defied orders from Bao Dai to transfer command of the army and come to France "for consultations." In the headiness of success, the prime minister flirted with a dubiously constituted National Revolutionary Congress and a self-appointed Revolutionary Committee of sect generals and other schemers, both of which demanded the ouster of the emperor. There was also talk of attacking French military personnel or civilians suspected of aiding the Binh Xuyen. Ely declared that Diem was an "irresponsible madman." Emotions ran high in Saigon, and accusations of blame for the tense situation flew back and forth between the French and Vietnamese and between the French and Americans. Collins immediately began successful efforts to persuade both Diem and Ely to proceed more cautiously.[77]

With the immediate crisis in Vietnam beginning to ebb, Collins made his final estimate of the situation there in preparation for the end of his mission, which had now lasted six months. Just as he had done in Washington, the president's special representative gave a frank warning on Diem and outlined the grim choices that the United States would likely face in Vietnam. The success against the Binh Xuyen notwith-standing, the general remained unconvinced that Diem had the leader-ship ability to implement the economic, political, and military programs that Saigon needed to compete successfully with the challenge from Hanoi. In fact, Collins worried that Diem might now be more resistant than ever to American advice to take competent men into his govern-ment and to decentralize his authority. For the moment, Collins believed, the United States should continue to work with Diem. If Diem still proved incapable of effective leadership, however, "we should either withdraw our support from Vietnam, because our money will be wasted, or we should take such steps as can legitimately be taken to secure an effective new Premier." Unless "wholehearted agreement" among the American, French, and Vietnamese (whomever headed the Saigon gov-ernment) could be achieved, Collins concluded in phrases strikingly similar to Heath's final report from Saigon, "we should withdraw from Vietnam."[78]

The State Department listened respectfully but again did not heed the general. During lengthy and difficult discussions with Premier Faure in Paris from May 8 to 12, Dulles argued forcefully that Diem was the only available nationalist alternative to the Vietnamese communists. British foreign ministry officials participated in most of these talks and generally backed Dulles but also emphasized the need for preserving Western unity. At the beginning of the talks, Faure adopted a hard line. Unlike Pierre Mendès-France, who had a reputation as a political brawler, the new premier was more of a fencer. He declared that Diem was mad ("fou") and that his regime was a catastrophe for both Vietnam and the West. In a largely theatrical gesture to emphasize his government's frus-tration with America's continued insistence on Diem, Faure offered to withdraw the FEC immediately from Vietnam. Although the proposal appealed to U.S. officials, the Americans knew that French forces still remained necessary for internal security in South Vietnam. If the United States and France were to continue to work together, Faure also wanted personnel from both nations "who make policy difficult" to be removed from Indochina. Dulles' advisers warned him that this ploy was aimed at Lansdale and Kidder, about whose attitude the French had com-plained during the battle in Saigon. The secretary of state side-stepped the FEC and personnel proposals, acknowledged that Diem might ulti-mately fail, but clung tenaciously to the argument that "we have to take

[a] gamble we can succeed with Diem" if he is given unreserved support.[79]

In making his case for Diem, Dulles astounded Faure by asserting: "In that part of the world, there was no such thing as a 'coalition' government, but one-man governments."[80] After all of Collins' efforts to broaden Diem's cabinet, Dulles was now beginning to rationalize away one of Diem's greatest shortcomings—lack of a popular political base. Primarily for the sake of good relations with the United States, Faure eventually agreed that France would support Diem's government, but his pledge was carefully hedged with qualifications. What Dulles termed an "understanding," the premier more accurately described as an "agreement not to disagree."[81] This meeting marked the end of efforts toward a joint Franco-American approach for which Collins and Ely had labored so hard in Saigon. Dulles had finally realized a major success in his desire to Americanize Western support of South Vietnam. Upon his return to Washington, Dulles proclaimed hopefully that "the government of Diem, which seemed to be almost on the ropes a few weeks ago, I think is reestablished with strength."[82] The secretary of state was referring to what had happened in Saigon and Paris, but he also may have been thinking of the policy debate between Collins and the State Department.

The failure to heed Collins' warnings had tragic results. Some of Dulles' closest advisers, such as Young, Robertson, and the secretary's special assistant John W. Hane, Jr., insisted in later years that the decision to stay with Diem was correct.[83] Diem's ill-fated rule, though, substantiated much of Collins' assessment. Diem's "success" against the Binh Xuyen was largely illusory. It was due more to the disunity and dissipation of his sect opponents than to Diem's ability. For a brief, critical moment the army rallied to Diem in a spirit of national unity, but the prime minister soon squandered this asset. The same officers who saved Diem in 1955 would remove him in 1963. As Collins expected, Diem became more stubborn and more reliant on his family government. As Dulles admitted, there was no coalition. The inflexible, self-serving regime, about which Collins had warned, grew more difficult than ever to influence. U.S. reaffirmation of support for Diem put American prestige and credibility at the mercy of Diem's ability alone.[84]

Shortly after Collins' departure from Saigon in May, Ely also left. Although occasionally prone to angry outbursts, Ely usually had joined

Collins as a voice of moderation.[85] Without the frank admonitions of these two pragmatic statesmen, Diem's fatal flaws were less obvious. For many in the United States, Diem became a symbol of anticommunism and righteousness in Vietnam. Some Americans who knew Diem well, such as Lansdale, fostered this view out of personal sympathy and fondness for a friend. Lansdale contended that Collins was a "big picture" official from Washington who never really understood the local conditions in Vietnam. Lansdale complained that Collins talked to Diem like a "country squire looking down his aristocratic nose at a bumpkin."[86] Yet, the president's special envoy perceived very clearly the reality of Diem's situation. Collins sincerely regretted having to recommend against Diem, whom he called a "fine little man."[87] Diem may have been a patriot, as almost everyone agreed, but his good qualities did not compensate for his lack of leadership ability or the narrowness of his political base.

In the long run, Collins was right and Dulles was wrong. At the time, though, the secretary's concern that there was no clear-cut alternative to Diem appeared well founded. To have followed Collins' counsel would have been a risky venture into the unknown. Since Collins' option was not tried, it cannot be known with certainty what would have happened had a government been established under Phan Huy Quat in 1955. Quat was a Northern intellectual whom many Vietnamese in the South, including the sect leaders and the Ngos, did not trust. Unlike the Catholic Diem, Quat was a member of the majority Buddhist religion, but Quat's small Dai Viet party gave him only a limited political base. Quat's success would have depended heavily on his own political skill, which was notable. After 1955, Quat survived politically as a low-key opponent of the Diem regime and served briefly as prime minister in 1965. In the face of virtually impossible political conditions, he demonstrated considerable finesse in both roles. On balance, Quat's chances for success in 1955 were, at least, no worse than Diem's.[88]

In the spring of 1955, with the advice of Kenneth Young and others in the State Department, Dulles decided that Diem was to be the father of his country. Despite Eisenhower's longtime respect for Collins, the administration rejected the general's repeated warnings about Diem's liabilities. Indeed, in a fashion similar to the prerevisionist image of Eisenhower, the president presided over but did not participate actively in most of this discussion. When Collins first recommended serious consideration of alternatives to Diem, Eisenhower admitted to Dulles that he did not know what to do. In the subsequent deliberations throughout April, Dulles briefed the president and obtained his approval of key instructions, such as the recall of Collins to Washington for consultations, but the issue never really diverted Eisenhower's attention from the concurrent Taiwan crisis.

With Diem, the United States was buying time but also buying trouble. America became the guarantor not only of an independent South Vietnam but also of a particular Vietnamese leader. The significance of the Collins recommendations was that the United States had a real, not speculative, opportunity to separate itself from the doomed Diem and simultaneously to open up the South Vietnamese political system to other nationalist leaders. There were alternatives in Vietnam to Ho Chi Minh and Ngo Dinh Diem, but Dulles' rejection of Collins' advice closed the door on those options. On May 19, Dulles recounted to the NSC the argument that he had used with Faure that "in the Orient it was necessary to work through a single head of government rather than a coalition," and he cited Syngman Rhee in Korea and even Ho Chi Minh as successful examples. At almost the same time as this secret briefing, French journalist Robert Guillain wrote that U.S. policy in Vietnam is "the cordon pattern, the Syngman Rhee pattern." Ngo Dinh Diem was to be America's Vietnamese Rhee, and his success was, according to Guillain, "for the Americans a question of 'face.' "[89] It was a policy based on image rather than substance.

VI

The Substance and Subterfuge
of Nation Building
(May 1955–January 1957)

In MAY 1955, the possibility was growing that Ngo Dinh Diem's government might actually fill the political void that the Geneva Conference had left south of the seventeenth parallel. Diem's leadership was far from secure, but the crisis in containment, which had begun at Geneva with France's and Britain's de facto recognition of the Democratic Republic of Vietnam (DRV), was easing. If South Vietnam was going to join West Germany, South Korea, and Taiwan as another truncated nation on the front line of the cold war, however, it would need a Conrad Adenauer, Syngman Rhee, or Chiang Kai-shek. Those leaders had a strong enough domestic following and adequate international standing upon which to build a viable state. Could Diem assume that role in South Vietnam? For the next two years, it appeared that he might.

The outwardly positive guise of nation building concealed the basically negative, reactive, and military nature of America's containment policy. Washington's strategists deemed military defense necessary to guard a vulnerable regime until there was time for it to become self-sufficient. In Europe, where containment was born, the economic, social, and political systems were already well established. Containment there could be a balanced blend of economic assistance (the Marshall Plan) and military security (the North Atlantic Treaty Organization). In Korea, where there had been a conventional military invasion, the ordering of choices among military and other efforts was largely predetermined. In Vietnam, though, the circumstances were unlike Europe or Korea. French colonial rule had prevented the development of indigenous economic and political institutions. The French-Vietminh war had left additional economic, social, and political disruption. Although Vietnam was divided like Korea, the seventeenth parallel was not the thirty-eighth. The rough mountain and jungle terrain along the Vietnamese-Laotian-Cambodian border or the Plain of Reeds near Saigon were more likely invasion routes than across the Geneva demarcation line. Of even greater threat was subversion. Indeed, the real battle for Vietnam was never defined by such targets as borders, invasion routes, or cities. It was the struggle for the Vietnamese population.

According to the Final Declaration of the Geneva Conference, there was to be a "free expression of the national will" in the form of a nationwide election on July 20, 1956. Presumably this vote would decide under whose authority Vietnam would be reunified, but precisely how this election was to be conducted remained completely unspecified by the authors of the declaration. They decreed only that "consultations will be held on this subject between the competent representative authorities of the two zones from 20 July 1955 onwards."[1] Since the DRV and France were the signatories of the Vietnam armistice agreement, it followed that these consultations were to be between Hanoi and Paris. By the summer of 1955, though, the French government had already begun relinquishing its responsibilities for South Vietnam because of both U.S. pressure and its own desire to be rid of the Indochina burden. In this situation, an election would occur only if officials in Hanoi and Saigon could enter into direct discussions on ground rules for a vote to decide the very survival of their regimes. No Vietnamese leader on either side had ever conducted a national election, and the difficulties inherent in this one were almost limitless. The most critical obstacle was that the government of South Vietnam and its patron, the United States, had never recognized the government of North Vietnam nor the legitimacy of the Geneva agreements. For Diem's representatives to even talk to their northern counterparts would have been a major political and psychological concession, if not surrender.

Although the likelihood of any election began to diminish almost as soon as the Geneva Conference adjourned, diplomats around the world devoted much effort over many months to the issue. Consequently, journalists and scholars have often characterized the negation of the Geneva election provisions as a decisive event in Vietnam's tragic history. Most of these accounts place the blame squarely on Diem for blocking the election with the urging, or at least willing acquiescence, of the Eisenhower administration. They generally note that Washington was uncomfortable with the role of opposing a seemingly democratic method of deciding Vietnam's future but that U.S. officials could argue that the vote would not be truly free and that Saigon had no formal obligation to adhere to the Geneva stipulations.[2]

It was inconceivable that Diem would have submitted willingly to an electoral contest with Ho Chi Minh under any terms. The Vietminh's popularity from its military victory over France, the DRV's control north of the seventeenth parallel (where the population surpassed the South's by two million), and electioneering by communist cadres who remained in the southern zone would have combined to produce a DRV victory. Political analysts in Saigon, Hanoi, and other interested capitals shared this assessment. Although Prime Minister Anthony Eden of Britain and Premier Edgar Faure of France contended that without Hanoi's observance of the Geneva armistice "there would not be any Mr. Diem," the southern leader remained adamant that his government was not a party to the agreement and was not bound by it.[3]

The Eisenhower administration insisted that Britain, France, and the United States not gang up on Diem. Dillon Anderson, the president's special assistant for national security affairs, termed it a "delicate problem" for the United States neither to oppose free elections nor to allow a communist takeover of South Vietnam. The Geneva agreements' vagueness on election procedures, Anderson contended, allowed Washington and Saigon to take a position supporting the principle of free elections but insisting on "terms of elections" that would avoid a communist victory in the South. This position, he maintained, was consistent with the U.S. stand in Germany and Korea. Still, Anderson emphasized, the bottom line of U.S. policy was to "look to the possibility of saving a separated South Vietnam from Communist domination, even if the non-Communist forces could not win an all Vietnam election."[4]

As they had throughout the Geneva proceedings, policy considerations far beyond the borders of Vietnam shaped the positions of various governments on the election issue. Since the World War II conferences at Yalta and Potsdam, the United States had championed free elections as a major weapon in its rhetorical and ideological offensive against Soviet tyranny. Diem's political weakness undermined the use of this standard tactic in an area that U.S. officials deemed strategically valuable. For many weeks, Washington's policy drifted while the administration sought to find a credible position that would gain more time to strengthen South Vietnam. Meanwhile, France and the United Kingdom urged that Diem allow the election to proceed. Both nations feared that otherwise armed hostilities would resume in Vietnam, and, unlike the United States, neither was willing to take that risk. Britain had shared the Geneva chairmanship with the Soviet Union, and France was a signatory to the armistice. Both felt obligated to defend the settlement. On the other hand, neither wanted a diplomatic rift with its American ally, and both faced challenges elsewhere (the French in North Africa and the British in Malaya) that would be made much more difficult by a new outbreak in Indochina. For Paris and London, an election would essentially terminate their responsibilities, but so too would an overt U.S. or South Vietnamese assumption of blame for the consequences of what might follow if an election was not held.[5]

On the communist side, the issue was similarly blurred. Hanoi's propagandists kept up a bold front, such as announcing in May 1955 that Saigon would be renamed Ho Chi Minh City after reunification. Like Paris, Hanoi would have welcomed a vote to complete the modus vivendi of the Geneva Final Declaration. Secretary of State John Foster Dulles wondered at times if there was not, in fact, some type of secret understanding between the French and Vietminh. On the other hand, the DRV would not have accepted an elaborate system of election supervision, and quite possibly no workable format would have emerged even if serious preparations had been undertaken. The International Commission for Supervision and Control in Vietnam (ICC) doubted that either side would allow close scrutiny within its zone, and Hanoi's leaders were probably pessimistic from an early date about the likelihood of a vote by July 1956. The DRV's best hope was to get strong diplomatic support from its socialist patrons in Moscow and Beijing, but the two communist powers had revealed at Geneva that they would place their own interests ahead of North Vietnam's. Like Britain and France, the USSR and PRC wanted no more trouble over Vietnam than necessary.[6]

In the spring of 1955, before Diem's showdown battle with the sects in Saigon, the State Department and Ambassador Collins began to urge Diem to take the initiative on the election issue. In fact, Dulles even contemplated briefly the possibility of a Diem victory after the prime minister made a very positive first impression on the secretary in their talks in Saigon on March 1. Collins and most other U.S. officials were less sanguine about Diem's prospects but believed that he could manipulate the election issue. Saigon could seize the propaganda advantage by announcing its willingness to begin talks on July 20, in preparation for a 1956 vote. If Diem insisted on numerous safeguards to guarantee a free election, the DRV would probably balk and thus appear to be the obstacle to the election process. True to his reputation for stubbornness, Diem refused this advice and allowed weeks to pass with no statement. His silence was due in part to the sect crisis but even more to his belief that any talks could be considered ipso facto acceptance of the Geneva Accords and the Hanoi regime. Diem complained that, unlike the governments "of Adenauer and Rhee who have universally recognized support of Western powers," his regime faced a reunification election with only U.S. backing while that of France and Britain was "half-hearted at best."[7]

By June, it appeared to Kenneth Young in the State Department that a potentially dangerous diplomatic situation was rapidly developing. He was sympathetic to Diem's wariness of elections but realized that the July 20 deadline for commencing consultations on this issue was going to fall in the midst of an East-West summit conference scheduled to begin in Geneva on July 18. The government of India, which chaired the ICC and considered itself the champion of neutralism in Asia, was asking the United Kingdom and the Soviet Union, as cochairmen of the 1954 Geneva Conference, to push Diem into election talks. If Soviet leaders Nikolai Bulganin and Nikita Khrushchev chose to support this demand at the summit or to call for reconvening the Indochina conference, the situation for Eisenhower, Eden, and Faure could be, in Young's word, "messy." After repeated prompting by Britain, France, and the United States, Diem finally broadcast a statement in Saigon on July 16. As the heads of the major powers traveled to Switzerland, Diem announced that his government desired unification of Vietnam and supported the idea of free elections. He added emphatically, however, that his regime had not signed the Geneva Accords and was not bound by them.[8]

Contrary to Young's fears, the coincidence of the Geneva summit and the Vietnam deadline proved to be a boon to American and South Vietnamese hopes for avoiding cr delaying an election. The summit occurred largely as a result of what Dulles deemed a Soviet "maneuver" to ease East-West tensions. The leaders devoted most of their time to issues such as the future of Germany and Eisenhower's "open skies" proposal on arms control. Foreign Minister Vyacheslav M. Molotov of the USSR raised the Vietnam question with Eden on July 23, but did not press it. He appeared satisfied with Eden's assurance that Britain, France, and the United States would recommend to Diem that he give the DRV a direct communication of his position on elections. Hence the important July 20, 1955 deadline passed with no significant communist protest. On August 9, Diem's government issued a statement reiterating its July 16 broadcast but again refused to engage the Hanoi regime in direct correspondence. In fact, the August 9 statement largely foreclosed any possibility of consultations with the declaration that "nothing constructive can be done towards this end, as long as the Communist regime in the North does not permit each Vietnamese citizen to enjoy democratic liberties and fundamental human rights."[9] Assistant Secretary of State Walter S. Robertson and Senator Mike Mansfield soon issued public endorsements of this position.[10]

Hanoi, Moscow, and Beijing went through the motions of protesting Diem's recalcitrance, but it was clear long before July 1956 that there was not going to be an all-Vietnam election in that month or any time soon. In September 1955, Premier Pham Van Dong of the DRV lodged a complaint about delays with the British and Soviet cochairmen. In November, at a meeting of big power foreign ministers, Molotov nudged Britain's Harold Macmillan on the subject but did not pursue it. The French appeared interested primarily in "liquidating their Geneva responsibilities in [the] most graceful and unobtrusive manner possible" and in allowing the Geneva Accords to "die [a] natural death."[11] The PRC called in January for a reconvening of the Geneva Conference, but both London and Washington dismissed the move as a propaganda ploy. In May 1956, the British and Soviet foreign ministers met in London and formally considered the Geneva agreements. They sent messages to North and South Vietnam, France, and the ICC urging compliance with the accords and offering to hear grievances, but that was as far as they would commit themselves. Reviewing the results of this meeting, Deputy

Assistant Secretary of State William J. Sebald declared that the Geneva Conference had turned out to be "a considerable diplomatic victory" for the West. It had gained time to strengthen South Vietnam, and now, after two years, there appeared to be no likelihood in the near future of either an election or a breakdown of the armistice. Although the Soviets had not abandoned Hanoi nor had the British guaranteed support of Saigon, the Geneva cochairmen were clearly anxious to avoid a crisis over Vietnam. There was no election in 1956 to decide the reunification of Vietnam. Saigon and Washington had sought this result, but they had accomplices in London, Paris, Moscow, and Beijing who were not eager to risk involvement in a rekindled conflict for the sake of Hanoi.[12]

Although there was not an all-Vietnam election, balloting to reconstitute South Vietnam's government did occur in 1955 and 1956. The restructuring of the State of Vietnam as a republic had been a high priority of American officials from the outset of Diem's rule. An important part of Collins' seven-point reform program to strengthen and broaden Diem's administration was the creation of a national assembly. Such a move would, in U.S. opinion, provide the Saigon regime a measure of popular authority enabling it to counter the sects, resist pressure for submission to the Geneva election provisions, and depose the indolent Bao Dai. Without an elected assembly to promulgate a new constitution, Bao Dai was the "thread of legitimacy" on which Diem's government hung. At the same time, the absentee emperor was a continuing vestige of French claims of influence in Vietnam and the source or foil of anti-Diem intrigues. As Dulles prepared for his pivotal talks with Faure in May 1955, Eisenhower firmly instructed the secretary that "we should not in any way seem to support [Bao Dai]."[13]

Although Americans preferred the creation of an assembly before the elimination of Bao Dai, Diem had his own agenda. While the national army mopped up remnants of the sect forces that had fled after the battle of Saigon, the U.S. embassy learned through covert channels that the prime minister planned an October 1955 referendum on the monarchy. G. Frederick Reinhardt, the new U.S. ambassador and an experienced foreign service officer, expressed concern about the clearly "undemocratic aspects" of Diem's move to oust the emperor without first establishing any alternative authority except his own. Diem's old rival Phan Huy Quat voiced the same objection privately to the U.S. embassy. Dai Viets and other opponents of the government risked arrest and other reprisals if they were openly critical. A Central Intelligence Agency (CIA) analysis acknowledged this discontent but downplayed it as predictable negativism from a hopelessly fragmented opposition. Reinhardt, too, rationalized his doubts with the contention that Diem's assertion of strong executive authority was a move toward stable government and preferable to doing nothing. Furthermore, it seemed that the regime was determined to proceed and that there was little Washington could do without provoking a debilitating crisis in U.S. relations with Saigon. Diem agreed with his brother Ngo Dinh Nhu that "Western democratic models could not simply be applied to Vietnam" and that an "assembly would render government unstable."[14]

On October 23, 1955, Diem's government staged a referendum on the question: "Do the people wish to depose Bao Dai and recognize Ngo Dinh Diem as the Chief of State of Vietnam with the mission to install a democratic regime?"[15] Over 98 percent of the votes cast favored the proposition, and a republic under Diem as president replaced the dissipated monarchy. Diem's victory in the balloting was not surprising, but the near unanimity of the vote revealed an ominous political cunning. Those close to Diem, such as Colonel Edward G. Lansdale, had suggested to the prime minister that a 60 percent share of the votes would be very respectable. Under Nhu's direction, however, the government's campaign left little to chance. The regime mounted an intense and effective propaganda effort aimed at teaching people how to vote, emphasizing national pride, and inciting hatred of Bao Dai and his debauchery. In the cities of South Vietnam, for example, effigies of the emperor appeared adorned with bags of money, packs of playing cards, and pictures of naked women. Conversely, campaigning for Bao Dai was not allowed. On election day, citizens voted by secret ballot with little sign of direct intimidation. When the official results were released, Diem was credited with almost two hundred thousand more votes in Saigon than there were registered voters. Similarly, in some rural areas notorious for weak government control and allegiance, returns were posted giving Diem almost unanimous endorsement.[16]

The government's lopsided victory was a "success" similar to the military defeat of the sects. It was not a true representation of Diem's power or popularity. The emperor's weakness, the disarray of the political opposition, and other such factors explained his triumph. Nevertheless, it was a significant performance. Diem's American sympathizers, such as Young and Lieutenant General John W. O'Daniel, were encouraged by the orderliness of the election and the regime's surprising grip on the voting process. Diem's agents delivered the votes, and Bao Dai managed only a symbolic and hollow protest. In what was essentially his last political act, the emperor fired Diem as his prime minister and appealed for international condemnation of the rigged referendum. He prepared a message denouncing Diem's dictatorship but was not surprised that it was not published in Vietnam or that Diem won the election. Despite their threat to block the balloting, the communists, too, were unable to stop it. Diem was not charismatic, but he and his brothers had demonstrated their talents for intrigue, manipulation, propaganda, and intimidation.[17]

On March 4, 1956, the voters of South Vietnam selected an assembly to produce a constitution for the Republic of Vietnam (RVN). The election was essentially a repeat of the October referendum. Initially, Young suggested that the United States not rush Diem into a free and secret balloting for fear it might result in a splintered assembly. "Democracies in newly independent Asian countries are unpredictable," he cautioned Reinhardt and warned that it was a "delicate task" to balance the strong leadership they needed with the establishment of broadly representative institutions. The State Department's director of the Office of Southeast Asian Affairs (SEA) was admitting Diem's weak mandate and contending, as had Dulles in defending one-man rule, that popular support and strong leadership were separable issues. Young even went so far as to assert, as had Nhu, that representative government may not be an appropriate model for Asia. More important to Young was that the election "institutionalize" the authority of Diem's heretofore "personalized" regime.[18]

Young need not have worried. The U.S. embassy in Saigon estimated that at least 90 of the 123 members chosen for the constituent assembly, despite a variety of party labels, could be expected to support completely Diem and the draft constitution that he had prepared. The Ngos simply disqualified all candidates with any organized support outside the government ranging from the conservative Dai Viet to the radical Vietminh. Furthermore, some seats were created for so-called refugee constituencies, one of which went to Madame Nhu (who ran as an "independent"), to further ensure government control of the assembly. Such moves were practically identical to those used by the Vietminh in selecting the DRV's first constituent assembly in 1946.[19]

With the referendum on Bao Dai and the election of the constituent assembly, Washington finally had what it had long desired in Saigon—at least the trappings if not the substance of representative government. American officials liked to claim that Diem's Republic of Vietnam was the "legally constituted" government of Vietnam. In the context of Vietnam's internal politics, "legally" was an extremely elastic adverb.

Reinhardt was much less complacent than his Washington superiors about what he termed the "increasingly totalitarian character" of Diem's government. Although sympathetic to the need for internal stability, he argued that "lasting stability" depended on the extent of popular support for the government. A hand-picked assembly and the squelching of all public criticism cost the regime much-needed domestic and international respect. Moreover, Reinhardt warned, American acceptance of this behavior convinced Diem that he could take U.S. aid and support for granted and made him unreceptive to suggestions for more democratic procedures. The ambassador specifically recommended that the State Department at least modify its practice of refusing to see any Vietnamese without prior approval of Diem's ambassador in Washington. Talking to people of "various political shades," Reinhardt reasoned, would make Diem less sure of America's unconditional support and less intransigent to advice from Americans and other anticommunist Vietnamese.[20]

Washington, however, turned a deaf ear to both Reinhardt's appeal and Diem's critics. On the eve of the constituent assembly election, the leader of the southern Dai Viet party, Nguyen Ton Hoan, sent an impassioned letter to Eisenhower warning that Diem's personal dictatorship was undermining Western hopes of making South Vietnam a bulwark against communism. The White House referred the letter to the State Department, and Paul Kattenburg of Young's SEA staff scrawled across the top of it: "This letter not to be answered; writer is inimical to achievement of US policy objectives in Viet-Nam."[21] Young's office responded similarly to Nguyen Bao Toan, who had headed the Revolutionary Committee that gave Diem a claim to popular support during the battle with the sects but who had subsequently opposed Diem's autocratic methods. When Toan visited Washington in March 1956,

SEA officials secured agreement from Congressmen Walter Judd (R–Minn.) and Clement Zablocki (D–Wis.), both strong backers of the Saigon regime, "to lecture him on national interest versus party politics."[22]

The RVN had obtained a democratic façade in the October and March elections, but underneath it was an authoritarian state. From their years of experience in the clandestine world of Vietnam's anticolonial struggle, the Ngos had developed a ruthless talent for self-preservation. Their nepotism and clannishness were extreme even within Vietnam's family-centered culture. They conceived of themselves as founders of a new dynasty, which, in part, explained their zeal for the filial bond. Despite Diem's Western, liberal designation as the president of a republic, he was, in fact, a new emperor claiming the mandate of heaven. In the Ngos' own peculiar blend of Catholicism and Confucianism, it was God's will that they assume leadership to restore morality, remove barbarian influence, and reunite the fragmented nation. Although he dedicated his almost totally Buddhist country to the Virgin Mary, it was revealing that his family compared him to Emperor Gia Long, the founder of the Nguyen dynasty of which Bao Dai was the last monarch. Diem sought to emulate Gia Long's great achievement of unifying northern and southern Vietnam and establishing law and order throughout the country. National survival, not popular government, was the overriding goal. The obedience and loyalty of the people was assumed as long as the ruler remained uncorrupted. The Ngos equated their landslide election victories with the mandate of heaven. Proud to claim Gia Long among her ancestors, Madame Nhu claimed years after the murders of her husband and brother-in-law that the Diem government was "the only legitimately elected one of Vietnam" and that "with that choice, the VN nation has indicated who she considers as legitimate heir of Emperor Gia-Long (1762–1820)."[23] Conversely, Bao Dai declared that, after his ouster in October 1955, "it was no longer the Vietnam that my ancestors and our dynasty had worked relentlessly to build, defend, and reconstitute."[24]

Gia Long ruled Vietnam as an absolute monarch, and Diem, too, would tolerate no opposition. He was paternalistic, suspicious, and rigid, and he had a low opinion of the morals and motives of most of his fellow countrymen. With the assistance of his brothers Nhu and Ngo Dinh Can, he managed what could only be termed a police state. From

Hue, Can operated a network of agents, informants, and (according to his critics) assassins as far south as Phan Thiet. In the Saigon region, Nhu's private clique functioned as a secret police force much like the Japanese Kempeitai of World War II. Although Nhu and Can headed a government party called the National Revolutionary Movement, their real instrument of political control was a largely secret group called the Can Lao. The Ngos used this clandestine network to dispense government favors, such as import-export licenses. An American official warned Diem that such practices ran counter to good government policy because "you simply cannot have authorized corruption without having unauthorized corruption."[25]

Through its strategically placed members in the bureaucracy and military, the Can Lao was the RVN's de facto government organization just as the Communist Party was for the DRV. In another parallel to the communists, the regime also promoted an official orthodoxy known as personalism (*Nhan Vi*). This arcane philosophy was the creation of Nhu, the family intellectual, whom Bao Dai described as "intelligent, courageous, and cruel." Personalism blended European and Asian concepts into a justification of absolute state power for the protection of the "human person."[26]

A January 1956 presidential ordinance effectively prohibited all political opposition. By the spring, according to a spokesman for the regime, 15,000 to 20,000 peasants labeled as Vietminh sympathizers had been detained in "reeducation camps." Also in 1956, the government abolished elected village councils and replaced them with appointed administrators. These new local chiefs and civic action officers sent out to the rural areas from Saigon were often Catholics who had moved down from the North and were unknown and unsympathetic to the villagers. One American observer described them as carpetbaggers. When the constituent assembly promulgated the RVN's constitution in October 1956, it came as no surprise that it sanctioned sweeping executive authority.[27]

In October 1954, Eisenhower had offered direct aid to South Vietnam on the condition that Saigon implement political, economic, and social reforms. Two years later, the same administration accepted Diem's authoritarianism with equanimity. In part, a certain ambiguity about Diem explained this U.S. attitude. His staunch American defenders, such as Professor Wesley Fishel, contended that he was not as draconian as he appeared, and Fishel eventually published an article urging greater understanding of Diem's "democratic one-man rule." The standard American apology for Diem's conduct was that Western democratic notions were not directly applicable to Vietnamese society, that Diem faced an overriding short-term threat to his survival, and that reform had to remain for the moment a long-term objective. It was enough for Dulles, Young, Reinhardt, and other American policy makers that Diem was vigorously anticommunist. Diem was trying to establish his leadership, Reinhardt recalled later, and not "running a Jeffersonian democracy." "I must say that Mr. Dulles made my life a lot easier by taking a pretty philosophic view of the question," the ambassador explained, "saying that a truly representative government was certainly our objective in the long run, but one shouldn't be unrealistic in thinking it was something to be achieved in a matter of weeks or days."[28] In the meantime, though, the RVN was less a state and more a "foreign-backed family."[29]

Since U.S. and RVN officials placed a higher priority on stability than reform, the overwhelming bulk of American assistance to South Vietnam was military. Indeed, General O'Daniel and Admiral Felix B. Stump, the commander in chief of U.S. Pacific forces, maintained in August 1955 that "a position of military strength is basic to the attitude necessary for popular support of the Diem government."[30] Their argument completely reversed the Defense Department's 1954 contention that evidence of political progress should be a prerequisite for increased military aid to Diem's government. The Pentagon now fell fully in step with the State Department on this issue, which Dulles had termed a "hen and egg" question. In August 1956, a Saigon embassy analysis labeled the army as Diem's "chief instrument" in the consolidation of his political power, which made possible "the transition of Viet Nam from a puppet monarchy into an independent constitutional democracy."[31] Such views coupled with the RVN's shortage of indigenous revenues produced a staggering preponderance of defense spending in the U.S. assistance program. From 1956 to 1960, 78 percent of U.S. aid to South Vietnam went into the RVN's military budget, and this figure did not include such security items as direct equipment transfers and police training. Conversely, about 2 percent of U.S. funds went into such programs as health, housing, and community development. In fact, the twenty-mile highway from Saigon to Bien Hoa, which was built because there was no road out of the capital that could carry heavy military traffic, cost more money than the United States provided for all community development, social welfare, health, housing, education, and like projects combined from 1954 to 1961.[32]

During the Collins mission, Washington, Saigon, and Paris had agreed to reduce South Vietnam's existing military force level of about 170,000 men down to 100,000 by July 1955. This move was intended to contain costs and was deemed safe in view of SEATO protection of South Vietnam in case of external attack. By September, however, the national army was still 142,000, and U.S. and RVN officials mutually agreed to a new ceiling of 150,000 by December 31. These figures temporarily excluded about 10,000 Cao Dai and Hoa Hao troops that had rallied to the government. The total force level tabulation also omitted the Civil Guard (CG) and Self-Defense Corps (SDC). The CG was akin to a provincial militia or national guard, and the SDC was composed of men designated in each village for local security. Although numbering in the thousands, the actual strength of these two elements was almost unknowable because they were so poorly organized and lacking in arms. Diem wanted these units enlarged and provided with U.S. military assistance and training. Initially, Americans considered his proposals as too costly and as a possible move toward the Ngos' creation of a private army. Also, consistent with the conventional post–Korean War preoccupation of U.S. military planners on how best to secure the seventeenth parallel, expenditures on counterinsurgency forces seemed less compelling than bolstering the regular army. Eventually the Civil Guard issue assumed great importance in U.S.–RVN military efforts, but at first it was overshadowed by more pressing concerns.[33]

One of the biggest problems facing the American assistance program in Vietnam was the small number of U.S. military personnel in the country. At the time of the Indochina cease-fire in July 1954, O'Daniel's Military Assistance Advisory Group (MAAG) had 342 members, and the armistice agreement specified that no additional foreign military forces could be introduced into either zone. As long as French forces remained in the South, this limitation was not a serious difficulty. Following the Collins-Ely agreement on joint training of the South Vietnamese Army, a combined Training Relations Instruction Mission (TRIM) appeared. After the Dulles-Faure talks in May 1955, however, the French began a rapid, staged reduction of their combat and training personnel in Vietnam. By the spring of 1956, the French Expeditionary Corps

(FEC), the French High Command, and the French contingent in TRIM were gone. A small element of French air force and naval trainers remained for another year before they also withdrew. Although American military professionals were glad to have an unfettered hand to employ their own training techniques and organizational doctrines, they faced a critical manpower shortage. With the concurrence of Stump and Reinhardt, O'Daniel managed to push the actual number of U.S. soldiers up near 400 through various reporting devices on such things as leaves and temporary duty assignments. When Lieutenant General Samuel T. Williams replaced the retiring O'Daniel as MAAG chief in October 1955, the 342 figure still remained official. With the endorsement of the Joint Chiefs of Staff (JCS), Williams' urgent request for lifting of the MAAG ceiling was brought before the National Security Council (NSC) in December.[34]

While it was sympathetic to the problem, the State Department opposed an outright U.S. repudiation of an explicit provision of the Geneva agreements. Despite the presence of Chinese communist military technicians in North Vietnam and America's nonparticipation in the armistice accords, Secretary Dulles and others at the top levels of the department did not want to invite the charge that the United States had undermined the Geneva settlement. Such a development could weaken the U.S. position in any future negotiations with the Geneva conferees and could risk prompting the DRV to make a serious violation of the cease-fire. Consequently, State Department officers argued for the use of civilian contractors or other alternatives to meet the personnel shortage. Admiral Arthur W. Radford, the JCS chairman, insisted that only uniformed U.S. military experts could do the job and that diplomatic squeamishness be hanged.[35]

From this debate, an ingenious proposal emerged for a "Temporary Equipment Recovery Mission" (TERM) of about 350 U.S. military logistics personnel with some additional civilian (Filipino and other non-American) technicians to go to South Vietnam. This group would be separate from MAAG but would augment its strength and relieve it of the logistics portion of its training. Just as important, TERM would help solve a difficult and critical problem, which served as a cogent rationale for its creation. This new problem was the disposition of enormous quantities of U.S. supplies and equipment given previously to the FEC that were being lost, abandoned, or misappropriated as the French left the country. French officers had refused to allow O'Daniel's men to inventory the matériel, and Williams complained that the French openly boasted about the amounts that they were sending to North Africa and France. TERM's mission would be to recover excess property from the French, protect it from rust and other deterioration, and arrange for its transfer either to the South Vietnamese, Laotian, and Cambodian forces or out of Indochina to U.S. aid programs in Turkey, Iran, and elsewhere. The removal and transfer of old equipment was not an armistice violation, but France and India questioned the introduction of the American military team. Dulles accepted the TERM plan and countered the critics with an assertion of America's right to salvage millions of dollars of its own matériel. Other U.S. officials also noted the unit's small size compared to the 190,000 French troops that had left Indochina while the DRV expanded its army from six to eighteen combat divisions. Washington implemented TERM in June 1956, and, within a year, most of the equipment had been recovered. TERM remained in place, however, as a subterfuge for keeping U.S. military technicians in Vietnam until it finally merged with MAAG in 1960. By the end of the Eisenhower administration in 1961, the American military mission in Vietnam still numbered less than 700.[36]

Even more critical than the number of American soldiers was the content and objectives of the training and advice that they provided the South Vietnamese. Numerous observers criticized the U.S. MAAG program as inappropriate for the true dangers that faced the southern regime. They charged that O'Daniel and Williams underestimated the importance of counterinsurgency warfare and organized Saigon's armed forces into conventional formations with artillery and other heavy equipment. There is little question that this structure proved ineffective against the armed insurrection that emerged after 1958, but up through 1957 the military picture in the South was much less clear. The RVN defenses were deficient in almost every respect while the DRV had a conventional army of some 300,000 men that had proven its ability at Dienbienphu. In this situation, it would have been folly not to have provided South Vietnam with a conventional force large enough to at least delay or harass an invading army. Diem and Nhu insisted on such a force as a matter of national integrity and as a hedge against a slow response from the United States and SEATO to a lightning assault. While the Army of the Republic of Vietnam (ARVN) was being regrouped into infantry divisions, however, the local security patrols and outposts of the old Vietnamese National Army were lost. O'Daniel, Williams, and Diem were aware of the external–internal defense dilemma, but in the absence of a well-developed CG and SDC, it seemed unavoidable. On the positive side, O'Daniel believed that, by mid-1956, a credible beginning had been made in terms of conventional forces.[37]

Collateral to the extreme military deficiencies that the ARVN had to overcome was the limitation of current American military doctrines. In the Korean War, the U.S. Army's land warfare tactics, developed primarily for Europe's open fields, encountered serious problems in mountainous terrain against probing and encircling guerrilla operations. Eventually, General Matthew B. Ridgway combined aggressive patrolling with tactical air support and artillery to create what his troops dubbed "meat grinder" tactics. A division and deputy corp commander in Korea, Williams was well-versed in the doctrinal reassessments inspired by the Korean experience. He understood the strengths and dangers of guerrilla fighters, but he considered guerrilla warfare itself essentially diversionary and harassing and believed that properly trained, equipped, and motivated conventional forces would ultimately control the battlefield.[38]

Williams' forty years of service as an infantry officer also placed him in agreement with Ridgway's view that ground troops remained essential to victory even in the nuclear age. This opinion was apparent in an exchange among Williams, Stump, Radford, and Chief of Naval Operations Admiral Arleigh A. Burke on how the United States should respond to a surprise attack across the seventeenth parallel. This discussion came in May and June 1956 as the Eisenhower administration wrestled with the difficult global challenge of coordinating conventional and nuclear strategy. The NSC Planning Board asked the Pentagon to use Vietnam as a test case for assessing U.S. capabilities for responding to local aggression. Burke proposed a scenario in which Saigon would end up in control of all of Vietnam with U.S. forces primarily in a supporting role. Stump envisioned the need for an American invasion of the North to achieve this result. The plan assumed that Williams would be the theater commander, and the MAAG chief estimated that six to eight U.S. divisions with full logistic support would be required to take over all of Vietnam. He noted, too, that such a "Western colonialist" intervention would cause Ho to appear as the national champion and Diem as a puppet. In his judgment, this planning exercise underscored the need for building a larger South Vietnamese ground force than had been authorized. The infantryman's "requirements" bothered Radford, an aviator, and the JCS chairman wondered whether Williams was suitable for the command. All four flag officers assumed that U.S. missiles with nuclear warheads would be available if needed against enemy troop concentrations.[39]

Against the background of this analysis, the NSC took up the question of dealing with local aggression in Vietnam at its meeting of June 7, 1956. Radford began by detailing a plan similar to Burke's scenario. Its purpose was to repulse an attack across the seventeenth parallel and not retake North Vietnam, but Radford advocated seizing that opportunity if it presented itself. He envisioned no large deployment of U.S. ground forces and contended that the ARVN could carry the bulk of the fighting with American advisers and air and naval support. The decisive battle would likely occur in the hills northwest of Tourane (Danang). There, U.S. fighter bombers and Honest John field-artillery rockets capable of delivering tactical nuclear warheads would drive the attackers back. As he had done at the time of the Dienbienphu decisions, the admiral foresaw good prospects of success with no serious disruption of America's global military posture. His confidence suggested that he would have welcomed an attack, but he asserted that there was no indication of any immediate invasion threat.[40]

Radford's presentation generated a broad-ranging discussion but no firm policy decisions. Prompted by State Department concerns about the Pentagon's overreliance on nuclear options, Assistant Secretary of State Robertson proposed that the NSC agree that atomic weapons not be used in Asia except in the gravest situations. Radford completely rejected the idea. He was adamant that defense planners had to be free to use nuclear strikes to prevent a "desperate" situation such as had emerged initially in Korea. There were no fixed military targets in Vietnam for conventional or atomic bombardment, the admiral admitted, but enemy troops, especially if Chinese communist forces joined the conflict, would provide ample targets. Acting Secretary of Defense Reuben B. Robertson, Jr., supported Radford and added that Diem, in recent talks, had indicated no aversion to nuclear weapons in Vietnam and considered them a "show of strength." Hearing this observation, the president raised the possibility of sending to Southeast Asia some Nike missiles with small atomic warheads.[41]

Apart from questions about the wisdom and necessity of nuclear arms, the "show of strength" idea also related to how to convince the North and South Vietnamese that the United States indeed would intervene forcefully in Indochina. Thinking of Dienbienphu, Secretary Dulles expressed relief that SEATO gave the administration the "political capabilities" to provide emergency military assistance. Under the Manila Pact, the president could authorize military intervention, Dulles believed, but he urged consultation with Congress if time permitted. The Defense Department representatives raised the possibility of a publicly announced prior commitment to defend South Vietnam, similar to the Taiwan Resolution of 1955, but Dulles and Eisenhower thought it unnecessary to assume a formal obligation. Alluding to the approaching presidential election, Eisenhower humorously reminded the council that they might not even be in Washington in January. Radford noted that there was a problem of familiarizing American commanders with Vietnam because of the limits on MAAG size. After a facetious comment about replacing orderlies with colonels, the president directed the Pentagon to find a way to rotate senior officers through Saigon to facilitate planning and to demonstrate to the South Vietnamese the American commitment to their defense. CIA Director Allen Dulles cited another problem area: the weakness of the Laotian and Cambodian regimes exposed the RVN's western border to attack. Eisenhower agreed that the broad Laotian frontier was a much more likely invasion route than the seventeenth parallel. Secretary Dulles promised to refill promptly the long-vacant ministerial post in Vientiane, although he joked that it might strain the budget to supply the bottled water necessary to ensure the envoy's health.[42]

The levity in this meeting conveyed a strong degree of self-confidence that the administration could handle whatever might develop in Vietnam, but the substance of U.S. policy was much less certain. The administration's New Look strategy and post-Geneva decisions had created military, diplomatic, clandestine, and aid options in Southeast Asia. A review of the New Look in January 1955 (NSC 5501) had added further flexibility through the pursuit of negotiations and the development of limited warfare capabilities for those "gray areas" on the periphery of Soviet–American rivalry where massive retaliation was a less credible threat. The Geneva summit was a part of this relaxation of New Look bellicosity. In Vietnam, however, the decision to stand behind Diem and oppose the Geneva elections even at the risk of U.S. military involvement ran counter to this supposed flexibility. Strategists inside the government, such as Ridgway and Assistant Secretary of State for Policy Planning Robert R. Bowie, and outside, such as Harvard Professor Henry A. Kissinger and Princeton Professor William W. Kaufmann, argued for graduated deterrence using a range of military alternatives from massive retaliation through tactical nuclear weapons to ground troops. This type of preparation was very costly, however, and Eisenhower himself remained committed to the New Look goal of containing defense spending through primary reliance on nuclear deterrence. A much less expensive and also potentially more promising approach in less-developed areas like Indochina was the nonmilitary strengthening of regimes friendly to the United States. Even more important in the long run than America's nuclear umbrella or MAAG training programs was American economic and technical assistance to the RVN to help it develop an indigenous capacity for survival.[43]

"Nation building" was the catch-phrase for the collection of only loosely coordinated U.S. programs and proposals intended to help South Vietnam progress from a narrow, rigid, and externally sustained state into an open, vital, and self-sufficient society. Collins' seven-point plan had targeted some of the most pressing problem areas, such as public administration, land reform, and economic development. Many of these deficiencies were the legacy of French colonialism. After decades of French management of Vietnamese affairs, for example, there were virtually no native civil servants with high-level executive experience. Furthermore, those Vietnamese who had served in the colonial bureaucracy had been conditioned to be *fonctionnaires,* who followed orders and avoided personal decisions at all cost. The Vietnamese civil police also had been structured to protect French interests or, more recently, to serve the Saigon and Cholon vice lords. The inequities of land holding were self-evident. In Cochinchina, the southern half of South Vietnam, 2 percent of the landowners held 45 percent of the land while 72 percent of the owners held 15 percent of the land. Also, since the South possessed almost no industrial raw materials, the French had not attempted industrialization in southern Vietnam. Its principal exports were rice and rubber (much of the latter produced on plantations owned by French companies like Michelin).[44]

Among the first of these problems to be addressed by the Eisenhower administration was public and police administration. It was not that the needs in this area were more urgent than land and economic reform, but that Professor Wesley Fishel of Michigan State University (MSU) was on the scene. Immediately on becoming prime minister in 1954, Diem had invited his friend Fishel and others from the university to serve as consultants in Saigon. Michigan State President John A. Hannah authorized a leave for Fishel, and, after receiving a telephone call from Secretary of State Dulles, he also agreed to send a survey team to assess how MSU might help the new regime.[45] Having served the Eisenhower administration as an assistant secretary of defense, Hannah was readily receptive to Dulles' request for help. Although Hannah maintained that the effort was essentially academic, education takes time, and the rescue aspect of the project portended a deeper involvement in Vietnamese affairs than simple instruction.

Edward W. Weidner, chairman of the Michigan State political science department, headed the survey team. The other three members were specialists in economics, public relations, and police training. After a two-week whirlwind visit to Saigon, the four professors submitted a recommendation in October 1954 that MSU enter into contracts with the Saigon government and the U.S. Foreign Operations Administration (FOA) to establish an extensive technical assistance program. FOA was the agency that administered nonmilitary aid. It was succeeded in June 1955 by the International Cooperation Administration and in November 1961 by the Agency for International Development. FOA was to fund the Vietnam program, which was to be operated independently by the university. In the survey team's plan, Michigan State would establish a training institute for public administrators and would provide technical advice and training in public administration, public finance, economics, public information, and police administration. The ambitious proposal even included building a television station for a nation without television sets.[46]

Weeks of negotiations followed between MSU and FOA. Not only were there many details, such as salaries, housing, and equipment, to be decided, but also the broad scope of the project presented problems. Leland Barrows, director of the United States Operations Mission (USOM), which was FOA's arm in Saigon, argued that much of the proposed assistance in finance and economics was already provided by his team. Ambassador Collins supported Barrows and insisted also that Michigan

State not "become involved in matters of government policy."[47] The contracts as finally worded scaled down the original proposal to two areas. Operating through a National Institute of Administration to be set up in Saigon, the Michigan State University Group (MSUG) would help train civil servants and establish a consulting program for the presidency and for local governments. The second area was to utilize MSU's expertise in law enforcement education to strengthen South Vietnam's police services. The television station was out, and most economic and finance activities were significantly reduced.[48]

The first Michigan State personnel arrived in Saigon on May 20, 1955, and the group operated there until June 30, 1962. During the first two years, the prevailing crisis atmosphere in South Vietnam gave MSUG little chance to concentrate on education, and most of its work was essentially emergency consulting activities. The Diem regime's authority beyond the Saigon city limits was tenuous and in some places nonexistent. Terrorist bombings continued in the cities, and rural travel was unsafe. By 1957, however, a surface normalcy had been achieved, and MSUG began to devote more effort to training and spent less time directly involved in the workings of government agencies. Eventually, MSU decided to concentrate solely on academic matters and turned over all direct advising to USOM's own staff.[49]

The initial participants in the MSU project were imbued with the cold war belief that "there is no nation in the world in which there is a more crucial clash between the free world and the communist world than in Vietnam."[50] They gave top priority to "the urgent task of propping up the Diem government."[51] It was a period of rapid transition for all the parties involved, and in their haste they made mistakes. Michigan State was changing from a primarily agricultural college to a multifaceted university, but many of its programs, such as international education, were still embryonic. The U.S. government, despite its experience with the Marshall Plan and Point Four programs, was still far short of having a global-aid capacity. Much of the expertise that MSU offered, especially in police training, was not available in 1955 through USOM. Most important, Vietnamese society itself was in upheaval. The professors assumed that America's democratic forms of public and police administration were readily transferable to South Vietnam, but that was an assumption based more on faith in the merits of the American system than on an understanding of the workings of an Asian society trying to liberate itself from a century of Western imperialism.[52]

It was a heady experience for these American Midwesterners. They were not entirely altruistic; they knew that they were serving American interests and also seizing a unique career opportunity. Weidner became the first chief adviser or head of the group and reported that "for once in our lives we feel we are making a contribution directly to the course of human events."[53] The professors quickly learned, however, that there was a vast discrepancy between the ideals that they cherished for Vietnam and the realities of Vietnamese politics and society. When plastic bombs and rioting mobs terrorized the wives and children of American aid officials and MSUG members in July 1955, the cultural and geographic distance between Southeast Asia and the American Midwest could not have seemed greater. Weidner was especially exasperated to learn that Diem himself was behind one of the worst of these incidents —a violent protest demonstration against foreign pressure to begin planning the Geneva mandated elections. "Our cultures are really worlds apart," Weidner mused, "and this I knew before I came, but I didn't realize that the President's [Diem's] frame of reference was so far apart from ours too."[54] By November, Weidner was even more discouraged about the possibility of forming a democratic government around Diem. In a letter to Fishel, who had returned to Michigan, Weidner warned: "They may really have an Army run country with Diem permitting no opposition."[55]

Over the remaining years of the MSU project, this tension continued between the university's desire for a democratic Vietnam and the Diem regime's overriding concern with its own survival and protection against ruthless opponents. MSUG never gave up on the hope for an independent and viable South Vietnam, but the group's support of Diem was a different matter. Some members of the Michigan State contingent were critical publicly of Diem's rule by the late fifties and early sixties. Citing academic freedom, MSU would not censor such criticism, and hence in 1962 Diem refused to renew the MSUG contract. Even Fishel became distressed and disillusioned about the Saigon regime before the end of the MSU project and long before Diem's assassination by disgruntled military officers in November 1963.[56]

As the cost in lives and money of the American involvement in

Vietnam escalated in the mid-1960s, Michigan State suddenly found itself the target of criticism for its decisions and actions a decade earlier. In April 1966, *Ramparts,* a stridently antiwar magazine, published a shrill attack on the MSU project. Part of the article was simply a smear of Fishel and Hannah. It described the MSU president as running a "service station" university that exemplified "the decay of traditional academic principles found in the modern university on the make." It characterized Fishel as "ambitious, looking for an angle" and as "the Biggest Operator of them all" who lived in luxury in Saigon as a virtual "proconsul." Hannah and others at Michigan State rebutted these charges and argued that *Ramparts* overlooked much of the constructive help that the university gave the struggling Vietnamese government in routine bureaucratic administration. More serious and more central to the magazine's broadside, though, were its allegations that MSUG served as a "front" for the CIA, that MSUG armed and trained the secret police, and that throughout all of this activity MSUG failed to criticize and expose the errors and abuses of the Saigon regime.[57]

With these charges, *Ramparts* placed a large portion of the responsibility for the growth of police-state repression in South Vietnam on MSUG and specifically on the group's police advisers. There was no question that the Saigon government had special officers who were brutal and oppressive, but so too did the Vietnamese communists without the benefit of American training. American advisers never had to train foreign police in torture and terror. Furthermore, the American police professionals, in contrast even to American political advisers, were by training and experience sensitive to the need to maintain good relations between the police and the general public, and they constantly admonished the Vietnamese police to be disciplined and restrained.[58]

There were CIA agents in MSUG. How many was secret, and the facts still remain hidden in classified government files. There were probably from five to eight agents among the MSUG staff, which numbered slightly over fifty American advisers at its peak in 1957–58. It was easy for the CIA to slip agents surreptitiously into MSUG because the university had to go outside its own faculty to recruit police advisers. Michigan State had a large and well-qualified police administration faculty, but it was not adequate for staffing programs in both East Lansing and Saigon. This problem was compounded when the U.S. government later pressed MSU to expand the number of police advisers because bandits and guerrillas continued to have free reign in many areas. Michigan State had no countersubversive or intelligence experts, and the Vietnamese police needed these skills to deal with the various insurgent groups. The International Cooperation Administration recommended some qualified "third agency personnel," and MSU hired them. This group was the CIA contingent.[59]

Officially, MSU did not know that these counterinsurgency advisers were covert CIA operatives, and hence the university could and did deny such knowledge later. On the other hand, the agents' true affiliation was known and accepted by some members of MSUG. Fishel, who was chief adviser from 1956 to 1958, knew they were CIA but later insisted that they were involved only in countersubversive training of the civil police and not "cloak-and-dagger work." Ralph Smuckler, Fishel's successor as chief adviser, was also aware of the CIA connection with MSUG, and he too insisted that there was no "spying or counterespionage" but only training consistent with the MSUG mandate to provide police advising. Still, MSUG was uncomfortable with intelligence training, which was outside the university's own expertise. Hence, in 1959, Smuckler arranged the transfer of that activity to USOM.[60]

Like their precise number, what the CIA agents in MSUG actually did is obscured by government secrecy. They were only a small part of what was a sizable covert operation initiated by the Eisenhower administration in Southeast Asia in 1954. Along with providing local police with counterintelligence training, CIA teams also engaged in airlifting supplies to Dienbienphu, paramilitary training of Laotian mountain tribes, infiltrating agents into North Vietnam, and other activities. Retired Major General William J. Donovan, America's World War II intelligence chief, was U.S. ambassador to Thailand in 1953–54. Regarding himself as a "warrior-ambassador" and possibly exceeding his instructions, he promoted counterinsurgency programs within and far beyond the Thai borders. He was also on the board of directors of the International Rescue Committee (IRC). Originally established to assist scientists, journalists, and other intellectuals fleeing from communist regimes in Europe, the IRC maintained a Saigon office. There were few refugee intellectuals in South Vietnam, but the IRC kept busy with programs to teach democracy to the Vietnamese and to provide humanitarian assistance. Its Saigon staff worked closely with a similar effort called Operation Brotherhood, which was advised by Lansdale and staffed by Filipinos.[61]

Although an active-duty Air Force officer, Lansdale worked for the CIA in Vietnam during 1954 and 1955. Besides Lansdale, according to various accounts, Fishel and Wolf Ladejinsky also served the agency. Ladejinsky was a land reform expert who quit USOM to work full time for the RVN government. When Ladejinsky first arrived in Vietnam, Young mysteriously cautioned Reinhardt that the new adviser was "far more than an agricultural expert."[62] Fishel absolutely denied that he was a CIA agent and joked about the accusations with Lansdale. A Hanoi radio broadcast in August 1957 characterized South Vietnam as an American colony with Fishel serving as governor, Lansdale as spy chief, and Williams, Reinhardt, and Ladejinsky rounding out the shadow government. "You will see at long last they've got your number!" Fishel wrote Lansdale in a letter that enclosed a copy of the broadcast. "I hope you will appreciate the importance of the position in which they have located me and will show me proper respect in the future," he quipped. Again in 1967, when an antiwar publication claimed that Fishel was CIA station chief in Saigon while MSUG chief adviser, he joked to Lansdale that now it was known what he was actually doing in Vietnam "when you, like all the other gullible ones, considered me an innocent university professor. Cagey weren't I?"[63]

Life for Americans in South Vietnam in the mid-1950s was like living amidst the intrigue of an Eric Ambler or Ian Fleming thriller. As one U.S. intelligence analyst described it to his family, it was "a wonderful combination of carefree lounging by the pool at lunchtime and haphazard rendezvous at night." There was a "Wonderland-ish" quality to the place with fact and fancy often equally incredible and difficult to distinguish.[64] Even without CIA records, however, available sources give some insights into how MSUG's philosophy and intent compared with the Eisenhower administration's objectives and programs in South Vietnam. Specifically, civic action, the supplying of weapons and equipment to the police, and the organization of the Civil Guard provide useful insights. The picture that emerges is not as scandalous as *Ramparts* charged and, if not quite as innocuous as Michigan State would have liked, more to the university's credit.

Civic action was an effort "to extend the central government to the villages as a government responsive to the needs of the people."[65] MSUG and U.S. officials in Saigon recognized the importance of broadening Diem's authority and political following beyond the capital, and Lansdale was the officer in charge of this effort. He was extremely dedicated to the task of building popular support for Diem, and, in fact, was shocked to learn that some Americans were encouraging the Can Lao's political intimidation of Vietnamese. Unable to stop it, he requested a transfer from Vietnam and received it at the end of 1956. Meanwhile, he solicited advice from Weidner, Fishel, Smuckler, and others in MSUG on civic action. The professors, who may not have been fully aware of Lansdale's other covert activities, liked the basic idea of civic action but raised specific objections to some of the particulars of implementation. A program of sending civic action teams from the government ministries into the villages was started and had some success, but it was plagued with bureaucratic rivalry and other problems that MSUG had predicted. Civic action could be considered an example of an MSUG connection with the CIA, but it was not a cloak-and-dagger operation.[66]

More questionable was Michigan State's role in the equipping of the Vietnamese police. In a strictly legal sense, there was no doubt that the handguns, riot guns, ammunition, tear gas, and other police matériel provided to South Vietnam came from USOM, not MSUG. On the other hand, the preparation of the equipment lists and the training in the use of the items was done by MSUG, since it, not USOM, possessed the necessary expertise. MSUG made the RVN police more efficient and effective, and hence, along with the U.S. government, assumed some accountability for its trainees' performance. As Smuckler later pointed out, however, there was an important but "fine line between being adviser and actor."[67] Since neither MSUG nor USOM had operational control of any municipal, national, or special police units, and since Diem often resisted American advice on internal security, the primary responsibility for the use and conduct of the police rested with the Saigon government. The United States supported Diem, but, as one MSUG member asserted, Diem was "a puppet who pulls the strings."[68]

The Civil Guard was one important internal security issue on which Diem's views clashed sharply with those of the Michigan State experts. A very poorly trained and ill-equipped force, the CG numbered perhaps 50,000—much larger than all other police units combined. Its broadly defined mission was to provide order and security to the rural areas of Vietnam through various types of guard and patrol activities. With the basic concurrence of USOM, MSUG viewed the CG as something like the Michigan State Police or the Texas Rangers, that is, a rural, civilian police agency. On the other hand, Diem, supported by Lansdale and Williams, viewed the CG as something like the national guard in America—a paramilitary force to augment the regular armed forces. This fundamental difference of opinion, involving disagreement among Americans as well as between Americans and Vietnamese, stalled the MSUG advisory effort with the Civil Guard for four years. In a 1959 compromise, USOM assumed the task of advising the Guard. Finally in December 1960, Diem and MAAG prevailed, and the CG began receiving American military arms and advisers in 1961.

The protracted debate over the Civil Guard demonstrated that MSUG was not an obedient and uncritical tool of Diem or of U.S. government agents. It was MSUG's judgment that, by keeping the Civil Guard as a civilian police force of no more than 30,000, the CG could be based in the villages and provide the villagers twenty-four-hour security against communist assassination squads and other forms of terrorism—thereby establishing a good relationship with the people. Diem wanted the CG to be organized into mobile strike forces with combat arms that could supplement the ARVN, if North Vietnam invaded the South or if communist guerrillas staged heavily armed uprisings. USOM and MSUG were concerned, however, that such a large paramilitary force would violate the Geneva armistice limitation on the size of the South Vietnamese army. Also, there was the possibility that the CG (which was composed largely of Catholic refugees from the North) might become a private, sectarian army for the Catholic Diem to use against the predominantly Buddhist ARVN. In later years, the apparent success of the communists' guerrilla tactics in rural areas led some members of MSUG to express retrospective doubts about their insistence that the CG remain a lightly armed civilian force, but in the 1950s they were unwavering in their position.[69]

MSUG made mistakes but also had some successes. It instructed Vietnamese civil servants and police officers both in job skills and in the virtues of a democratic and public spirited bureaucracy. How these trainees used their knowledge in the service of President Diem was difficult to assess.[70] Despite its own well-established bill of rights and legal system, the United States has often experienced controversy over how American police and public officials use their expertise. In the unsettled environment of a developing and strife-torn country, the challenges to fair and enlightened leadership were enormous. The Diem government gravitated steadily away from the promise of a progressive, nationalist alternative to the DRV toward an autocratic, self-serving, and politically isolated regime. MSUG was not responsible for that transition and ultimately found itself unable to coexist with it. Michigan State University decided in 1962 that its institutional interests and values were inconsistent with the policies of the RVN government, and MSU pulled out.

In the struggle for the allegiance of the Vietnamese people, both Diem and his communist adversaries followed the classic advice of the political philosopher Niccolo Machiavelli that "it is much safer to be feared than loved."[71] The DRV appealed for loyalty on the basis of its anticolonial credentials earned fighting the French and its socialist tenets of social and economic equality. The RVN had a weaker but potentially effective claim to be the guardian of Vietnamese tradition against an alien Marxist philosophy. Both sides, however, backed up their emotional and intellectual appeals with force and intimidation. Threats do not win love, and coercion ran counter to the elevated rhetoric of the two antagonists. The question was not just one of theories and ideologies but effectiveness. Who would be most persuasive or ruthless or both? Initially, Americans had doubted Diem's leadership capability, and they found his early successes surprising, encouraging, and confusing. With each week and month that his regime survived, he was fulfilling the Eisenhower administration's strategy of buying time to strengthen the defense of Asia against the communist threat. It was not clear, however, whether he was building a nation that could itself become a cornerstone of that defense or he was presiding over a subterfuge like TERM that provided a cover for what was essentially an American cold war outpost.

VII

The Miracle and the Muddle
of South Vietnam
(January 1955–January 1959)

Fʀᴏᴍ 1956 through the end of the Eisenhower presidency in January 1961, the administration's basic Vietnam policy goals remained the same. As outlined in a series of similarly phrased National Security Council (NSC) documents over that period, the U.S. objectives were to (1) "assist Free Viet Nam to develop a strong, stable and constitutional government," (2) work toward "the eventual peaceful reunification of a free and independent Viet Nam under anti-Communist leadership," (3) support Saigon's insistence that a reunification vote be held only if "genuinely free elections" could occur in both zones, (4) aid the building of "indigenous armed forces" in the South capable of providing internal security and some resistance to external attack, (5) encourage the South Vietnamese to plan their defense in accordance with "U.S. planning concepts" and the provisions of the SEATO Treaty, and (6) undertake political, economic, and psychological efforts to weaken the Vietnamese communists.[1] For the most part, Washington was optimistic about the eventual achievement of these goals, but the program to implement them was slow, tedious, and often contentious.

Also, Vietnam was essentially a second-echelon issue for the Eisenhower administration after 1955. Following the president's recovery from his September 1955 heart attack, he devoted his personal attention to such issues as his reelection, budget balancing, civil rights, disarmament, Sputnik, and crises in Hungary, the Middle East, and the Taiwan Straits. Secretary of State John Foster Dulles remained his strong right arm until the secretary's death from abdominal cancer in May 1959, but, from the fall of 1956, Dulles' declining health limited his energy.[2] These factors left the detailed articulation of Vietnam policy to the nation's foreign policy bureaucracy. Eisenhower and Dulles made their own commitment to the survival of an independent, noncommunist Republic of Vietnam (RVN) and to President Ngo Dinh Diem very clear, however, in their lavish official reception for Diem in Washington in May 1957. During this visit, the administration and much of the American press praised Diem's "miracle" in Vietnam. They marveled at his apparent success in forming and maintaining a state in the South despite international doubts and domestic obstacles.

If there was to be any lasting substance to his miracle, the American and RVN nation-building effort had to go far beyond the military and civil-service programs begun during Diem's first year in office. In a country whose population and economy were 80 percent agrarian, with rice and rubber being its principal products, one cornerstone of nation building was a sound program of land transfers to peasant proprietors and general agricultural reform. Ambassadors Donald R. Heath and J. Lawton Collins had singled out the essential need for quick progress in this area to help establish a popular, democratic base for the Saigon regime. As American agricultural expert Wolf Ladejinsky documented, there were extreme inequities of land holdings in southern Vietnam, and communist propaganda made "land to the tiller" one of its central appeals to the people.[3]

Despite the political and humanitarian logic of land reform, the problem and its solution were far from simple. Under U.S. pressure, Diem promulgated a land ordinance in January 1955 that limited rent to a maximum of 25 percent of a farmer's major crop in fertile areas with smaller maximums elsewhere. It allowed additional rent if the owner provided such extras as implements or fertilizer, but the total payment was to be less than the 50 to 70 percent rents that had prevailed. Progressive in appearance, this law accomplished little. Diem paid scant personal attention to rural problems through 1955 and 1956. Ladejinsky tried to convince him of the "weak link" between the government and the farmers, but Diem protested that he had to deal first with the sects, the danger of invasion, and other issues that he considered more urgent.

Diem demonstrated little awareness of any relationship between the security of his regime and the personal security of the individual Vietnamese peasant.[4]

Besides the lack of leadership from Saigon, agrarian reform in the South faced other obstacles. Although 40 percent of the southern population were tenants, they did not respond enthusiastically to the idea of rent controls. Because of civil war conditions, rents had not been collected in some areas for nine years, and any talk of new payment procedures was unwelcome. The government program also seemed inadequate to many farmers in comparison to communist promises of sweeping land transfers. Many landlords, though, thought that the ordinance was too radical. Such discontent among both owners and tenants, along with the regime's elimination of local administrative structures provided by the sects and by elected village councils, left a rural malaise and leadership vacuum to be exploited by the communists.[5]

In an attempt to revive the RVN's flagging effort in the countryside, Ladejinsky developed a land transfer plan. Having left the United States Operations Mission (USOM) in Saigon to work full time for Diem, the American proposed that tenants purchase the land that they worked in installments equal to the current rent. To induce landlord cooperation, the owner was to receive a cash down payment from money provided by the government. Since the RVN did not have the estimated $30 million needed to subsidize the project, Diem requested that the United States provide it. He broached the subject directly with Ambassador G. Frederick Reinhardt and USOM Director Leland Barrows and submitted a written appeal for the funding to Richard Nixon when the vice president visited Saigon in July 1956. The U.S. government's foreign aid bureaucracy practically choked on this request. Doubting the propriety of American cash payments to Vietnamese landlords, worrying about inflationary effects on the RVN economy, and fearing criticism from Congress, the International Cooperation Administration (ICA), USOM's parent agency in Washington, proceeded to "talk it to death." Kenneth Young, the State Department's ever-vigilant guardian of South Vietnam's interest, argued forcefully that the time had come to back American rhetoric about land reform with adequate funds to determine whether or not Vietnamese farmers in the North and South could be won over to support Saigon and oppose Hanoi.[6]

The State Department and ICA finally reached a compromise agreement to authorize $3.5 million to help pay Saigon's administrative costs of the land transfer plan and to provide funds for other development programs to free some Vietnamese piasters for the down payments. This assistance fell far short of the subsidy needed. Lacking decisive initiative from either the Eisenhower or Diem administrations, land reform languished and died in South Vietnam. One USOM official in Saigon reacted bitterly. He found it difficult to rationalize how the United States could spend $200 million a year to support the RVN military but not spend 1 percent of that amount for a few years for agrarian reform, a program that the United States had sponsored around the world for many years.[7]

Despite official pretensions to the contrary, South Vietnam's agricultural-based economy made little real progress while Eisenhower was president. A December 1956 report by the chairman of Eisenhower's Council on Foreign Economic Policy proclaimed that South Vietnam had made a "miraculous recovery over the past two years" from the formidable economic dislocation caused by the Indochina War. In December 1961, a similar State Department report still trumpeted the "economic miracle in South Viet-Nam."[8] The reality was quite different. South Vietnam's economic foundation was a tripod of rice, rubber, and relief in the form of U.S. aid. Rice production grew in the mid-1950s to around 5.3 million metric tons of unmilled paddy rice, which had been the 1938 yield, but began to decline late in the decade as insurgents sought to weaken the regime and as rural violence increased. At no time during the Diem era did per capita rice production even come close to pre–World War II levels. Rubber production grew modestly, although the cultivation of rubber trees is a slow process compared to the expansion of paddy fields. Rubber generally comprised two-thirds or more of the South's exports for 1955–1962. Although the RVN was potentially a very productive agricultural area, rice, rubber, and other farm products provided only a small fraction of the gross national product necessary to support a military establishment of the size Saigon and Washington deemed necessary or to provide export earnings for economic development. Consequently, the U.S. Treasury annually provided about 85 percent of Diem's military budget (two-thirds of his overall budget) and paid for 75 to 85 percent of South Vietnam's imports.[9]

Besides the South's inadequate gross national product, there were additional pressures for sizable American aid. Both Saigon and Washington were determined to demonstrate that the South's capitalist way of life provided a better standard of living than that of the communist Democratic Republic of Vietnam (DRV). Hence, they designed a large assistance effort to satisfy immediate political and military needs rather than to build an economic infrastructure—a choice that handicapped real growth. Another problem was the inevitable tension between patron and protégé. Dulles visited Saigon in March 1956 and wanted to talk with Diem about the Geneva agreements, elections, and relations with France. When his host inquired about raising U.S. assistance from its current $250 million to 300 or 350 million, Dulles put Diem off with the suggestion that he take up his request with the embassy.[10]

The Ngos were always wanting more U.S. help and faster delivery of aid with less red tape. Conversely, Washington was concerned about its own budget and its commitments elsewhere in the world. It also believed that detailed, if cumbersome, procedures and record keeping were a necessary evil in the management of a large program and in the auditing required for congressional oversight. Even some of Diem's staunchest supporters on Capitol Hill, such as Senator Mike Mansfield (D–Mont.), raised questions at times about the level and uses of American spending in Vietnam. After decades of experience with French colonial officials, the Vietnamese were inherently suspicious of U.S. rules, regulations, and dictates regardless of the rationale. They were sensitive to any hint of insult to their sovereignty. Their resistance to U.S. advice was at times more emotional than rational and revealed resentment of their own dependence.[11]

American officials needed to be sensitive to the Ngos' nationalistic feelings. The brothers could be stubborn and even self-destructive, but they acutely sensed the danger to their political survival posed by a large-scale U.S. presence in their country. They made clear to Washington that they did not desire an infusion of U.S. troops or any appearance that their regime was an American protectorate. When discussing specific nation-building plans, U.S. experts often exhibited a neocolonial impatience with Vietnamese resistance to seemingly sensible proposals. Self-assured Americans failed to perceive that their proud but insecure allies might prefer self-government to good government.[12]

The United States channeled its dollars into the Vietnamese economy primarily through the Commercial Import Program (CIP). Modeled on the Marshall Plan in Europe, the CIP provided U.S. funds for the purchase of products in the United States and elsewhere in the currency of the country of origin. Vietnamese importers with special licenses obtained these goods by depositing piasters into a "counterpart fund" in Saigon. The RVN also collected tariffs on these U.S. subsidized imports. The counterpart fund and customs duties paid almost all the costs of the South's military establishment and civil administration. In theory, the CIP was a well-conceived device to infuse huge sums into the Vietnamese economy without runaway inflation, since U.S. currency would not circulate freely and the level of aid would be tied to commercial transactions. In fact, the CIP was a failure with only a surface façade of success.

U.S.–RVN nation-building efforts in the commercial and industrial, that is, urban, sector fared no better than the agrarian program. From the inception of the CIP in January 1955 through Eisenhower's departure from office in January 1961, the United States supplied well over one billion dollars in counterpart funds plus additional tens of millions in other forms of aid. There was no crippling inflation, and there was a politically and psychologically appealing sense of middle- and upper-class prosperity in South Vietnam's cities. Unlike Europe's economic recovery under the Marshall Plan, the RVN's progress was phony. Instead of purchasing manufacturing equipment and industrial raw materials, millions of counterpart dollars went into the acquisition of luxury items like Japanese motorbikes and American refrigerators. The reasons were complex, including political priorities, the inexperience and sometimes corruption of importers, and pressure to maintain high military budgets tied to counterpart funding. This third factor may have been paramount, since many officials in Saigon and Washington conceived of the CIP as more a means of financing a large military force than of promoting economic development. Regardless of the causes, the result was an artificial urban vitality while the countryside languished and industry remained virtually nonexistent.[13]

Diem, Nhu, and Vice President Nguyen Ngoc Tho (a loyal subordinate put in charge of economic development but with no economic expertise) bore the responsibility for some of the most questionable and debilitating decisions. Whether they were economically ignorant, as some American aid officials believed, or simply distrustful of the hand that fed them, they were stubbornly resistant to change or compromise on several key points. Some questions, such as how to apportion funds between military and civilian expenditures or how to decide the merits of private versus public investment schemes, were open to debate. The rate of exchange between the piaster and dollar, however, was an absolutely crucial issue on which the effects of Saigon's recalcitrance could be documented.

Considered in its entirety, the exchange rate involved many complex and often competing variables. Put simply, the problem was that the official rate, used for CIP transactions, was thirty-five piasters to the dollar, but there were also other rates: an unofficial rate, used for many other transactions, of about sixty-five to one and a black-market or open-market rate of as high as one hundred to one. U.S. officials repeatedly urged Diem to devalue the piaster in order to bring the official rate into closer conformity with the other rates. He countered that such a move would cut American aid in half and increase the cost of living of his people. Although partially correct, Diem's argument revealed that his regime was shirking responsibility for the nation's development. It was taxing CIP imports, not its own people; it was using artificially underpriced goods to imitate not stimulate economic progress; and its manipulation of currency exchange was accumulating unused cash reserves in domestic and foreign bank accounts maintained by the government, the Can Lao, individual government officials, and government-licensed importers. Between 1955 and 1961, South Vietnam's trade deficit ranged from 150 to 200 percent annually and surpassed one billion dollars collectively. Yet, by 1961 the RVN had a cash reserve—an idle rainy-day account—of over $200 million in various foreign currencies. Nhu tapped this hoarded cash in 1963 when the United States suspended the CIP, but meanwhile the Ngos had kept millions of dollars of U.S. aid funds out of productive use in the national economy and had perpetuated the South's complete dependence on American sustenance.[14]

South Vietnam built the form, not the substance, of a nation, but the Eisenhower administration chose to believe that the progress was real and lasting. With the CIP providing funds, with the Military Assistance Advisory Group (MAAG) reorganizing and strengthening the armed forces, with the Michigan State University Group at work on public and police administration, and with Diem's electoral successes, Washington exuded confidence and delight. Mansfield issued a report in October 1955 concluding that his 1954 argument for the support of Diem as the best hope for South Vietnam had proved correct. In December 1955, the Operations Coordinating Board (OCB), the administration's interdepartmental working group that implemented national security policy, prepared an equally self-congratulatory progress report declaring that the United States was "largely responsible" for the survival of free government in Vietnam. These assessments and others also noted Diem's autocratic treatment of his southern opposition, his narrow political base, and the continued economic dependence of his nation, but their overall tone was buoyant and positive. Dulles assured the Senate Foreign Relations Committee that "Diem has done a wonderful job, of course with our help," in defeating his sect rivals, laying the foundation for representative government, and beginning to build "a strong and effective anti-Communist regime." These encouraging analyses of late 1955 and 1956 largely ended the shadow of doubt that had hung over Diem in U.S. circles and helped establish the arrogantly optimistic "can do" attitude that pervaded U.S. policies in Vietnam in subsequent years.[15]

During the final year of Eisenhower's first term, a solid consensus emerged among the administration, congressional leaders, and interested members of the public that South Vietnam was the "finger in the dike," as Senator John F. Kennedy (D-Mass.) phrased it, that kept "the red tide of Communism" from inundating Southeast Asia.[16] The investment of American money and prestige was not only merited, in this view, but was, in fact, paying handsome dividends in strengthening the security of the United States and its allies. Many prominent Americans accepted the notion that Vietnam was an important strategic and ideological battleground in the cold war.

A number of these individuals associated themselves with the American Friends of Vietnam (AFV), a nonpartisan lobby founded late in 1955. Kennedy's "finger in the dike" remark—a reiteration of Eisenhower's domino theory—came in a June 1, 1956 speech to a meeting of the AFV in Washington. To some extent the group was a public outgrowth of the previously less overt Vietnam Lobby of Wesley Fishel, Mansfield, and others who had long worked to aid Diem's regime. Among the founders were Leo Cherne and Joseph Buttinger of the International Rescue Committee and Elliott H. Newcomb and Harold L. Oram of the public relations firm that the RVN employed to promote its interests in the United States. The organization's members represented a broad spectrum of American political opinions ranging from the conservatism of Republican senators William F. Knowland (Calif.) and Karl E. Mundt (S.Dak.) to the liberalism of Democratic senators Kennedy and Hubert H. Humphrey (Minn.). Well-known crusaders against Asian communism, such as publisher Henry R. Luce, endorsed the AFV and so too did Governor Christian A. Herter (R–Mass.), who would succeed Dulles as secretary of state, and future Vietnam War critic Congressman Eugene J. McCarthy (D–Minn.).[17]

In a 1965 exposé, the muckraking *Ramparts* magazine suggested that the AFV may have exerted inordinate influence toward deepening the U.S. commitment in Vietnam. Actually, the organization was preaching to the converted in the administration and Congress. Its first two presidents were William J. Donovan and John W. O'Daniel. Both of these retired generals were so intimately connected with the government and especially its clandestine operations that there was more than a hint that the AFV had the blessing if not covert support of the CIA and other agencies. On behalf of the AFV, Donovan wrote to Eisenhower in February 1956 to urge that the administration oppose international efforts to force Saigon into the elections specified by the Geneva Final Declaration. The president replied that he was in full agreement. In fact, when discussing the answer to Donovan, Dulles indicated to Eisenhower that U.S. policy went even further than Donovan's concern about elections and sought the "gradual termination of the old Geneva Accords."[18]

Eisenhower accepted uncritically a briefing by O'Daniel in late February that declared Saigon's army was now prepared "to do a first-class fighting job" and that dismissed the lack of land reform as a problem that could be dealt with after pacification. There was no acknowledgment in the report that land ownership and domestic peace might have some relationship. "Diem has the ship of state headed in the right direction," O'Daniel assured the president and predicted that the RVN would succeed with continued U.S. backing. The United States should not be impatient, the retired MAAG chief warned. It might take twenty-five years, but he was convinced that "the Communists will eventually stew in their own juices."[19] Eisenhower told Dulles that he found O'Daniel's report "refreshing" and urged that it be presented to Congress. The AFV president appeared before a House subcommittee on Far Eastern affairs chaired by Clement J. Zablocki (D–Wis.) that included Walter H. Judd (R–Minn.), Edna F. Kelly (D–N.Y.), Marguerite S. Church (R–Ill.), Frances P. Bolton (R–Ohio), and John M. Vorys (R–Ohio). The members not only accepted his account without question but took the opportunity to lavish praise on O'Daniel, Diem, and the U.S.

159

record in Vietnam. A State Department officer at the hearing noted: "It is obvious that the Committee was prepared to take General O'Daniel's word without question on most of the points raised."[20]

Expressing little concern about the potential costs or risks of a protracted commitment to the Diem regime, the administration looked confidently to the future. Assistant Secretary of State Walter S. Robertson appeared before the same gathering of the AFV that Kennedy had addressed and reaffirmed the administration's support of Diem and of the Vietnamese people's desire for freedom and independence. Robertson's speech had been carefully reviewed by Young and others and constituted a major policy statement—one that the State Department was still citing two years later.[21] Candid discussions within the executive branch admitted Diem's democratic shortcomings but downplayed them as long as he remained adamantly opposed to any rapprochement with North Vietnam. These analyses also warned that subversive activity would likely increase as the communists sought to undermine Diem's surprising staying power. Lieutenant General Samuel T. Williams, the MAAG chief, insisted, though, that Diem was popular with the people. Chairman of the Joint Chiefs of Staff Admiral Arthur W. Radford returned from an inspection tour in July 1956 to proclaim that the internal security situation was the best in ten years, and O'Daniel buttressed this assessment with a declaration that "Free Viet-Nam was now entirely pacified and secure."[22] Secretary Dulles maintained his own high opinion of Diem, but the secretary was aware of one troubling reality. He noted that, unlike Korea and Taiwan, Vietnam offered no important targets for America's massive retaliatory power, and, consequently, a strong local government and military structure were essential in the South.[23] His observation proved quite prescient when, in the 1960s, the United States attempted to use its enormous firepower to compensate for South Vietnam's internal political and military weakness.

Against the background of practically universal American satisfaction with his performance, Diem arrived in Washington on May 8, 1957 for an elaborately staged state visit. The timing and symbolism of the event were opportune and important for both Diem and Eisenhower. The South Vietnamese president gained recognition, publicity, and an incalculable boost to his domestic political position and his standing among world leaders. With the help of both the U.S. Information Service and the AFV, the films, news stories, and other public relations materials generated by the American trip were fully exploited. For Eisenhower, the Diem visit was part of an intense effort of his own to cultivate and flatter key Asian and African leaders. During the Suez Canal crisis of 1956, he had learned firsthand the value of good relations with the Third World, and he embarked in early 1957 on a blitz of personal diplomacy. One scholar has suggested that the excessive attention that Eisenhower and Dulles paid to such Asian "potentates" as Diem, Chiang Kai-shek, and Syngman Rhee may have been prompted in part by frustration and irritation in dealing with European leaders. Habib Bourguiba of Tunisia, Jawaharlal Nehru of India, and King Saud of Saudi Arabia began a 1957 procession of visiting dignitaries, who were fêted with honors and ceremonies and given extended opportunities to discuss their nations' problems with the president, secretary of state, and other top U.S. officials.[24]

The administration, Congress, AFV, and media gave Diem a reception that was nothing less than triumphal. Eisenhower made his personal plane available for Diem's use in the United States and greeted his visitor at Washington National Airport, a physically tiring practice that he had initiated reluctantly with King Saud's visit. During four days in Washington, Diem met with Eisenhower, Dulles, and other officials of the State and Defense Departments, addressed a joint session of Congress, and appeared before the National Press Club. Moving on to New York, he lunched with John D. Rockefeller III and David Rockefeller at Pocantico Hills, visited his former residence at the Maryknoll Seminary, received an honorary degree at Seton Hall University, was honored with a parade and welcoming ceremony by Mayor Robert F. Wagner of New York City, was hosted by the Council on Foreign Relations, the AFV, and the International Rescue Committee, and attended a private mass by Francis Cardinal Spellman. He then proceeded to Detroit for further honors and some plant visits before going to East Lansing for receipt of an honorary degree from Michigan State University and a grand dinner and reception hosted by MSU president John A. Hannah. He made additional stops in Tennessee, where he toured Tennessee Valley Authority sites and some farms, and Los Angeles, where he visited petroleum facilities and received more honors. He ended his two-week circuit in Hawaii as the guest of Admiral Felix B. Stump, commander-in-chief of U.S. Pacific forces.[25]

The public rhetoric along his way hailed Diem as a "tough miracle man" and the "savior" of South Vietnam and of all of Southeast Asia. Administration leaders complimented his success and referred proudly to his leadership "miracle" in the joint communiqué issued as he left Washington.[26] Behind closed doors, however, they were more restrained. They mostly just listened to his troubles and promised little. In his meeting with Eisenhower on May 9, Diem asked pointedly that the United States keep its aid at the current annual level of $250 million of which about $170 million went into the RVN military budget. The money was needed, he maintained, to expand his country's armed forces to 170,000 men (an increase of 20,000) organized in heavy infantry divisions. South Vietnam faced danger from a Vietminh invasion or commando raids, which were already occurring along the Cambodian border, and Diem insisted that only a large ground force could counter this threat. He claimed that frequently cloudy weather and lack of good targets limited the usefulness of U.S. air power in Vietnam and that promises of SEATO help, such as troops from Thailand or the Philippines, were inadequate. Ngo Dinh Nhu had made these same arguments for a larger Army of the Republic of Vietnam (ARVN) during a visit to Washington a month earlier. Nhu also added that it would not be desirable "to send American troops into Vietnam since this would be, after all, a civil war."[27]

Eisenhower assured Diem that he understood the need for a strong army, but he reminded his guest that the United States had global obligations from NATO to Korea and had to apply its limited resources in the best interests of everyone. This noncommittal rejoinder was not pro forma diplomatic caution but was, for the president, a frustrating truth. Only a few weeks earlier, he had seen Congress, including conservative members of his own party, make deep slashes in his proposed foreign aid budget. Much of this money had been targeted, as was his initiative in personal diplomacy, toward the Third World in recognition of the need for greater U.S. influence there.[28]

In addition to maintaining the total amount of U.S. aid and increasing military force levels, which were Diem's top priorities, his agenda contained numerous other items, mostly security related. He sought equipment for the Civil Guard and Self-Defense Corps. He made a request for stronger broadcasting facilities to enable better propaganda competition with Radio Hanoi. Even when he raised the need for tractors and bulldozers for construction of roads and agricultural settlements in the central highlands, his concern for the military security of the region was as apparent as any economic benefits of the program. Before the Washington meetings began, American officials in Saigon had criticized Diem's agenda. "It would have been more statesmanlike had it contained some positive indication of what [the RVN was] prepared to do," the embassy commented, rather than being a "heavy shopping list and pleas for special treatment." [29]

Many of the topics that State Department officials identified for Eisenhower and Dulles to raise with Diem brought much the same type of noncommittal response from him that he received in answer to his aid requests. When the Americans mentioned the disparity in piaster exchange rates, Diem and his entourage dodged the question. The Vietnamese claimed that devaluation was dangerous for a developing nation's economy and sought to redirect the conversation into a critique of the CIP. Ignoring the inflationary pressures, they appealed for more direct aid for capital improvements over which they had more control rather than counterpart funds tied to consumer goods. The Americans broached another sensitive subject when they expressed concern about the regime's recent restrictions on the activities of South Vietnam's Chinese businessmen. The government had prohibited Vietnamese of Chinese origin from participating in eleven occupations and demanded that they declare Vietnamese citizenship. A complex mixture of ethnic discrimination, favoritism for Ngo family cronies, and concern about political subversion among the Chinese motivated these regulations. Because of complaints from the Republic of China, Robertson and Under Secretary of State Herter urged Eisenhower and Dulles to try to convince Diem that the issue could have serious repercussions. Taipei claimed to protect the interests of overseas Chinese, and this harassment of Vietnamese Chinese was embarrassing Chinese nationalists and was providing fertile recruiting opportunities for Chinese communists. Diem downplayed the problem and Taipei's concern and insisted that "this matter will work itself out." [30]

The Eisenhower-Diem summit and the tour of America were personal triumphs for Diem but produced no fundamental changes in U.S.–RVN relations. Upon his return to Saigon, the president let himself bask for a while in the warmth of the reception that he had received, and he expressed no overt criticism or disappointment that he had not received assurances of greater aid. He was not fooled by praise, however, and, before leaving America, he had expressed doubts about the extent of U.S. military commitment to South Vietnam. He pointed out to Ambassador Elbridge Durbrow, the new U.S. envoy to Saigon who accompanied him on his travels, that the United States had not used atomic weapons in Korea nor intervened at Dienbienphu, which suggested that in some future crisis Washington might refrain from employing its mighty arsenal. His brother Nhu was more openly pessimistic about the psychological letdown of the U.S. trip. In both Saigon and Washington, the objective was to make South Vietnam a "showcase" that would outshine the North, but U.S. and RVN officials knew that it was going to be a difficult effort. Away from the glare and glamour of state dinners and high-level conferences, much work remained to be done in economic, political, and military improvements. Eisenhower and Dulles moved on to tackle other problems, such as civil rights in Little Rock, space and arms competition with the Soviet Union, hostilities in Lebanon, and renewed shelling of Quemoy and Matsu. Diem, Durbrow, and those with whom they worked directly were left with the problems of South Vietnam.[31]

During the remainder of 1957 and into 1958, South Vietnam's two biggest challenges were (1) a shrinking U.S. aid budget with associated disagreements and indecision over how best to utilize it, and (2) a mounting rural unrest that made the aid program more critical than ever. The interrelationship and gravity of these two problems was apparent in two tense conversations between Durbrow and Diem on October 1 and 2, 1957. The ambassador, accompanied by Williams, emphatically informed Diem that recent congressional action on global aid programs would probably mean a 20−percent reduction in U.S. assistance to the RVN in fiscal year 1958. Citing internal security requirements, the president and his advisers insisted that their military budget could not be reduced, that they did not have sufficient tax revenue to make additional contributions to the budget, and that they needed more U.S. support for the rural Self-Defense Corps. Diem stated categorically that, if U.S. aid was reduced, military needs would have to be met before economic needs. He feared that the flattering but unrealistic miracle image of his nation popular in the United States had made Washington complacent about the challenges that he still faced. Durbrow's comment to Washington was that Diem neither had the inclination for reform nor understood the urgent need to establish "what we consider the necessary economic and agricultural foundations for his regime." The RVN president wanted to make South Vietnam into a showcase in order to gain popular support in both North and South Vietnam, the ambassador noted, but instead the regime's only discernible development project was to create a huge army whose payroll it could not meet from its own resources.[32]

On February 22, 1957, before his trek to Washington, Diem had barely escaped an assassin's bullet that seriously wounded an official standing next to him during a ceremony at Banmethuot in the Central Highlands. Some American observers believed that, from the time of this incident, Diem displayed an inordinate concern with internal security at the expense of almost all other programs. He possessed a pietistic fatalism about his personal safety and tended to interpret such close calls as signs of divine providence. His political survival instincts were strong, however, and he had good reason to be concerned about the mountainous region around Banmethuot, Pleiku, and Kontum that the French called Pays Montagnard du Sud (PMS), named for the rugged Montagnard tribes of the area. Its sparse population and strategic location along the Cambodian and Laotian borders made the area a likely invasion and infiltration route. In late summer of 1957, Durbrow listed Diem's plan to create a "human wall" of settlements in the PMS as the president's "currently most preoccupying question." With little regard for economic viability or the sensibilities of the hill people, the Saigon government began erecting resettlement centers for Catholic refugees, discharged ARVN soldiers, and others presumed loyal to the regime. By 1958, economic hardship in the settlements and Montagnard anger began to combine in antigovernment protests. It was a discontent that the DRV, using minority cadres trained in a special school in Hanoi, sought to encourage.[33]

The unrest in the highlands was part of a scattered but growing undercurrent of resistance to the regime. During Diem's miracle or honeymoon period from 1954 to 1956, he had benefited from the absence of unified opposition from the old Vietnamese National Army, the sects, the Dai Viets, and others. The peasants, whom Durbrow described as "phlegmatic," had generally adopted a traditionally impassive, waiting attitude. Although the Vietminh had thousands of cadres in the South after 1954, they also kept a low profile. Needing to consolidate its own regime in the North, Hanoi initially opted for "legal struggle" through the Geneva election apparatus. Even when it was apparent by

1956 that a reunification election was unlikely, the DRV counseled its southern adherents to avoid armed struggle. The communists still faced some serious problems in the North, such as a major peasant uprising in Nghe An province in protest of land reforms. Ho Chi Minh's government also sought to remain in step with Moscow's current "peaceful coexistence" line in order not to risk loss of Soviet aid. Yet, even without orders from Hanoi, violent incidents began to increase in the South, and, in many cases, these had their origin in the RVN's own repressive policies.[34]

A veteran conspirator himself, Diem had from the beginning of his rule sought to eliminate all organized opposition to his authority. His brothers Can and Nhu and their Can Lao henchmen intimidated and often silenced government critics. The RVN waged a "Denunciation of Communism" campaign that identified thousands of suspects, who were dismissed from civil service jobs, subjected to various penalties, jailed, and sometimes executed. Many caught in the dragnet were communist cadres, but many others were former Bao Dai supporters, members of minor parties, or nationalists who did not share Washington's view that Diem was a "benevolent authoritarian."[35] It was a "dark hour" for the communists and other anti-Diem Vietnamese, and some began to strike back violently with assassinations, arson, sabotage, and other acts of terrorism. A "challenge and response" pattern escalated the violence. Through 1957, murders of local officials and government loyalists occurred at the rate of 15 to 35 per month, while monthly arrests of communist suspects averaged over 5000 and executions over 150.[36]

Although RVN and U.S. officials blamed the Lao Dong (Workers' Party), which was the official name of the Vietnamese Communist Party, for the hostilities, the Party's leadership in Hanoi continued to oppose armed resistance throughout 1957 and 1958. The magnitude of American support for Diem had surprised communist strategists, and they were understandably wary of U.S. intentions. Armed insurrection in the South could, in their view, invite American military retaliation against the DRV. Consequently, Party directives to southern cadres stressed strengthening the North and encouraging the southern revolution through propaganda. Rather than a call to arms, the orders were to win the sympathy of the people with promises of reform, including eventual national reunification. Many leaders of the antigovernment violence in the RVN were not Lao Dong members, and those Party activists who joined the resistance kept their partisan identity secret from their allies in order to preserve the integrity of the Party line. The communists were attempting to coordinate carefully the revolution in the North and South and to contain, at least momentarily, the spread of spontaneous rebellion.[37]

While officials in Hanoi weighed their alternatives, American leaders too faced difficult choices. The Eisenhower administration had never had a clearly developed policy for dealing with subversion in Vietnam. There were two basic approaches to the problem: (1) a strict policing of the population to identify, apprehend, and eradicate dissidents, and (2) a meaningful social and economic reform program that would eliminate the causes of disaffection. Diem and some U.S. officials favored the first option while some of Diem's American and Vietnamese critics stressed the second. The two elements were not necessarily incompatible, but they posed a dilemma for Saigon. Heavy-handed attempts by the government to control and indoctrinate the people without improving their living conditions would drive more into opposition. If the regime was not forceful enough, however, the insurgents' strategy of terror and sabotage might succeed in causing a breakdown in any economic, educational, and social reforms that Saigon attempted in order to attract people to the government.

Besides the Ngos' marked preference for repression over reform, disagreement among American officials exacerbated the difficulties of developing a sound policy. Foreign service officers in Vietnam often expressed concern about the "diminishing or even negative returns" of intimidation and control in place of economic development.[38] They also cited the regime's inattention to the poverty of the people, which was epidemic even in some of the agriculturally richer provinces. Durbrow thought that U.S. policy should be more flexible and that, if necessary, the United States should pressure Diem through the aid program to reorient his efforts to more of an economic than military emphasis. Williams dissented and argued that Diem was correct to focus on armed force and internal security as prerequisites to building economic and political stability. The general also alleged that some U.S. civilians in Saigon were referring to Diem as "our son-of-a-bitch" and in other vulgar ways belittling RVN leaders. Not only did the MAAG chief "resent a friend of mine being referred to as a SOB," but he also detected an attitude in such language that was damaging to U.S-RVN relations and mutual interests.[39] Top Eisenhower administration officials were aware of Durbrow's and Williams' judgments, and Robertson stated the compromise view in Washington that the United States would like to shift more aid from military to economic needs "but no lasting economic development is possible without security against aggression."[40]

As Robertson's remark revealed, the debate over counterinsurgency policy related directly to the fashioning of the U.S. aid program for South Vietnam. From the Truman administration's initial commitment of aid to the French in Indochina through the Eisenhower administration's decision to assist the new Diem regime, the overwhelming preponderance of U.S. help had been for military purposes. Ironically, as armed resistance to Diem's government began to mount for the first time since the sect uprising, total U.S. aid for Vietnam dropped as part of a global retrenchment in what were known as mutual security programs. In late October 1957, Durbrow and Barrows made a forceful appeal to their superiors that funds for Saigon be spared from the budget ax or at least not cut as drastically as the proposed 20 percent. Besides the growing terrorism within the RVN, they claimed that spreading neutralism among South Vietnam's neighbors made all of Southeast Asia unstable. Furthermore, if Diem carried out his threat to cut economic programs in order to maintain his armed forces, he would, in their opinion, increase his domestic political isolation. If he fell, Durbrow warned, "we could lose a fairly staunch friend in the Asian mainland" and a "vital piece of real estate" in Southeast Asia.[41] Dulles informed Durbrow that the State Department and ICA did not find these arguments convincing and that the proposed aid level of $175 million was an "equitable allocation." South Vietnam, South Korea, and Taiwan were all staunch friends of the United States, Dulles observed, and must all bear the burden of the cuts.[42]

Confronted with the reality of fewer dollars to go around, relations between the U.S. embassy and the Saigon government became more strained. Durbrow tried to convince Diem to balance the limited resources available between military and economic programs and argued that large defense expenditures delayed economic development and were counterproductive. Diem responded that, even with a high standard of living, the communists would not allow domestic peace unless the government had a strong armed force to suppress them. The president complained bitterly to Durbrow that his government had been a loyal friend and merited more generous treatment. He contended that the RVN was more deserving of extra help than Taiwan, Korea, and Thailand, all of which were receiving jet aircraft that had been denied his air force on the grounds that such modernization violated the Geneva armistice agreement.[43]

Diem shared many of his grievances with Williams, whom he trusted as an American who agreed with his emphasis on military security, and the general privately advised Stump of personal dissension between Diem and Durbrow. Diem also sought to circumvent the embassy by dispatching Ladejinsky to Washington in the fall of 1958 to convince U.S. officials that the RVN was not a dictatorship and deserved greater aid. Upon his return to Saigon, however, Ladejinsky brought back a frank report that the mood among members of Congress, including Mansfield, was for less foreign aid everywhere and that Diem was wasting his time asking for increases. He also told the president that concern about RVN authoritarianism was a genuine problem and needed to be alleviated by a more liberal civil rights attitude in Saigon.[44]

The source of friction among U.S. diplomats and RVN officials was a complex mixture of personality clashes and profound policy differences. Diem and Williams believed strongly that the Civil Guard and Self-Defense Corps should be paramilitary forces, for example, but USOM and the Michigan State University Group held as firmly that the Guard should be a civil police force and that the SDC was of dubious utility. Also, just as Williams often supported Diem, occasionally an RVN official would take Durbrow's side. Most notable was Nguyen Huu Chau, secretary of state for the presidency and minister of the interior, who resigned from the cabinet. He complained that the regime should be more tolerant of U.S. aid decisions, since American support was vital to the life of the country. Can Lao harassment, initiated by Madame Nhu after Chau decided to divorce her sister, explained the boldness of the minister's break with the regime, but he had been at odds with the Ngos for some time.

Chau had often disagreed on economic policy with Vice President Tho, a former security officer who also had the title of secretary of state for national economy. American economic experts charged that Tho knew more about political control than the "basic laws of the market place." Tho was a close associate of Nhu, and Diem's brother was a strong advocate of what he called mixed economy, which meant close government supervision and even ownership of key enterprises. Given the attitude of Nhu and Tho, the RVN exercised extensive control over even minute economic details, which, according to U.S. experts, contributed to the low level of commercial activity and represented a "general harassment of business operations."[45] Barrows believed that Diem had no understanding that a modern economic state must be pluralistic and that Nhu "had all the attributes of an authoritarian and hence communistic regime except he was a Catholic not a Communist."[46]

Despite embassy and USOM disagreements and frustrations with Diem, both Durbrow and Barrows maintained that the United States had no choice but to provide the RVN with the moral and material resources needed for survival. Returning to Washington in January 1959 for a new assignment, Barrows noted the difficulties with Diem during 1958 over aid but urged that assistance be kept as high as possible to prevent a political break with Saigon. The outgoing USOM director acknowledged that extensive aid could delay economic independence but still maintained that, with help, South Vietnam had made excellent progress since 1954. Durbrow could recite readily the RVN's economic and political weaknesses. Diem had "drawbacks," he advised Washington in August 1958, but the president "is solidly on our side and is [the] sort of leader we can work with." The ambassador argued that the United States should seek to strengthen South Vietnam even if it meant having to compromise on issues like state-run industries. Consistent with the administration's desire to buy time in Vietnam, Durbrow expressed hope that, if some tragedy removed Diem, "our program would have had time to build political and economic structures" secure enough to survive the transition and to preserve U.S. influence.[47]

The Eisenhower administration's formal expressions of Vietnam policy in 1958 were very similar to the assessments of Durbrow and Barrows. In May, on the anniversary of Diem's 1957 visit to Washington, Eisenhower sent the South Vietnamese leader a warm personal greeting. The letter noted with pleasure Diem's recent trips to Thailand, Australia, South Korea, India, and the Philippines and lauded the RVN as an example to all free nations in its determination to maintain its sovereignty and independence. Referring to Diem as "the foremost advocate of our interests in that area," Dulles advised sending this letter to encourage Diem at a time of instability in Southeast Asia. Laos, Cambodia, and Indonesia were following a neutralist path in international relations.

In fact, Cambodia's Prince Norodom Sihanouk had accepted economic assistance from the People's Republic of China and, on July 24, 1958, established diplomatic relations with Beijing.[48]

According to the Operations Coordinating Board, the issue in Vietnam was the balance of power in the Far East between the "free world" and Sino-Soviet bloc. In its operations plan for Vietnam dated June 4, 1958, the OCB declared that the U.S. objective was to maintain South Vietnam's affiliation with the free world and to develop a stable, free, and representative government there able to resist communism from within and without. The RVN was "an outpost of the free world face-to-face with a powerful and threatening communist regime occupying part of its territory." The United States had made a substantial investment, the OCB believed, that had helped stop the communist advance throughout Southeast Asia. In other words, the dominoes were still standing. To ensure continued success, the plan called for further assistance in a manner designed to avoid delays and the appearance of unilateral U.S. action. On the critical question of how much and what type of aid, the OCB decreed: "Care should be taken in developing U.S. operations that sufficient resources are provided for an effective military establishment while leaving sufficient margin for sound economic development." In plain English, military needs took priority over economic needs.[49]

The OCB retained these basic policy guidelines when it revised its operations plan in January 1959, but it added some new sections that reflected the increasing turmoil inside South Vietnam. It called for a discreet effort to get Diem and his brothers to liberalize their political control in order to avoid further alienation of key elements of the population. The plan emphasized that U.S. policy was to promote private investment, but it opened the door slightly to the acceptance of some state-owned or controlled businesses. The OCB also singled out the "discernible increase in armed dissident activities" and the accompanying disruption of the RVN's economic and social development as a "most serious problem," which was being addressed in current discussions on the size and role of the ARVN and Civil Guard. In another change from previous documents, this OCB plan used the term "Vietcong" in place of Vietminh. Coincident with this first use of what became Washington's generic label for South Vietnamese communists was a secret decision in Hanoi to approve more armed struggle in the

South. In its "Resolution 15" of January 1959, the Communist Party Central Committee emphasized political over military tactics, but, like the ongoing U.S.–RVN discussion of the Civil Guard, it anticipated an increasingly violent confrontation.[50]

As Eisenhower reached the midpoint of his second term, the policy of the United States was well fixed on a course it would follow in Vietnam for years to come. With the basic, if largely passive, approval of Congress and the press, the administration decreed South Vietnam to be a valuable property to be retained by the West and denied to the communist bloc. "At whatever cost" was not added to that assertion because, up to that time, the objective did not appear to require such extreme considerations. Diem had survived longer and bought more time for the development of a strong counterweight to the DRV than Eisenhower, Dulles, or any architect of American policy had expected. This result had been obtained primarily by a heavy emphasis on military security and government control at the expense of economic development and political reform, and neither Saigon nor Washington was inclined to alter this formula significantly.

Buying time—the Eisenhower administration's negative goal of simply staving off disaster—had been achieved, but to gain that success Washington was also buying trouble. The longer the Diem regime depended on U.S. assistance for its survival, the higher became the U.S. investment in South Vietnam in both dollars and global credibility. The positive side of American policy, the strengthening of the RVN, was sacrificed to the negative side as U.S. officials repeatedly deferred to Diem on key points like the exchange rate, land transfers, and political controls. Hanoi's propagandists labeled South Vietnam's government the My-Diem regime, combining the Vietnamese word for America with the name of the RVN president, to characterize Diem as an American puppet.[51] The Ngos were obstreperous clients, though, who never fully trusted the United States, who clamored continuously for more assistance and less criticism, and who made clear above all else that their first priority was the preservation of their own authority in the name of the national interest. Collins had tried to warn Washington of the self-serving nature of the Diem regime, but Dulles and his advisers had decided that the United States should cast its lot with the Ngos. During the Dienbienphu crisis, the secretary had worried that direct U.S. involvement in Indochina would mean that "the prestige of the United

States would be engaged to a point where we would want to have a success" and that defeat "would have worldwide repercussions."[52] The Eisenhower administration had left the United States little choice but to see through its decision to stick with Diem, and the greatest dangers of that course still lay ahead.

VIII

Trapped by Success
(January 1959–January 1961)

As DWIGHT D. EISENHOWER yielded the presidency to John F. Kennedy on January 20, 1961, U.S. policy in Vietnam was in trouble. Literally as the new president took the oath of office, officials in the Pentagon were reading a disturbing report by Brigadier General Edward G. Lansdale, Ngo Dinh Diem's friend and erstwhile confidant who was deputy assistant for special operations to the secretary of defense. Having just returned from a twelve-day inspection tour of Vietnam, Lansdale declared that Vietnam was in "critical condition" and required "emergency treatment." He professed to be "shocked" by the strength and extent of Vietcong infiltration throughout South Vietnam. There was genuine risk, he warned, that the "free Vietnamese" and the "U.S. team in Vietnam" would be unable to prevent a communist victory, which "would be a major blow to U.S. prestige and influence, not only in Asia but throughout the world." He recommended "a changed U.S. attitude, plenty of hard work and patience, and a new spirit by the Vietnamese." [1]

Lansdale was an experienced but biased observer of South Vietnam and the U.S. effort there. His report was only one man's opinion, but it revealed that American policy in Vietnam had come to a crossroads during the last two years of the Eisenhower administration. Diem faced both the unrelenting pressure of the Vietcong's armed insurgency and the mounting criticism of noncommunist Vietnamese. His regime was in real danger and that threat transformed long-standing disagreements between Diem and U.S. officials into serious tensions. These same stresses brought out debilitating strains within American circles on how to respond. Over its eight years in office, the Eisenhower administration had gone from caution to confidence to confusion in Vietnam.

The confusion arose in part from the swift rise and unanticipated strength of anti-Diem resistance in 1959–60. In the Central Highlands, the thick forests of the Mekong Delta, and the environs of Saigon itself, locally led peasant forces with captured weapons successfully attacked villages and military installations. This tide of insurgency caught not only American and South Vietnamese officials unprepared, but it also surpassed levels desired by communist (Lao Dong) leaders in Hanoi. Although the Party hierarchy increasingly allowed armed struggle through 1959 and 1960, it still desired a balance between military and political tactics. Southern resistance fighters angrily countered that Diem's ruthless U.S.-backed regime, which in May 1959 began beheading Lao Dong members, threatened them with immediate physical and organizational liquidation. In January 1961, the Politburo in Hanoi finally gave its sanction to military struggle in rural, but not urban, areas. In December 1960, however, the southern cadres already had instituted their own alternative to the government in Saigon. They called their movement the National Liberation Front (NLF), and it became the Party's vehicle for revolution in the South. Diem and the Americans persisted in referring to the NLF as the Vietcong. The Front declared its objective was to overthrow the "disguised colonial regime of the U.S. imperialists" and to abolish "the Ngo Dinh Diem dictatorial administration—lackey of the U.S."[2]

Despite a shared determination to extinguish the mounting insurrection, U.S. and Republic of Vietnam (RVN) officials continued their ongoing debate over American aid policies. During the first half of 1959, newspaper articles appeared in Saigon, presumably placed by Ngo Dinh Nhu, complaining of the insufficiency, slowness, and onerous regulations of the U.S. assistance program. Citing increased Vietcong activity in Laos, the Camau peninsula, and north of Saigon, Diem informed Ambassador Elbridge Durbrow that his government would not accept any reduction of military aid to the RVN and might refuse to accept economic aid if military support was cut. Diem argued further that military aid was prompter and had fewer strings attached than economic development funds. Diem and Nhu held firm to their belief that they must first defeat militarily the antigovernment guerrillas before trying to ameliorate the peasants' economic plight or devoting major resources to other economic projects.[3]

Durbrow understood these concerns but disagreed with the Ngos' analysis. The ambassador cautioned Washington to avoid a reduction of the RVN's defense support below the "danger point" and also urged his superiors not to "attach banking conditions" to aid funds and thus tie the hands of the U.S. Operations Mission (USOM) in Saigon.[4] At the same time, however, he supported firm limits on U.S. military assistance in order to force Diem's government to devise a more austere military budget that would free resources for building a much-needed economic infrastructure in the South. In making this argument, Durbrow minimized the Vietcong threat and even suggested that government reports of increased guerrilla activity might be part of Diem's "usual spring offensive to influence volume of US aid to VN."[5] The former deputy chief of the U.S. Military Assistance Advisory Group (MAAG) reported in April 1959 that "the Viet Minh guerrillas [have] ceased to be a major menace to the government."[6]

Durbrow's judgment that economic needs took priority over internal security problems was arguable but based upon the facts as he saw them. Whereas the U.S. embassy listed Vietcong strength figures as unconfirmed, South Vietnam's economic data was known and grim. The embassy's economic statistics for the last quarter of 1958 supported the conclusion that the RVN was no closer to a self-sustaining economy than it had been a year earlier. In no area was the lack of progress more apparent or more critical than in rice production. The harvest was up about 10 percent, but the typical farm family, which represented two-thirds of all Vietnamese, had only $25 a year to spend after rent, taxes, and basic maintenance. The RVN exported some 250,000 tons of milled riced, which combined with 75,000 tons of rubber to comprise 85 percent of the nation's exports. The total value of all exports was about $80 million, according to USOM's Division of Agriculture, which left a trade imbalance of about $200 million to be made up mostly by American aid. In a similar vein, embassy experts warned Washington to be wary of the "unrelieved optimism" in an April 1959 series of *New York Times* articles extolling the accomplishments of the RVN's agrarian reforms.[7]

The issue of military versus economic aid to developing nations was so critical and complex that Eisenhower established a special committee in November 1958 to study the problem and to make an assessment of all military assistance programs. William H. Draper, Jr., an investment banker, former general, and experienced government official, headed the committee. Dillon Anderson, one of Eisenhower's previous national security advisers, chaired the Southeast Asia subcommittee that included J. Lawton Collins as senior military adviser and Lansdale as a staff member. Anderson's subcommittee visited South Vietnam in early February 1959. Still resentful of Collins' earlier criticism, Diem at first refused to meet with the delegation. He relented after Lansdale arranged for Nhu and Madame Nhu to sit unseen behind a silk screen and listen to the discussion. Although the scene conjured up an image of the Nhus as literally the power behind the throne, Anderson later recounted the incident as only a quaint footnote to the visit.[8]

While in Saigon, Anderson predicted that Washington's concern with the U.S. budget deficit would lead to a reduction of aid to the RVN in fiscal year 1960. Collins joined Durbrow in expressing alarm that a significant cut could terminate recently initiated efforts to improve the Civil Guard. With an air of bureaucratic detachment, Anderson rejoined that there will always be some valid issue that will prompt an appeal to delay reduction one more year. Collins raised doubts about the need for Saigon to maintain an armed force of 150,000. He believed that supporting this number of troops drained resources needed for economic development and that lowering the number would not undermine security since RVN forces were already too small to wage a war. This view and his concern for the lack of a "loyal opposition" in South Vietnam recalled positions that he had taken while he served in Saigon in 1954–55. After Collins and Anderson departed, Durbrow wrote Assistant Secretary of State for Far Eastern Affairs Walter Robertson that his "hunch" was that the Draper Committee would recommend some cuts in aid programs. In a personal letter to MAAG chief Lieutenant General Samuel T. Williams, Collins mused that "things have certainly worked out far better than we had any right to expect when I first went there in the fall of 1954." Contrary to Durbrow's hunch, Collins hoped that the Draper report would help Eisenhower get more support for "aid programs which are in for some very hard sledding in Congress this year."[9]

When the Draper Committee published its findings in August 1959, it highlighted U.S. military assistance in Vietnam as an example of effective use of aid that "made it possible for the Vietnamese to establish and maintain a free nation." [10] Overall the report was an endorsement of aid programs, but the committee minutes and background survey on Vietnam noted problems. These documents discussed the RVN's multiple exchange rates, fiscal and economic policies, and other areas needing reform. They also reflected Collins' questions about the size of the Vietnamese armed forces. Even with reforms and reductions, the Anderson subcommittee concluded, "the military burden on the Vietnamese economy is so great, that large amounts of MAP [Military Assistance Program] and defense support aid will be required from the U.S. for the indefinite future." [11]

Collins' concerns about costs and Durbrow's misgivings about the lack of economic development did not sway Assistant Secretary of State Robertson from a firm commitment to military support of Diem. Joining with Joseph A. Mendenhall, the State Department's officer in charge of Vietnamese affairs, Robertson explicitly rejected Collins' idea of reducing the size of the RVN's military forces. He also disputed the Anderson Subcommittee's proposals for requiring a modification of Vietnamese currency exchange rates. On April 22, two days after Christian Herter assumed the post of secretary of state from the dying John Foster Dulles, Robertson took direct aim at "the current fashion in some circles" of arguing that economic aid is more important than military aid. If the United States allowed the RVN to become militarily weak in the face of strong communist forces in the North, he told USOM Director Arthur Z. Gardiner, America would face the choice "of either letting Viet-Nam be taken over by the Communists or counter-attacking with thermonuclear weapons." To avoid this predicament, conventional forces had to be maintained. Economic development was "no defense against actual aggression," Robertson asserted, and "prosperity does not, therefore, mean security." [12] Consistent with the assistant secretary's arguments, Eisenhower gave a public pledge in a speech at Gettysburg College in early April to provide South Vietnam "the military strength necessary to its continued existence in freedom." [13]

Robertson, who would retire from the State Department in June, was a hardline anticommunist. He admired Diem's toughness and maintained that, although the RVN president was a "sort of dictatorial fanatic," he "had glued South Viet Nam together" and prevented a communist takeover. Unlike his younger colleagues, Robertson had personally confronted a situation in China in 1946–47 very similar to that now presented by Vietnam. As chargé d'affaires at the U.S. embassy in Nanjing, he had been directly involved in the debate over how much and what kind of U.S. help to give Chiang Kai-shek. A close associate of China lobbyists such as Congressman Walter Judd (R–Minn.), Robertson may have seen a parallel between Chiang and Diem and drawn a lesson from the 1940s that there must be strong and unequivocal American support for its client. There was, however, a contrary lesson from the China experience. As a nationalist who equated the interests of China with his own political survival, Chiang had pursued his own course regardless of whether the U.S. gave or withheld aid. The lesson was that aid alone was not a panacea nor did it necessarily provide leverage on the client.[14]

With the size and purpose of U.S. aid to Vietnam becoming an increasingly divisive issue both within the administration and between the American and RVN governments, another participant entered the fray: Congress. Besides budget-conscious conservatives, some congressional liberals questioned the level of foreign aid. A special Senate committee issued a report in 1957 warning that too much American assistance to a foreign government could dangerously involve the United States in the recipient's internal politics and impede efforts toward self-sufficiency. Senator Wayne Morse (D–Ore.) became an obstreperous advocate of this view. In another initiative in 1958, Senators Mike Mansfield (D–Mont.), William Fulbright (D–Ark.), John Kennedy (D–Mass.), and others joined Morse in a pointed request to Eisenhower to place more emphasis on economic than military aid in Vietnam and elsewhere. Indeed, Mansfield, the Senate's acknowledged specialist on South Vietnam, even urged serious consideration of reducing and eventually eliminating aid to the RVN on the grounds that Diem's regime had moved beyond the need for emergency and extraordinary assistance.[15]

Against this backdrop of congressional opinion, charges of scandal in America's Vietnam aid program leaped from the headlines of several U.S. newspapers in late July 1959. In six articles published by the Scripps-Howard chain, investigative reporter Albert M. Colegrove alleged that Washington had "forked over bundles of American cash to the fledgling, inexperienced Vietnam Government, and then looked piously at the ceiling while the money melted away."[16] In a style similar to the 1966 *Ramparts* exposé of the Michigan State University Group, these reports painted a lurid picture of waste and corruption in the aid program and of incompetence and luxurious living among American officials in Saigon. Much of Colegrove's evidence was vague and circumstantial, but appearing in the wake of the 1958 best-selling novel *The Ugly American,* which purported to unmask the hypocrisy of U.S. policy in developing areas, the articles prompted public outrage and calls for a congressional investigation.[17]

Two subcommittees, chaired by Clement Zablocki (D–Wis.) in the House and Mansfield in the Senate, held hearings in Washington and followed up with inspection visits to Saigon. Durbrow, Williams, and Gardiner came to Washington to testify, and their staffs dropped most other business to devote many hours to preparing information for the investigators. Much of the inquiry focused on such things as the construction of radio towers, contracts for bridges and fertilizer plants, furniture in the USOM director's house, and general audit and control procedures. The probe lacked sufficient coherence to be conclusive, but no hard, damaging evidence emerged to support the allegations of gross waste or serious misconduct.

Congressional opinions remained largely as they had been before the hearings. A longtime supporter of U.S. aid to South Vietnam, Zablocki labeled Colegrove's articles "irresponsible journalism," and his subcommittee's report basically exonerated the U.S. team in Saigon.[18] Consistent with his previous doubts about U.S. aid policy, Mansfield criticized the management of the assistance effort, but his subcommittee found no specific wrong-doing. In an interview many years later, Durbrow recalled Mansfield as "cold as ice" during the hearings, and the ambassador concluded that the senator "was turned off to Diem by that time."[19] In a more recent interview, however, Mansfield asserted that "my very strong belief was that [Diem] was the only one who could do the job in South Vietnam. That was my stand from the beginning to the end [and] never wavered. There were questions in my mind, very serious questions, about his brother and sister-in-law, but about Diem himself none."[20]

The Colegrove hearings, the only congressional inquiry to center specifically on Vietnam in the 1950s, had little impact on Eisenhower administration policy but further complicated American relations with Diem. The RVN president was furious at the credence given Colegrove's accusations and the diversion of U.S. embassy, USOM, and MAAG personnel from more urgent work. The dispatch of investigators to Saigon especially irked Diem because it reminded him of old French colonial practices that impugned the sovereignty of the Vietnamese and the integrity of their fiscal management. Even after the worst charges had been refuted and he had received assurances of continued confidence from Mansfield and the White House, Diem still believed that the episode placed American aid to his country under a cloud. There was no doubt that damage had been done. Other press stories followed Colegrove's series. In November, the *New York Times* reported the enormous cost overrun, some $48 million beyond initial projections, for the eighteen-mile Saigon–Bien Hoa highway. The paper described it as a "road that runs nowhere" but that "resembles an American turnpike."[21] Although the Vietnamese press in Saigon tried to downplay all these stories as *une tempête dans un verre d'eau* (the French equivalent of "a tempest in a teapot"), communist commentators had a propaganda bonanza. Broadcasting in Vietnamese, Radio Moscow described the U.S. aid program in the RVN as being in the hands of "a bunch of embezzling rowdies," and transmissions from Beijing and Hanoi carried similar commentaries.[22]

In August, after the airing of the Colegrove charges already had imparted an impression of mismanagement and malfeasance, the Diem regime's conduct of elections for the national assembly further tarnished the RVN's image. The voting clearly demonstrated an absence of democracy in the South. As they had done in the 1956 elections, Nhu, Ngo Dinh Can, and their Can Lao henchmen used various forms of intimidation to rig the candidate lists and thus guarantee practically unanimous government control of the assembly. Under the scrutiny of the U.S. embassy and foreign press, however, they allowed the regime's most well-known critic, Dr. Phan Quang Dan, to remain on the ballot for one of the Saigon seats. Like Phan Huy Quat, Dan was a physician with excellent nationalist credentials. Unlike Quat, he had avoided any association with the discredited emperor Bao Dai and had since 1955 assumed a courageous and outspoken role as public gadfly despite repeated government efforts to silence him. In the 1959 balloting, Dan defeated his government opponent by a six-to-one margin but never took his seat because of a conviction on charges of "electoral fraud." The case against Dan was trumped-up and contributed to Durbrow's conclusion that the entire election process showed "no progress towards liberalization [of the] regime."[23] On the same day that the ambassador penned this critical assessment, Assistant Secretary of State for Congressional Relations William B. Macomber, Jr., assured Senator Jacob K. Javits (R–N.Y.) that "full democracy with all its freedom is not functioning in Viet-Nam, but the seeds have been planted and some of the plants are growing."[24]

The issue of liberalization deeply concerned Durbrow as it had his predecessors in the U.S. embassy. He sent Washington detailed information on Can Lao political intimidation, politicization of the RVN military, peculation, and other corrupt activities. Following the election and the much publicized Dan case, the old criticism of a Ngo family dynasty reappeared in American discussions of Vietnam. Durbrow believed that Nhu, isolated in the government palace "making his Machiavellian plans," was the evil eminence in the regime.[25] The ambassador realized that Diem was extremely sensitive to any criticism of his family, but the American envoy thought that the president might be more amenable to change if his brother's influence could be reduced. With Washington's permission, Durbrow made a frank presentation to Diem on April 7, 1960 covering some of the specific allegations against Nhu, his wife, and the Can Lao and pointing out the danger of such conduct to the welfare of the government. The president dismissed the charges as gossip, but Wolf Ladejinsky, the American who was Diem's agricultural adviser, later indicated to Durbrow that the complaints troubled Diem. In a personal letter to Michigan State University Professor Wesley Fishel, Ladejinsky also described the president as "profoundly disturbed" by the disinterest and disaffection of the people toward the government. "He had better court his people," Ladejinsky added, "if he wishes to remain in the saddle."[26]

Three weeks after Durbrow's blunt conversation with Diem, eighteen South Vietnamese "notables" addressed an open letter to the president making many of the same charges and adding others. This Caravelle Manifesto, named for the hotel in which it was drafted, was restrained. It declared its signers' concern for the future of their country without demanding the ouster of the regime. It was also bold because it articulated specific grievances. The letter expressed disappointment with Diem's rule, noted the sham elections and other failures to liberalize the government, protested the system of one-party and one-family rule, cited the practice of promotion by loyalty instead of merit in the military, and deplored the economic hardships of the peasants and the forced labor on agrovilles—specially designed rural settlements intended to be secure from guerrilla attacks. Despite the suspicious similarity between these views and opinions held by some U.S. embassy personnel, there was no evidence that Durbrow or his staff was behind the protest. The embassy was concerned, however, that a disgruntled American businessman in Saigon who had supplied information to Colegrove was trying again to discredit U.S. officials by attempting to link the Caravelle group with the embassy.[27]

No Saigon newspaper dared publish the Caravelle Manifesto. Diem publicly ignored it, although he eventually retaliated against the signers with arrests and harassment on various pretexts. The complete ineffectiveness of the protest laid bare the truth of its charges. Most of the eighteen authors were former cabinet members and high-ranking officials who had served under Bao Dai or Diem; yet, they generated no popular response and exerted no influence on the government. Some observers dismissed them as has-beens, opportunists, or obstructionists, but the words of their manifesto were sincere and courageous.[28] Two of the group were Phan Huy Quat and Tran Van Do, leaders that the United States had been prepared momentarily to support in 1955 as replacements for Diem and his brothers. The battle with the sects and Washington's desire to revert to wholehearted support of Diem ended the Quat and Do alternative, and the two men stood in 1960 as impotent reminders of a missed opportunity. South Vietnam might have benefited from the service of moderate nationalists like the Caravelle eighteen in 1955 or 1960, but Diem would tolerate no rivals or sharing of power. Some of these progressives would appear again briefly as national leaders in the months after Diem's 1963 assassination, but by then the armed conflict raging within the country would not allow time for their gradual reform methods.

Following the appearance of Western news reports of the Caravelle Manifesto, including a front-page story in the *New York Times* on May 1, Diem's longtime American patron and booster, Wesley Fishel, sent his "very dear friend" a letter of encouragement and advice. He cautioned Diem that there was considerable uneasiness in the United States about Vietnam. Fishel itemized concerns about the integrity and competence of Vietnamese officials, the slow pace of democratization, and the deterioration in internal security. He also noted anxiety about administrative reform and reorganization that flowed from insinuations about Can Lao corruption and repression. Although conceding that there might be some isolated examples of these problems in Vietnam, Fishel suggested that Diem's basic need was for a better public relations effort in America. The professor emphasized to Diem his own "profound belief in what you are trying to accomplish in Vietnam." As for the Caravelle group, Fishel recalled that Diem had often referred to "the failure of Vietnamese intellectuals to understand the nature of the struggle with Communism, and especially the security problem."[29]

The issues Fishel raised illustrated the nature of the dilemma and debate gripping U.S. policy toward Vietnam in 1960. On one side was the view that the Diem regime must reform politically, economically, and militarily or it would collapse and take the American effort to contain communism in Southeast Asia down with it. On the other side was the conviction that what Diem needed was not U.S. criticism but rather the confidence that he had full American support in a joint struggle for his own and his nation's survival against ruthless communist adversaries. In one form or another, these two positions had existed since Bao Dai had first appointed Diem prime minister. As communist and anticommunist opposition to Diem's regime mounted and as the Eisenhower administration entered its final months, however, the tension within U.S. circles grew critical. Durbrow put increasing pressure on Diem for change until the personal as well as policy friction between them became intense. As this confrontation worsened, General Williams took on the role of the loyal Diem supporter with a resulting conflict between the U.S. diplomatic and military chiefs in South Vietnam. Their respective agencies in Washington, the State and Defense Departments, tended to support their own man, and hence the policy clash deepened. Noticeably absent from much of this bureaucratic fight, especially in contrast to the time of the Dienbienphu siege and the Geneva Conference, was any significant White House or cabinet-level leadership. With the backing of J. Graham Parsons, Robertson's successor as assistant secretary of state for Far Eastern affairs, Durbrow slugged it out with Williams, seconded usually by Lansdale in the Pentagon.

Williams believed that Durbrow hated Diem and that the ambassador was unfit professionally for the sensitive position that he held. The general judged Durbrow "better suited to be the senior salesman in a good ladies shoe store than to be representing the U.S. in an Asian country." Williams also concluded that Durbrow's "CIA henchman [Saigon station chief Nick Natsios] was more properly suited to be a cigar counter operator in a middle class hotel."[30] Durbrow and Natsios detested Nhu and his wife even more than Diem, according to the MAAG chief, and were constantly frustrated by their inability to uncover solid proof of Ngo family corruption. Assuming that Durbrow bitterly disliked him for his friendship with Diem, Williams vented his anger toward the ambassador privately to Lansdale.[31]

Durbrow admitted that he did not get along well with Williams, but he twice endorsed extension of the general's tour as MAAG chief on the grounds that Williams was a good soldier and was able to work effectively with Diem. With the armed insurgency gaining momentum in the spring of 1960, however, the ambassador and some military analysts became increasingly critical of Williams. They insinuated that the poor performance of the Army of the Republic of Vietnam (ARVN) against the guerrillas was partly the fault of Williams' emphasis on organizing and training a large-unit, road-bound conventional force to defend against a Korean War–type invasion from the North. The general countered that the ARVN's problems were not the result of MAAG training doctrines but rather of too little training of any kind. He complained that the arbitrary force ceiling of 150,000 men, the interminable bureaucratic wrangling over the Civil Guard, Vietnamese resistance to his advisers' suggestions, the pressing need for conventional as well as counterinsurgency training, and other such obstacles were to blame. Both at the time and in the years following his retirement from active duty in August 1960, Williams staunchly maintained that, if his recommendations concerning force levels and training had been adopted in the mid-1950s as many were in the early 1960s, the entire course of the Vietnam War could have been altered in favor of the RVN.[32]

Lansdale assured Williams that he was aware of the MAAG chief's frustration with "backseat drivers." Lansdale was confident that Williams "understood what was going on" and that, moreover, he "had a tremendous feeling for the Vietnamese."[33] From his desk in the Pentagon, Lansdale waged his own duel with Durbrow and the State Department. Recalling his previous experience in the Philippines and Vietnam, Lansdale favored an American-sponsored program of political advisers at the local level to improve the Saigon government's relations with the people and its ability to counter the guerrillas. Durbrow had his doubts about Diem's openness to reform and pointedly advised the State Department's Office of Southeast Asian Affairs "that we have left the 'Lansdale days' behind."[34]

As the ambassador was offering his views on Lansdale in April 1960, Diem made a move to circumvent the U.S. embassy in Saigon. He had the RVN embassy in Washington ask the State Department for its approval of a Lansdale visit to Saigon to discuss the communist threat. This invitation touched off some fierce bureaucratic in-fighting. Durbrow made it clear that he did not want Lansdale in South Vietnam. Lansdale then wrote privately to Williams and suggested that the MAAG chief might propose to Diem that he send the invitation "over the heads of the bureaucrats directly to his friend Eisenhower."[35]

The Defense Department favored a Lansdale visit to Saigon as a show of sympathy and support for Diem, if for no other reason. The State Department believed that Lansdale's presence would be a complicating factor at a time when U.S. officials needed to force Diem to face some unpleasant realities. A conference on May 13 between representatives of the two departments proved unable to reach agreement on a Lansdale mission, and the conferees dropped the question into Durbrow's lap as head of the Saigon Country Team. With little leadership from Washington, the ambassador equivocated. He acknowledged that Diem might listen to Lansdale. Durbrow cabled the secretary of state that he would concur, if Lansdale would follow the State Department's instructions and cooperate fully with the U.S. embassy. A month later, Washington still had made no decision, and Lansdale wrote Williams that the State Department wants the military "wa-a-a-ay back in anything to do with foreign aid or foreign countries." In a bit of election-year analysis, he added that "State is running roughshod over the military right now" and would probably continue to do so if the next president was someone other than Vice President Richard Nixon or Senate Majority Leader Lyndon B. Johnson (D–Tex.).[36]

On May 3, 1960, with the Lansdale visit still under discussion, Durbrow asked Washington for permission to put "teeth" into his efforts to persuade Diem to "come to his senses."[37] Specifically, the ambassador recommended the withholding of some helicopters and other promised matériel until the RVN showed evidence of more effective and less repressive administration. This provocative proposal prompted a Pentagon memorandum that criticized sharply what it termed a petty "spanking" of Diem at a time when he was locked in combat with an armed enemy.[38]

The State Department and CIA deemed the issue of how to handle Diem urgent enough that they brought it to the National Security Council (NSC) meeting on May 9—a meeting devoted almost entirely to the Soviet Union's announcement on May 7 of the capture of an American U–2 spy plane pilot and the related damage to plans for a U.S.–USSR summit meeting scheduled for the following week. Spokesmen for State and CIA noted Diem's isolation from his people and cautioned of a possible parallel with Syngman Rhee, the authoritarian president of the Republic of Korea who had just been forced to resign on April 27 under heavy public pressure. Eisenhower acknowledged that Diem seemed arbitrary and blind to his problems. "We rescued this country [the RVN] from a fate worse than death," the president reflected, "and it would be bad to lose it at this stage." Without referring specifically to Collins, Eisenhower recalled that the NSC had once received a recommendation that the U.S. oppose Diem. Now he urged State, Defense, and CIA to study ways to respond to Diem's weakening position.[39]

The State Department instructed Durbrow to give Diem a stern warning about U.S. opposition to "irresponsible acts," but Washington prohibited the embassy from threatening to withhold specific equipment. The same telegram also made explicit the dilemma in which the United States found itself: how to "bargain" with Diem without dangerously weakening South Vietnam. Durbrow replied that Diem's attitude remained unrealistic and stubborn and that the Vietnamese leader dismissed the events in Korea as the results of Rhee's senility and hence irrelevant to the situation in the RVN. "We are continuing to do what we can to influence Diem," the ambassador reported, "but our leverage on certain sensitive matters is quite evic_ntly limited, particularly at this time when there is some question in Diem's mind about continued U.S. support of him."[40] As Collins had predicted over five years earlier and as other American officials had often encountered with such forceful leaders as Rhee and Chiang Kai-shek, the embassy could do little to reform the RVN whether the United States gave or withheld support.

While American officials struggled for an approach to Diem, the internal security problems in South Vietnam worsened in the summer of 1960. In units typically numbering two to three hundred soldiers, the Vietcong inflicted mounting casualties on government troops and captured weapons, radios, and other supplies. Guerrilla assaults constantly disrupted rubber production and rice shipments, and terrorist violence reached the streets of Saigon. The South Vietnamese military was, according to Williams, "in a tizzy" and exhibited an ominous inability to respond effectively to the attacks.[41] In late August, Durbrow judged that the "survival of Free Viet-Nam [is] at stake," and he resorted to the shopworn recommendation that the United States "reinforce assistance to Diem, who is [the] only dedicated anti-Communist nationalist leader in sight."[42]

In Durbrow's estimation, however, the situation was so grave that new and drastic action was required. He proposed that he confront Diem with frank and specific proposals on personnel changes and transfers within the government. Diem would not like it, the ambassador admitted, and, indeed, it was possible that the president's authoritarian handling of internal problems was correct. Regardless, the embassy felt compelled to follow its own best judgment. The most explosive of Durbrow's ideas were the transfer of Nhu, his wife, and his chief of secret intelligence out of Vietnam, the American naming of specific individuals for key cabinet posts, and the disbanding of the Can Lao.[43]

As it had in the spring, Durbrow's desire to pressure Diem triggered debate in the corridors of Washington. Lansdale thought it proper for the United States to offer Diem friendly advice but doubted that Durbrow, whom Lansdale characterized as "insulting, misinformed and unfriendly" toward Diem, was the best messenger.[44] Lansdale's implication was that he would be a better choice to counsel Diem. At the NSC meeting on September 21, CIA Director Allen W. Dulles and Under Secretary of State C. Douglas Dillon suggested an effort along the lines proposed by Durbrow, and on October 7 Dillon authorized the ambassador to proceed. Washington's instructions advised against designating specific cabinet appointments and deemed dissolution of the Can Lao impossible, but, on the touchy question of Nhu, Durbrow had a green light. Meeting with Diem on October 14, the ambassador sweetened the pill with news that MAAG would begin training the Civil Guard, a move long desired by Diem. He then delivered the bitter prescription for internal reform of the RVN, including the transfer of Nhu to a foreign assignment. The president listened with surprising calm and gave little reaction except to charge that the communists were the source of rumors about his brother and sister-in-law.[45]

The Eisenhower administration followed Durbrow's demarche with an awkward combination of pressure and promises. Meeting with Diem in Saigon on October 18, Assistant Secretary Parsons firmly backed the ambassador's proposals. At the same time, however, Eisenhower sent Diem a letter praising the past progress of the RVN and pledging continued U.S. support. By early November, Durbrow thought that he could detect some positive response from the Saigon government. The RVN suspended the controversial agroville program, for example, but the ambassador noted that such moves might only be "window dressing designed to try to fool us Americans as well as discontented Vietnamese circles."[46]

As the November election to choose Eisenhower's successor drew near, the administration's policy of buying time with Diem was running out of time. Parsons praised Durbrow for playing a "thankless but courageous role" in trying to force Diem to listen to unwanted advice. Reflecting over the record since 1954, Parsons asserted that Diem's sense of self-reliance had served him well in the beginning but now was his undoing. Diem might prove "inherently incapable of adapting and of doing those things which are needful in political, psychological, and social fields," the assistant secretary concluded, and, if so, "we must revise downward our estimate of [the] republic's future under Diem."[47]

Diem's personality had not changed in six years. Parsons' characterization of the RVN president echoed that of Collins, Donald Heath, Frederick Reinhardt, and others. Also, the administration remained unable to come to agreement on how to approach Diem. Parsons supported Durbrow's hard line with Diem, but the assistant secretary and the ambassador disagreed on how far to push it. Parsons believed that the time had come to grant Diem's long-standing demand for an increase of 20,000 in his armed forces. Durbrow continued to insist that yielding the point would only encourage Diem's hope for a military panacea for his nation's social and economic deficiencies.[48]

Parsons' receptiveness to an increase in ARVN strength was due in part to the outbreak of a civil war in Laos that diverted Washington's attention from Saigon to Vientiane. Indeed, Parsons' October visit to Saigon to underscore Durbrow's demarche was only a momentary detour from a special mission by the assistant secretary of state and Assistant Secretary of Defense John N. Irwin, Jr., to the Laotian capital. Poor and sparsely populated, the neutral kingdom of Laos had been independent since the 1954 Geneva Conference and occupied a strategically significant location in Southeast Asia. The long, densely forested frontier between Laos and Vietnam made Laos a corridor through which the Democratic Republic of Vietnam (DRV) could reinforce and supply the guerrillas in the RVN. Aware of this danger and the threat of a communist-controlled Laos becoming a staging area for assaults on Thailand and Cambodia, the Eisenhower administration deemed Laos a domino that must not be allowed to fall.[49]

The United States had been deeply involved in Laotian politics since 1954. Washington's efforts were intended to strengthen the Royal Laotian Government and Army and to defeat the Pathet Lao, a communist-led guerrilla force that the Vietminh helped establish during the First Indochina War and that remained closely linked to the DRV. Using diplomacy, aid leverage, military assistance, and clandestine operations, the Eisenhower administration went through many twists and turns as it attempted to weave its way through interagency politics in Washington and internecine conflict in Vientiane. As U.S. ambassador in Laos from 1956 to 1958, Parsons had been a principal architect of American efforts to prevent Prince Souvanna Phouma from forging a national unity coalition with the Pathet Lao. Using a suspension of commercial import payments, Washington helped force Souvanna out as prime minister in July 1958.

In August 1960, a military coup seized power from the U.S.-backed government, and Souvanna returned to office. The Parsons–Irwin mission of October failed to dissuade Souvanna from negotiating with the Pathet Lao. Soon afterward, troops led by a member of the government ousted in August attacked Souvanna's forces, and Souvanna began receiving military matériel from the Soviet Union and DRV. The escalation of fighting and the involvement of the Soviets confronted the Eisenhower administration with a crisis comparable to Dienbienphu. The possibility emerged of direct U.S. military intervention to prevent a communist success in Laos. Also reminiscent of Dienbienphu, America's European allies, specifically Britain and France, were disinclined to become militarily involved in Laos. These Laotian developments—coupled with increasing difficulties with the new Fidel Castro government in Cuba and preoccupation with a dangerous depletion of U.S. gold reserves in international money markets—made it very difficult for Washington to concentrate on Diem and his problems during Eisenhower's last weeks in office.[50]

Diem's problems remained critical, however, and intensified dramatically on November 11, 1960 when an attempted military coup came very near to toppling his regime. Before dawn, elite paratroopers under the command of two colonels attacked the presidential palace and quickly isolated Diem, Nhu, and Madame Nhu in the wine cellar. The paratroopers probably could have captured or killed the president and his brother, but the rebels, motivated by personal and patriotic frustrations, sought only to compel Diem to agree to reforms and not to force him out. The Ngos proceeded to negotiate with the colonels and even pledged to reorganize the government, to allow more press freedom, and to accede to other demands. All the while, the president's personal radio net crackled with distress calls to ARVN units outside Saigon. The junior officers leading the revolt failed to coordinate effectively their move with other military commanders or with dissident politicians. Although some military units and some government critics, such as Phan Quang Dan, took a neutral or sympathetic stand toward the revolt, other armed forces, including armor from My Tho and infantry from Bien Hoa under the command of Colonel Nguyen Van Thieu, entered Saigon and dispersed the paratroopers. The rebel leaders escaped to Cambodia on the afternoon of November 12. The government arrested Dan and other political and military suspects, and Diem reneged on his promises of reform.[51]

The revolt of the paratroopers was brief and unsuccessful, but it further exacerbated the tensions and troubles within American policymaking circles. The U.S. embassy initially adopted a neutral stance toward the surprise uprising. If Diem fell or was reduced to a figurehead, this hands-off approach would leave the way open to work with the new leadership. At the same time, Durbrow urged that there be an "active role" for Diem and that the two sides compromise for the sake of anticommunist unity. Lansdale quickly alerted others in Washington that the ambassador was clearly failing to support Diem and, in fact, implied that Durbrow welcomed the challenge to the Ngos. Durbrow later insisted that he "was 100% in support of Diem."[52] Conversely, the recollection of William Colby, the new CIA station chief in Saigon, was that the U.S. embassy was "not 100% in support of Diem in this fight."[53]

General Williams described Durbrow as delighted with the incident. Although retired and no longer in Saigon, the former MAAG chief remained in touch with events in South Vietnam through various MAAG officers. A few weeks after the coup attempt, he suggested to Lansdale that there had been "much scullduggery . . . with the striped pants boys."[54] Williams' innuendo reflected the belief of the Ngos and their friends that some Americans may have actually helped initiate the paratrooper revolt. That charge remained unsubstantiated, but U.S. personnel from the embassy, CIA, and MAAG were in communication with the Ngos, the rebels, and the fence-sitters throughout the incident in an effort to minimize a bloody internal war that would weaken the RVN and open a window of opportunity for the Vietcong.[55]

There were numerous lessons and portents in this incident. Since the failure of General Nguyen Van Hinh's effort to unseat Diem in 1954 and the defeat of the sects in 1955, the South Vietnamese military had not been directly involved in politics. It was clear that the military was now a political force. The Ngos could be expected to further politicize the army and to retain their authoritarian controls. Any future military rebels could be expected to be better organized and more ruthless.[56] Durbrow's neutrality in contrast to the support Diem received from Heath and Collins against Hinh also sent a message to the Ngos. Diem did not have unqualified American support. The regime needed to shore up that support, if possible, but Diem could not rely solely on Americans for his political survival.

Wholehearted support of Diem had been the cornerstone of the Eisenhower administration's policy toward the RVN since Diem's battle with the sects in 1955. The wisdom of that position had been questioned many times, and, during the final two months of Eisenhower's presidency, Durbrow and Lansdale continued the argument. Both men agreed that Diem's regime faced danger both from within South Vietnam and from the DRV, and both wanted to see the RVN strengthened militarily and politically. Durbrow continued to believe that concerted pressure on Diem would be needed, and he even advised the State Department not to prepare a pro forma congratulatory letter from Eisenhower to Diem on the outcome of the paratrooper incident. Durbrow thought that it was unwise to praise Diem at a time when the United States should be confronting him with a "stern attitude." Conversely, Lansdale argued that the coup attempt made it more imperative than ever that Diem be reassured of U.S. confidence in him. At the same time, the general conceded, Diem must be made to understand the need to "change some of his ways."[57] Durbrow was singularly ill-suited for this delicate task, in Lansdale's view, and should be recalled from Saigon, at least temporarily. In addition, the general warned his Pentagon superiors that the State Department's Southeast Asia division was responsible for Durbrow's "demoralizing meddling in Vietnam's affairs" and that the Defense Department needed to monitor carefully State's instructions to Saigon.[58]

In late November, Deputy Secretary of Defense James H. Douglas formally asked the State Department to allow Lansdale to visit Saigon to make an evaluation and policy recommendation. Lansdale wanted also to make several other official stops throughout Southeast Asia. An extended Asian tour would give him more direct influence on policy, and it would also get him out of Washington. As the Pentagon's spokesman on special operations, he had clashed with Allen Dulles over the military wisdom of a CIA proposal for U.S.-backed Cuban refugees to make an amphibious landing in Cuba to destabilize the Castro regime. If he was out of the country for several weeks, Lansdale believed, he could avoid any later blame for participating in the planning of what he deemed to be a doomed exploit. The ambassadors in the Philippines, Thailand, Cambodia, and Laos made clear that the notorious special operations officer was not welcome in their areas. They feared that local leaders would interpret Lansdale's presence as evidence of a U.S. plot to intervene further in their affairs. Durbrow, Parsons, and others in the State Department had no such basis on which to refuse permission for a visit to Vietnam, since Diem had previously invited Lansdale. The State Department agreed to a twelve-day trip only to South Vietnam and insisted that the general carefully adhere to instructions to cooperate with Durbrow.

Lansdale resented the imposed restrictions. As he put it, his orders were to "keep my nose clean" and "not to disturb the quiet existence of Ambassadors anywhere." Despite his short leash, Lansdale still thought it important that he go because, as he told Williams, "Diem and the Vietnamese need a friend present right now, and this is the important thing for the U.S. or, as the saying should say: if you can't join 'em, lick 'em!"[59] Writing from San Francisco during a December 29 stopover en route to Saigon, Lansdale further confided to Williams that "our mutual Foreign Service friends are howling that I shouldn't visit, and if I do, it should only be for a week. To hell with them."[60] This attitude recalled some of Lansdale's and Lieutenant General John O'Daniel's differences with Heath in 1954.

During December, while Lansdale battled the diplomats and the escalating civil war in Laos generated emergency White House discussions of possible intervention there, Durbrow presented his final recommendations to the departing Eisenhower administration. He suggested that a promise to approve the 20,000–man increase in the armed forces could be used as a carrot to entice Diem into political reform, but Secretary Herter, in a rare moment of direct involvement in Vietnamese affairs, rejected the idea. The fighting in Laos and the insurgency in Vietnam necessitated fixing troop levels on their merits and not as a bargaining ploy. Durbrow accepted that analysis, but he remained adamant that Diem's biggest failure was his lack of broad political support and his preference for greater military power over pursuit of internal reform. It was the ambassador's considered opinion that Diem's ineffective response to the twin problems of Vietcong violence and popular dissatisfaction might force the United States soon "to undertake [the] difficult task of identifying and supporting alternate leadership."[61] Whether Durbrow's conclusion was a prediction or a wish or both, the State Department deemed such talk "extremely sensitive." Parsons agreed that liberalization was the key to Diem's future but advised Durbrow to keep such discussion top secret and for limited distribution only.[62]

On January 17, 1961, Lansdale submitted his report to the secretary of defense warning of the imminent danger of a communist victory in South Vietnam. In a private letter to Williams on the same day, Lansdale summarized his findings: "While our Embassy has been busily doing business with the noisy oppositionists in Saigon, the Viet Cong have started to steal the country and expect to be done in 1961."[63] On January 19, Eisenhower and Herter briefed President-elect Kennedy on foreign policy. Their discussion of Southeast Asia concentrated on Laos, not Vietnam, and Eisenhower reiterated forcefully the domino theory that, if one state in the region fell to the communists, "then we would have to write off the whole area." He and Herter advised the new president that the SEATO treaty obligated the United States to aid Laos, and they urged Kennedy to seek a political or, if necessary, military settlement there. The United States should act in concert with the SEATO nations if possible, they recommended, but "if we were unable to persuade our allies, then we must go it alone."[64]

On January 28, a week after Kennedy's inauguration, Lansdale and Parsons joined the president, Vice President Lyndon Johnson, Secretary of State Dean Rusk, Secretary of Defense Robert McNamara, and others to discuss both Lansdale's report and the counterinsurgency plan that had been under development for the past six months. On January 30, Kennedy approved the plan, including the increase of 20,000 in the RVN armed forces and the expansion of the Civil Guard at a combined cost to the United States of approximately $40 million. On May 10, 1961, Frederick Nolting, a career diplomat with no Southeast Asia experience, officially replaced Durbrow as U.S. ambassador in Saigon. Some consideration was given to naming Lansdale to the post, but State Department officers such as Parsons objected that Diem's friend, although not without his talents, was not enough of a "team player" for such a sensitive post.[65]

The Eisenhower team had held together on Vietnam policy for eight years. As Eisenhower's administration closed, however, Washington's Saigon protégés were politically besieged and facing armed insurrection. U.S. officials were engaged in heated debate over whether to increase or reduce the American identification with Diem. Along with plans for the invasion of Cuba at the Bay of Pigs, the Vietnam question—complicated by growing strife in Laos—greeted the new Kennedy administration. Kennedy and his team would make their own decisions, but Eisenhower had left them some very stark options in Vietnam. One choice was to abandon Diem and risk the collapse of the South as an untenable cold war outpost. The other option was to stick with Diem, reinforce the RVN, and prepare for a larger and costlier American effort. With another six months in office, the Eisenhower administration would have likely decided, as did Kennedy and his advisers, to select the second course. In the discussions of January 1961, neither the outgoing nor incoming administrations questioned Eisenhower's earlier decision that the seventeenth parallel dividing North and South Vietnam was an important symbolic and strategic place to dig in America's heels against expansive communism.

After the French defeat at Dienbienphu and the partition of Vietnam at the Geneva Conference of 1954, the Eisenhower administration's goal in Indochina was to buy time to establish a workable defense of South Vietnam against aggression from the North and subversion from within. Through 1957 there were outward signs of success, and, indeed, the administration and the American press applauded the "miracle" of South Vietnam's survival and progress. The shallowness of this success, however, was apparent in economic reports, political analyses, and other information available to U.S. officials. By 1961 the goal of buying time had been achieved. The Saigon regime had stood for over six years, but South Vietnam was not a viable nation and was not becoming one. The objective of an independent South Vietnam was proving increasingly unrealistic and unachievable without greater cost and risk to the United States. With its proclivity to perceive and proclaim success where, in fact, failure abounded, the Eisenhower administration trapped itself and its successors into a commitment to the survival of its own counterfeit creation.

IX

Conclusion

THE EISENHOWER administration presided over the birth of an independent South Vietnam and nursed it through early infancy. Yet, as Eisenhower left office, this offspring of the cold war was weak and unhealthy. Whether it could be invigorated or even saved and, if so, how was left to the "action intellectuals" of the Kennedy administration. The experiment in nation building, begun in the spirit of promoting and protecting American moral and material benefits, was floundering on the reality that Ngo Dinh Diem and his reactionary family were on the wrong side of the revolution for social and political justice that was sweeping through Asia, Africa, and Latin America. Because the Diem government had survived for over six years as a hallmark of American commitment to its own vision of a stable and peaceful Asia, however, the United States was trapped by the very success of the Eisenhower administration in keeping Diem in power and in promoting his symbolic role.

In the spring of 1954, the Eisenhower administration did not intervene militarily in Vietnam to support France in the war against the Vietminh. Over a decade later, the Johnson administration deployed U.S. forces to support the Republic of Vietnam (RVN) in the war against the Vietcong and the Democratic Republic of Vietnam (DRV). Eisenhower's restraint, especially in contrast to Lyndon Johnson's use of

Conclusion

American power was notable. Indeed, historical analyses of Eisenhower's Vietnam policies often limit themselves to the decisions surrounding the dramatic battle at Dienbienphu and the Geneva Conference that marked the conclusion of France's Indochina War. This attention on 1954 gives the Eisenhower administration an image of successfully managing the strategic challenge of war and unrest in Southeast Asia.

Although enormously significant, these events comprised only one part of the history of the Eisenhower administration's efforts in Vietnam. Taken as a whole, the Eisenhower years were a time of deepening American commitment to South Vietnam premised on superficial assumptions about the government in Saigon, its future prospects, and the importance of its survival to U.S. global strategic interests. The United States successfully achieved its objective of creating an ally for itself in South Vietnam. Once established, however, the Saigon regime proved to be an unruly and impotent client whose requirements for survival trapped its patron in ever-increasing costs and risks.

The Eisenhower team entered the White House committed to the containment of communism, by military force if necessary, but wary of the cost and feasibility of policing the world. In Vietnam, they first attempted to strengthen the French to protect U.S. interests in Asia and to bolster an important ally in the North Atlantic alliance. When the French option failed, they turned hesitantly to Diem, whose survival of the challenge from the sects in 1955 encouraged the belief in Washington that a viable pro-Western South Vietnam might be possible under him. The policy of buying time while building a self-sustaining nation in the South seemed successful well into 1957. This outward success, however, was a fragile shell. Throughout Eisenhower's second term, the Saigon regime's narrow political base and lack of economic development left the RVN vulnerable and increasingly thwarted by armed insurrection and other forms of popular dissatisfaction.

The danger to Diem's government sparked Ambassador Elbridge Durbrow's clash with Lieutenant General Samuel Williams and Brigadier General Edward Lansdale, but their debate over South Vietnamese political reform versus wholehearted support of Diem was not new. Like Durbrow, Ambassadors Donald Heath and J. Lawton Collins believed that U.S. support of Diem's regime had to be conditioned on Diem's progress on reform. Among the chief American diplomats in Saigon, Frederick Reinhardt came closest to the wholehearted support position, but he too had his doubts about Diem and occasionally expressed misgivings or advised caution. The ambassadors were willing to give Saigon time and opportunity for change, but, if improvements were not forthcoming at some point (when was the critical question), they were prepared to decree that American aid was not serving its intended purpose. The implication was that the United States should separate itself from a failed effort. The failure would have been Diem's, not America's, and the United States could look to some other leader or some other country for a liberal capitalist showcase in the developing world.

Joining Lansdale and Williams as advocates of full support for Diem were Lieutenant General John O'Daniel, Assistant Secretary of State Walter Robertson, and, after some initial hesitation, Kenneth Young in the State Department. Characterizing Diem and his government as beleaguered and insecure, they insisted that Saigon's leaders needed the assurance of unqualified U.S. support and loyalty in order to gain the confidence, boldness, and momentum to carry them through perilous times. This faction within the Eisenhower administration was more optimistic about Diem than the other school and put more faith in the positive effects of psychological blandishments and esprit de corps.

There were some difficult questions in the policy split personified by Durbrow and Lansdale by the end of 1960. Both men wanted to strengthen South Vietnam, but Durbrow's hard-line approach was singularly incompatible with Lansdale's preference for friendly persuasion. Who was correct was hard to determine because the real difficulty was Diem himself. He and his brothers were well aware of the division within the American ranks and sought to exploit it. The RVN president was a courageous, stubborn, and private person. These qualities could be advantages when battling the sects, the Caravelle group, and even the communists, but they also bred suspicion and discontent within South Vietnam. Similarly, the clever but ruthless Ngo Dinh Nhu was a strength and a weakness for his brother. It was said in Saigon that the Ngos never forgot and that they never learned.[1] Their paranoia, pride, loyalty to family, and particular brand of patriotism made them understandably leery of Americans and others. In reality, however, the immediate security of Diem and his government depended on U.S. support, and the Ngos were unwise, regardless of their reasons, to antagonize American officials. Diem used Williams and Lansdale to play politics with the U.S. ambassador and the director of the U.S. Operations Mission (USOM).

Conclusion

These American officials knew it and resented it. USOM Director Leland Barrows concluded that Diem had no "real desire to reduce his dependence on us." "Aid creates dependence no matter how good it is," Barrows reflected. "Therefore, if you don't insist upon getting something else you are going to do harm."[2]

All of the principal parties mismanaged the critical situation in Vietnam during the final months of the Eisenhower presidency. Diem was too recalcitrant and manipulative with American officials. Lansdale was too romantic about Diem's reciprocating U.S. loyalty. Durbrow was too rigid and impatient with Diem's faults. Eisenhower and Secretary of State Christian Herter provided inadequate leadership. Herter had not been involved in the extensive Indochina discussions of 1954–55 and was unfamiliar with Southeast Asian affairs. Eisenhower was preoccupied with pressing issues such as the U–2 incident and Laos, and, as he prepared for retirement, was not inclined to add to his personal agenda. Allen Dulles still headed the Central Intelligence Agency (CIA), but he too was busy with the U–2, Laos, Cuba, and other problems. The CIA was part of the swirl of controversy over Diem, but its precise role still remains shrouded in secrecy.

In the absence of top-level direction, the American bureaucratic infighting became intense and overly personal, and the policy became oversimplified. The Eisenhower administration had forgotten its caution and reservations of 1954 and had narrowed its choices in Vietnam. Complete withdrawal of U.S. support or openness to leaders other than Diem became increasingly difficult. During the early hours of the November 1960 coup attempt, Durbrow's neutral stance preserved U.S. options and sought to maintain U.S. influence regardless of who occupied the presidential palace. Yet, Lansdale pilloried the ambassador for his coyness and maneuvered for Durbrow's job. This incident, the candid criticisms of Nhu, and other efforts to assess objectively both problems and possibilities in U.S. relations with the RVN destroyed Durbrow's effectiveness in Saigon. The Eisenhower administration's experience in Vietnam underscored the need to preserve flexibility and to keep open exits in unstable bilateral relations. Some commitment to the client state was necessary to maintain U.S. credibility and the cooperation of the aid recipient, but U.S. interests became hostage to exaggerated notions of loyalty, credibility, and strategic danger.

The fate of Southeast Asia was important to the United States as both symbol and substance in the world balance of power, but that importance was not so great as to override reasonable prudence and reserve. The policy debate over the degree of support for Diem revealed the trap in which Washington had placed itself. The United States could not cut its support of Diem without risking collapse of the entire nation-building effort in South Vietnam.

The intensity of the internal debate among American officials over who would be the leader of South Vietnam revealed several things. It showed how much U.S. decision makers cared about the issue and how important they believed the political viability of the Saigon government was to U.S. welfare. It demonstrated the weakness of Diem's government and the power, albeit not absolute power, that the United States had in and over South Vietnam's affairs. It showed the Americans' presumption of control, if not dominion, over their Vietnamese client-allies. By the 1960s, after a decade of this thinking, it was very difficult for U.S. leaders to conceive of South Vietnam in any other terms. Washington had been attempting to direct events in Vietnam for years, and, between 1960 and 1975, it sent over two million troops to do America's bidding in the country.[3]

In an April 1959 address at Gettysburg College, Eisenhower declared that "the loss of South Vietnam would set in motion a crumbling process that could, as it progressed, have grave consequences for us and for freedom."[4] The president's rhetoric was as foreboding and confining as it had been when he first made his famous domino analogy in 1954. As Eisenhower described them, the stakes were so great that the United States had no choice but to stand by South Vietnam. Paradoxically, however, the proclaimed danger was too imprecise to prompt direct U.S. military or civil intervention in Vietnam. Prepared neither to retreat nor fight, the Eisenhower administration turned to nation building. With profuse American military and economic aid, Diem managed to bring a degree of order to the South, reorganize the Army, and initiate some governmental programs. Washington chose to label Diem a "miracle man." The miracle was primarily in public relations, but the president and his advisers chose to accept and promote it as fact. In an October 1960 letter to Diem, Eisenhower observed the RVN's fifth anniversary by praising "its successful struggle to become an independent Republic."[5] As Eisenhower prepared to relinquish the presidency to John F. Kennedy, he believed that Diem was successfully governing his nation and thereby waging the frontline fight against communist expansion at little relative cost to the United States.

In 1962, after the Kennedy administration had enlarged the U.S. military advisory role in South Vietnam, one American adviser experienced personally the nature of his nation's self-created problem. Lieutenant Colonel John Paul Vann decided to create a heroic image for his South Vietnamese military counterpart in order to inspire the Vietnamese colonel to rise to meet successfully the challenge of combat command. The two officers conducted numerous field operations with impressive statistics on enemy losses, but the RVN forces were not winning control of the countryside. In time, Vann realized that his charade had produced a façade of battlefield progress that disguised serious military deficiencies within Saigon's conduct of the war against the Vietcong. When Vann attempted to address the weakness with candid reporting of his counterpart's failures, he found that his superiors turned a deaf ear to his warnings. The spurious symbol that he had helped produce became the substance of specious strategies. As his biographer has written, "Vann was, in effect, trapped by his own outward-seeming success."[6] Long before Vann, the Eisenhower administration had set the same trap.

The Eisenhower administration bears a considerable part of the responsibility for what was known in Saigon as "la présence américaine," but how much of that responsibility was ascribable to the president personally is problematical.[7] As the revisionists have noted, Eisenhower was directly involved in the 1954 Indochina decisions, and he urged prudence, if also resolve. From 1955 through the end of his second term, however, there is little evidence of the president's hand, hidden or otherwise, in Vietnam policy making. His 1955 heart attack certainly limited his work load for a while. Also, Vietnam ceased to be perceived as a crisis issue after the Collins mission and hence was less demanding of presidential attention. On those occasions when he did address questions about Southeast Asia, his contribution was basically an unreflective reiteration of the domino theory and of the earlier decisions to support Diem and to continue the pursuit of containment in South Vietnam.

After leaving office, Eisenhower was a hawk on the war. In 1965, Lyndon Johnson sought the former president's guidance on the question of direct U.S. military intervention in Vietnam. As Senate majority leader during the 1950s, Johnson had been a close observer and frequent supporter of Eisenhower's foreign policies, and his conversations and correspondence with Eisenhower on Vietnam in 1965 give evidence of genuine respect for Eisenhower's views. As he had done in 1954, Eisenhower believed that military intervention was a tenable U.S. option in Vietnam, and he agreed with Johnson's escalation. His principal criticism, in fact, was that the president was not applying enough force. He gave every indication that, in Johnson's place, he would have approved military intervention. In April 1965 at Johns Hopkins University, Johnson explained that America was fighting in Vietnam because, since 1954 the United States had honored "a national pledge" to defend the Vietnamese people against terror and aggression.[8] A few weeks later, Eisenhower privately reassured the incumbent that this rationale for military intervention was correct. "You have to go all out" with military help for South Vietnam, he advised, because "we are not going to be run out of a free country that we helped to establish."[9]

The United States believed that it could control the political, economic, and social evolution of postcolonial Vietnam. The goal was unattainable without larger and difficult-to-justify cost to the United States. Some historians of the Vietnam War have argued that the cost may have been acceptable as part of the moral and strategic struggle against communist totalitarianism.[10] Washington could not be indifferent to victory by the DRV, which was allied with nations that proclaimed themselves the enemies of the United States. America had some important interests in Southeast Asia, such as trade for itself and its allies, regional power balance, and access to harbors and airfields. The question was how to protect those interests and how to measure their importance. Similar interests existed in Japan, Korea, Taiwan, and the Philippines, and each country presented its own problems and possibilities for the United States. In Vietnam, both the Diem government and SEATO defense pact were weak expedients, and that weakness was only thinly masked in the 1950s by the slowness of the DRV to exploit it.

A time bomb was ticking in Southeast Asia while Eisenhower was president. It was similar to the civil rights conflagration smoldering under the surface in America. In May 1954, while American diplomats sat at the Geneva Conference on Indochina, the U.S. Supreme Court issued its landmark decision that racial segregation of public schools was unconstitutional. Through the rest of the decade, the Eisenhower White House provided more rhetoric than results toward implementing desegregation.[11] The eventual eruption of black discontent and protest in the 1960s was in part a result of these years of frustration with executive inaction. In like manner, the Vietnam time bomb did not explode while Eisenhower was in office. This result was more a product of good luck than of sound policy. There was mounting evidence in the 1950s that the bomb was there; some precautions were taken; but the bomb was not defused. There was fear of detonating the bomb, but there was also an underestimation of its size and destructive force. Primarily, there was an absence of ideas of what to do about it except leave it alone and hope that it was a dud.

Administration officials in the 1950s could not foresee the magnitude of the U.S. effort in Vietnam in the 1960s nor could they anticipate the high cost that Vietnam would exact from the United States in lives, money, prestige, and self-confidence. Even an advocate of restraint like Collins did not characterize Hanoi as a foe so formidable that it could withstand U.S. power. The concern of the wary was whether the fate of South Vietnam merited any significant cost at all. In the catalog of Eisenhower's foreign policies, Vietnam did not occupy as much attention as the Soviet Union, the North Atlantic alliance, Suez, or Taiwan. With the exception of the flurry surrounding Dienbienphu and Geneva, Vietnam was a secondary issue. By the end of Eisenhower's second term, the United States had no counterinsurgency plan to meet the armed insurrection in South Vietnam. Concern over Laos revealed that the domino theory remained the touchstone of U.S. strategy, and lack of allied interest in Laos exposed SEATO to be a hollow shell.[12]

In Vietnam, the Eisenhower team was more skilled in tactics than in strategy. It was cautious, procrastinating, and concerned about congressional and public support. The president and his advisers were managing the cold war in Asia but not mastering it. They used the miracle myth of South Vietnam as evidence of their global resolve to combat communism but had no clear definition of the nature of the Vietnamese communists' threat to the United States. They equated the danger of communist totalitarianism with the World War II challenge of fascist dictatorship. Eisenhower and especially John Foster Dulles were more sensitive to European than Asian issues. For them, one of the key links between Europe and Asia was colonialism. Once France had acceded to American designs for Vietnam in 1955, the administration assumed that it had liberated Western policies from the colonial stigma. It failed to recognize the neocolonialism of U.S. controls over the commercial import program, of the compromises with landlords on land reform, and of the attempts to bolster a Westernized elite like the Catholic Ngo family. The United States did not extract huge profits from Vietnam and, in fact, spent vast sums there. Yet, the American presence made South Vietnam as dependent and as devoid of national self-respect as would have the most exploitative of colonial masters.[13]

By the end of the 1950s, the cold war certainties of good versus evil were considerably blurred in Vietnam. The Saigon regime's corruption and repression raised numerous moral issues, but the communist side too was brutal and autocratic. From these moral vagaries arose the dilemma over Diem. As Congressman Walter Judd phrased it, "our choice was between a 'bad' government that was friendly, and a worse government that was *hostile* to us."[14] General Williams objected when some U.S. officials referred to Diem as "our son-of-a-bitch."[15] For Americans there were a series of questions: Was Diem an SOB? Was he America's SOB? Was Ho Chi Minh an SOB? Whose SOB was he? Was the United States to support its SOB over "their" SOB? These queries suggest that the basic historical issue in Vietnam was not a moral question alone. Most historians characterize the American war in Vietnam as a tragedy and argue that it was wrong in either purpose or method or both. Yet, such conclusions do not address how a great nation like the United States, which was admired and respected by millions throughout the world at the end of World War II, could go so wrong in Vietnam in the three decades after World War II.[16]

Eisenhower was a popular and respected leader who, as supreme allied commander during World War II, seemed to personify America's moral and material ascendancy among the nations. That image helped carry him to the White House and helped explain the popularity that he enjoyed throughout his presidency. The world and America's place in it changed, however, during the 1950s. The death of Soviet leader Joseph Stalin in 1953 began to alter subtly the international moral equation. The postwar economic recovery revitalized both victors and vanquished around the globe. The rise and success of nationalist movements throughout the developing world under local leaders with various ideologies further changed the political, economic, and moral complexion of the international system. Eisenhower and his advisers made some tactical adjustments to the growing complexity of the world, but their goals remained fixed to an unremitting anticommunism grounded in the moral and material preeminence of America in 1945.

The Eisenhower administration was both the creator and the captive of an illusion in Vietnam. A combination of factors—cold war bipolarism and paranoia, the arrogance of power, cultural and racial chauvinism—blinded U.S. leaders to social, political, historical, and military realities in Vietnam. Eisenhower's restraint seemed realistic during the early months of his administration, when he avoided a direct American military involvement in the collapsing French colonial war in Indochina. Although laudable in retrospect, his caution was the product of the moment. Eisenhower and Secretary of State Dulles were fundamentally committed to preventing the success of the Vietnamese communists' bid for control of the country. They viewed the French defeat as only a temporary setback and, in fact, an opportunity for the United States to assume the leadership role. Throughout the remaining years of his presidency, Eisenhower and his lieutenants worked assiduously to build up South Vietnam as a key defensive outpost guarding the strategic, political, and economic interests of the United States in Southeast Asia. They achieved a seemingly miraculous success in Vietnam merely with the survival of Diem's government. In 1961, South Vietnam still stood as an American outpost in the cold war. The ultimate burden of sustaining this miracle was obscured by the rhetoric and expectations of nation building. The United States had embarked upon a costly and tragic course in Vietnam. Kennedy, and later Johnson, accepted and pursued the same specious success that beguiled and trapped Eisenhower.

The U.S. strategy of containment failed in Vietnam partly because there was no self-sustaining state in the South for the United States to support. From its inception in 1954, South Vietnam was largely a political vacuum into which the United States became deeply drawn in a futile attempt to fill the void. American involvement helped sustain the Diem regime, but it handicapped the Saigon government in its competition with the communists for national legitimacy. Eisenhower's foreign policy may have been astute in some areas, as the Eisenhower revisionists argue, but in Vietnam, as the more judicious revisionist studies acknowledge, the administration oversimplified and overcommitted. The United States fostered dependence, not independence, in South Vietnam. In the early 1960s, the Diem façade became increasingly untenable as internal

Vietnamese opposition to him and his family mounted. The trap snapped on America in 1963. Diem's assassination led to a series of short-lived successor regimes that further exposed the frailty of South Vietnam's autonomy.[17] There was no viable government in Saigon, and by the mid-1960s only U.S. military force could maintain the fiction that there was.

NOTES

Preface

1. For a review of Vietnam War historiography see Divine, "Vietnam Reconsidered."

2. Eisenhower, *Mandate for Change*, p. 452. See also Kimball, *To Reason Why*, pp. 6–11.

3. Schlesinger, *Bitter Heritage*, p. 32. For other examples of the quagmire thesis see the books by Halberstam, *Making of a Quagmire* and *Best and the Brightest*.

4. For examples of the stalemate thesis see Gelb and Betts, *Irony of Vietnam*, and Ellsberg, *Papers on the War*.

5. Hixon, "Containment on the Perimeter." For an example of the flawed containment thesis see Herring, *America's Longest War*.

6. For some examples of the revisionist view see Lewy, *America in Vietnam;* Summers, *On Strategy;* Podhoretz, *Why We Were in Vietnam;* and Nixon, *No More Vietnams.*

7. Divine, "Vietnam Reconsidered," p. 92. Some examples of postrevisionist studies are Kahin, *Intervention;* Kolko, *Anatomy of a War;* and Gardner, *Approaching Vietnam.* See also Herring, "America and Vietnam"; and Kimball, *To Reason Why*, pp. 18–22.

8. Discussion at the 194th National Security Council meeting, April 29, 1954, *FRUS, 1952–54*, 13:1440.

9. Paterson, "Historical Memory and Illusive Victories." There are many studies of the lessons of Vietnam from many different perspectives. See, for example, Ravenal, *Never Again;* Thompson and Frizzell, *Lessons of Vietnam;* and Braestrup, *Vietnam as History.*

10. Mueller, *War, Presidents and Public Opinion*, pp. 52–58; Sperlich and Lunch, "American Public Opinion and the War in Vietnam." For critiques of the "win" thesis see Herring, "The 'Vietnam Syndrome' and American Foreign Policy"; LaFeber, "The Last War, the Next War, and the New Revisionists"; and Kattenburg, "Reflections on Vietnam."

1. Vietnam, Colonialism, and Cold War
(1941–January 1953)

1. Shafer, *Deadly Paradigms*, pp. 240–75; Hoffmann, *Primacy or World Order*, pp. 23–24.

2. Fifield, *Diplomacy of Southeast Asia*, p. 27; von der Mehden, *South-East Asia*, pp. 39–50; Hess, *United States' Emergence as a Southeast Asian Power*, pp. 159–60.

3. Duiker, *Communist Road to Power*, pp. 68–69, 98–100; Lomperis, *The War Everyone Lost—and Won*, p. 31; Fall, *Two Viet-Nams*, pp. 47–59.

4. Buttinger, *Vietnam*, 1:221–22; Hammer, *Struggle for Indochina*, p. 104; Bui Diem and Chanoff, *In the Jaws of History*, p. 29. See also Bao Dai, *Le dragon d'Annam*.

5. Halberstam, *Ho*, p. 12. See also Duiker, *Communist Road to Power*, pp. 7–89.

6. McAlister and Mus, *Vietnamese and Their Revolution*, pp. 16–17, 50–51, 102.

7. McAlister, *Vietnam*, pp. 134–35, 154, 216–17, 315–16; Bui Diem and Chanoff, *In the Jaws of History*, pp. 20–28.

8. McAlister, *Vietnam*, pp. 316–22; Lomperis, *The War Everyone Lost—and Won*, pp. 4–8.

9. Bui Diem and Chanoff, *In the Jaws of History*, pp. 48–50; Lomperis, *The War Everyone Lost—and Won*, pp. 34–36; Warner, *The Last Confucian*, pp. 66–67; Fall, *Two Viet-Nams*, pp. 210–11.

10. Buttinger, *Vietnam*, 1:308–37.

11. Quoted in Fall, *Two Viet-Nams*, p. 73.

12. *Ibid.*, pp. 68–77; Duiker, *Communist Road to Power*, p. 125.

13. Hammer, *Struggle for Indochina*, pp. 223–33.

14. Kahin and Lewis, *United States in Vietnam*, pp. 28–29; Kolko, *Anatomy of a War*, p. 80.

15. Fall, *Two Viet-Nams*, pp. 204–224; Hammer, *Struggle for Indochina*, pp. 214–19; Bui Diem and Chanoff, *In the Jaws of History*, pp. 62–70; Gardner, *Approaching Vietnam*, p. 68.

16. Fall, *Two Viet-Nams*, p. 214; Hess, *United States' Emergence as a Southeast Asian Power*, pp. 217–50.

17. Robert Blum memorandum of conversation with Bao Dai, November 19, 1953, enclosed in Blum to C. D. Jackson (special assistant to the president), February 19, 1954, box 2, Jackson Records.

18. Fall, *Two Viet-Nams*, pp. 204–6.

19. Hammer, *Struggle for Indochina*, pp. 266, 350.

20. Kahin, *Intervention*, pp. 5–6; LaFeber, "Roosevelt, Churchill and Indochina"; Hess, "Franklin D. Roosevelt and Indochina"; Thorne, "Indochina and Anglo-American Relations"; Hess, *United States' Emergence as a Southeast Asian Power*, pp. 1–2, 161–63, 214–15; Gardner, *Approaching Vietnam*, pp. 53, 76–80.

21. Kahin, *Intervention*, p. 7; Herring, "Truman Administration and the Restoration of French Sovereignty in Indochina."

22. Herring, *America's Longest War*, pp. 9–11; Hess, *United States' Emergence as a Southeast Asian Power*, pp. 325–26; Williams, et al., *America in Vietnam*, pp. 90–97.

23. Quoted in Hammer, *Struggle for Indochina*, p. 270. See also *ibid.*, pp. 247–54, 267–70; Duiker, *Communist Road to Power*, pp. 139–41; and Kelly, *Lost Soldiers*, pp. 60–65.

24. Hess, "First American Commitment in Indochina," pp. 331–50; Hess, *United States' Emergence as a Southeast Asian Power*, pp. 333–65; Rotter, *Path to Vietnam;* Spector, *Advice and Support*, pp. 115–16; Gardner, *Approaching Vietnam*, pp. 80–87; Williams, et al., *America in Vietnam*, pp. 82–87.

25. Hess, *United States' Emergence as a Southeast Asian Power*, pp. 367–71; Gardner, *Approaching Vietnam*, p. 92; Goldman, *Crucial Decade—And After*, pp. 91–145; NSC 68, April 14, 1950, *FRUS, 1950*, 1:234–85; Ambrose, *Rise to Globalism*, p. 164; Blum, *Drawing the Line*, pp. 198–220; Matray, *Reluctant Crusade*, pp. 247–58.

26. Kahin, *Intervention*, pp. 36–37, 42; Spector, *Advice and Support*, pp. 119–65.

27. Herring, *America's Longest War*, pp. 22–23.

28. NSC 124/2, June 25, 1952, United States Department of Defense, *Pentagon Papers*, 1:385–86.

2. Eisenhower, Dulles, Dominoes, and Dienbienphu
(January 1953–May 1954)

1. United States President, *Public Papers: Eisenhower, 1953*, p. 16.

2. United States Department of State, *Bulletin* (February 9, 1953): 212–16.

3. John Foster Dulles memorandum of conversation with Eisenhower, March 24, 1953, *FRUS, 1952–54*, 13:419. See also Gardner, *Approaching Vietnam*, pp. 135–40; and Immerman, "Perceptions by the United States of Its Interests in Vietnam."

4. Duiker, *Communist Road to Power in Vietnam*, pp. 141–43.

5. United States President, *Public Papers: Eisenhower, 1954*, pp. 382–84 (emphasis added). See also Eisenhower, *Mandate for Change*, pp. 332–33.

6. Divine, *Eisenhower and the Cold War*, pp. 12–14; Ambrose, *Rise to Globalism*, p. 187.

7. Gaddis, *Strategies of Containment*, p. 127; Ambrose, *Eisenhower*, 1:547–

49, 572; Mueller, *War, Presidents and Public Opinion*, pp. 235–37; Brands, *Cold Warriors*, pp. 185–200.

8. This revisionist literature has become quite extensive. Some examples of the genre and some historiographical analyses are Parmet, *Eisenhower and the American Crusades;* Lyon, *Eisenhower;* Alexander, *Holding the Line;* De Santis, "Eisenhower Revisionism"; Divine, *Eisenhower and the Cold War;* McAuliffe, "Eisenhower, the President"; Greenstein, *The Hidden-Hand Presidency;* Ambrose, *Eisenhower,* vol. 2; Joes, "Eisenhower Revisionism and American Politics"; and Reichard, *Politics as Usual,* pp. 85–186.

9. McMahon, "Eisenhower and Third World Nationalism"; Gaddis, *Strategies of Containment,* p. 197; Schlesinger, *Cycles of American History,* pp. 387–405; Challener, "National Security Policy from Truman to Eisenhower," pp. 48–50, 67–72; Brands, "Age of Vulnerability." Two of the most judicious revisionists, Divine and Ambrose, qualify their conclusions but basically give Eisenhower high marks for the restraint that he displayed in foreign affairs. See Divine, *Eisenhower and the Cold War,* pp. 153–55; and Ambrose, *Eisenhower,* 2:625–26.

10. Eisenhower interview, pp. 27–28, PUL. See also Divine, *Eisenhower and the Cold War,* pp. 20–23; Lyon, *Eisenhower,* pp. 510–11, 645–47; Gaddis, *Strategies of Containment,* pp. 129, 163; Brands, *Cold Warriors,* pp. 3–26; Immerman, "Eisenhower and Dulles"; and Nelson, " 'Top of the Policy Hill.' " For biographies of Dulles see Hoopes, *Devil and John Foster Dulles;* Pruessen, *John Foster Dulles;* and Toulouse, *Transformation of John Foster Dulles.*

11. Eisenhower, *Mandate for Change,* pp. 178–81, 211; Divine, *Eisenhower and the Cold War,* pp. 25–29; Alexander, *Holding the Line,* pp. 42–48; Lyon, *Eisenhower,* p. 520; Reichard, *Reaffirmation of Republicanism,* pp. 51–52; Graebner, *America as a World Power,* pp. 185–222.

12. Anderson, "China Policy and Presidential Politics."

13. Gaddis, *Strategies of Containment,* pp. 145–46; Challener, "National Security Policy," pp. 50–72; Kinnard, *President Eisenhower,* pp. 1–36; Weigley, *American Way of War,* pp. 399–402.

14. United States Department of State, *Bulletin* (January 25, 1954): 107–110; Gaddis, *Strategies of Containment,* pp. 147–61; Alexander, *Holding the Line,* pp. 66–69; Kinnard, *President Eisenhower,* pp. 126–27.

15. United States Senate, *Executive Sessions of the Senate Foreign Relations Committee (Historical Series),* 5:385–88.

16. United States President, *Public Papers: Eisenhower, 1953,* pp. 540–41. See also Dulles to C. Douglas Dillon, May 7, 1953, *FRUS, 1952–54,* 13:550–51; Spector, *Advice and Support,* pp. 170–81; Herring, *America's Longest War,* pp. 25–29; and Kahin, *Intervention,* p. 42.

17. Spector, *Advice and Support,* p. 182; Karnow, *Vietnam,* pp. 189–91; Kelly, *Lost Soldiers,* pp. 70–75; John W. O'Daniel brief attached to Andrew J. Goodpaster (Eisenhower's staff secretary) memorandum to Eisenhower, March 2, 1956, box 50, International series, Ann Whitman File, Eisenhower Papers (hereafter cited as Whitman File); memorandum of conversation with Ngo Dinh

Diem, August 18, 1955, *FRUS, 1955–1957,* 1:520. For details of the siege and battle at Dienbienphu see Fall, *Hell in a Very Small Place;* and Roy, *Battle of Dien Bien Phu.*

18. Discussion at the 179th NSC meeting, January 8, 1954, *FRUS, 1952–54,* 13:947–54. See also Burke and Greenstein, *How Presidents Test Reality,* pp. 31–35, 60–61.

19. C. D. Jackson (special assistant to the president) memorandum for the president, January 18, 1954, memorandum of the meeting of the President's Special Committee on Indochina, January 29, 1954, and Walter Bedell Smith (under secretary of state) memorandum to Eisenhower, March 11, 1954, *FRUS, 1952–54,* 13:981–82, 1002–6, 1108–16; United States Department of Defense, *Pentagon Papers,* 1:90–91.

20. Memorandum of meeting of the President's Special Committee on Indochina, January 29, 1954, *FRUS, 1952–54,* 13:1006; Millett, *Short History of the Vietnam War,* pp. xviii–xix. For a biography of Lansdale see Currey, *Lansdale.*

21. Dulles to Eisenhower, February 9, 1954, *FRUS, 1952–54,* 13:1025. See also Dulles to Eisenhower, February 6, 1954, Department of State press release, February 19, 1954, *ibid.,* 1021, 16:415; and United States Senate, *Executive Sessions of the Senate Foreign Relations Committee (Historical Series),* 6:154–84.

22. Duiker, *Communist Road to Power,* pp. 158–61; Hammer, *Struggle for Indochina,* pp. 327–28; Spector, *Advice and Support,* p. 190.

23. Discussion at the 189th NSC meeting, March 18, 1954, discussion at the 192d NSC meeting, April 6, 1954, *FRUS, 1952–54,* 13:1132–33, 1253; Eisenhower, *Mandate for Change,* pp. 372–73.

24. Capt. G. W. Anderson (assistant to Adm. Radford) memorandum for the record, March 21, 1954, *FRUS, 1952–54,* 13:1137–40. See also James C. Hagerty (presidential press secretary) Diary, March 20, 1954, Hagerty Papers.

25. Radford memorandum for Eisenhower, March 24, 1954, *FRUS, 1952–54,* 13:1159.

26. Eisenhower, *Mandate for Change,* p. 345. See also Ridgway, *Soldier,* pp. 274–78.

27. Ely, *Mémoires,* pp. 64–77; Radford, *From Pearl Harbor to Vietnam,* pp. 391–95; Césari and de Folin, "Military Necessity, Political Impossibility"; United States Department of Defense, *Pentagon Papers,* 1:97–98; Radford memorandum for Eisenhower, March 24, 1954, Radford memorandum for the file, April 24, 1954, *FRUS, 1952–54,* 13:1158–59, 1396–97. For a detailed examination of Operation Vulture see Prados, *The Sky Would Fall.*

28. Dulles memorandum for Eisenhower, March 23, 1954, *FRUS, 1952–54,* 13:1141–42. See also Guhin, *John Foster Dulles,* pp. 221–42; Spector, *Advice and Support,* pp. 199–202; Prados, *The Sky Would Fall,* pp. 152–56; Gardner, *Approaching Vietnam,* pp. 143, 150; Douglas MacArthur II (Department of State counselor), memorandum for Dulles, April 7, 1954, Robert Cutler (special

assistant to the president for national security affairs) memorandum for Smith, April 30, 1954, *FRUS, 1952–54*, 13:1270–72, 1447–48; Nixon, *Memoirs*, pp. 150, 154; Radford interview, pp. 46–56; Twining (Air Force chief of staff) interview, pp. 29–32; Murray Marder, "When Ike Was Asked to Nuke Vietnam," *Washington Post*, August 22, 1982.

29. Dulles memorandum of conversation with Eisenhower, March 24, 1954, *FRUS, 1952–54*, 13:1150. See also Eisenhower, *Mandate for Change*, p. 373; and Eisenhower interview, p. 65, DDEL.

30. Discussion at the 190th NSC meeting, March 25, 1954, *FRUS, 1952–54*, 13:1163–68. L. Arthur Minnich, Jr. (assistant staff secretary to the president), notes of Cabinet meeting, March 26, 1954, box 4, Cabinet series, Records of the White House Office, Office of the Staff Secretary, DDEL, recorded "a number of alternatives being considered without decision yet."

31. Hoopes, *Devil and John Foster Dulles*, p. 211. For studies that emphasize the Eisenhower administration's caution during the Dienbienphu crisis, see Ambrose, *Eisenhower*, 2:173–85; Parmet, *Eisenhower and the American Crusades*, pp. 353–72; Divine, *Eisenhower and the Cold War*, pp. 40–51; Cooper, *Lost Crusade*, pp. 69–74; Spector, *Advice and Support*, pp. 198–214; Gardner, *Approaching Vietnam*, pp. 179–247; Scribner, "Eisenhower and Johnson Administrations' Decisionmaking on Vietnamese Intervention"; Billings-Yun, *Decision against War;* Saunders, "Military Force in the Foreign Policy of the Eisenhower Presidency." For accounts that suggest a greater possibility of U.S. military intervention in 1954, see Herring, *America's Longest War*, pp. 29–39; Karnow, *Vietnam*, pp. 197–98; Alexander, *Holding the Line*, pp. 78–81; Kahin, *Intervention*, pp. 45–48; Prados, *The Sky Would Fall;* and Gurtov, *First Vietnam Crisis*, pp. 92–105. For an interpretation that specifically characterizes Eisenhower's policies as militant and aggressive, see Bator, *Vietnam*. For a study that credits Eisenhower with successful management of Vietnam policy in 1954 but that avoids the hawk and dove dichotomy in its analysis see Burke and Greenstein, *How Presidents Test Reality*.

32. Ridgway memorandum to JCS, April 6, 1954, *FRUS, 1952–54*, 13:1269–70. See also Radford memorandum to Wilson, March 31, 1954, Donald R. Heath (ambassador in Saigon) to Dulles, April 1, 1954, Ridgway memorandum to JCS, April 2, 1954, Adm. Robert B. Carney (chief of naval operations) memorandum to JCS, April 2, 1954, Twining memorandum to Radford, April 2, 1954, Gen. Lemuel C. Shepherd, Jr. (Marine Corps commandant), memorandum to JCS, April 2, 1954, *ibid.*, 1198–1200, 1220–23; and Hagerty Diary, March 26, 1954.

33. United States Department of State, *Bulletin* (April 12, 1954): 539–42. See also Dulles to Eisenhower, March 26, 1954, box 80, Dulles Papers, PUL; and United States President, *Public Papers: Eisenhower, 1953*, pp. 183–84, for evidence of the president's support of the principle of united action.

34. Quoted in Nixon, *Memoirs*, p. 151.

35. Discussion at the 191st NSC meeting, April 1, 1954, *FRUS, 1952–54*, 13:1201–2.

36. *Ibid.*, 1202, n.3. See also memorandum of telephone conversation between Eisenhower and Dulles, April 1, 1954, box 5, Diary series, Whitman File.

37. Hagerty Diary, April 1, 1954.

38. Eisenhower, *Mandate for Change*, p. 345.

39. *Ibid.*, pp. 278–85; Hagerty Diary, April 20, 1954; Ferrell, *Eisenhower Diaries*, pp. 269–70; Reichard, *Reaffirmation of Republicanism*, pp. 58–68.

40. Draft joint resolution, April 2, 1954, *FRUS, 1952–54*, 13:1211–12.

41. Dulles memorandum of conversation with Eisenhower, April 2, 1954, *ibid.*, 1210–11.

42. Dulles memorandum for the file, April 5, 1954, *ibid.*, 1224–25.

43. Memorandum of telephone conversation between Eisenhower and Dulles, April 3, 1954, *ibid.*, 1230.

44. Roberts, "The Day We Didn't Go to War." See also United States House of Representatives, Committee on Armed Services, *United States-Vietnam Relations*, 9:686; Gibbons, *U.S. Government and the Vietnam War*, 1:191–92; Challener, "National Security Policy," pp. 60–61; and Gardner, *Approaching Vietnam*, pp. 204–7. For a detailed analysis of the April 3 meeting see Herring and Immerman, "Eisenhower, Dulles, and Dienbienphu."

45. Adams, *Firsthand Report*, p. 122.

46. Dillon to Dulles, April 5, 1954, *FRUS, 1952–54*, 13:1236–38. See also Dillon interview, p. 14, DDEL.

47. Dulles to Dillon, April 5, 1954, *FRUS, 1952–54*, 13:1242. See also Dulles to Winthrop W. Aldrich (ambassador at London), April 4, 1954, memorandum of telephone conversation between Eisenhower and Dulles, April 5, 1954, *ibid.*, 1238–42; and United States Department of Defense, *Pentagon Papers*, 1:94–95, 100–101.

48. Eisenhower, *Mandate for Change*, p. 347; discussion at the 192d NSC meeting, April 6, 1954, *FRUS, 1952–54*, 13:1254; Parmet, *Eisenhower*, pp. 366–68.

49. Memorandum of telephone conversation between Eisenhower and Dulles, April 5, 1954, discussion at the 192d NSC meeting, April 6, 1954, *FRUS, 1952–54*, 13:1241–42, 1253–54. See also Gibbons, *U.S. Government and the Vietnam War*, 1:187–95; and Billings-Yun, *Decision against War*, pp. 99–102.

50. Burke and Greenstein, *How Presidents Test Reality*, pp. 67, 98.

51. Memorandum of discussion at the 192d NSC meeting, April 6, 1954, *FRUS, 1952–54*, 13:1253–57.

52. Kahin, *Intervention*, pp. 48–50. For a Southeast Asian collective defense proposal as early as June 1952 see NSC 124/2, June 25, 1952, United States Department of Defense, *Pentagon Papers*, 1:384–90.

53. Discussion at the 192d NSC meeting, April 6, 1954, *FRUS, 1952–54*, 13:1259–62. See also Charles C. Stelle (member of the Policy Planning Staff) memorandum to Robert R. Bowie (director of the Policy Planning Staff), March 31, 1954, and James C. H. Bonbright, Jr. (deputy assistant secretary of state for European affairs), memorandum of conversation, April 4, 1954, *ibid.*, 1195–98, 1232.

54. Quoted in Fall, *Hell in a Very Small Place*, p. 310. See also "Chronology of Actions on the Subject of Indochina prior to the Geneva Meeting on Korea and Indochina in the Spring of 1954," January 27, 1956, box 82, Dulles Papers, PUL; Gardner, *Approaching Vietnam*, pp. 182–97; Eden, *Full Circle*, pp. 93–94; United States Department of Defense, *Pentagon Papers*, 1:98–104; Pemberton, "Australia, the United States, and the Indochina Crisis of 1954"; Warner, "Britain and the Crisis over Dien Bien Phu"; and Césari and de Folin, "Military Necessity, Political Impossibility."

55. Hagerty Diary, April 24, 1954; Nixon, *Memoirs*, pp. 151–52. See also Livingston T. Merchant (assistant secretary of state for European affairs) memorandum to Dulles, April 17, 1954, *FRUS, 1952–54*, 13:1346–48; Radford, *From Pearl Harbor to Vietnam*, p. 405; Nixon interview, p. 44; and McClintock, *Meaning of Limited War*, p. 169.

56. Smith to Dulles, April 25, 1954, *FRUS, 1952–54*, 13:1403–4. See also Dulles to Smith, April 23, 1954, Radford memorandum for the file, April 24, 1954, Dulles to Smith, April 25, 1954, Bowie memorandum to Dulles, May 2, 1954, *ibid.*, 1374, 1396–97, 1404–5, 16:651–54; Eisenhower, *Mandate for Change*, p. 351; United States Department of Defense, *Pentagon Papers*, 1:106; and Herring and Immerman, "Eisenhower, Dulles, and Dienbienphu," pp. 355–62.

57. Dulles to Dillon, June 14, 1954, *FRUS, 1952–54*, 13:1689–90. See also Dillon to Dulles, May 10, 1954, MacArthur memorandum of conversation, May 11, 1954, Dulles to Dillon, May 11, 1954, Dulles to Dillon, May 17, 1954, Merchant memorandum of conversation, June 16, 1954, Dulles to delegation at Geneva, June 14, 1954, *ibid.*, 1522–28, 1534–36, 1575–76, 1710–13, 16:1147; "Procedural Steps for Intervention in Indochina," no date, box 8, Subject series, Dulles Papers, DDEL; Dillon interview, pp. 13–19, PUL; Eisenhower, *Mandate for Change*, pp. 357–66; and Kahin, *Intervention*, pp. 50–52.

58. Minnich memorandum to Eisenhower, no date, *FRUS, 1952–54*, 13:1412.

59. Eisenhower to Gen. Alfred M. Gruenther (supreme Allied commander, Europe), April 26, 1954, *ibid.*, 1419. See also Eisenhower to Capt. E. E. Hazlett, Jr. (personal friend of Eisenhower), April 27, 1954, *ibid.*, 1427–28; and Eisenhower, *Mandate for Change*, pp. 373–74.

60. Minnich memorandum to Eisenhower, no date, *FRUS, 1952–54*, 13:1412.

61. Eisenhower, *Crusade in Europe*, p. 476.

62. Hagerty Diary, April 26, 1954; Minnich memorandum to Eisenhower, no date, *FRUS, 1952–54*, 13:1412–13. See also Eisenhower interview, pp. 26–27, PUL; United States President, *Public Papers: Eisenhower, 1953*, pp. 179–88; and Reichard, *Reaffirmation of Republicanism*, p. 69.

63. Cutler memorandum of conference at the White House, May 5, 1954, *FRUS, 1952–54*, 13:1469 (emphasis in the original).

64. Hagerty Diary, April 26, 1954; Minnich memorandum to Eisenhower, no date, discussion at the 194th NSC meeting, April 29, 1954, *FRUS, 1952–54*, 13:1414, 1439–42.

65. Hagerty Diary, April 26, 1954; Minnich memorandum to Eisenhower, no

date, discussion at the 194th NSC meeting, April 29, 1954, *FRUS, 1952–54*, 13:1413, 1445. See also "R. Cutler's Summary of Principal Points Made by the President in his Talk with Republican Leaders," April 26, 1954, box 11, Briefing Notes subseries, NSC series, Records of the Office of the Special Assistant for National Security Affairs, DDEL; Alfred Politz research survey, March 20, 1954, box 105, Subject series, White House Central Files (Confidential File), DDEL; and Challener, "National Security Policy," pp. 62–63.

66. Larson (director of United States Information Agency) interview, p. 2.

67. Eisenhower to Hazlett, April 27, 1954, *FRUS, 1952–54*, 13:1428. See also Prados, *The Sky Would Fall*, p. 197.

68. Fall, *Two Viet-Nams*, p. 229.

69. Quoted in Hughes, *Ordeal of Power*, p. 182.

70. Kahin, *Intervention*, p. 72; Bissell (CIA) interview, pp. 7–8.

3. The Geneva Conference and the "Diem Card" (May–June 1954)

1. United States Department of State, *Bulletin* (August 2, 1954): 163–64.

2. Herring, *America's Longest War*, pp. 37–40; Cameron, *Vietnam Crisis*, 1:275–77; Gardner, *Approaching Vietnam*, pp. 248–56, 281–84; Lacouture, *Mendès France*, pp. 3–16.

3. Immerman, "United States and the Geneva Conference," pp. 56–59; Brands, *Cold Warriors*, pp. 71–77.

4. Carlton, *Anthony Eden*, pp. 339–56.

5. Immerman, "United States and the Geneva Conference."

6. Hess, "Redefining the American Position in Southeast Asia," pp. 126–31; Guhin, *John Foster Dulles*, pp. 244–51; Sullivan, *France's Vietnam Policy*, pp. 43–48; Cable, *Geneva Conference*, pp. 111–12; Dawson, "The 1954 Geneva Conference."

7. Burke and Greenstein, *How Presidents Test Reality*, pp. 93–94.

8. For detailed accounts of the Geneva negotiations see Randle, *Geneva 1954*; and Devillers and Lacouture, *Viet Nam*. For the DRV's internal problems see Kolko, *Anatomy of a War*, pp. 60–65; and Cable, *Geneva Conference*, p. 98. On the PRC's role see Joyaux, *La Chine et le règlement du premier conflit d'Indochine*.

9. Dulles to delegation at Geneva, May 22, 1954, *FRUS, 1952–54*, 16:892–94. See also Robert McClintock (chargé d'affaires in Saigon) to Dept. of State, desp. 522, May 13, 1954, United States Department of State General Records, Record Group 59, 751G.00/5–1354 (hereafter cited as RG 59 with file number); and Hammer, *Struggle for Indochina*, p. 218.

10. McClintock to Dulles, tel. 2432, May 17, 1954, RG 59, 751G.00/5–1754. For more on Nguyen De's influence on Bao Dai, see Buttinger, *Vietnam*, 2:784, 1065–66; and Cooper, *Lost Crusade*, p. 126. Buttinger indicates that De had parted with the French long before 1949 but remained "the most cunning

and reactionary" of the emperor's advisers. See also Bui Diem and Chanoff, *In the Jaws of History*, pp. 65–70.

11. Buttinger, *Vietnam*, 2:728–35, 787; Hammer, *Struggle for Indochina*, pp. 275–86, 321–22.

12. Fall, *Two Viet-Nams*, p. 216.

13. Buttinger, *Vietnam*, 2:815; Hammer, *Struggle for Indochina*, p. 287; Spector, *Advice and Support*, pp. 131–34.

14. Donald R. Heath (ambassador in Saigon) to Dulles, tel. 1847, March 31, 1954, RG 59, 751G.00/3–3154; Paul J. Sturm (consul in Hanoi) to Dulles, tel. 584, April 15, 1954, RG 59, 751G.00/4–1554; McClintock to Dulles, May 12, 1954, *FRUS, 1952–54*, 13:1544–45; Buttinger, *Vietnam*, 2:763.

15. "Phan Huy Quat," January 29, 1965, CIA Biographic Register, *Declassified Documents Reference Systems*, 1978, 31B; "Major Non-Communist Political Parties and Religious and Armed Groups in the State of Vietnam," September 28, 1953, pp. 3–4, RG 59, Intelligence Report No. 6431 (hereafter cited as IR 6431).

16. Cooper, *Lost Crusade*, p. 116. See also Shaplen, *Lost Revolution*, p. 104; Fitzgerald, *Fire in the Lake*, pp. 110–11; C. J. Little (member of Far East Program Division staff) memorandum to Shannon McCune (deputy directory of Far East Program Division), September 13, 1950, box 10, Dallas M. Coors (director of Indochinese affairs) memorandum of conversation with Ngo Dinh Diem, January 30, 1951, Thomas J. Cory (member of U.S. mission to the United Nations) memorandum of conversation with Diem, June 21, 1951, box 7, Records of the Philippine and Southeast Asian Division, Country Files, RG 59, Lot 54–190; and Dean Rusk (assistant secretary of state) to Rev. Frederick A. McGuire (National Catholic Welfare Conference), October 2, 1950, RG 59, 851G.413/10–250.

17. Warner, *Last Confucian*, pp. 66–71, 96–97; Buttinger, *Vietnam*, 2:1253–55; Shaplen, *Lost Revolution*, pp. 105–13; IR 6431, pp. 12–13; "Ngo Dinh Diem," Briefing Book of Ngo Dinh Diem Visit, May 8, 1957, box 73, Subject series, White House Central Files (Confidential File), DDEL; Duncanson, *Government and Revolution in Vietnam*, pp. 103, 215.

18. Fall, "Political-Religious Sects"; IR 6431, pp. 8–11.

19. Warner, *Last Confucian*, pp. 76–77; Fall, "Political-Religious Sects," p. 250; IR 6431, p. 11; Bloodworth, *Eye for the Dragon*, pp. 210, 214.

20. Heath to Dulles, January 18, 1954, *FRUS, 1952–54*, 13:977–81.

21. Heath to Dulles, tel. 1847, March 31, 1954, RG 59, 751G.00/3–3154. See also Gerald Warner (counselor in Bangkok embassy) to Dept. of State, desp. 588, March 18, 1954, RG 59, 751G.00/3–1854; Sturm to Dulles, tel. 531, March 29, 1954, RG 59, 751G.00/3–2954; Heath to Dept. of State, desp. 428, April 2, 1954, RG 59, 751G.00/4–254; Heath to Dept. of State, desp. 435, April 5, 1954, RG 59, 751G.00/4–554; Heath to Dulles, tel. 1970, April 12, 1954, RG 59, 751G.13/4–1254; and Heath to Dulles, March 24, 1954, *FRUS, 1952–54*, 13:1152–55.

22. Report of President's Special Committee on Indochina, p. 12, enclosed in

Smith memorandum to Eisenhower, March 11, 1954, box 2, Dulles-Herter series, Ann Whitman File, Eisenhower Papers. The president's own lengthy account of the siege at Dienbienphu and the Geneva Conference focuses primarily on the strain that Indochina placed on U.S. relations with France and Britain with almost no mention of any specific Vietnamese. See Eisenhower, *Mandate for Change,* 344–74. Bao Dai and Diem are mentioned on p. 366 and Bao Dai again on p. 372.

23. In reviewing the Eisenhower Library's copy of the top secret report cited in note 22, declassification officers excised three letters from the action line that follows the quoted paragraph, but, in this context, the three letters could only be "CIA." See memorandum of meeting of the President's Special Committee on Indochina, January 29, 1954, *FRUS, 1952–54,* 13:1006. Collins (president's special representative in Vietnam) interview with author indicates that Lansdale worked initially in Vietnam under Allen Dulles' direction.

24. O'Daniel to Dulles, Army message 1173A, April 25, 1954, RG 59, 751G.00/4–2554. See also Lansdale, *In the Midst of Wars,* p. 128; and United States Department of Defense, *Pentagon Papers,* 1:574.

25. McClintock to Dulles, April 30, 1954, McClintock to Dulles, May 7, 1954, *FRUS, 1952–54,* 13:1450, 1503–4; McClintock to Dulles, tel. 2616, June 1, 1954, RG 59, 751G.00/6–154.

26. McClintock to Dulles, tel. 2207, May 4, 1954, RG 59, 751G.00/5–454. See also McClintock to Dulles, tel. 2236, May 6, 1954, RG 59, 751G.00/5–654; McClintock to Dulles, tel. 2278, May 8, 1954, RG 59, 751G.00/5–854; McClintock to Dulles, tel. 2293, May 9, 1954, RG 59, 751G.00/5–954; and McClintock to Dulles, May 6, 1954, *FRUS, 1952–54,* 13:1477–78.

27. Richard K. Stuart (member of Southeast Asian affairs staff) memorandum to Robert E. Hoey (officer in charge of Vietnam-Laos-Cambodia affairs), May 10, 1954, RG 59, 751G.00/5–1054.

28. Drumright memorandum to Robert D. Murphy (deputy under secretary of state), May 11, 1954, RG 59, 751G.00/5–1154.

29. McClintock to Dept. of State, desp. 515, May 10, 1954, RG 59, 751G.00/5–1054.

30. Discussion at the 195th NSC meeting, May 6, 1954, discussion at the 196th NSC meeting, May 8, 1954, discussion at the 197th NSC meeting, May 13, 1954, discussion at the 198th NSC meeting, May 20, 1954, National Intelligence Estimate 63–5–54, May 21, 1954, discussion at the 200th NSC meeting, June 3, 1954, discussion at the 202d NSC meeting, June 17, 1954, *FRUS, 1952–54,* 13:1481–93, 1505–11, 1547–49, 1586–90, 1595–98, 1660–62, 1713–18; Dulles to Sen. James H. Duff (R–Pa.), June 28, 1953, box 69, Dulles Papers, PUL; Heath to Dept. of State, desp. 17, July 16, 1954, RG 59, 751G.521/7–1654; Kattenburg, *Vietnam Trauma,* p. 67, n.28. For some of the theories on American efforts to secure Diem's appointment as prime minister see United States Department of Defense, *Pentagon Papers,* 1:296; Herring, *America's Longest War,* p. 49; Kahin, *Intervention,* p. 78; Cooper, *Lost Crusade,* pp. 120–21; Scheer, *How the United States Got Involved in Vietnam,* pp. 13–15; Prouty,

Secret Team, pp. 59–60; Gibbons, *U.S. Government and the Vietnam War*, 1:260–62; and Chaffard, *Indochine*, pp. 19–20, 26–29.

31. Buttinger, *Vietnam*, 2:849; Warner, *Last Confucian*, pp. 65–66; Shaplen, *Lost Revolution*, p. 101; Kattenburg, *Vietnam Trauma*, p. 53; Reinhardt (ambassador in Saigon) interview, pp. 10–11.

32. Bui Diem and Chanoff, *In the Jaws of History*, pp. 71–72, 86.

33. Lansdale interview.

34. Memorandum of conversation, May 18, 1954, *FRUS, 1952–54*, 16:846. See also Dillon to Dulles, May 12, 1954, *ibid.*, 13:1543; Bui Diem and Chanoff, *In the Jaws of History*, pp. 82–86; Cooper, *Lost Crusade*, pp. 121–27; and Karnow, *Vietnam*, pp. 217–18.

35. Bao Dai, *Le dragon d'Annam*, p. 329. (Translation is mine.)

36. Bao Dai to Smith, May 13, 1954, RG 59, 751G.00/5–1354. (Translation is mine.) For a different, published translation of this letter see Smith to Dulles, May 20, 1954, *FRUS, 1952–54*, 16:863.

37. Memorandum of conversation, May 18, 1954, *FRUS, 1952–54*, 16:843–46.

38. Bonsal memorandum to Smith, May 19, 1954, Bonsal memorandum of conversation with Luyen, May 20, 1954, *ibid.*, 848–49, 859–62.

39. Bao Dai, *Le dragon d'Annam*, p. 328; Heath memorandum of conversation, April 24, 1954, Dulles to delegation at Geneva, May 22, 1954, Bonsal memorandum of conversation with Tezenas du Montcel (French minister of the Associated States), May 22, 1954, Smith to Dulles, May 24, 1954, *FRUS, 1952–54*, 13:1384–85, 16:892–95, 900–902.

40. Dillon to Dulles, May 24, 1954, Dillon to Dulles, May 26, 1954, Dillon to Dulles, June 15, 1954, *FRUS, 1952–54*, 13:1608–9, 1614–16, 1695–96; Dillon to Dulles, tel. 4756, June 8, 1954, RG 59, 751G.00/6–854; McClintock to Dulles, tel. 2799, June 16, 1954, RG 59, 751G.00/6–1654; Dillon to Dulles, tel. 4933, June 18, 1954, RG 59, 751G.13/6–1854; Bao Dai, *Le dragon d'Annam*, pp. 328–29.

41. McClintock to Dulles, June 13, 1954, *FRUS, 1952–54*, 13:1685.

42. Heath to Dept. of State, desp. 17, July 16, 1954, RG 59, 751G.521/7–1654. See also McClintock to Dulles, June 11, 1954, Dillon to Dulles, June 20, 1954, *FRUS, 1952–54*, 13:1681, 1725–27; McClintock to Dulles, tel. 2564, May 27, 1954, RG 59, 751G.00/5–2754; Turner C. Cameron, Jr. (consul in Hanoi) to Dulles, tel. 710, June 5, 1954, RG 59, 751G.00/6–554; Cameron to Dulles, tel. 711, June 5, 1954, RG 59, 751G.00/6–554; and McClintock to Dulles, tel. 2819, June 18, 1954, RG 59, 751G.00/6–1854.

43. Dept. of State to Joseph A. Yager (adviser to delegation in Geneva), tel. 450, June 20, 1954, RG 59, 751G.00/6–2054.

44. Dillon to Dulles, May 26, 1954, *FRUS, 1952–54*, 13:1616–18.

45. Dillon to Dulles, May 24, 1954, *ibid.*, 1608–9.

46. McClintock to Dulles, tel. 2916, June 27, 1954, RG 59, 751G.00/6–2754. See also McClintock to Dulles, tel. 2918, June 27, 1954, RG 59, 751G.13/6–2754; and Lansdale, *In the Midst of Wars*, pp. 155–57.

47. Dillon to Dulles, tel. 971, September 3, 1954, RG 59, 751G.00/9–354.

48. Douglas MacArthur II (Dept. of State counselor) memorandum of conversation, May 14, 1954, McClintock to Dulles, May 25, 1954, Dillon to Dulles, June 15, 1954, Dillon to Dulles, June 21, 1954, Smith to Dulles, June 14, 1954, *FRUS, 1952–54,* 13:1562–64, 1610–11, 1695–96, 1727–28, 16:1134–36; McClintock to Dulles, tel. 2293, May 9, 1954, RG 59, 751G.00/5–954; McClintock to Dulles, tel. 2576, May 28, 1954, RG 59, 751G.00/5–2854; Bui Diem and Chanoff, *In the Jaws of History,* pp. 85–86; Cooper, *Lost Crusade,* p. 128.

49. Dillon to Dulles, June 15, 1954, *FRUS, 1952–54,* 13:1696.

50. Heath memorandum of conversation with Bao Dai, June 28, 1954, *ibid.,* 1759–61. See also McClintock to Dulles, June 29, 1954, McClintock to Dulles, July 4, 1954, *ibid.,* 1762–64, 1782–84; and McClintock to Dulles, tel. 2924, June 28, 1954, RG 59, 751G.00/6–2854.

51. Eisenhower to Gen. Alfred M. Gruenther (supreme Allied commander, Europe), June 8, 1954, *FRUS, 1952–54,* 13:1667–69.

52. McClintock to Dulles, June 24, 1954, *ibid.,* 1737–38. See also McClintock to Dulles, June 10, 1954, *ibid.,* 1674–75.

53. Murphy to Dillon, June 10, 1954, Dulles to McClintock, June 26, 1954, *ibid.,* 1678, 1752–54; Spector, *Advice and Support,* pp. 221–23.

54. Wesley R. Fishel (professor at Michigan State University) memorandum of conversation with Tran Van Do, April 14, 1971, box 27, Fishel Papers; U. Alexis Johnson (head of delegation in Geneva) to Dulles, July 2, 1954, *FRUS, 1952–54,* 16:1271–72; Bui Diem and Chanoff, *In the Jaws of History,* p. 87; Scigliano, *South Vietnam,* p. 61.

55. Fishel memorandum of conversation with Do, April 14, 1971, Do to Fishel, December 29, 1969, box 27, Fishel Papers; Johnson to Dulles, July 3, 1954, Johnson to Dulles, July 8, 1954, delegation in Geneva to Dept. of Defense, July 9, 1954, Bonsal to Dulles, July 13, 1954, *FRUS, 1952–54,* 16:1277, 1298–1300, 1313–14, 1347.

56. Dulles to C. Douglas Dillon (ambassador in Paris), June 28, 1954, *FRUS, 1952–54,* 16:1256–57. See also Eisenhower, *Mandate for Change,* p. 401; Kahin, *Intervention,* p. 54; Ambrose, *Eisenhower,* 2:207–8; United States Department of Defense, *Pentagon Papers,* 1:141–46; Hess, "Redefining the American Position in Indochina," pp. 131–36; Gardner, *Approaching Vietnam,* pp. 289–306; and Lacouture, *Mendès France,* pp. 219–30.

57. Fishel memorandum of conversation with Nguyen Huu Chau, no date, box 27, Fishel Papers. See also Fishel memorandum of conversation with Do, April 14, 1971, Do to Fishel, December 29, 1966, *ibid.;* and Smith to Dulles, July 17, 1954, Smith to Dulles, July 18, 1954, Smith to Dulles, July 20, 1954, Smith to Dulles, July 21, 1954, *FRUS, 1952–54,* 16:1418–19, 1426–28, 1439–41, 1477–78, 1494.

58. Heath to Bonsal, July 4, 1954, *FRUS, 1952–54,* 16:1280–82. For McClintock's views see McClintock to Dulles, June 24, 1954, and McClintock to Dulles, July 4, 1954, *ibid.,* 13:1734–41, 1782–84.

59. Dulles to delegation in Geneva, July 10, 1954, *ibid.*, 1324–27.

60. Discussion at the 206th NSC meeting, July 15, 1954, *ibid.*, 13:1834–40. See also United States Department of Defense, *Pentagon Papers*, 1:145–53.

61. Discussion at the 206th NSC meeting, July 15, 1954, *FRUS, 1952–54,* 13:1837.

62. Dulles to delegation at Geneva, July 16, 1954, Smith to Dulles, July 18, 1954, Smith to Dulles, July 21, 1954, *ibid.*, 16:1397–98, 1426–28, 1500–1501; Johnson and McAllister, *Right Hand of Power*, pp. 222–27.

63. For texts of these agreements see *FRUS, 1952–54,* 16:1505–42. See also Kahin, *Intervention*, p. 61.

64. Smith to Dulles, July 21, 1954, *FRUS, 1952–54,* 16:1500–1501.

65. Final Declaration on Indochina, July 21, 1954, *ibid.*, 1541. See also United States Department of Defense, *Pentagon Papers*, 1:165–66; and Sullivan, *France's Vietnam Policy*, pp. 48–50.

66. Agreement on the Cessation of Hostilities in Vietnam, July 20, 1954, *FRUS, 1952–54,* 16:1508–9.

67. Declaration of the Government of the French Republic, July 21, 1954, *ibid.*, 1545.

68. Smith to Dulles, July 21, 1954, *ibid.*, 1497–99; Fall, *Two Viet-Nams*, pp. 222–23, 232–33; Lacouture, *Mendès France*, pp. 231–41; Cable, *Geneva Conference*, pp. 123–24.

69. Quoted in Dulles, *American Policy toward Communist China*, p. 146. See also CBS Radio Division, "The Leading Question," May 16, 1954, transcript, box 7, Foreign Relations series, Mansfield Papers; and Guhin, *John Foster Dulles*, p. 249.

70. "Geneva: Failure of a Policy," speech by Mansfield, July 8, 1954, box 7, Foreign Relations series, Mansfield Papers.

71. Discussion at the 207th NSC meeting, July 22, 1954, *FRUS, 1952–54,* 13:1869–70. See also Smith statement upon arrival in Washington, July 23, 1954, *ibid.*, 16:1551–52; Herring, *America's Longest War*, pp. 41–42; and Brands, *Cold Warriors*, pp. 90–92.

72. Discussion at the 207th NSC meeting, July 22, 1954, *FRUS, 1952–54,* 13:1867–71.

73. Memorandum of telephone conversation between Foster Dulles and Allen Dulles, July 22, 1954, box 2, Telephone Conversations series, Dulles Papers, DDEL. See also Prouty, *Secret Team*, pp. 192–96.

74. Discussion at the 207th NSC meeting, July 22, 1954, *FRUS, 1952–54,* 13:1870.

4. SEATO and Other Stopgaps to Shore-up South Vietnam (June–November 1954)

1. The State Department posed most of these questions soon after the Geneva Conference in John Foster Dulles to C. Douglas Dillon (ambassador in Paris), July 28, 1954, *FRUS, 1952–54,* 13:1888–89. For studies that note the historical

significance of the post-Geneva period in shaping America's Vietnam policy see Herring, *America's Longest War*, pp. 50–51; Kahin, *Intervention*, pp. 66–70; Herring and Immerman, "Eisenhower, Dulles, and Dienbienphu," p. 363; and Cooper, *Lost Crusade*, pp. 134–44.

2. Ambrose, *Rise to Globalism*, pp. 212–15.

3. United States Department of State, *Bulletin* (August 2, 1954): 163–64.

4. United States Department of Defense, *Pentagon Papers*, 1:177–78. For NSC 5405 see *ibid.*, 434–43. On the interdepartmental working group see memorandum of telephone conversation between Foster Dulles and Allen Dulles, July 22, 1954, box 2, Telephone Conversations series, Dulles Papers, DDEL; and Dulles to Donald R. Heath (ambassador in Saigon), August 7, 1954, *FRUS 1952–54*, 13:1924–25.

5. G. Hayden Raynor (director of British Commonwealth and Northern European affairs) memorandum of conversation, June 29, 1954, *FRUS, 1952–54*, 12:585–86.

6. Memorandum of telephone conversation between Foster Dulles and Allen Dulles, July 27, 1954, box 2, Telephone Conversations series, Dulles Papers, DDEL.

7. O'Daniel to Department of the Army, July 27, 1954, *FRUS, 1952–54*, 13:1885. See also O'Daniel to Department of the Army, August 3, 1954, and National Intelligence Estimate, August 3, 1954, *ibid.*, 1903–14.

8. Heath to Dulles, July 30, 1954, Heath to Dulles, August 10, 1954, *ibid.*, 1891–92, 1932–33.

9. Review of U.S. Policy in the Far East (NSC 5429), August 12, 1954, box 12, Policy Papers subseries, NSC series, Records of the Office of the Special Assistant for National Security Affairs (OSANSA), DDEL; discussion at the 210th NSC meeting, August 12, 1954, *FRUS, 1952–54*, 12:724–33; United States Department of Defense, *Pentagon Papers*, 1:204.

10. NSC 5429, August 12, 1954, box 12, Policy Papers subseries, NSC series, Records of OSANSA.

11. Discussion at the 210th NSC meeting, August 12, 1954, *FRUS, 1952–54*, 12:728–30.

12. Discussion at the 211th NSC meeting, August 18, 1954, box 6, NSC series, Ann Whitman File, Eisenhower Papers (hereafter cited as Whitman File). For a critique of the administration's difficulties in developing a coherent national security policy that could respond effectively to a perceived Chinese threat and to local insurrection see Gurtov, *First Vietnam Crisis*, pp. 156–65.

13. See for example McMahon, "Eisenhower and Third World Nationalism"; Rabe, *Eisenhower and Latin America;* and Immerman, *CIA in Guatemala.*

14. Robert McClintock (chairman of interdepartmental working group on Indochina) memorandum of conversation, August 16, 1954, box 69, Subject series, White House Central Files (Confidential File), DDEL. See also discussion at the 210th NSC meeting, August 12, 1954, box 5, NSC series, Whitman File.

15. Dillon to Dulles, August 20, 1954, *FRUS, 1952–54*, 13:1964–66. See also Dulles to Dillon, August 18, 1954, and William R. Tyler (deputy director of

Western European affairs) memorandum of conversation, August 27, 1954, *ibid.*, 1957–59, 1991–93; Dillon interview, p. 9, DDEL; and Devillers and Lacouture, *Viet Nam*, pp. 348–51, 359–61.

16. Wilson to Dulles, August 12, 1954, Dulles to Wilson, August 18, 1954, *FRUS, 1952–54*, 13:1938–39, 1954–56.

17. Discussion at the 210th NSC meeting, August 12, 1954, *ibid.*, 12:730. See also *Life* (January 19, 1953): 106.

18. Thompson, "Strengths and Weaknesses of Eisenhower's Leadership," pp. 21–22; Melanson, "Foundations of Eisenhower's Foreign Policy," p. 58; Kinnard, "Civil-Military Relations," pp. 217–20.

19. Discussion at the 210th NSC meeting, August 12, 1954, *FRUS, 1952–54*, 12:731–32.

20. Raynor memorandum of conversation, June 29, 1954, *ibid.*, 588.

21. United States Department of State, *Bulletin* (September 20, 1954): 394–96. See also Herman Phleger (Dept. of State legal adviser) memorandum to Dulles, July 27, 1954, *FRUS, 1952–54*, 16:1552–56; and Hess, "Redefining the American Position in Southeast Asia," pp. 141–44.

22. United States Department of State, *Bulletin* (September 20, 1954): 393; Dulles to Nelson W. Aldrich (ambassador in London), July 28, 1954, Dulles memorandum of conversation with Eisenhower, August 17, 1954, *FRUS, 1952–54*, 12:680–81, 13:1953; discussion at the 214th NSC meeting, September 12, 1954, box 6, NSC series, Whitman File; Gerson, *John Foster Dulles*, pp. 195–97.

23. Bissell interview, pp. 8–11. See also United States Department of State, *Bulletin* (September 20, 1954): 393.

24. Nixon interview, p. 49. See also Goodpaster interview by Erwin, pp. 119–20, DDEL.

25. United States Senate, Committee on Foreign Relations, *Vietnam Hearings*, p. 11. See also Kahin, *Intervention*, p. 72; Gibbons, *U.S. Government and the Vietnam War*, 1:271–76; and Eisenhower, *Mandate for Change*, p. 374.

26. Dulles press conference, December 18, 1954, pp. 12–15, box 82, Dulles Papers, PUL. See also summary minute of a meeting in the office of the secretary of state, October 8, 1954, *FRUS, 1952–54*, 13:2125; Kahin, *Intervention*, pp. 70–71, 75; Melanson, "Foundations of Eisenhower's Foreign Policy," pp. 54–55; Spanier, *American Foreign Policy*, pp. 92–93; and Eisenhower, *Waging Peace*, p. 364.

27. Eisenhower, *Mandate for Change*, pp. 402–9, 459–66; Ambrose, *Eisenhower*, 2:212–14; Dulles, *American Policy toward Communist China*, pp. 149–52.

28. *Cleveland Plain Dealer*, November 14, 1971.

29. Paul M. Kattenburg (Philippine and Southeast Asian affairs [PSA] staff) memorandum for Robert E. Hoey (officer in charge of Vietnam-Laos-Cambodia affairs), July 7, 1954, United States Department of State General Records, Record Group 59, 611.51G/7–754 (hereafter cited as RG 59 with file number).

30. Fishel manuscript, no title or date, box 8, Fishel Papers. See also Scigliano and Fox, *Technical Assistance in Vietnam*, pp. 1–2.

31. Gibbons, *U.S. Government and the Vietnam War*, 1:90; Warren Hinckle et al., "The University on the Make," *Ramparts* (April 1966): 11–22. For Fishel's denials of CIA membership see Fishel to Lansdale, April 6, 1967, box 53, Lansdale Papers; Fishel to editor of *Providence Journal*, May 12, 1966, box 28, Fishel Papers; and clipping from *National Observer*, April 18, 1966, box 55, Hannah Records.

32. Jack W. Lydman (PSA staff) memorandum to Hoey, July 16, 1954, RG 59, 611.51G/7–1654; American Friends of Vietnam biography of Dr. Wesley Robert Fishel, no date, box 27, Fishel Papers; Heath to Dulles, tel. 830, August 31, 1954, RG 59, 751G.oo/8–3154; Gen. J. Lawton Collins (president's special representative in Vietnam) to Dulles, tel. 1876, November 18, 1954, box 1, Collins Papers.

33. Collins interview with author.

34. Lansdale interview.

35. Lansdale, *In the Midst of Wars*, pp. 157–59. See also United States Department of Defense, *Pentagon Papers*, 1:573–83; Charlton and Moncrieff, *Many Reasons Why*, pp. 55–56; and Prouty, *Secret Team*, p. 174.

36. Lacouture, *Vietnam*, p. 66. See also William M. Gibson (first secretary of the embassy in Paris) memorandum of conversation, November 30, 1954, *FRUS, 1952–54*, 13:2330–34.

37. Lansdale, *In the Midst of Wars*, p. 129. See also Charlton and Moncrieff, *Many Reasons Why*, pp. 42–43; and Lansdale, "Thoughts about a Past War," p. xiv. For some accounts of Lansdale's activities see Currey, *Lansdale*; Gibbons, *U.S. Government and the Vietnam War*, 1:141–42, 259–64; Shaplen, *Lost Revolution*, pp. 101–4, 111–16; Fitzgerald, *Fire in the Lake*, pp. 102–6; Wise and Ross, *Invisible Government*, pp. 156–57; Karnow, *Vietnam*, pp. 220–24; and Ambrose and Immerman, *Ike's Spies*, pp. 245–48.

38. Fall, *Viet-Nam Witness*, pp. 59–60. See also Heath to Dulles, tel. 83, July 7, 1954, and Heath to Dulles, tel. 85, July 7, 1954, RG 59, 751G.02/7–754.

39. Kahin, *Intervention*, pp. 75–77; Gibbons, *U.S. Government and the Vietnam War*, 1:265–66; Charlton and Moncrieff, *Many Reasons Why*, pp. 44–45; Hooper, Allard, and Fitzgerald, *United States Navy and the Vietnam Conflict*, 1:270–99; Dooley, *Deliver Us from Evil*; O'Daniel, *Nation That Refused to Starve*, pp. 37–55.

40. Dillon to Dulles, August 20, 1954, *FRUS, 1952–54*, 13:1966. See also Heath to Dulles, August 17, 1954, *ibid.*, 1951–52; and Kahin, *Intervention*, p. 77.

41. Heath to Dulles, tel. 751, August 26, 1954, and Heath to Dulles, tel. 752, August 26, 1954, RG 59, 751G.oo/8–2654. See also Dillon to Dulles, tel. 420, July 29, 1954, RG 59, 751G.oo/7–2954; and Hammer, *Death in November*, pp. 64–69.

42. Heath to Dulles, August 27, 1954, *FRUS, 1952–54*, 13:1990–91. See

also Heath to Dulles, August 29, 1954, and Heath to Dulles, August 31, 1954, *ibid.*, 1995–96, 1999–2000; Heath to Dulles, tel. 780, August 27, 1954, RG 59, 751G.00/8–2754; Heath to Dulles, tel. 790, August 28, 1954, RG 59, 751G.00/8–2854; and Heath to Dulles, tel. 833, August 31, 1954, RG 59, 751G.00/8–3154.

43. Douglas MacArthur II (Dept. of State counselor) memorandum of conversation, September 6, 1954, *FRUS, 1952–54*, 13:2007–10. See also Heath to Dulles, August 27, 1954, *ibid.*, 1988–90; and Heath to Dulles, tel. 850, September 1, 1954, RG 59, 751G.00/9–154.

44. Heath to Dulles, September 9, 1954, Heath to Dulles, September 10, 1954, Heath to Dulles, September 11, 1954, *FRUS, 1952–54*, 13:2014–16, 2018–20.

45. Heath to Dulles, September 16, 1954, *ibid.*, 2030–31.

46. Heath to Dulles, tel. 991, September 13, 1954, RG 59, 751G.00/9–1354; Heath to Dulles, tel. 1023, September 15, 1954, RG 59, 751G.00/9–1554; Heath to Dulles, tel. 1099, September 18, 1954, RG 59, 751G.13/9–1854; Heath to Dulles, October 13, 1954, *FRUS, 1952–54*, 13:2135–38; Heath to Dulles, October 27, 1954, RG 59, 751G.00/10–2754; Fishel memorandum to Collins, March 7, 1955, *FRUS, 1955–57*, 1:111–13; Lansdale interview.

47. Jack K. McFall (U.S. United Nations delegation) memorandum of conversation, September 23, 1954, *FRUS, 1952–54*, 12:918–19. See also Agreement on the Cessation of Hostilities in Vietnam, July 20, 1954, Heath to Dulles, September 5, 1954, Heath to Dulles, September 17, 1954, Walter Bedell Smith (acting secretary of state) to Dillon, September 17, 1954, *ibid.*, 16:1508–9, 13:2004–5, 2033–35; and Heath to Dulles, tel. 1059, September 17, 1954, RG 59, 751G.13/9–1754.

48. Dulles memorandum of conversation with Mendès-France, October 3, 1954, *FRUS, 1952–54*, 13:2115. See also Smith to Heath, September 28, 1954, and Smith to Dillon, September 28, 1954, *ibid.*, 2080–84.

49. Heath to Dulles, tel. 1401, October 10, 1954, RG 59, 751G.00/10–1054; Herbert Hoover, Jr., (acting secretary of state) to Heath, tel. 1516, October 12, 1954, RG 59, 751G.00/10–1254; Heath to Dulles, October 13, 1954, Hoover to Dulles, October 21, 1954, *FRUS, 1952–54*, 13:2135–38, 2149–51; minutes of Cabinet meeting, October 19, 1954, box 4, Cabinet series, Whitman File; Devillers and Lacouture, *Viet Nam*, pp. 362–69.

50. Heath to Dulles, September 13, 1954, Heath to Dulles, September 18, 1954, Heath to Dulles, September 23, 1954, Dulles memorandum of conversation with Mendès-France, October 3, 1954, *FRUS, 1952–54*, 13:2025, 2035–37, 2048, 2115; Smith to Dillon, tel. 1074, RG 59, 751G.13/9–2354; Heath to Dulles, September 24, 1954, RG 59, 751G.13/9–2454.

51. Heath to Dulles, September 29, 1954, *FRUS, 1952–54*, 13:2092–93. See also Dillon to Dulles, September 24, 1954, Smith to Heath, September 28, 1954, and Turner C. Cameron, Jr., (chargé d'affaires in Saigon) to Dulles, October 1, 1954, *ibid.*, 2056–57, 2085–86, 2105–6.

52. Dillon to Dulles, October 4, 1954, Cameron to Dulles, October 7, 1954, *ibid.*, 2115–18.

53. Discussion at the 215th NSC meeting, September 24, 1954, *ibid.*, 2058–59.

54. Vice Adm. Arthur C. Davis (deputy assistant secretary of defense) to Dulles, October 20, 1954, *ibid.*, 2146–47. See also Dulles to Wilson, October 11, 1954, and Robert Cutler (special assistant to the president for national security affairs) memorandum for the record, October 19, 1954, *ibid.*, 2132–35, 2142.

55. United States Senate, Committee on Foreign Relations, *Report on Indochina*, pp. 11, 14–15. See also Special National Intelligence Estimate, September 15, 1954, Mansfield to Dulles, September 24, 1954, Robertson memorandum to Dulles, September 25, 1954, summary minute of a meeting at the Dept. of State, September 25, 1954, *FRUS, 1952–54*, 13:2028–30, 2055–56, 2061–70; Dulles memorandum, August 23, 1954, box 3, General Correspondence and Memoranda series, Dulles Papers, DDEL; and Judd interview.

56. Heath to Dulles, October 22, 1954, *FRUS, 1952–54*, 13:2151–53.

57. Discussion at the 215th NSC meeting, September 24, 1954, *ibid.*, 2059. See also Smith to Heath, tel. 857, September 1, 1954, RG 59, 751G.00/9–154; and Gardner, *Approaching Vietnam*, 324.

58. Heath to Robertson, September 16, 1954, RG 59, 751G.00/9–1654. See also Heath to Dulles, tel. 987, September 13, 1954, RG 59, 751G.00/9–1354; Heath to Dulles, tel. 1067, September 17, 1954, RG 59, 751G.13/9–1754; O'Daniel interview, pp. 17–19; and Gurtov, *First Vietnam Crisis*, pp. 133–34.

59. Heath to Dulles, tel. 1226, September 25, 1954, RG 59, 751G.00/0–2554; Heath to Dulles, September 23, 1954, Heath to Dulles, September 27, 1954, *FRUS, 1952–54*, 13:2048–52, 2075–78; United States Department of Defense, *Pentagon Papers*, 1:577–78.

60. Charlton and Moncrieff, *Many Reasons Why*, pp. 42, 45–46. See also Kahin, *Intervention*, p. 81.

61. Discussion at the 218th NSC meeting, October 22, 1954, *FRUS, 1952–54, 13*:2153–58.

62. Discussion at State–JCS meeting, August 20, 1954, Livingston T. Merchant (assistant secretary of state for European affairs) memorandum of conversation, October 23, 1954, Dillon to Dulles, October 23, 1954, Eisenhower to Diem, undated, Dillon to Dulles, October 24, 1954, Dillon to Dulles, October 25, 1954, Dulles to Dillon, October 29, 1954, *ibid.*, 1962–64, 2164–69, 2176–81, 2193–94; Devillers and Lacouture, *Viet Nam*, p. 379; Mélandri, "Repercussions of the Geneva Conference."

63. Discussion at the 219th NSC meeting, October 26, 1954, *FRUS, 1952–54, 13*:2183–86.

64. MacArthur memorandum of conversation, October 30, 1954, *ibid.*, 2194–95. See also Goodpaster interview by Erwin, pp. 115–17, DDEL; and Gibbons, *U.S. Government and the Vietnam War*, 1:286.

65. Collins, *Lightning Joe*, p. 344; Goodpaster interview, p. 35, PUL; Eisenhower to Collins, February 20, 1948, Eisenhower to Chevy Chase Club, April 29, 1948, Eisenhower to Collins, March 15, 1952, Collins to Eisenhower, March 21, 1952, box 25, Name series, Eisenhower Pre-Presidential Papers.

66. Eisenhower to Collins, November 3, 1954, *FRUS, 1952–54*, 13:2205–7.

67. Dulles to Dillon, November 1, 1954, *ibid.*, 2200–2201; Bernard M. Shanley (president's special counsel) memorandum to Herbert G. Brownell (attorney general), November 3, 1954, J. William Barba (White House staff) memorandum for record, no date, Eisenhower to Collins, November 22, 1954, box 69, Subject series, White House Central Files (Confidential File), DDEL.

68. Collins, *Lightning Joe*, p. 379.

69. Eisenhower to Collins, November 3, 1954, *FRUS, 1952–54*, 13:2207. See also Goodpaster memorandum of conference at the residence of the secretary of state, October 31, 1954, *ibid.*, 2198–99; Goodpaster memorandum of conference with the president, November 3, 1954, box 3, Diary series, Whitman File; and Collins interview, pp. 3–5, PUL.

70. Heath to Dulles, tel. 1643, October 29, 1954, RG 59, 751G.00/10–2954.

5. The Collins Mission and Washington's "Point of No Return" (November 1954–May 1955)

1. Collins interview with author. See also Lansdale, *In the Midst of Wars*, pp. 203–7; and O'Daniel interview, pp. 19–20.

2. Robert Scheer and Warren Hinckle, "The Viet-Nam Lobby," *Ramparts* (July 1965): 16–24; John Foster Dulles memorandum, August 23, 1954, box 3, General Correspondence and Memoranda series, Dulles Papers, DDEL; Mike Mansfield to Dulles, September 24, 1954, Dulles to Donald R. Heath, October 30, 1954, *FRUS, 1952–54*, 13:2055–56, 2196; Dulles to Heath, tel. 1761, October 28, 1954, United States Department of States General Records, Record Group 59, 751G.00/10–2854 (hereafter cited as RG 59 with file number); C. Douglas Dillon (ambassador in Paris) to Dulles, tel. 1833, October 30, 1954, RG 59, 751G.00/10–3054; Dillon to Dulles, tel. 1908, November 4, 1954, RG 59, 751G.00/11–454.

3. Dillon to Dulles, November 5, 1954, Collins to Dulles, November 12, 1954, *FRUS, 1952–54*, 13:2210–13, 2238–41; Dillon to Dulles, tel. 1841, October 30, 1954, RG 59, 751G.00/10–3054; Dillon to Dulles, tel. 1908, November 4, 1954, RG 59, 751G.00/11–454; Collins to Dulles, tel. 1915, November 20, 1954, RG 59, 751G.00/11–2054; Collins to Dulles, tel. 1819, November 13, 1954, Collins to Dulles, tel. 2006, November 29, 1954, box 1, Collins Papers; Collins, *Lightning Joe*, pp. 385–86.

4. Eisenhower to Collins, November 3, 1954, *FRUS, 1952–54*, 13:2206.

5. Fall, *Viet-Nam Witness*, p. 278.

6. Heath to Dulles, November 7, 1954, *FRUS, 1952–54*, 13:2221–24.

7. Dillon to Livingston T. Merchant (assistant secretary of state for European affairs), December 3, 1954, *ibid.*, 2333. See also Heath to Dulles, November 3,

1954, *ibid.*, 2203–4; Thomas J. Corcoran (consul in Hanoi) to Dulles, tel. 684, January 21, 1955, RG 59, 751G.00/1–2155; Collins, *Lightning Joe,* pp. 384–85; Ely, *Mémoires,* pp. 294–300; and Devillers and Lacouture, *Viet Nam,* pp. 380–82.

8. Collins to Dulles, November 16, 1954, Dulles to Collins, November 20, 1954, Dulles to Collins, November 22, 1954, Collins to Dulles, December 14, 1954, Dillon to Dulles, December 17, 1954, *FRUS, 1952–54,* 13:2259–62, 2274–75, 2277–79, 2366–68, 2387–90; Collins to Dulles, February 11, 1955, *FRUS, 1955–57,* 1:84–86; Collins, *Lightning Joe,* pp. 386–87; Spector, *Advice and Support,* pp. 238–40; Devillers and Lacouture, *Viet Nam,* pp. 386–99; Rouanet, *Mendès France au pouvoir,* pp. 485–93; Ruscio, "Le Mendèsisme et l'Indochine," pp. 338–42.

9. Dillon to Dulles, November 15, 1954, Collins to Dulles, November 29, 1954, Dillon to Dept. of State, December 19, 1954, *FRUS, 1952–54,* 13:2246–50, 2315–19, 2400–2405; Dillon to Dulles, January 6, 1955, Collins to Dulles, January 10, 1955, William J. Sebald (deputy assistant secretary of state) memorandum to Dulles, January 17, 1955, Dillon to Dulles, October 31, 1955, *FRUS, 1955–57,* 1:19–20, 30–32, 41–45, 568–71; Collins, *Lightning Joe,* p. 392; Spector, *Advice and Support,* p. 236; Devillers and Lacouture, *Viet Nam,* pp. 370–78.

10. Collins to Dulles, December 6, 1954, *FRUS, 1952–54,* 13:2341–44. See also Collins to Dulles, November 15, 1954, *ibid.,* 2250.

11. Fishel memorandum to Collins, December 16, 1954, box 6, Collins Papers. See also Collins to Dulles, November 20, 1954, *FRUS, 1952–54,* 13:2272. Cooley (intelligence analyst on Collins's personal staff) interview includes recollection of Quat as being Sturm's candidate for an alternative to Diem for U.S. support.

12. Collins to Dulles, December 16, 1954, *FRUS, 1952–54,* 13:2379–82. See also Collins to Dulles, December 13, 1954, *ibid.,* 2362–66; Young to Collins, December 15, 1954, *FRUS, 1955–57,* 1:1–3; Collins to Dulles, tel. 2006, November 29, 1954, box 1, Lansdale memorandum to Collins, December 4, 1954, box 4, Fishel memorandum to Collins, December 10, 1954, box 6, Collins Papers; and Bui Diem and Chanoff, *In the Jaws of History,* p. 89.

13. Heath memorandum to Robertson, December 17, 1954, *FRUS, 1952–54,* 13:2391–92. See also Young memorandum of conversation, December 7, 1954, Herbert Hoover, Jr., (under secretary of state) to Collins, December 15, 1954, and Hoover to Dillon, December 17, 1954, *ibid.,* 2350–52, 2378–79, 2393–94.

14. Hoover to Dillon, December 17, 1954, *ibid.,* 2394–96.

15. Dulles to Collins, December 23, 1954, *ibid.,* 2415. See also Dulles to Collins, December 24, 1954, McClintock to Dulles, December 24, 1954, and Dillon to Dulles, December 30, 1954, *ibid.,* 2419–23, 2437–40; and discussion at the 229th National Security Council (NSC) meeting, December 21, 1954, box 6, NSC series, Ann Whitman File, Eisenhower Papers (hereafter cited as Whitman File).

16. Collins to Dulles, tel. 2811, January 17, 1955, box 3, Collins Papers. See also Collins to Dulles, tel. 2388, December 21, 1954, Collins to Dulles, tel. 2583, January 6, 1955, box 1, *ibid.*; and Collins to Dulles, January 15, 1955, *FRUS, 1955–57,* 1:37–40.

17. Collins report on Vietnam for the NSC, January 20, 1955, *FRUS, 1955–57,* 1:54–57.

18. Discussion at the 234th NSC meeting, January 27, 1955, *ibid.*, 66.

19. Young memorandum to Robertson, January 19, 1955, RG 59, 751G.00/1–1955; Collins, *Lightning Joe,* pp. 395–97; Eisenhower to Diem, February 3, 1955, box 3, Collins Papers; Collins interview by U.S. Army Military History Institute, pp. 412–17.

20. Discussion at the 234th NSC meeting, January 27, 1955, *FRUS, 1955–57,* 1:66. See also Collins report on Vietnam for the NSC, January 20, 1955, *ibid.*, 54–55.

21. Kidder to Dulles, tel. 3102, February 1, 1955, box 1, Collins Papers. See also Paul J. Sturm memorandum to Collins, December 16, 1954, box 5, and Kidder to Dulles, tel. 3190, February 4, 1955, box 1, *ibid.*; and Hammer, *Struggle for Indochina,* pp. 346–48.

22. Collins, *Lightning Joe,* pp. 397–98; Spector, *Advice and Support,* pp. 243–45; Buttinger, *Vietnam,* 2:865–68; Currey, *Lansdale,* pp. 172–73.

23. Dulles to Dept. of State, March 1, 1955, *FRUS, 1955–57,* 1:102. See also Young and Kidder memorandum of conversation, March 1, 1955, *ibid.*, 103–4; and Dulles statement upon arrival at Saigon, February 28, 1955, box 91, Dulles Papers, PUL.

24. Collins to Young, March 10, 1955, RG 59, 751G.00/3–1055.

25. Dulles, "Report from Asia," March 8, 1955, p. 8, box 99, Dulles Papers, PUL. See also Dulles to Eisenhower, March 1, 1955, *FRUS, 1955–57,* 1:97.

26. Dulles to Collins, draft cable, March 8, 1955, box 11, Chronological series, Dulles Papers, DDEL. See also Kidder to Dulles, March 4, 1955, *FRUS, 1955–57,* 1:106–8; proclamation of the Binh Xuyen, Cao Dai, and Hoa Hao sects, March 4, 1955, box 5, Collins Papers; and *Vietnam Presse,* March 5, 1955.

27. Collins to Dulles, March 10, 1955, *FRUS, 1955–57,* 1:119–22; Collins to Dulles, tel. 3798, March 10, 1955, box 1, Collins Papers; Kidder to Dept. of State, desp. 221, January 10, 1955, RG 59, 751G.00/1–1055.

28. Lansdale memorandum to Collins, March 11, 1955, box 4, Sturm memorandum of conversation, March 18, 1955, box 5, Lt. Joe Redick (Saigon) memorandum to Lansdale, March 19, 1955, box 4, Collins to Dulles, tel. 4011, March 20, 1955, box 1, Cooley memorandum to Collins, March 21, 1955, box 5, Collins Papers; Collins to Dulles, March 15, 1955, *FRUS, 1955–57,* 1:125–28.

29. Collins to Dulles, tel. 4039, March 22, 1955, Collins to Dulles, tel. 4050, March 23, 1955, Collins to Dulles, tel. 4053, March 23, 1955, Collins to Dulles,

tel. 4096, March 24, 1955, box 1, Collins Papers; Collins to Dulles, March 23, 1955, *FRUS, 1955–57*, 1:142–43.

30. Collins to Dulles, tel. 4138, March 26, 1955, box 1, Collins Papers; Lansdale memorandum to Collins, March 27, 1955, Collins to Dulles, March 29, 1955, Collins to Dulles, March 30, 1955, *FRUS, 1955–57*, 1:148–49, 158–63.

31. Collins to Dulles, March 30, 1955, *FRUS, 1955–57*, 1:159–63. See also Sturm memorandum of conversation, March 25, 1955, *ibid.*, 145–46; Collins to Dulles, tel. 4112, March 25, 1955, box 1, Collins Papers; and Kidder to Dulles, tel. 3264, February 8, 1955, RG 59, 751G.00/2–855.

32. Collins to Dulles, March 30, 1955, Collins to Dulles, March 31, 1955, *FRUS, 1955–57*, 1:163, 171–74; USARMA Saigon to Dulles, tel. MC 952–55, March 30, 1955, RG 59, 751G.00/3–3055; Collins to Dulles, tel. 4220, March 30, 1955, Collins to Dulles, tel. 4241, March 31, 1955, box 1, Collins Papers; Collins, *Lightning Joe*, pp. 400–401; Ely, *Mémoires*, pp. 305–7; Lansdale, *In the Midst of Wars*, pp. 260–67.

33. Collins to Dulles, tel. 4220, March 30, 1955, Collins to Dulles, tel. 4242, March 31, 1955, box 1, Collins Papers; Collins to Dulles, March 30, 1955, *FRUS, 1955–57*, 1:164–67.

34. Collins to Dulles, March 31, 1955, *FRUS, 1955–57*, 1:168–71.

35. Dulles telephone conversation with Eisenhower, April 1, 1955, box 10, Telephone Conversations series (White House), Dulles Papers, DDEL. See also Ambrose, *Eisenhower*, 2:231–46; and Gordon, "United States Opposition to Use of Force in the Taiwan Strait," pp. 637–41.

36. Collins to Dulles, April 2, 1955, *FRUS, 1955–57*, 1:180–89.

37. Dulles to Collins, April 3, 1955, *FRUS, 1955–57*, 1:190–93; Theodore C. Achilles (minister in Paris) to Dulles, tel. 4285, April 2, 1955, Achilles to Collins, tel. 630, April 3, 1955, box 3, Collins Papers; "Rift with French Widens in Saigon," *New York Times*, April 5, 1955.

38. Dulles memorandum of conversation with Eisenhower, April 4, 1955, box 3, White House Memoranda series, Dulles Papers, DDEL.

39. Dulles to Collins, April 4, 1955, *FRUS, 1955–57*, 1:196–97. See also Devillers and Lacouture, *Viet Nam*, p. 378.

40. Ambrose, *Eisenhower*, 2:251–52; Nelson, "John Foster Dulles and the Bipartisan Congress"; Collins, *Lightning Joe*, p. 388.

41. Collins to Dulles, April 7, 1955, *FRUS, 1955–57*, 1:218–21. See also Collins to Dulles, April 7, 1955, Collins to Dulles, April 12, 1955, *ibid.*, 215–18, 244; Collins to Dulles, tel. 5223, May 12, 1955, box 3, Collins Papers; and Collins interview with author.

42. Collins to Dulles, tel. 4448, April 9, 1955, box 3, Collins Papers. See also Dulles to Collins, tel. 4412, April 8, 1955, *ibid.*

43. Dulles to Collins, tel. 4438, April 9, 1955, box 3, Collins Papers.

44. Collins to Dulles, April 10, 1955, *FRUS, 1955–57*, 1:231–35.

45. Foster Dulles memorandum of telephone conversation with Allen Dulles, April 11, 1955, *ibid.*, 235.

46. Young memorandum to Robertson, April 11, 1955, RG 59, 751G.oo/
4–1155. See also Dulles to Collins, draft telegram, April 11, 1955, *FRUS,
1955–57*, 1:236; and Dulles memorandum of conversation with Eisenhower,
April 11, 1955, box 3, White House Memoranda series, Dulles Papers,
DDEL.

47. Dulles to Collins, April 11, 1955, *FRUS, 1955–57*, 1:239–41; Dulles
memorandum of telephone conversation with Robertson, April 11, 1955, box 3,
Telephone Conversations series, Dulles Papers, DDEL.

48. Collins to Dulles, April 14, 1955, *FRUS, 1955–57*, 1:248–49. See also
Dulles to Collins, April 12, 1955, *ibid.*, 247–48; and Sturm memorandum for
the record, April 14, 1955, box 5, Collins Papers.

49. Dulles memorandum of conversation with Eisenhower, April 17, 1955,
box 3, White House Memoranda series, Dulles Papers, DDEL.

50. In addition to the document cited in note 49, see also Dulles to Collins,
April 16, 1955, *FRUS, 1955–57*, 1:250–51; and James C. Hagerty (presidential
press secretary) Diary, April 12–20, 1955, pp. 5–7, Hagerty Papers.

51. Collins to Dulles, April 19, 1955, *FRUS, 1955–57*, 1:260–70. The quotation is from p. 270.

52. Mansfield memorandum for the record, April 1, 1955, *ibid.*, 176–77. See
also Young to Dulles, March 23, 1955, Young memorandum for Robertson,
April 1, 1955, and Young memorandum of conversation, April 11, 1955, *ibid.*,
144, 177–78, 221–222; and Mansfield interview, pp. 7–10, PUL.

53. Dulles to Collins, April 20, 1955, *FRUS, 1955–57*, 1:270–72 (Dulles'
italics). See also Dulles to Collins, tel. 4603, April 18, 1955, box 3, Collins
Papers.

54. C. L. Sulzberger, "Vietnam's Crisis Harms Our Relations with France,"
New York Times, April 18, 1955. "Point of no return" quotation is from Dulles
to Collins, April 4, 1955, *FRUS, 1955–57*, 1:196.

55. Vice Adm. A. C. Davis (deputy assistant secretary of defense) memorandum to H. Struve Hensel (assistant secretary of defense), April 25, 1955, *FRUS,
1955–57*, 1:284–87. See also William M. Gibson (first secretary of Paris embassy) memorandum of conversation, April 21, 1955, and Young memorandum
for Robertson, April 30, 1955, *ibid.*, 272–76, 337; and Dillon to Dulles, tel.
4576, April 21, 1955, box 3, Collins Papers.

56. Dillon Anderson (special assistant to the president for national security
affairs) memorandum for the record, April 22, 1955, box 1, Chronological
subseries, Special Assistant series, Records of the Office of the Special Assistant
for National Security Affairs, DDEL. See also Sebald memorandum for Dulles,
April 23, 1955, *FRUS, 1955–57*, 1:281, and Hoover memorandum for Dulles,
April 23, 1955, RG 59, 751G.oo/4–2355.

57. Mansfield memorandum for the record, April 21, 1955, *FRUS, 1955–57*,
1:277.

58. Dulles to Dillon, April 27, 1955, *ibid.*, 294–96. See also Dulles to Dillon,
April 27, 1955, and Young memorandum to Robertson, April 30, 1955, *ibid.*,
297–98, 337–38; Legislative Leadership meeting, supplementary notes, April

26, 1955, box 1, Legislative Meetings series, Whitman File; Collins, *Lightning Joe*, p. 405; and Shaplen, *Lost Revolution*, pp. 122–23.

59. Dulles to Dillon, April 27, 1955, Dulles to Dillon, April 28, 1955, *FRUS, 1955–57*, 1:301, 312–14; Foster Dulles telephone conversations with Allen Dulles, April 28, 1955, and Collins, April 28, 1955, box 3, Telephone Conversations series, Dulles Papers, DDEL.

60. Dillon to Dulles, April 30, 1955, *FRUS, 1955–57*, 1:332–36; Ely, *Mémoires*, pp. 311–12; Shaplen, *Lost Revolution*, pp. 124–25.

61. Kidder to Dulles, tel. 4780, April 24, 1955, box 3, Collins Papers; Kidder to Dulles, tel. 4805, April 26, 1955, Kidder to Dulles, tel. 4845, April 27, 1955, box 1, *ibid.*; A. M. Rosenthal, "Rebels in Saigon Face Curbs Today," *New York Times*, April 28, 1955; Bloodworth, *Eye for the Dragon*, pp. 211–15.

62. Buttinger, *Vietnam*, 2:879; editorial note, *FRUS, 1955–57*, 1:302.

63. Ely's report in Kidder to Dulles, April 28, 1955, *FRUS, 1955–57*, 1:303–5. For Lansdale's description see Lansdale, *In the Midst of Wars*, pp. 282–83. Lansdale gives the location of the fighting as place Khai-Dinh, which was a major intersection on rue Petrus Ky.

64. Kidder to Dulles, tel. 4860, April 28, 1955, box 3, Collins Papers; Kidder to Dulles, April 29, 1955, *FRUS, 1955–57*, 1:315–16; Warner, *Last Confucian*, p. 82; Scigliano, *South Vietnam*, p. 21.

65. Lansdale, *In the Midst of Wars*, pp. 282–84. Currey, *Lansdale*, pp. 174–77, basically follows Lansdale's account but makes several factual errors, including confusing the events of March 29–30 and April 28.

66. Robertson to Gen. Nathan F. Twining (Air Force chief of staff), September 13, 1956, box 35, Lansdale Papers. See also Shaplen, *Lost Revolution*, pp. 122–24; and Dulles to Dillon, tel. 3837, April 27, 1955, RG 59, 751G.00/4–2755.

67. Lansdale, *In the Midst of Wars*, p. 289; Fisher Howe memorandum, April 28, 1955, and editorial note, *FRUS, 1955–57*, 1:281; 301–3.

68. Collins interview with author. For more on Lansdale's "channel" see United States Department of Defense, *Pentagon Papers*, 1:574; Homer Bigart, "Rise of Vietnam's Religious Crisis Caught Many by Surprise," *New York Times*, August 22, 1963; and Fishel to Lansdale, April 15, 1955, box 35, Lansdale Papers.

69. Barrows (director, U.S. Operations Mission, Vietnam) interview. See also Dillon to Dulles, tel. 4767, May 2, 1955, box 3, Collins Papers; Preston Grover, "U.S. Believes Diem Can Save Indochina from Communists," *Newport News (VA) Times-Herald*, June 15, 1955, clipping, box 35, Lansdale Papers; and Bao Dai, *Le dragon d'Annam*, pp. 334–35, 339.

70. Discussion at the 246th NSC meeting, April 28, 1955, *FRUS, 1955–57*, 1:307–10.

71. *Ibid.*, 310–12. Collins' prediction that the Binh Xuyen would become guerrillas proved correct, and in 1960 the gang became part of the National Liberation Front or Vietcong. See Pike, *Viet Cong*, pp. 69, 435; and Karnow, *Vietnam*, p. 223.

72. Kidder manuscript. See also Kidder to Dulles, April 30, 1955, Kidder to Dulles, May 1, 1955, *FRUS, 1955–57*, 1:327–28, 340–44; and Frédéric-Dupont, *Mission de la France en Asie*, p. 218.

73. Speech prepared for Senate delivery by Senator Mansfield, April 29, 1955, box 121, Smith Papers. See also Gibbons, *U.S. Government and the Vietnam War*, 1:297.

74. O'Daniel to Adm. Robert B. Carney (chief of naval operations), April 29, 1955, Young memorandum for Robertson, April 30, 1955, *FRUS, 1955–57*, 1:324–25, 337–39. Lansdale also sent a similar message on April 29. See Lansdale, *In the Midst of Wars*, p. 300.

75. Dulles to Dillon, April 30, 1955, *FRUS, 1955–57*, 1:340. See also "U.S. Still Backing Vietnam Premier," *New York Times*, April 29, 1955. For an extremely biased but fascinating account of some of the behind-the-scenes maneuvering see du Berrier, *Background to Betrayal*, pp. 91–108. Du Berrier acted as interpreter for Luyen's agent.

76. Dulles to Collins, May 1, 1955, *FRUS, 1955–57*, 1:344–45. See also Young memorandum to Robertson, April 30, 1955, *ibid.*, 338.

77. Kidder to Dulles, April 29, 1955, *FRUS, 1955–57*, 1:316–19. See also Kidder to Dulles, April 30, 1955, Kidder memorandum of conversation, May 3, 1955, Collins to Dulles, May 3, 1955, *ibid.*, 325–26, 350–53; Collins to Dulles, tel. 5006, May 2, 1955, box 3, Collins Papers; Collins, *Lightning Joe*, pp. 406–7; Lansdale, *In the Midst of Wars*, pp. 299–311; and Buttinger, *Vietnam*, 2:880–85.

78. Collins to Dulles, May 5, 1955, *FRUS, 1955–57*, 1:362–68. Collins' views buttressed the CIA's Special National Intelligence Estimate, May 2, 1955, *ibid.*, 346–50. See also Collins, *Lightning Joe*, pp. 407–8.

79. Dulles to Dept. of State, May 12, 1955, *FRUS, 1955–57*, 1:401–5. See also Dulles to Dept. of State, May 8, 1955, Dillon to Dept. of State, May 11, 1955, *ibid.*, 372–78, 393–99; Hoover to Dulles, tel. 26, May 12, 1955, RG 59, 751G.00/5–1255; and Colard, *Edgar Faure*, pp. 70–71.

80. Dulles memorandum of conversation with M. Faure, May 11, 1955, box 9, Subject series, Dulles Papers, DDEL.

81. Dulles to Dept. of State, May 13, 1955, *FRUS, 1955–57*, 1:406–9; Winthrop W. Aldrich (ambassador in London) to Dulles, tel. 5031, May 15, 1955, RG 59, 751G.00/5–1555.

82. Dulles, "An Historic Week—Report to the President," May 17, 1955, pp. 4–5, box 91, Dulles Papers, PUL. See also Dulles to Eisenhower, May 12, 1955, *FRUS, 1955–57*, 1:399–400; Collins, *Lightning Joe*, pp. 406–9; and Sullivan, *France's Vietnam Policy*, pp. 55–57.

83. Hane interview, pp. 197, 201; "John Foster Dulles and the Far East," p. 55, Dulles Oral History Project; Shaplen, *Lost Revolution*, pp. 127–28.

84. Scigliano, *South Vietnam*, p. 22; Tran Van Don, *Our Endless War*, pp. 62–65; Kahin, *Intervention*, pp. 93–101; Halberstam, *Best and the Brightest*, pp. 286–93; Karnow, *Vietnam*, p. 265.

85. For a detailed and perceptive account of Ely's efforts during the spring of 1955 see Artaud, "Spring 1955."

86. Lansdale to Shaplen, May 30, 1965, box 39, Lansdale Papers. See also Lansdale, *In the Midst of Wars*, pp. 202–7, 301. Ely disagreed with Lansdale. See Ely, *Mémoires*, pp. 316–17.

87. Collins interview with author. See also Collins interview, pp. 14–15, PUL.

88. "Phan Huy Quat," January 29, 1965, CIA Biographic Register, and "The Situation in South Vietnam," June 4, 1965, CIA Monthly Report, in *Declassified Documents Reference Systems*, 1978, 31B, 35A; Bui Diem interview; Young to Collins, December 15, 1954, Mansfield memorandum for the record, April 1, 1955, *FRUS, 1955–57*, 1:1–3, 176–77; Shaplen, *Lost Revolution*, pp. 158–59, 306–7, 342–45; Johnson and McAllister, *Right Hand of Power*, pp. 208, 435–37.

89. Robert Guillain, "Le tragédie du Viet Nam," *Le Monde*, May 18, 1955. See also discussion at the 249th NSC meeting, May 19, 1955, box 6, NSC series, Whitman File; Devillers and Lacouture, *Viet Nam*, pp. 413–15; and Frédéric-Dupont, *Mission de la France en Asie*, p. 213.

6. The Substance and Subterfuge of Nation Building (May 1955–January 1957)

1. Final Declaration on Indochina, July 21, 1954, *FRUS, 1952–54*, 16:1541. See also "Considerations Bearing on the Problem of the 1956 Election in Vietnam," February 1, 1955, United States Department of State General Records, Record Group 59, Intelligence Report No. 6818 (hereafter cited as RG 59 with file number).

2. For some examples of this standard interpretation see Herring, *America's Longest War*, pp. 55–56; Kahin, *Intervention*, pp. 88–92; Cooper, *Lost Crusade*, pp. 149–52; Gibbons, *U.S. Government and the Vietnam War*, 1:299–300; Spector, *Advice and Support*, pp. 303–4; and Duncanson, *Government and Revolution in Vietnam*, pp. 223–24.

3. Lt. Col. Vernon A. Walters (interpreter) memorandum of conversation, July 21, 1955, *FRUS, 1955–57*, 1:491–93. See also National Intelligence Estimate, November 23, 1954, and Richard M. Bissell (assistant to the CIA director) memorandum, December 20, 1954, *FRUS, 1952–54*, 13:2286–2301, 2407–9.

4. [Dillon Anderson] Briefing Note on U.S. Policy on All Vietnam Elections (NSC 5519), June 9, 1955, box 1, Chronological subseries, Special Assistant series, Records of the Office of the Special Assistant for National Security Affairs, DDEL. See also U.S. Policy on All Vietnam Elections (NSC 5519), May 17, 1955, Dulles to G. Frederick Reinhardt (ambassador in Saigon), May 27, 1955, and William J. Sebald (deputy assistant secretary of state) memorandum to Dulles, June 14, 1955, *FRUS, 1955–57*, 1:410–12, 421–22, 449–55.

5. Donald R. Heath (ambassador in Saigon) to Dulles, November 6, 1954,

FRUS, 1952–54, 13:2218–20; Theodore C. Achilles (minister in Paris) to Dulles, tel. 3582, February 24, 1955, RG 59, 751G.00/2–2455; Reinhardt to Dulles, June 24, 1955, C. Douglas Dillon (ambassador in Paris) to Dulles, July 6, 1955, *FRUS, 1955–57,* 1:468–70, 478–79; Achilles to Dulles, tel. 1002, September 2, 1955, RG 59, 751G.00/9–255.

6. Randolph A. Kidder (chargé d'affaires in Saigon) to Dulles, March 3, 1955, *FRUS, 1955–57,* 1:104–6; Thomas J. Corcoran (consul in Hanoi) to Dulles, tel. 1319, May 18, 1955, RG 59, 751G.00/5–1855; Anita C. Lauve (Saigon embassy staff) memorandum, September 1, 1955, RG 59, 751G.00/10–1554; Shaplen, *Lost Revolution,* p. 137; Joyaux, *La Chine et le règlement du premier conflit d'Indochine,* pp. 321–25; Smith, *International History of the Vietnam War,* 1:29–33; Cable, *Geneva Conference,* pp. 140–41.

7. Reinhardt to Dulles, tel. 5711, June 7, 1955, RG 59, 751G.00/6–755. See also Kenneth Young (director of Philippine and Southeast Asian affairs [PSA]) and Kidder memorandum of conversation, March 1, 1955, Collins to Dulles, March 19, 1955, Dulles to Collins, March 19, 1955, Dulles to Collins, April 6, 1955, Dulles to Collins, May 27, 1955, and Young to Reinhardt, June 2, 1955, *FRUS, 1955–57,* 1:103–4, 130–35, 210–11, 422–23, 428–31; Collins to Dulles, tel. 5191, box 1, Collins Papers; and Kidder to Dulles, tel. 5323, May 17, 1955, RG 59, 751G.00/5–1755.

8. Patricia M. Byrne (PSA staff) memorandum of conversation, June 18, 1955, Young memorandum to Walter S. Robertson (assistant secretary of state), July 5, 1955, Reinhardt to Dulles, July 16, 1955, *FRUS, 1955–57,* 1:460–63, 477–78, 489–90; Cameron, *Viet-Nam Crisis,* 1:383–84.

9. Cameron, *Viet-Nam Crisis,* 1:389–90. See also Dulles to Reinhardt, July 22, 1955, and Dulles to Reinhardt, July 26, 1955, *FRUS, 1955–57,* 1:495–96, 497–98; and LaFeber, *America, Russia, and the Cold War,* pp. 180–83.

10. Cooper, *Lost Crusade,* p. 150.

11. Dillon to Dulles, tel. 2633, December 1, 1955, RG 59, 751G.00/12–155; Dillon to Dulles, tel. 2692, December 5, 1955, RG 59, 751G.00/12–555. See also "Probable Developments in South Vietnam through July 1956," September 15, 1955, RG 59, Intelligence Report No. 7045; Daniel V. Anderson (counselor in Saigon embassy) to Dulles, September 20, 1955, and Dulles to Dept. of State, November 14, 1955, *FRUS, 1955–57,* 1:540–42, 579–80; and Duncanson, *Government and Revolution in Vietnam,* p. 224.

12. Sebald memorandum to Dulles, May 10, 1956, *FRUS, 1955–57,* 1:680–82. See also Young to Reinhardt, July 28, 1955, and minutes of bilateral foreign ministers meeting with United Kingdom, January 31, 1956, *ibid.,* 499–503, 628–30; "Probable Developments in Vietnam through Mid-1957," May 23, 1956, RG 59, Intelligence Report No. 7256; Anderson to Dept. of State, desp. 22, July 24, 1956, RG 59, 751G.00/7–2456; Cameron, *Viet-Nam Crisis,* 1:432–36; and Hammer, *Death in November,* pp. 93–95.

13. Dulles memorandum of conversation with the president, May 6, 1955, box 11, Chronological series, Dulles Papers, DDEL. See also "The Legality of Bao Dai," May 5, 1955, RG 59, Intelligence Report No. 6918; and Collins

memorandum to Reinhardt, May 10, 1955, Dulles to Reinhardt, May 19, 1955, Young to Reinhardt, June 10, 1955, Dulles to Reinhardt, July 1, 1955, and Dulles to Dept. of State, September 27, 1955, *FRUS, 1955–57*, 1:391, 416–18, 444–45, 474, 546.

14. Reinhardt to Dulles, tel. 494, July 29, 1955, RG 59, 751G.00/7–2955. See also Reinhardt to Dept. of State, desp. 57, August 26, 1955, RG 59, 751G.13/8–2655; Reinhardt to Dulles, tel. 1468, September 28, 1955, RG 59, 751G.00/9–2855; Reinhardt to Dulles, June 2, 1955, Frank G. Wisner (CIA deputy director) memorandum to Robertson, June 3, 1955, and Reinhardt to Dulles, September 29, 1955, *FRUS, 1955–57*, 1:431–34, 547–48; Collins to Dulles, draft telegram, May 11, 1955, box 5, Collins Papers; and Cooper, *Lost Crusade*, p. 149.

15. Anderson to Dept. of State, desp. 124, October 18, 1955, RG 59, 751G.00/10–1855.

16. Reinhardt to Dept. of State, November 29, 1955, *FRUS, 1955–57*, 1:589–92; Cooper, *Lost Crusade*, pp. 151–52; Fall, *Two Viet-Nams*, pp. 257–58; Lansdale, *In the Midst of Wars*, pp. 333–34; Herring, *America's Longest War*, p. 55; Kahin, *Intervention*, p. 95; "Outcome Predictable in South Vietnamese Elections," April 3, 1961, RG 59, Intelligence Report No. 8444.

17. Reinhardt to Dulles, October 25, 1955, Young to Reinhardt, October 27, 1955, Reinhardt to Dept. of State, November 29, 1955, *FRUS, 1955–57*, 1:565–68, 592–94; Dillon to Dulles, tel. 1721, October 13, 1955, RG 59, 75G.00/10–1355; Dillon to Dulles, tel. 1853, October 18, 1955, RG 59, 751G.00/10–1855; O'Daniel memorandum to Reinhardt, October 25, 1955, SEA-RS-603LL; O'Daniel, *Nation That Refused to Starve*, pp. 64–67; Bao Dai, *Le dragon d'Annam*, p. 343.

18. Young memorandum to Robertson, October 5, 1955, Young to Reinhardt, October 5, 1955, *FRUS, 1955–57*, 1:550–54.

19. Reinhardt to Dulles, tel. 3502, February 29, 1956, RG 59, 751G.00/2–2956; Reinhardt to Dulles, tel. 3556, March 3, 1956, RG 59, 751G.00/3–356; Reinhardt to Dulles, 3655, March 8, 1956, RG 59, 751G.00/3–856; Anderson to Dept. of State, desp. 332, April 9, 1956, RG 59, 751G.00/4–956; Fall, *Two Viet-Nams*, pp. 131, 258–59.

20. Reinhardt to Dulles, tel. 2378, December 6, 1955, RG 59, 751G.00/12–655; Reinhardt to Young, March 3, 1956, RG 59, 751G.00/3–356.

21. Hoan to Eisenhower, February 27, 1956, RG 59, 751G.00/2–2756.

22. Sebald memorandum to Robert D. Murphy (deputy under secretary of state), March 12, 1956, RG 59, 751G.00/3–1256. See also Eric Kocher (deputy director of SEA) memorandum to Robertson, February 13, 1957, RG 59, 751G.00/2–857; and Buttinger, *Vietnam*, 2:1112, 1245–46.

23. Madame Nhu to Lawrence E. Spivak (producer of "Meet the Press"), October 26, 1972, box 5, Lansdale Papers. See also Fall, *Two Viet-Nams*, pp. 237–38; Scigliano, *South Vietnam*, pp. 55–58; Kahin, *Intervention*, p. 101; and Buttinger, *Dragon Defiant*, p. 52.

24. Bao Dai, *Le dragon d'Annam*, p. 343.

25. Barrows interview.

26. Bao Dai, *Le dragon d'Annam*, p. 348; Durbrow to Dept. of State, December 22, 1958, Durbrow to Dept. of State, March 2, 1959, *FRUS, 1958–60*, 1:109–13, 144–70.

27. Scigliano, *South Vietnam*, pp. 28–33, 54–61, 75–81; Fall, *Two Viet-Nams*, pp. 246–68; Duncanson, *Government and Revolution in Vietnam*, pp. 211–28; Kahin, *Intervention*, pp. 96–101; Paul J. Sturm (Saigon embassy staff) memorandum of conversation, May 11, 1955, box 5, Collins Papers; Chaffard, *Indochine*, pp. 151–71.

28. Reinhardt interview, p. 20. See also Kahin, *Intervention*, p. 94; Fall, *Two Viet-Nams*, p. 272; Gibbons, *U.S. Government and the Vietnam War*, 1:300–301; and Fishel, "Vietnam's Democratic One-Man Rule."

29. Kolko, *Anatomy of a War*, pp. 88–87, 91. See also Herring, *America's Longest War*, p. 63.

30. O'Daniel to Stump, August 9, 1955, Stump to Dept. of the Army, August 10, 1955, *FRUS, 1955–57*, 1:506–12.

31. Reinhardt to Dept. of State, desp. 34, August 2, 1956, RG 59, 751G.5–MSP/8–256.

32. Scigliano, *South Vietnam*, pp. 113–15.

33. O'Daniel memorandum to Reinhardt, September 23, 1955, SEA–RS–603z; O'Daniel to Reinhardt, September 30, 1955, SEA–RS–603f; Kidder to Dulles, February 3, 1955, Herbert J. Hoover (acting secretary of state) to Reinhardt, September 27, 1955, Reinhardt memorandum of conversation, November 7, 1955, Reinhardt to Dept. of State, November 17, 1955, Reinhardt to Dulles, December 5, 1955, *FRUS, 1955–57*, 1:76–78, 544–45, 571–72, 581, 596–97; Spector, *Advice and Support*, pp. 237–39, 263–65; Duncanson, *Government and Revolution in Vietnam*, pp. 288–93.

34. Adm. Arthur W. Radford (JCS chairman) memorandum to Charles E. Wilson (secretary of defense), December 9, 1955, *FRUS, 1955–57*, 1:598–99; Spector, *Advice and Support*, pp. 239–40, 250–52, 255–56.

35. Reinhardt to Dulles, December 31, 1955, Robertson memorandum to Dulles, January 18, 1956, Dulles to Reinhardt, January 23, 1956, Robertson memorandum to Murphy, February 2, 1956, memorandum of conversation, February 4, 1956, *FRUS, 1955–57*, 1:615–16, 618–21, 622–23, 631–33, 635–37.

36. Williams to Gen. Walter Krueger, April 14, 1956, box 5, Williams Papers; Dulles to Reinhardt, February 9, 1956, Reinhardt to Dulles, February 13, 1956, Young memorandum of conversation, February 28, 1956, Mansfield D. Sprague (assistant secretary of defense) to Robertson, April 15, 1956, Howard P. Jones (deputy assistant secretary of state) memorandum to Murphy, July 26, 1957, *FRUS, 1955–57*, 1: 640–41, 642–44, 648–49, 780–82, 827–28; Col. Robert F. Evans memorandum to Rear Adm. Edward J. O'Donnell, June 16, 1959, Williams to Mansfield, May 13, 1960, *FRUS, 1958–60*, 1:209–12, 467–71; Spector, *Advice and Support*, pp. 257–62; Scigliano, *South Vietnam*, p. 193.

37. O'Daniel, "Military Training Assistance in Vietnam," no date, SEA–RS–

814b; O'Daniel memorandum to Reinhardt, September 30, 1955, SEA–RS–603bb; Corcoran memorandum of conversation, April 5, 1957, *FRUS, 1955–57,* 1:773–76; Spector, *Advice and Support,* pp. 263–65, 272–73; Herring, *America's Longest War,* pp. 58–59; Shaplen, *Lost Revolution,* pp. 138–39.

38. Williams paper on guerrilla operations, December 28, 1955, *FRUS, 1955–57,* 1:606–10; Weigley, *History of the United States Army,* pp. 519–23. For a resume of Williams's career see his retirement orders, August 15, 1960, box 42, Lansdale Papers.

39. Burke to Stump, May 30, 1956, Stump to Burke, June 1, 1956, Williams to Stump, June 4, 1956, Robert R. Bowie (assistant secretary of state) memorandum to Dulles, June 6, 1956, Williams to Stump, June 7, 1956, Radford to Stump, June 14, 1956, *FRUS, 1955–57,* 1:687–95, 709–13.

40. Radford paper presented at 287th NSC meeting, June 7, 1956, *ibid.,* 703–9.

41. Discussion at the 287th NSC meeting, June 7, 1956, *ibid.,* 695–703.

42. *Ibid.* See also discussion at the 295th NSC meeting, August 31, 1956, box 8, NSC series, Ann Whitman File, Eisenhower Papers, for further consideration of the president's authority to commit troops without congressional action.

43. Bowie memorandum to Dulles, June 6, 1956, *FRUS, 1955–57,* 1:693–95; Gibbons, *U.S. Government and the Vietnam War,* 1:306–8; Gaddis, *Strategies of Containment,* pp. 161, 178; Weigley, *American Way of War,* pp. 410–11; Kinnard, *President Eisenhower,* pp. 43–65; Rosenberg, "Origins of Overkill," pp. 152–55.

44. Scigliano, *South Vietnam,* pp. 38, 102–10; Fall, *Two Viet-Nams,* pp. 289–98, 308; Hammer, *Death in November,* pp. 62–63.

45. Hannah interview.

46. Report of the Special FOA Mission from Michigan State College for Public Administration, Public Information, Police Administration, and Public Finance and Economics, October 16, 1954, box 658, Vietnam Project; Montgomery, *Politics of Foreign Aid,* pp. 213, 298.

47. Collins to Hannah, January 11, 1955, box 42, Hannah Records. See also Barrows to Dulles, tel. TOUSFO 614, November 2, 1954, Barrows to Dulles, tel. TOUSFO 687, November 12, 1954, Collins to Dulles, tel. 1877, November 18, 1954, and Barrows to Dulles, tel. TOUSFO 1011, January 4, 1955, box 1, Collins Papers.

48. Agreement between the Government of the United States represented by the Foreign Operations Administration and Michigan State University, April 19, 1955, Agreement between the Government of Vietnam and Michigan State University, April 19, 1955, box 627, Vietnam Project.

49. Scigliano and Fox, *Technical Assistance in Vietnam,* pp. 4–12; Ralph Smuckler (MSUG) interview.

50. Report of the Special FOA Mission from Michigan State College, October 16, 1954, box 658, Vietnam Project.

51. FOA record of meeting on Vietnam with Michigan State public administration team, October 28, 1954, box 2, Collins Papers.

52. Scigliano and Fox, *Technical Assistance in Vietnam,* pp. 56–58, 66–71; Hannah interview; Smuckler interview; Turner (MSUG) interview.

53. Weidner to Joseph G. LaPalombara (MSU), July 22, 1955, box 634, Vietnam Project.

54. *Ibid.* See also Reinhardt to Dulles, tel. 348, July 22, 1955, RG 59, 751G.00/7–2255.

55. Weidner to Fishel, November 9, 1955, box 23, Fishel Papers.

56. Scigliano and Fox, *Technical Assistance in Vietnam,* pp. 52–54; Scigliano, *South Vietnam,* pp. 204–6; Fishel to Hannah, February 17, 1962, box 11, Fishel Papers; Wesley Fishel, "Diem Miracle Petered Out in Viet-Nam," *Washington Post,* September 1, 1963.

57. Warren Hinckle, et al., "The University on the Make," *Ramparts* (April 1966): 11–22; Statement by John A. Hannah, April 22, 1966, box 657, Smuckler Report on the MSU-Vietnam Project, April 1966, box 658, Vietnam Project; Smuckler memorandum for the record on "factual misstatements in the *Ramparts* article of April 1966," no date, box 55, Hannah Records; Gibbons, *U.S. Government and the Vietnam War,* 1:264.

58. Barrows interview; Smuckler interview; Scigliano and Fox, *Technical Assistance in Vietnam,* pp. 19, 43.

59. Smuckler interview; Scigliano and Fox, *Technical Assistance in Vietnam,* pp. 6, 8, 21, 40–41, 60; Reinhardt to Dulles, August 25, 1955, *FRUS, 1955–57,* 1:527–30; Kattenburg memorandum to Young, October 9, 1956, RG 59, 751G.5–MSP/10–956.

60. Statement by Hannah, April 22, 1966, box 657, Smuckler Report on the MSU-Vietnam Project, April 1966, box 658, Vietnam Project; Smuckler interview; Turner interview; Weidner memorandum to Hannah, November 8, 1956, box 42, clipping from *National Review,* April 18, 1966, box 55, Hannah Records; Fishel to editor of *Providence Journal,* May 12, 1966, box 28, Fishel Papers.

61. Prados, *Presidents' Secret Wars,* pp. 108–19, 261–74; Prouty, *Secret Team,* p. 60; Gibbons, *U.S. Government and the Vietnam War,* 1:310–11; Cave Brown, *Wild Bill Donovan,* pp. 822–29; Lansdale, *In the Midst of Wars,* pp. 169–70; Leo Cherne (IRC chairman) to Donovan, September 29, 1954, Donovan Papers. For IRC activities in South Vietnam see Angier Biddle Duke (IRC president) report to the board of directors, October 15, 1955; and Robert A. MacAlister (IRC director in Saigon), Reports No. 7–15 from IRC-Saigon, May 8, 1955–July 28, 1955, *ibid.*

62. Young to Reinhardt, June 2, 1955, *FRUS, 1955–57,* 1:429–30. See also Elbridge Durbrow (ambassador in Saigon) to Kocher, October 10, 1958, *FRUS, 1958–60,* 1:90, n.6.

63. Fishel to Lansdale, November 19, 1957, box 37, Fishel to Lansdale, April 6, 1967, box 53, Lansdale Papers.

64. Cooley letters to his family, February 15 and April 12, 1955. James Cooley's assignment in Vietnam was to help Collins sort out fact from fancy in information coming into the U.S. embassy from various sources.

65. Lansdale memorandum to Fishel, September 6, 1955, box 24, Fishel Papers.

66. Lansdale interview; Kenneth P. Landon (Operations Coordinating Board) memorandum of discussion, November 7, 1955, *FRUS, 1955–57*, 1:572–76; Weidner to Charles C. Killingsworth (MSU), June 2, 1955, box 634, Smuckler to Weidner, September 13, 1955, Walter W. Mode (MSUG) to Weidner, September 23, 1955, Weidner to Barrows, September 26, 1955, box 660, Vietnam Project; Lansdale, *In the Midst of Wars*, pp. 209–31, 339–45; Montgomery, *Politics of Foreign Aid*, pp. 70–71, 79–81.

67. Smuckler interview.

68. Scigliano, *South Vietnam*, p. 216. See also Turner interview; Statement by Hannah, April 22, 1966, box 657, Vietnam Project; Scigliano and Fox, *Technical Assistance in Vietnam*, pp. 55, 60; and Montgomery, *Politics of Foreign Aid*, pp. 82–83.

69. Lansdale interview; Smuckler interview; Turner interview; Collins to Dulles, tel. 3452, February 17, 1955, box 1, Collins Papers; Fishel to Durbrow, November 7, 1957, box 24, Fishel Papers; Lansdale to Williams, March 14, 1958, Lansdale to Sprague, March 19, 1958, Howard Elting, Jr., (chargé d'affaires in Saigon) to Dulles, April 1, 1958, Robertson to Dillon (under secretary of state), January 8, 1959, Dulles to Durbrow, January 16, 1959, *FRUS, 1958–60*, 1:26–29, 30–34, 128–30, 134–35; Basic Counterinsurgency Plan for Viet-Nam, January 4, 1961, *FRUS, 1961–63*, 1:7; Montgomery, *Politics of Foreign Aid*, pp. 64–70; Scigliano and Fox, *Technical Assistance in Vietnam*, pp. 17, 67; Scigliano, *South Vietnam*, pp. 163–64, 201, 210; Spector, *Advice and Support*, pp. 320–25.

70. Scigliano and Fox, *Technical Assistance in Vietnam*, pp. 19, 66–67, 73–74; Smuckler Report on the MSU-Vietnam Project, April 1966, box 658, Vietnam Project.

71. Machiavelli, *The Prince*, p. 90.

7. The Miracle and the Muddle of South Vietnam (January 1955–January 1959)

1. U.S. Policy in Mainland Southeast Asia (NSC 5809), April 2, 1958, and U.S. Policy in Mainland Southeast Asia (NSC 6012), July 25, 1960, *FRUS, 1958–60*, 1:34–35, 523–24. See also United States House of Representatives, Committee on Armed Services, *United States-Vietnam Relations*, 10:1082–95, 1113–33, 1281–97.

2. Divine, *Since 1945*, pp. 77–99.

3. Scigliano, *South Vietnam*, p. 107; Fitzgerald, *Fire in the Lake*, pp. 115–16, 201–4.

4. G. Frederick Reinhardt (ambassador in Saigon) to Dept. of State, desp. 453, June 15, 1955, United States Department of State General Records, Record Group 59, 751G.00/6–1555 (hereafter cited as RG 59 with file number). See also Leland Barrows (director of United States Operations Mission in Saigon) to

Dulles, tel. TOUSFO 1153, January 21, 1955, RG 59, 851G.16/1–2155; and Duncanson, *Government and Revolution in Vietnam*, pp. 252–53.

5. Daniel V. Anderson (counselor in Saigon embassy) to Dept. of State, desp. 340, April 23, 1956, RG 59, 751G.5–MSP/4–2356.

6. Young memorandum to Walter S. Robertson (assistant secretary of state), October 26, 1956, *FRUS, 1955–57*, 1:756–57. See also Reinhardt to Dulles, July 9, 1956, and Reinhardt to Dulles, July 21, 1956, *ibid.*, 715–19, 721–24; and Gardner E. Palmer (counselor in Saigon embassy) to Dept. of State, desp. 7, July 12, 1956, RG 59, 851G.20/7–1256.

7. Wesley C. Haraldson (acting director of USOM) to Howard P. Jones (deputy assistant secretary of state), March 2, 1957, RG 59, 751G.00/3–257. See also John B. Hollister (ICA director) to Barrows, November 23, 1956, and Christian A. Herter (acting secretary of state) to Reinhardt, April 12, 1957, *FRUS, 1955–57*, 1:753–54, 779–80; Arthur L. Richards (under secretary of state) memorandum to Robertson, February 20, 1957, RG 59, 751G.00/2–2057; and Duncanson, *Government and Revolution in Vietnam*, pp. 242–46.

8. Clarence B. Randall (chairman of Council on Foreign Economic Policy) report, December 1956, *FRUS, 1955–57*, 9:32; United States Department of State, *Threat to the Peace*.

9. Anderson to Dept. of State, desp. 340, April 23, 1956, RG 59, 751G.5–MSP/4–2356; National Intelligence Estimate, July 17, 1956, *FRUS, 1955–57*, 1:720–21; Reinhardt to Dept. of State, desp. 34, August 2, 1956, RG 59, 751G.5–MSP/8–256; Arthur Z. Gardiner (counselor in Saigon embassy) to Dept. of State, desp. 269, February 18, 1959, RG 59, 851G.00/2–1859; "The Outlook for North and South Vietnam," May 5, 1959, RG 59, Intelligence Report No. 8008; Fall, *Two Viet-Nams*, pp. 289–96.

10. Reinhardt to Dept. of State, March 15, 1956, *FRUS, 1955–57*, 1:659–61.

11. Gardiner to Dept. of State, desp. 464, June 24, 1955, RG 59, 751G.5–MSP/6–2455; Robertson memorandum to Herbert J. Hoover (under secretary of state), November 22, 1955, Thomas J. Corcoran (Southeast Asian affairs staff) memorandum of conversation, April 4, 1957, *FRUS, 1955–57*, 1:585–86, 770–73; Reinhardt to Dept. of State, desp. 339, April 23, 1956, RG 59, 751G.00/4–2356; Reinhardt to Dulles, tel. 1888, December 10, 1956, RG 59, 851G.00/12–1056; Montgomery, *Politics of Foreign Aid*, p. 174.

12. Herring, " 'Peoples Quite Apart,' " pp. 1–2, 22–23.

13. C. E. Lilien memorandum of conversation, December 10, 1957, RG 59, 751G.131/12–1057; Fitzgerald, *Fire in the Lake*, pp. 138, 466; Kahin, *Intervention*, p. 86; Scigliano, *South Vietnam*, p. 112; Herring, *America's Longest War*, pp. 60–61.

14. Haraldson to Dept. of State, desp. 157, November 26, 1956, RG 59, 751G.13/11–2656; Reinhardt to Dulles, tel. 1888, December 10, 1956, RG 59, 851G.00/12–1056; Eric Kocher (deputy director of Southeast Asian affairs) memorandum to Jones, December 31, 1956, RG 59, 751G.13/12–3156; J. C. Corbett memorandum to C. Douglas Dillon (deputy under secretary of state),

May 22, 1957, RG 59, 751G.13/5–2257; Gene Gregory (RVN publicist) to Sen. Mike Mansfield, April 3, 1957, box 8, Foreign Relations series, Mansfield Papers; Fall, *Two Viet-Nams*, pp. 297, 302–6; Duncanson, *Government and Revolution in Vietnam*, pp. 284–87; Kahin, *Intervention*, pp. 87–88; Scigliano, *South Vietnam*, pp. 125–29.

15. United States Senate, *Executive Sessions of the Senate Foreign Relations Committee (Historical Series)*, 8:159–61. See also OCB Progress Report on Southeast Asia (NSC 5405), December 21, 1955, box 9, NSC Policy Papers series, Records of the Office of the Special Assistant for National Security Affairs, DDEL; United States Senate, Committee on Foreign Relations, *Viet Nam, Cambodia, and Laos;* Mansfield to Chester Bowles (former ambassador in New Delhi), January 17, 1956, box 8, Foreign Relations series, Mansfield Papers; Status of United States Programs for National Security as of June 30, 1955 (NSC 5525), August 31, 1955, discussion at the 274th NSC meeting, January 26, 1956, and intelligence brief, February 7, 1956, *FRUS, 1955–57*, 9:544, 1:624–25, 637–39; Anderson to Dept. of State, desp. 218, January 12, 1956, RG 59, 851G.413/1–1256; Kahin, *Intervention*, p. 93; and Goodpaster (Eisenhower's staff secretary) interview by Soapes, p. 120, DDEL. See Sheehan, *Bright Shining Lie*, for an exposition of the "can do" mentality.

16. Kennedy's speech "America's Stake in Vietnam" was published by the American Friends of Vietnam in *Symposium on America's Stake in Vietnam*, pp. 8–14.

17. Reinhardt to Dept. of State, desp. 209, January 3, 1956, RG 59, 751G.00/1–356; Herring, *America's Longest War*, p. 57; Fitzgerald, *Fire in the Lake*, pp. 111–12; Gibbons, *U.S. Government and the Vietnam War*, 1:301–5.

18. Dulles memorandum to Eisenhower, February 10, 1956, *FRUS, 1955–57*, 1:641–42. See also Frank G. Wisner (CIA deputy director) memorandum to Robertson, September 27, 1956, *ibid.*, 742–43; Eisenhower to Donovan, February 7, 1956, box 13, Eisenhower Diary series, Ann Whitman File, Eisenhower Papers (hereafter cited as Whitman File); Robert Scheer and Warren Hinckle, "The Viet-Nam Lobby," *Ramparts* (July 1965): 16–24; and Scheer, *How the United States Got Involved in Vietnam*, pp. 31–33, 39–46.

19. O'Daniel brief attached to Goodpaster memorandum to Eisenhower, March 2, 1956, box 50, International series, Whitman File.

20. Robert E. Hoey (special assistant to the secretary of state) memorandum to Kocher, March 2, 1956, RG 59, 751G.00/3–256. See also O'Daniel, *Nation That Refused to Starve*, pp. 69–117.

21. Walter S. Robertson, "United States Policy Towards Vietnam," in *Symposium on America's Stake in Vietnam*, pp. 15–19; "Vietminh Breaks Truce, U.S. Holds," *New York Times*, June 2, 1956; Young memorandum to Robertson, May 29, 1956, RG 59, 751G.00/5–2956; Hoover to Reinhardt, tel. 3922, June 1, 1956, RG 59, 751G.5/5–2456; Herter to Elbridge Durbrow (ambassador in Saigon), tel. 1622, March 11, 1958, RG 59, 751G.00/3–1158.

22. Paul M. Kattenburg (officer in charge of Vietnam affairs) memorandum of conversation, September 25, 1956, *FRUS, 1955–57*, 1:739–41. See also

Williams to Admiral Felix B. Stump (commander-in-chief Pacific), May 15, 1956, Dept. of Defense memorandum, August 22, 1956, and Reinhardt to Young, December 20, 1956, *ibid.*, 682–83, 733, 759–60; "Probable Developments in Vietnam through Mid-1957," May 23, 1956, RG 59, Intelligence Report No. 7256; and Reinhardt to Dept. of State, desp. 389, June 23, 1956, RG 59, 751G.00/6–2356.

23. Dulles to Eisenhower, March 15, 1956, *FRUS, 1955–57,* 1:658; Dulles memorandum of conversation, April 25, 1956, box 1, General Correspondence and Memoranda series, Dulles Papers, DDEL.

24. Ulam, *Rivals,* pp. 237–38; Ambrose, *Eisenhower,* 2:383–85; Status of U.S. Programs for National Security as of June 30, 1957, *FRUS, 1955–57,* 9:609.

25. Program for Ngo Dinh Diem Visit, May 3, 1957, box 73, Subject series, White House Central Files (Confidential File), DDEL.

26. Joint communiqué, May 11, 1957, United States Department of State, *Bulletin* (May 27, 1957): 851; United States President, *Public Papers: Eisenhower, 1957,* p. 417; John Osborne, "The Tough Miracle Man of Vietnam," *Life* (May 13, 1957): 156–76; Gibbons, *U.S. Government and the Vietnam War,* 1:332–33.

27. Corcoran memorandum of conversation, April 5, 1957, *FRUS, 1955–57,* 1:773–76. See also Durbrow memorandum of conversation, May 9, 1957, and Capt. B. A. Robbins (U.S. Navy) memorandum of conversation, May 10, 1957, *ibid.*, 794–99, 807–11.

28. Durbrow memorandum of conversation, May 9, 1957, *FRUS, 1955–57,* 1:794–99; Ambrose, *Eisenhower,* 2:376–81; Kaufman, *Trade and Aid,* pp. 99–110.

29. Anderson to Dulles, tel. 3358, May 6, 1957, box 73, Subject series, White House Central Files (Confidential File). See also Durbrow to Dulles, tel. 3292, April 30, 1957, *ibid.*; Corcoran memorandum of conversation, May 9, 1957, *FRUS, 1955–57,* 1:799–801; and Gardner, *Approaching Vietnam,* p. 341.

30. Corcoran memorandum of conversation, May 9, 1957, *FRUS, 1955–57,* 1:803–6. See also Durbrow memorandum of conversation, May 9, 1957, and Corcoran memorandum of conversation, May 10, 1957, *ibid.*, 794–99, 812–16; Durbrow to Dulles, tel. 3293, April 30, 1957, and Robertson memorandum to Dulles, May 8, 1957, box 73, Subject series, White House Central Files (Confidential File); and Herter memorandum to Eisenhower, May 7, 1957, RG 59, 751G.11/5–757.

31. Durbrow to Dulles, July 1, 1957, *FRUS, 1955–57,* 1:825–26. See also Durbrow memorandum of conversation, May 17, 1957, *ibid.*, 820–22; Durbrow to Dept. of State, desp. 386, June 15, 1957, RG 59, 751G.11/6–1557; and Leo Cherne to Mansfield, February 3, 1958, box 8, Foreign Relations series, Mansfield Papers.

32. Durbrow to Dept. of State, desp. 115, October 8, 1957, RG 59, 751G.00/10–857.

33. Durbrow to Dulles, August 30, 1957, *FRUS, 1955–57,* 1:841–42. See

also Anderson to Dulles, February 27, 1957, and Anderson to Dulles, March 30, 1957, *ibid.*, 764, 768–69; Haraldson to Dept. of State, desp. 233, January 6, 1958, RG 59, 851G.16/1–658; Montgomery, *Politics of Foreign Aid*, pp. 72–83; Duiker, *Communist Road to Power*, pp. 184–85; and Pike, *Viet Cong*, pp. 59–60.

34. Corcoran memorandum of conversation, October 7, 1957, RG 59, 751G.00/ 10–757; Durbrow to Dept. of State, September 30, 1958, *FRUS, 1958–60*, 1:82–85; Fitzgerald, *Fire in the Lake*, p. 197; Fall, *Two Viet-Nams*, pp. 154–57; Fall, *Last Reflections on a War*, p. 198; Porter, *Vietnam*, pp. 194–96; Spector, *Advice and Support*, pp. 310–16.

35. Biography of Diem in briefing book for Diem visit, May 1957, box 73, Subject series, White House Central Files (Confidential File).

36. Anderson to Dulles, March 30, 1957, *FRUS, 1955–57*, 1:768–69; Kocher memorandum to Robertson, August 12, 1958, Robertson memorandum to Dillon, January 8, 1959, *FRUS, 1958–60*, 1:71–73, 128–31; Duiker, *Communist Road to Power*, pp. 183–84; Pike, *Viet Cong*, pp. 59, 71–73; Fitzgerald, *Fire in the Lake*, pp. 197–98.

37. Kahin, *Intervention*, pp. 101–9; Kolko, *Anatomy of A War*, pp. 99–101; Race, *War Comes to Long An*, 81–84.

38. Robert E. Barbour (consul in Hue) to Dept. of State, desp. 18, March 19, 1958, RG 59, 751G.00/3–1958.

39. Williams to Stump, November 16, 1957, *FRUS, 1955–57*, 1:862–63.

40. Joseph A. Mendenhall (officer in charge of Vietnam affairs) memorandum of conversation, November 17–18, 1958, *FRUS, 1958–60*, 1:100–102. See also Durbrow to Dulles, August 13, 1958, *ibid.*, 74–77; Williams memorandum to Durbrow, October 9, 1957, and Durbrow to Dulles, December 5, 1957, *FRUS, 1955–57*, 1:846–48, 869–84; and Thomas D. Bowie (counselor in Saigon embassy) to Dept. of State, desp. 452, June 13, 1958, RG 59, 751G.00/6–1358.

41. Durbrow to Dulles, October 28, 1957, *FRUS, 1955–57*, 1:854–56. See also Williams to Vice Adm. G. W. Anderson (U.S. Navy), October 2, 1957, *ibid.*, 844–45; and Durbrow to Dept. of State, desp. 106, September 26, 1957, RG 59, 751G.00/9–2657.

42. Dulles to Durbrow, November 19, 1957, *FRUS, 1955–57*, 1:863–64.

43. Durbrow to Dept. of State, December 5, 1957, *FRUS, 1955–57*, 1:869–84; Durbrow to Dulles, February 8, 1958, Durbrow to Dulles, August 5, 1958, Howard Elting, Jr., (chargé d'affaires in Saigon) to Dept. of State, October 31, 1958, *FRUS, 1958–60*, 1:10–15, 66–69, 93–96; Durbrow to Dept. of State, desp. 305, March 5, 1958, RG 59, 751G.11/3–558.

44. Williams to Stump, December 23, 1957, *FRUS, 1955–57*, 1:888–89, n.1; Durbrow to Dulles, October 3, 1958, Elting memorandum of conversation, December 12, 1958, *FRUS, 1958–60*, 1:86–87, 103–5.

45. Gardiner to Dept. of State, desp. 321, March 14, 1958, RG 59, 851G.00/ 3–1458. See also Williams to Stump, October 18, 1958, and Col. James I. Muir (U.S. Army) memorandum for the record, November 5, 1957, *FRUS, 1955–57*, 1:851–53, 856–61; Durbrow memorandum of conversation, January 30, 1958,

Durbrow to Dulles, February 25, 1958, and Amory Houghton (ambassador in Paris) to Dept. of State, December 31, 1958, *FRUS, 1958–60,* 1:5–8, 15–16, 114–17; Haraldson to Dept. of State, desp. 157, November 26, 1956, RG 59, 751G.13/11–2656; and Kocher memorandum to Jones, December 31, 1956, RG 59, 751G.13/12–3156.

46. Barrows interview.

47. Durbrow to Dulles, August 13, 1958, *FRUS, 1958–60,* 1:74–77. See also Mendenhall memorandum of conversation, January 8, 1959, *ibid.,* 127–28.

48. Dulles memorandum to Eisenhower, May 22, 1958, *ibid.,* 1:39, n.1. See also Eisenhower to Diem, May 23, 1958, *ibid.,* 39–40; Durbrow to Dulles, tel. 243, August 8, 1958, RG 59, 751G.11/8–858; and Smith, *International History of the Vietnam War,* 1:74–75, 112–14, 117.

49. OCB Operations Plan for Vietnam, June 4, 1958, *FRUS, 1958–60,* 1:40–54. Quotations are from pp. 41–42.

50. OCB Operations Plan for Vietnam, January 7, 1959, *ibid.,* 117–24. See also Kolko, *Anatomy of a War,* pp. 102–3; Porter, *Vietnam,* p. 196; and Smith, *International History of the Vietnam War,* 1:162–66.

51. Scigliano, *South Vietnam,* pp. 196–208.

52. Dulles memorandum to Eisenhower, March 23, 1954, *FRUS, 1952–54,* 13:1141.

8. Trapped by Success
(January 1959–January 1961)

1. Lansdale memorandum to secretary of defense and deputy secretary of defense, January 17, 1961, box 49, Lansdale Papers.

2. Ten-Point Program of the NLF, December 20, 1960, quoted in Kahin and Lewis, *United States in Vietnam,* pp. 390–95. See also Kahin, *Intervention,* pp. 109–15; Race, *War Comes to Long An,* pp. 105–22; Kolko, *Anatomy of a War,* 102–6; and Duiker, *Communist Road to Power,* 187–99.

3. Durbrow to John Foster Dulles, March 28, 1959, Durbrow memorandum of conversation, April 24, 1959, Durbrow to Dept. of State, June 24, 1959, *FRUS, 1958–60,* 1:176–77, 188–90, 213–17; Arthur Z. Gardiner (counselor in Saigon embassy) to Dept. of State, desp. 264, February 14, 1959, United States Department of State General Records, Record Group 59, 751G.5–MSP/2–1459 (hereafter cited as RG 59 with file number); Gardiner to Dept. of State, desp. 301, March 18, 1959, RG 59, 751G.5–MSP/3–1859.

4. Durbrow to Christian A. Herter (secretary of state), June 12, 1959, *FRUS, 1958–60,* 1:207; Durbrow to Dulles, tel. 1963, March 19, 1959, RG 59, 751G.5–MSP/3–1959.

5. Durbrow to Dulles, March 28, 1959, *FRUS, 1958–60,* 1:176–77. See also Durbrow to Dulles, April 11, 1959, *ibid.,* 181–82.

6. Quoted in Spector, *Advice and Support,* p. 334.

7. Joseph Rosa (first secretary in Saigon embassy) to Dept. of State, desp. 345, April 20, 1959, RG 59, 851G.16/4–2059. See also Gardiner to Dept. of

State, desp. 269, February 18, 1959, RG 59, 851G.oo/2–1859; and Henry D. Wyner (second secretary in Saigon embassy) to Dept. of State, desp. 327, April 7, 1959, RG 59, 851G.20/4–759.

8. Anderson interview, p. 27.

9. Collins to Williams, March 12, 1959, box 4, Williams Papers. See also Durbrow to Robertson, February 16, 1959, *FRUS, 1958–60*, 1:138–44; Tracy Voohrees (Draper Committee counsel) to Senator Mike Mansfield, August 20, 1959, box 40, Subject series, White House Central Files (Confidential File), DDEL; and Currey, *Lansdale*, pp. 200–6.

10. President's Committee to Study the United States Military Assistance Program, *Composite Report*, 1:143.

11. Appendix F to Minutes of the Sixth Meeting, February 24–26, 1959, box 2, Records of President's Committee to Study the United States Military Assistance Program. See also Initial Draft Southeast Asia (Anderson Subcommittee), February 27, 1959, *ibid.*; Anderson interview, pp. 21–30; Wolf Ladejinsky (adviser to Diem) to Lansdale, April 22, 1959, box 3, Lansdale Papers; and Smith, *International History of the Vietnam War*, 1:182–84.

12. Mendenhall memorandum of conversation, April 22, 1959, *FRUS, 1958–60*, 1:185–86. See also Robertson to Durbrow, March 10, 1959, *ibid.*, 172–74; and Eisenhower, *Waging Peace*, pp. 358–59.

13. Quoted in Williams, et al., *America in Vietnam*, p. 143.

14. "John Foster Dulles and the Far East," pp. 55–57, Dulles Oral History Project. See also May, *Truman Administration and China*, pp. 6, 12–19, 45–47; Judd interview. For an analysis that drew an explicit parallel between Chiang and his Guomindang party and Diem and his Can Lao party see Durbrow to Dept. of State, March 2, 1959, *FRUS, 1958–60*, 1:155–56.

15. Gibbons, *U.S. Government and the Vietnam War*, 1:320–22; Montgomery, *Politics of Foreign Aid*, pp. 221–24; Reichard, "Domestic Politics of National Security," p. 252.

16. Quoted in Gibbons, *U.S. Government and the Vietnam War*, 1:323.

17. Montgomery, *Politics of Foreign Aid*, pp. 224–25; Lederer and Burdick, *Ugly American*.

18. Montgomery, *Politics of Foreign Aid*, p. 232. See also Gibbons, *U.S. Government and the Vietnam War*, 1:323–25; J. Graham Parsons (assistant secretary of state) memorandum to Herter, August 6, 1959, C. Douglas Dillon (under secretary of state) memorandum of conversation, December 18, 1959, and editorial note, *FRUS, 1958–60*, 1:225–27, 273–74, 289; L. J. Saccio (International Cooperation Administration [ICA] deputy director) memorandum to James R. Riddleberger (ICA director), August 13, 1959, RG 59, 751G.oo/8–1359; and Durbrow to embassy in Saigon, tel. 293, August 15, 1959, RG 59, 751G.5–MSP/8–1559.

19. Elbridge Durbrow, interview by Congressional Research Service, October 25, 1978, quoted in Gibbons, *U.S. Government and the Vietnam War*, 1:326–27.

20. Mansfield interview with author.

21. Herter to Durbrow, tel. 971, November 23, 1959, RG 59, 751G.5–MSP/11–2359.

22. Saigon press and Radio Moscow quoted in Montgomery, *Politics of Foreign Aid*, pp. 233–35. See also Howard Elting, Jr., (counselor in Saigon embassy) to Herter, tel. 396, August 7, 1959, RG 59, 751G.5–MSP/8–759; Durbrow to Herter, tel. 575, August 22, 1959, RG 59, 751G.5–MSP/8–2259; and Herter memorandum to Eisenhower, August 25, 1959, RG 59, 751G.5–MSP/8–2559.

23. Durbrow to Herter, August 28, 1959, *FRUS, 1958–60,* 1:227–29. See also Durbrow to Herter, August 31, 1959, Durbrow to Herter, September 2, 1959, *ibid.,* 229–33; Durbrow to Herter, tel. G-43, September 18, 1959, RG 59, 751G.oo/9–1859; Durbrow to Herter, tel. G-56, October 19, 1959, RG 59, 751G.oo/10–1959; Fall, *Two Viet-Nams,* pp. 258–59; and Scigliano, *South Vietnam,* pp. 82–85.

24. Macomber to Javits, August 28, 1959, RG 59, 751G.oo/8–2459.

25. Durbrow to Dept. of State, March 2, 1960, *FRUS, 1958–60,* 1:297. See also Durbrow to Dept. of State, March 2, 1959, *ibid.,* 144–70; Herter to Durbrow, tel. 1028, December 3, 1959, RG 59, 751G.11/12–359; and Herter to Durbrow, tel. 1048, December 7, 1959, RG 59, 751G.11/12–759.

26. Ladejinsky to Fishel, March 1, 1960, box 28, Fishel Papers. See also Durbrow to Dept. of State, March 2, 1960, Durbrow to Herter, April 7, 1960, *FRUS, 1958–60,* 1:293–99, 375–77.

27. Fall, *Two Viet-Nams,* pp. 442–48; Montgomery, *Politics of Foreign Aid,* p. 312; H. Francis Cunningham, Jr. (chargé d'affaires in Saigon) to Herter, March 16, 1960, Durbrow to Herter, April 19, 1960, *FRUS, 1958–60,* 1:330–31, 404–6.

28. Duncanson, *Government and Revolution in Vietnam,* pp. 267–68, 282; Buttinger, *Vietnam,* 2:960–65; Hugh S. Cumming, Jr. (director of intelligence and research) memorandum to Dillon, May 3, 1960, Durbrow to Herter, May 9, 1960, *FRUS, 1958–60,* 1:438, 450–51.

29. Fishel wrote this letter to Diem in two parts, dated April 30 and May 2, 1960. It is in box 11, Fishel Papers. See also *New York Times,* May 1, 1960.

30. Williams to Col. R. E. Lawless, May 15, 1962, box 8, Williams Papers. For a similar judgment of Durbrow see Alsop (journalist) interview, pp. 10–13.

31. Williams to Lansdale, July 12, 1960, box 42, Lansdale Papers; Williams to Rev. Raymond J. De Jaegher, February 27, 1962, Williams to Adm. Felix Stump, October 26, 1962, Williams to Col. G. D. Jacobsen, November 5, 1962, box 8, Williams Papers.

32. Durbrow to Parsons, March 10, 1959, Williams to Tran Trung Dung (RVN assistant secretary of state for national defense), February 29, 1960, Durbrow to Parsons, April 19, 1960, Williams memorandum to Durbrow, June 1, 1960, Durbrow to Parsons, July 27, 1960, *FRUS, 1958–60,* 1:170–72, 291–93, 396–400, 471–73, 524–25; Thomas D. Bowie (counselor in Saigon embassy) to Dept. of State, desp. 245, January 26, 1959, RG 59, 751G.5/1–2659; Williams to De Jaegher, February 27, 1962, Williams to Lawless, May 15, 1962,

Williams Papers; *U.S. News and World Report,* September 12, 1964, November 9, 1964; Spector, *Advice and Support,* pp. 349–55.

33. Lansdale interview. See also Lansdale to Williams, March 18, 1960, *FRUS, 1958–60,* 1:324–25, n.3.

34. Durbrow to Richard E. Usher (acting director of Southeast Asian affairs), April 18, 1960, *FRUS, 1958–60,* 1:392–94. See also Lansdale to James H. Douglas (deputy secretary of defense), March 17, 1960, *ibid.,* 336–38.

35. Lansdale to Williams, April 30, 1960, *ibid.,* 425–26. See also Durbrow to Herter, April 22, 1960, *ibid.,* 409.

36. Lansdale to Williams, June 21, 1960, *ibid.,* 501–2. See also Chalmers B. Wood (officer in charge of Vietnam affairs) memorandum of conversation, May 13, 1960, and Durbrow to Herter, May 17, 1960, *ibid.,* 457–59, 462–63.

37. Durbrow to Herter, May 3, 1960, *ibid.,* 433–37.

38. Memorandum prepared in the Dept. of Defense, May 4, 1960, *ibid.,* 439–41.

39. Discussion at the 444th NSC meeting, May 9, 1960, *ibid.,* 446–47. See also Allen, *Korea's Syngman Rhee.*

40. Durbrow to Daniel V. Anderson (director of Southeast Asian affairs), July 18, 1960, *FRUS, 1958–60,* 1:514–15. See also Herter to Durbrow, May 9, 1960, and Durbrow to Herter, May 9, 1960, *ibid.,* 448–51.

41. Quoted in Spector, *Advice and Support,* p. 338. See also *ibid.,* pp. 337–48; Durbrow to Herter, August 30, 1960, *FRUS, 1958–60,* 1:544–47; and "Restive Political Situation in South Vietnam," August 29, 1960, RG 59, Intelligence Report No. 8325.

42. Durbrow to Herter, August 30, 1960, *FRUS, 1958–60,* 1:544–45.

43. Durbrow to Herter, September 16, 1960, *ibid.,* 575–79.

44. Lansdale memorandum to Rear Adm. Edward J. O'Donnell, September 20, 1960, *ibid.,* 579–85.

45. Editorial note, Dillon to Durbrow, October 7, 1960, Durbrow to Herter, October 15, 1960, *ibid.,* 585–86, 591–96.

46. Durbrow to Herter, November 3, 1960, *ibid.,* 622–25. See also Durbrow to Herter, October 20, 1960, and Herter memorandum to Eisenhower, October 20, 1960, *ibid.,* 605–8, 609–11.

47. Parsons to Durbrow, October 21, 1960, *ibid.,* 611–13.

48. Parsons to Durbrow, October 21, 1960, Durbrow to Parsons, November 8, 1960, Durbrow to Parsons, November 30, 1960, *ibid.,* 611–13, 626–27, 694–95.

49. Smith, *International History of the Vietnam War,* 1:238–40; Eisenhower, *Waging Peace,* pp. 607–8.

50. Eisenhower, *Waging Peace,* pp. 608–12; Hilsman, *To Move a Nation,* pp. 98, 105–26; Prados, *Presidents' Secret Wars,* pp. 261–67. See also Stevenson, *End of Nowhere.*

51. Durbrow to Herter, November 11, 1960, Lt. Col. Butler B. Toland (air attaché in Vietnam) to Lt. Gen. Isaac D. White (Air Force chief of staff), November 11, 1960, Durbrow to Herter, November 12, 1960, Lt. Gen. Lionel

C. McGarr (MAAG chief) to Adm. Harry D. Felt (commander-in-chief Pacific), November 12, 1960, *FRUS, 1958–60,* 1:632–39, 641–47, 649–52; Spector, *Advice and Support,* pp. 369–70; Colby and Forbath, *Honorable Men,* pp. 163–64; Karnow, *Vietnam,* pp. 235–37.

52. Elbridge Durbrow, interview by Dept. of State historian, April 2–May 4, 1984, quoted in *FRUS, 1958–60,* 1:663. See also Durbrow to Herter, November 11, 1960, and Lansdale to Thomas S. Gates, Jr. (secretary of defense), November 12, 1960, *ibid.,* 634–35, 653–54.

53. William Colby, interview by Dept. of State historian, January 6, 1984, quoted *ibid.,* 663.

54. Williams to Lansdale, January 19, 1961, box 42, Lansdale Papers.

55. Durbrow to Herter, November 17, 1960, *FRUS, 1958–60,* 1:670–72; Fishel memorandum to Mansfield, November 12, 1960, box 11, Fishel Papers; Gene Adrian Gregory (editor and publisher of *The Times of Vietnam*), "What Is behind the Buddhist Affair in Vietnam?" [1963], p. 12, box 11, Williams Papers; Colby and Forbath, *Honorable Men,* pp. 163–65; Karnow, *Vietnam,* pp. 236–37; Spector, *Advice and Support,* pp. 369–70.

56. For some examples of the direct impact of the 1960 coup attempt on later events see Sheehan, *Bright Shining Lie,* pp. 76–78, 122, 233; Hammer, *Death in November,* pp. 154–55, 166, 192, 287; and Chaffard, *Indochine,* pp. 182–83.

57. Lansdale to Gates, November 12, 1960, *FRUS, 1958–60,* 1:653. See also Durbrow to Herter, November 18, 1960, *ibid.,* 682–83.

58. Lansdale memorandum to Douglas, November 15, 1960, *ibid.,* 667–68.

59. Lansdale to Williams, December 23, 1960, box 8, Williams Papers. See also Durbrow to Herter, November 27, 1960, *FRUS, 1958–60,* 1:691–92; and Currey, *Lansdale,* pp. 210–16.

60. Lansdale to Williams, December 29, 1960, box 8, Williams Papers.

61. Durbrow to Herter, December 4, 1960, *FRUS, 1958–60,* 1:707–11. See also Durbrow to Herter, November 18, 1960, Herter to Durbrow, December 9, 1960, Durbrow to Herter, December 15, 1960, and Durbrow to Herter, December 24, 1960, *ibid.,* 683–85, 720–21, 731–32, 741–45; and Eisenhower, *Waging Peace,* pp. 608–14.

62. Parsons to Durbrow, December 31, 1960, *FRUS, 1958–60,* 1:751–52. See also Wood memorandum to Anderson, December 2, 1960, Dillon to Durbrow, December 16, 1960, John M. Steeves (deputy assistant secretary of state) to Durbrow, December 20, 1960, and Durbrow to Herter, December 29, 1960, *ibid.,* 705–7, 735–38, 749–50; and Williams to Lansdale, January 19, 1961, box 42, Lansdale Papers.

63. Lansdale to Williams, January 17, 1961, box 8, Williams Papers. See also Lansdale memorandum to secretary of defense and deputy secretary of defense, January 17, 1961, box 49, Lansdale Papers.

64. Clark Clifford (presidential adviser) memorandum to Lyndon Johnson, September 29, 1967, United States Department of Defense, *Pentagon Papers,* 2:635–37. See also Ambrose, *Eisenhower,* 2:614–15; and Schlesinger, *Thousand Days,* p. 299.

65. Wood notes on a meeting between Rusk and Parsons, January 28, 1961, *FRUS, 1961–63*, 1:19–20. See also Parsons summary of meeting at the White House, January 28, 1961, Walt W. Rostow (deputy special assistant for national security affairs) memorandum to McGeorge Bundy (special assistant for national security affairs), January 30, 1961, *ibid.*, 13–19; United States House of Representatives, Committee on Armed Services, *United States-Vietnam Relations*, 11:13; Lansdale to Williams, October 10, 1964, box 10, Williams Papers; Robert Shaplen to Lansdale, May 25, 1965, box 39, Lansdale Papers; Currey, *Lansdale*, pp. 222–29; and Spector, *Advice and Support*, p. 371.

9. Conclusion

1. Sheehan, *Bright Shining Lie*, p. 122.
2. Barrows interview.
3. Halberstam, *Best and the Brightest*, pp. 184–85; Shafer, *Deadly Paradigms*, pp. 251–54.
4. United States President, *Public Papers: Eisenhower, 1959*, pp. 311–13.
5. United States Department of State, *Bulletin* (November 14, 1960): 758. See also Graebner, *America as a World Power*, pp. 223–25.
6. Sheehan, *Bright Shining Lie*, pp. 92–93.
7. Scigliano, *South Vietnam*, p. 192; Billings-Yun, *Decision against War*, pp. 159–60.
8. United States President, *Public Papers: Johnson, 1965*, pp. 394–99. See also Kahin, *Intervention*, p. 66.
9. Memorandum of telephone conversation between Eisenhower and Johnson, July 2, 1965, box 10, Palm Desert-Indio series, Eisenhower Post-Presidential Papers. See also Ambrose, *Eisenhower*, 2:655–65.
10. See for example Lewy, *America in Vietnam;* and Podhoretz, *Why We Were in Vietnam*.
11. Burk, *Eisenhower Administration and Black Civil Rights*.
12. Kahin, *Intervention*, pp. 122–26; Ambrose, *Eisenhower*, 2:614–15; Goodpaster interview by Erwin, pp. 118–19, DDEL.
13. Fitzgerald, *Fire in the Lake*, p. 579; Gardner, *Approaching Vietnam*, pp. 126, 351; Brands, *Cold Warriors*, pp. 75, 87, 195–200; McMahon, "Eisenhower and Third World Nationalism," pp. 455–56, 460; Bui Diem (former RVN ambassador in Washington) interview.
14. Judd letter to author (Judd's italics).
15. Williams to Adm. Felix Stump (commander-in-chief Pacific), November 16, 1957, *FRUS, 1955–57*, 1:862.
16. Divine, "Vietnam Reconsidered," p. 92; Gelb and Betts, *Irony of Vietnam*, p. 363; Hoffman, *Primacy or World Order*, pp. 21–22.
17. Hammer, *Death in November*, p. 312; Shafer, *Deadly Paradigms*, pp. 271–75; Gardner, *Approaching Vietnam*, p. 353; Ambrose, *Eisenhower*, 2:622; Kahin, *Intervention*, pp. 33, 249, 399; Herring, *America's Longest War*, pp. 72, 279–80; Kolko, *Anatomy of a War*, p. 296.

BIBLIOGRAPHY

Manuscripts and Archives

Collins, Joseph Lawton, Papers (Vietnam File). Dwight D. Eisenhower Library, Abilene, Kans. (The Eisenhower Library will be abbreviated hereafter and in the notes as DDEL.)

Cooley, James. Letters to his family provided to the author by Cooley.

Donovan, William J., Papers. U.S. Army Military History Institute, Carlisle Barracks, Pa.

Dulles, John Foster, Papers. Chronological series, General Correspondence and Memoranda series, Subject series, Telephone Conversations series, White House Memoranda series. DDEL.

Dulles, John Foster, Papers. Princeton University Library, Princeton, N.J. (The Princeton University Library will be abbreviated hereafter and in the notes as PUL.)

Eisenhower, Dwight D., Papers. Ann Whitman File: Cabinet series, Diary series, Dulles-Herter series, International series, Legislative Meetings series, NSC series. DDEL.

Eisenhower, Dwight D., Pre-Presidential Papers. Name series. DDEL.

Eisenhower, Dwight D., Post-Presidential Papers. Palm Desert–Indio series. DDEL.

Fishel, Wesley R., Papers. Michigan State University Archives and Historical Collections, East Lansing, Mich.

Hagerty, James C., Papers. DDEL.

Hannah, John A., Records. Michigan State University Archives and Historical Collections, East Lansing, Mich.

Jackson, C. D., Records. DDEL.

Bibliography

Judd., Walter H. Letter to author, June 2, 1987.

Kidder, Randolph A. Unpublished manuscript provided to the author by Ambassador Kidder.

Lansdale, Edward G., Papers. Hoover Institution Archives, Stanford, Calif.

Mansfield, Michael J., Papers. Foreign Relations series. University of Montana Library, Missoula, Mont.

Records of President's Committee to Study the United States Military Assistance Program (Draper Committee). DDEL.

Records of the Office of the Special Assistant for National Security Affairs. NSC series, NSC Policy Papers series, Special Assistant series. DDEL.

Records of the White House Office. Office of the Staff Secretary: Cabinet series. DDEL.

SEA-RS [Southeast Asia-Ronald Spector] File. Center of Military History, Washington, D.C.

Smith, H. Alexander, Papers. PUL.

United States Department of State General Records. Record Group 59. National Archives, Washington, D.C.

United States Department of State Intelligence Reports. Record Group 59. National Archives, Washington, D.C.

United States Department of State Records of the Philippine and Southeast Asian Division. Country Files. Record Group 59. National Archives, Washington, D.C.

Vietnam Project. Michigan State University Archives and Historical Collections, East Lansing, Mich.

White House Central Files (Confidential File). Subject series. DDEL.

Williams, Samuel T., Papers. Hoover Institution Archives, Stanford, Calif.

Interviews and Oral Histories

Alsop, Joseph. Interview by Richard D. Challener, March 4, 1966. John Foster Dulles Oral History Project, PUL.

Anderson, Dillon. Interview by John Luther, December 30, 1969. Columbia University Oral History Project, DDEL.

Barrows, Leland. Interview with author. Washington, D.C., April 19, 1985.

Bui Diem. Interview with author. Fairfax, Va., July 1, 1987.

Bissell, Richard M., Jr. Interview by Richard D. Challener, September 7, 1966. John Foster Dulles Oral History Project, PUL.

Collins, J. Lawton. Interview by Richard D. Challener, January 13, 1966. John Foster Dulles Oral History Project, PUL.

—— Interview by U.S. Army Military History Institute, 1972. U.S. Army Military History Institute, Carlisle Barracks, Pa.

—— Interview with author. Washington, D.C., April 14, 1985.

Cooley, James. Interview with author. Washington, D.C., April 19, 1985.

Dillon, C. Douglas. Interview by John Luther, May 2 and June 28, 1972. Columbia University Oral History Project, DDEL.

—— Interview by Richard D. Challener, June 24, 1965. John Foster Dulles Oral History Project, PUL.

Eisenhower, Dwight D. Interview by Ed Erwin, July 20, 1967. Columbia University Oral History Project, DDEL.

—— Interview by Philip A. Crowl, July 28, 1964. John Foster Dulles Oral History Project, PUL.

Goodpaster, Andrew J. Interview by Ed Erwin, September 8, 1967. Columbia University Oral History Project, DDEL.

—— Interview by Richard D. Challener, January 11, 1966. John Foster Dulles Oral History Project, PUL.

—— Interview by Thomas Soapes, January 16, 1978. DDEL.

Hane, John W., Jr. Interview by Philip A. Crowl, January 29 and August 12, 1966. John Foster Dulles Oral History Project, PUL.

Hannah, John A. Interview with author. East Lansing, Mich., June 14, 1985.

"John Foster Dulles and the Far East: A Transcript of a Special Meeting of the Advisory Committee." July 17, 1964. John Foster Dulles Oral History Project, PUL.

Judd, Walter H. Interview with author. Washington, D.C., June 29, 1987.

Lansdale, Edward G. Interview with author. McLean, Va., June 25, 1986.

Larson, Arthur. Interview by Richard D. Challener, September 22, 1965. John Foster Dulles Oral History Project, PUL.

Mansfield, Michael J. Interview by Richard D. Challener, May 10, 1966. John Foster Dulles Oral History Project, PUL.

—— Interview with author. Tokyo, August 12, 1986.

Nixon, Richard. Interview by Richard D. Challener, March 5, 1965. John Foster Dulles Oral History Project, PUL.

O'Daniel, John W. Interview by Charles P. McDonald and Charles V. P. von Littichau, March 9, 1970, Center of Military History, Washington, D.C.

Radford, Arthur W. Interview by Philip A. Crowl, May 8, 1965. John Foster Dulles Oral History Project, PUL.

Reinhardt, G. Frederick. Interview by Philip A. Crowl, October 30, 1965. John Foster Dulles Oral History Project, PUL.

Smuckler, Ralph. Interview with author. East Lansing, Mich., June 10, 1985.

Turner, Ralph. Interview with author. East Lansing, Mich., June 12, 1985.

Twining, Nathan F. Interview by Philip A. Crowl, March 18, 1965. John Foster Dulles Oral History Project, PUL.

Newspapers and Periodicals

Cleveland Plain Dealer. 1971.

Le Monde. 1955.

Life. 1953, 1957.

New York Times. 1955–56, 1960, 1963.

Ramparts. 1965–66.

U.S. News and World Report. 1964.

Bibliography

Vietnam Presse. 1955.
Washington Post. 1963, 1982.

Books, Articles, and Dissertations

Adams, Sherman. *Firsthand Report: The Story of the Eisenhower Administration.* New York: Harper, 1961.

Alexander, Charles C. *Holding the Line: The Eisenhower Era, 1952–1961.* Bloomington: Indiana University Press, 1975.

Allen, Richard C. *Korea's Syngman Rhee: An Unauthorized Portrait.* Rutland, Vt.: Tuttle, 1960.

Ambrose, Stephen E. *Eisenhower.* 2 vols. New York: Simon & Schuster, 1983–84.

—— *Rise to Globalism: American Foreign Policy, 1938–1980.* 2d rev. ed. New York: Penguin, 1980.

Ambrose, Stephen E., with Richard H. Immerman. *Ike's Spies: Eisenhower and the Espionage Establishment.* Garden City, N.Y.: Doubleday, 1981.

Anderson, David L. "China Policy and Presidential Politics, 1952." *Presidential Studies Quarterly* (Winter 1980), 10:79–90.

Artaud, Denise. "Spring 1955: Crisis in Saigon." In Lawrence S. Kaplan, Denise Artaud, and Mark Rubin, eds., *Dien Bien Phu and the Crisis of Franco-American Relations, 1954–1955,* pp. 211–25. Wilmington, Del.: Scholarly Resources, 1990.

Bao Dai. *Le dragon d'Annam.* Paris: Plon, 1980.

Bator, Victor. *Vietnam: A Diplomatic Tragedy.* Dobbs Ferry, N.Y.: Oceana, 1965.

Billings-Yun, Melanie. *Decision Against War: Eisenhower and Dien Bien Phu, 1954.* New York: Columbia University Press, 1988.

Bloodworth, Dennis. *An Eye for the Dragon: Southeast Asia Observed, 1954–1970.* New York: Farrar, Straus & Giroux, 1970.

Blum, Robert M. *Drawing the Line: The Origin of the American Containment Policy in East Asia.* New York: Norton, 1982.

Braestrup, Peter, ed. *Vietnam as History: Ten Years after the Paris Peace Accords.* Washington, D.C.: University Press of America, 1984.

Brands, H. W., Jr. "The Age of Vulnerability: Eisenhower and the National Insecurity State." *American Historical Review* (October 1989), 94:963–89.

—— *Cold Warriors: Eisenhower's Generation and American Foreign Policy.* New York: Columbia University Press, 1988.

Bui Diem with David Chanoff. *In the Jaws of History.* Boston: Houghton Mifflin, 1987.

Burk, Robert. *The Eisenhower Administration and Black Civil Rights.* Knoxville: University of Tennessee Press, 1984.

Burke, John P., and Fred I. Greenstein, with the collaboration of Larry Berman and Richard Immerman. *How Presidents Test Reality: Decisions on Vietnam, 1954 and 1965.* New York: Russell Sage Foundation, 1989.

Buttinger, Joseph. *A Dragon Defiant: A Short History of Vietnam.* New York: Praeger, 1971.

—— *Vietnam: A Dragon Embattled.* 2 vols. New York: Praeger, 1967.

Cable, James. *The Geneva Conference of 1954 on Indochina.* New York: St. Martin's Press, 1986.

Cameron, Allen W., ed. *Vietnam Crisis: A Documentary History.* 2 vols. Ithaca, N.Y.: Cornell University Press, 1971.

Carlton, David. *Anthony Eden: A Biography.* London: Allen Lane, 1981.

Cave Brown, Anthony. *Wild Bill Donovan: The Last Hero.* New York: Times Books, 1982.

Césari, Laurent, and Jacques de Folin. "Military Necessity, Political Impossibility: The French Viewpoint on Operation *Vautour.*" In Lawrence S. Kaplan, Denise Artaud, and Mark Rubin, eds., *Dien Bien Phu and the Crisis of Franco-American Relations, 1954–1955,* pp. 105–20. Wilmington, Del.: Scholarly Resources, 1990.

Chaffard, Georges. *Indochine: dix ans d'indépendance.* Paris: Calmann-Lévy, 1964.

Challener, Richard D. "The National Security Policy from Truman to Eisenhower: Did the 'Hidden Hand' Leadership Make Any Difference?" In Norman A. Graebner, ed., *The National Security: Its Theory and Practice, 1945–1960,* pp. 39–75. New York: Oxford University Press, 1986.

Charlton, Michael, and Anthony Moncrieff. *Many Reasons Why: The American Involvement in Vietnam.* New York: Hill & Wang, 1978.

Colard, Daniel. *Edgar Faure.* Paris: Jean Dullis, 1975.

Colby, William, with Peter Forbath. *Honorable Men: My Life in the CIA.* New York: Simon & Schuster, 1978.

Collins, J. Lawton. *Lightning Joe: An Autobiography.* Baton Rouge: Louisiana State University Press, 1979.

Cooper, Chester L. *The Lost Crusade: America in Vietnam.* New York: Dodd, Mead, 1970.

Currey, Cecil B. *Edward Lansdale: The Unquiet American.* Boston: Houghton Mifflin, 1988.

Dawson, Francis N. "The 1954 Geneva Conference: Eisenhower's Indochina Policy." Ph.D. dissertation, West Virginia University, 1985.

Declassified Documents Reference Systems. Washington, D.C.: Carrollton Press, 1978.

De Santis, Vincent P. "Eisenhower Revisionism." *Review of Politics* (April 1976), 38:190–207.

Devillers, Philippe, and Jean Lacouture. *Viet Nam: de la guerre française à la guerre américaine.* Paris: Editions du Seuil, 1969. Translated by Alexander Lieven and Adam Roberts, under the title *End of a War: Indochina, 1954.* New York: Praeger, 1969.

Bibliography

Divine, Robert A. *Eisenhower and the Cold War*. New York: Oxford University Press, 1981.

—— *Since 1945: Politics and Diplomacy in Recent American History*. 2d ed. New York: Wiley, 1979.

—— "Vietnam Reconsidered." *Diplomatic History* (Winter 1988), 12:79–93.

Dooley, Thomas A. *Deliver Us from Evil: The Story of Viet Nam's Flight to Freedom*. New York: Farrar, Straus & Cudahy, 1956.

du Berrier, Hilaire. *Background to Betrayal: The Tragedy of Vietnam*. Boston: Western Islands, 1965.

Duiker, William J. *The Communist Road to Power in Vietnam*. Boulder, Colo.: Westview Press, 1981.

Dulles, Foster Rhea. *American Policy toward Communist China, 1949–1969*. New York: Crowell, 1972.

Duncanson, Dennis J. *Government and Revolution in Vietnam*. New York: Oxford University Press, 1968.

Eden, Anthony. *Full Circle: The Memoirs of Anthony Eden*. Boston: Houghton Mifflin, 1960.

Eisenhower, Dwight D. *Crusade in Europe*. Garden City, N.Y.: Doubleday, 1948.

—— *Mandate for Change, 1953–1956*. Garden City, N.Y.: Doubleday, 1963.

—— *Waging Peace, 1956–1961*. Garden City, N.Y.: Doubleday, 1965.

Ellsberg, Daniel. *Papers on the War*. New York: Simon & Schuster, 1972.

Ely, Paul. *Mémoires: L'Indochine dans la tourmente*. Paris: Plon, 1964.

Fall, Bernard B. *Hell in a Very Small Place*. Philadelphia: Lippincott, 1967.

—— *Last Reflections on a War*. Garden City, N.Y.: Doubleday, 1967.

—— "The Political-Religious Sects of Viet-Nam." *Pacific Affairs* (September 1955), 28:235–49.

—— *The Two Viet-Nams: A Political and Military Analysis*. Rev. ed. New York: Praeger, 1964.

—— *Viet-Nam Witness, 1953–66*. New York: Praeger, 1966.

Ferrell, Robert H., ed. *The Eisenhower Diaries*. New York: Norton, 1981.

Fifield, Russell H. *The Diplomacy of Southeast Asia: 1945–1958*. New York: Harper, 1958.

Fishel, Wesley R. "Vietnam's Democratic One-Man Rule." *The New Leader* (November 2, 1959): 10–13.

Fitzgerald, Frances. *Fire in the Lake: The Vietnamese and the Americans in Vietnam*. New York: Vintage Books, 1973.

Frédéric-Dupont, Edouard. *Mission de la France en Asie*. Paris: Editions France-Empire, 1956.

Gaddis, John L. *Strategies of Containment: A Critical Appraisal of Postwar American National Security Policy*. New York: Oxford University Press, 1982.

Gardner, Lloyd C. *Approaching Vietnam: From World War II through Dienbienphu, 1941–1954*. New York: Norton, 1988.

Gelb, Leslie H., with Richard K. Betts. *The Irony of Vietnam: The System Worked.* Washington, D.C.: Brookings Institution, 1979.

Gerson, Louis L. *John Foster Dulles.* In Robert H. Ferrell and Samuel Flagg Bemis, eds., *The American Secretaries of State and Their Diplomacy,* vol. 17. New York: Cooper Square, 1967.

Gibbons, William Conrad. *The U.S. Government and the Vietnam War: Executive and Legislative Roles and Relationships.* Part 1. *1945–1960.* Princeton, N.J.: Princeton University Press, 1986.

Goldman, Eric F. *The Crucial Decade—And After: America, 1945–1960.* New York: Vintage Books, 1960.

Gordon, Leonard H. D. "United States Opposition to Use of Force in the Taiwan Strait, 1954–1962." *Journal of American History* (December 1985), 72:637–60.

Graebner, Norman A. *America as a World Power: A Realist Appraisal from Wilson to Reagan.* Wilmington, Del.: Scholarly Resources, 1984.

Greenstein, Fred I. *The Hidden-Hand Presidency: Eisenhower as Leader.* New York: Basic Books, 1982.

Guhin, Michael A. *John Foster Dulles: A Statesman for His Times.* New York: Columbia University Press, 1972.

Gurtov, Melvin. *The First Vietnam Crisis: Chinese Communist Strategy and United States Involvement.* New York: Columbia University Press, 1967.

Halberstam, David. *The Best and the Brightest.* New York: Random House, 1972.

—— *Ho.* New York: Knopf, 1987.

—— *The Making of a Quagmire.* New York: Random House, 1964.

Hammer, Ellen J. *A Death in November: America in Vietnam, 1963.* New York: Oxford University Press, 1988.

—— *The Struggle for Indochina, 1940–1955.* Stanford, Calif.: Stanford University Press, 1966.

Herring, George C. "America and Vietnam: The Debate Continues." *American Historical Review* (April 1987), 92:350–62.

—— *America's Longest War: The United States and Vietnam, 1950–1975.* 2d ed. New York: Knopf, 1986.

—— " 'Peoples Quite Apart': Americans, South Vietnamese, and the War in Vietnam." *Diplomatic History* (Winter 1990), 14:1–23.

—— "The Truman Administration and the Restoration of French Sovereignty in Indochina." *Diplomatic History* (Spring 1977), 1:97–117.

—— "The 'Vietnam Syndrome' and American Foreign Policy." *Virginia Quarterly Review* (Autumn 1981), 57:594–612.

Herring, George C., and Richard H. Immerman. "Eisenhower, Dulles, and Dienbienphu: 'The Day We Didn't Go to War' Revisited." *Journal of American History* (September 1984), 71:343–63.

Hess, Gary R. "The First American Commitment in Indochina: The Acceptance of the 'Bao Dai Solution,' 1950." *Diplomatic History* (Fall 1978), 2:331–50.

Bibliography

Hess, Gary R. "Franklin D. Roosevelt and Indochina." *Journal of American History* (September 1972), 59:353–68.

—— "Redefining the American Position in Southeast Asia: The United States and the Geneva and Manila Conferences." In Lawrence S. Kaplan, Denise Artaud, and Mark R. Rubin, eds., *Dien Bien Phu and the Crisis of Franco-American Relations, 1954–1955*, pp. 123–48. Wilmington, Del.: Scholarly Resources, 1990.

—— *The United States' Emergence as a Southeast Asian Power, 1940–1950*. New York: Columbia University Press, 1987.

Hilsman, Roger. *To Move a Nation: The Politics of Foreign Policy in the Administration of John F. Kennedy*. Garden City, N.Y.: Doubleday, 1967.

Hixson, Walter L. "Containment on the Perimeter: George F. Kennan and Vietnam." *Diplomatic History* (Spring 1988), 12:149–63.

Hoffman, Stanley. *Primacy or World Order: American Foreign Policy since the Cold War*. New York: McGraw-Hill, 1978.

Hooper, Edwin B., Dean C. Allard, and Oscar P. Fitzgerald. *The United States Navy and the Vietnam Conflict*. Vol. 1. *The Setting of the Stage to 1959*. Washington, D.C.: GPO, 1976.

Hoopes, Townsend. *The Devil and John Foster Dulles*. Boston: Little, Brown, 1973.

Hughes, Emmet J. *The Ordeal of Power: A Political Memoir of the Eisenhower Years*. New York: Dell, 1962.

Immerman, Richard H. *The CIA in Guatemala: The Foreign Policy of Intervention*. Austin: University of Texas Press, 1982.

—— "Eisenhower and Dulles: Who Made the Decisions?" *Political Psychology* (Autumn 1979), 1:21–38.

—— "Perceptions by the United States of Its Interests in Indochina." In Lawrence S. Kaplan, Denise Artaud, and Mark R. Rubin, eds., *Dien Bien Phu and the Crisis of Franco-American Relations, 1954–1955*, pp. 1–26. Wilmington, Del.: Scholarly Resources, 1990.

—— "The United States and the Geneva Conference: A New Look." *Diplomatic History* (Winter 1990), 14:43–66.

Joes, Anthony J. "Eisenhower Revisionism and American Politics." In Joann P. Krieg, ed., *Dwight D. Eisenhower: Soldier, President, Statesman*, pp. 283–96. Westport, Conn.: Greenwood Press, 1987.

Johnson, U. Alexis, with Jef Olivarius McAllister. *The Right Hand of Power: The Memoirs of an American Diplomat*. Englewood Cliffs, N.J.: Prentice-Hall, 1984.

Joyaux, François. *La Chine et le règlement du premier conflit d'Indochine (Genève 1954)*. Paris: Publications de la Sorbonne, 1979.

Kahin, George McT. *Intervention: How America Became Involved in Vietnam*. New York: Knopf, 1986.

Kahin, George McT., and John W. Lewis. *The United States in Vietnam*. New York: Dial Press, 1967.

Karnow, Stanley. *Vietnam: A History*. New York: Viking Press, 1983.

Kattenburg, Paul M. "Reflections on Vietnam: Of Revisionism and Lessons Yet to Be Learned." *Parameters* (Autumn 1984), 14:42–50.

—— *The Vietnam Trauma in American Foreign Policy, 1945–1975.* New Brunswick, N.J.: Transaction Books, 1980.

Kaufman, Burton I. *Trade and Aid: Eisenhower's Foreign Economic Policy.* Baltimore: Johns Hopkins University Press, 1982.

Kelly, George A. *Lost Soldiers: The French Army and Empire in Crisis, 1947–1962.* Cambridge, Mass.: MIT Press, 1965.

Kimball, Jeffrey P., ed. *To Reason Why: The Debate about the Causes of U.S. Involvement in the Vietnam War.* New York: McGraw-Hill, 1990.

Kinnard, Douglas. "Civil-Military Relations: The President and the General." In Norman A. Graebner, ed., *The National Security: Its Theory and Practice, 1945–1960,* pp. 199–225. New York: Oxford University Press, 1986.

—— *President Eisenhower and Strategy Management: A Study in Defense Politics.* Lexington: University Press of Kentucky, 1977.

Kolko, Gabriel. *Anatomy of a War: Vietnam, the United States, and the Modern Historical Experience.* New York: Pantheon, 1985.

Lacouture, Jean. *Pierre Mendès France.* Translated by George Holoch. New York: Holmes and Mier, 1984.

—— *Vietnam: Between Two Truces.* Translated by Konrad Kellen and Joel Carmichael. New York: Vintage Books, 1966.

LaFeber, Walter. *America, Russia, and the Cold War, 1945–1984.* 5th ed. New York: Knopf, 1985.

—— "The Last War, the Next War, and the New Revisionists." *democracy* (January 1981), 1:93–103.

—— "Roosevelt, Churchill and Indochina, 1942–1945." *American Historical Review* (December 1975), 80:1277–95.

Lansdale, Edward G. *In the Midst of Wars: An American's Mission to Southeast Asia.* New York: Harper & Row, 1972.

—— "Thoughts about a Past War." In Allan R. Millett, ed., *A Short History of the Vietnam War,* pp. vi–xiv. Bloomington: Indiana University Press, 1978.

Lederer, William J., and Eugene Burdick. *The Ugly American.* New York: Norton, 1958.

Lewy, Guenter. *America in Vietnam.* New York: Oxford University Press, 1978.

Lomperis, Timothy J. *The War Everyone Lost—and Won: American Intervention in Viet Nam's Twin Struggles.* Washington, D.C.: CQ Press, 1987.

Lyon, Peter. *Eisenhower: Portrait of a Hero.* Boston: Little, Brown, 1974.

McAlister, John T., Jr. *Vietnam: The Origins of Revolution.* Garden City, N.Y.: Doubleday, 1971.

McAlister, John T., Jr., and Paul Mus. *The Vietnamese and Their Revolution.* New York: Harper & Row, 1970.

McAuliffe, Mary S. "Eisenhower, the President." *Journal of American History* (December 1981), 68:625–32.

McClintock, Robert. *The Meaning of Limited War.* Boston: Houghton Mifflin, 1967.

Bibliography

McMahon, Robert J. "Eisenhower and Third World Nationalism: A Critique of the Revisionists." *Political Science Quarterly* (Fall 1986), 101:453–73.

Machiavelli, Niccolo. *The Prince*. Translated by Luigi Ricci and revised by E. R. P. Vincent. New York: New American Library, 1952.

Matray, James I. *The Reluctant Crusade: American Foreign Policy in Korea, 1941–1950*. Honolulu: University of Hawaii Press, 1985.

May, Ernest P. *The Truman Administration and China, 1945–1949*. Philadelphia: Lippincott, 1975.

Mélandri, Pierre. "The Repercussions of the Geneva Conference: South Vietnam under a New Protector." In Lawrence S. Kaplan, Denise Artaud, and Mark R. Rubin, eds., *Dien Bien Phu and the Crisis of Franco-American Relations, 1954–1955*, pp. 197–210. Wilmington, Del.: Scholarly Resources, 1990.

Melanson, Richard A. "The Foundations of Eisenhower's Foreign Policy: Continuity, Community, and Consensus." In Richard A. Melanson and David Myers, eds., *Reevaluating Eisenhower: American Foreign Policy in the Fifties*, pp. 31–64. Urbana: University of Illinois Press, 1987.

Millet, Allen R., ed. *A Short History of the Vietnam War*. Bloomington: Indiana University Press, 1978.

Montgomery, John D. *The Politics of Foreign Aid: American Experience in Southeast Asia*. New York: Praeger, 1967.

Mueller, John E. *War, Presidents and Public Opinion*. New York: Wiley, 1973. Reprint. Lanham, Md.: University Press of America, 1985.

Nelson, Anna K. "John Foster Dulles and the Bipartisan Congress." *Political Science Quarterly* (Spring 1987), 102:43–55.

—— "The 'Top of the Policy Hill': President Eisenhower and the National Security Council." *Diplomatic History* (Fall 1983), 7:307–26.

Nixon, Richard. *No More Vietnams*. New York: Arbor House, 1985.

—— *RN: The Memoirs of Richard Nixon*. New York: Grosset & Dunlap, 1978.

O'Daniel, John W. *The Nation That Refused to Starve: The Challenge of the New Vietnam*. New York: Coward-McCann, 1960.

Parmet, Herbert S. *Eisenhower and the American Crusades*. New York: Macmillan, 1972.

Paterson, Thomas G. "Historical Memory and Illusive Victories: Vietnam and Central America." *Diplomatic History* (Winter 1988), 12:1–18.

Pemberton, Gregory J. "Australia, the United States, and the Indochina Crisis of 1954." *Diplomatic History* (Winter 1989), 13:45–66.

Pike, Douglas. *Viet Cong: The Organization and Techniques of the National Liberation Front of Vietnam*. Cambridge, Mass.: MIT Press, 1966.

Podhoretz, Norman. *Why We Were in Vietnam*. New York: Simon & Schuster, 1982.

Porter, Gareth, ed. *Vietnam: A History in Documents*. New York: New American Library, 1981.

Prados, John. *Presidents' Secret Wars: CIA and Pentagon Covert Operations since World War II*. New York: Morrow, 1986.

—— *The Sky Would Fall: Operation Vulture: The Secret U.S. Bombing Mission to Vietnam, 1954.* New York: Dial Press, 1983.

President's Committee to Study the United States Military Assistance Program. *Composite Report.* 2 vols. Washington, D.C.: GPO, 1959.

Prouty, L. Fletcher. *The Secret Team: The CIA and Its Allies in Control of the United States and the World.* Englewood Cliffs, N.J.: Prentice-Hall, 1973.

Pruessen, Ronald W. *John Foster Dulles: The Road to Power.* New York: Free Press, 1982.

Rabe, Stephen G. *Eisenhower and Latin America: The Foreign Policy of Anti-communism.* Chapel Hill: University of North Carolina Press, 1988.

Race, Jeffrey. *War Comes to Long An: Revolutionary Conflict in a Vietnamese Province.* Berkeley: University of California Press, 1972.

Radford, Arthur W. *From Pearl Harbor to Vietnam: The Memoirs of Admiral Arthur W. Radford.* Edited by Stephen Jurika, Jr. Stanford, Calif.: Hoover Institution Press, 1980.

Randle, Robert F. *Geneva 1954: The Settlement of the Indochina War.* Princeton, N.J.: Princeton University Press, 1969.

Ravenal, Earl C. *Never Again: Learning from America's Foreign Policy Failures.* Philadelphia: Temple University Press, 1978.

Reichard, Gary. "The Domestic Politics of National Security." In Norman A. Graebner, ed., *The National Security: Its Theory and Practice, 1945–1960,* pp. 243–74. New York: Oxford University Press, 1986.

—— *Politics as Usual: The Age of Truman and Eisenhower.* Arlington Heights, Ill.: Harlan Davidson, 1988.

—— *The Reaffirmation of Republicanism: Eisenhower and the Eighty-Third Congress.* Knoxville: University of Tennessee Press, 1975.

Ridgway, Matthew B. *Soldier: The Memoirs of Matthew B. Ridgway.* New York: Harper, 1956.

Roberts, Chalmers M. "The Day We Didn't Go to War." *Reporter* (September 14, 1954), 11:31–35.

Rosenberg, David Alan. "The Origins of Overkill: Nuclear Weapons and American Strategy." In Norman A. Graebner, ed., *The National Security: Its Theory and Practice, 1945–1960,* pp. 123–95. New York: Oxford University Press, 1986.

Rotter, Andrew J. *The Path to Vietnam: Origins of the American Commitment to Southeast Asia.* Ithaca, N.Y.: Cornell University Press, 1987.

Rouanet, Pierre. *Mendès France au pouvoir.* Paris: Robert Laffont, 1965.

Roy, Jules. *The Battle of Dien Bien Phu.* New York: Harper & Row, 1965.

Ruscio, Alain. "Le Mendèsisme et l'Indochine." *Revue d'histoire moderne et contemporaine* (April-June 1982), 29:324–42.

Saunders, Richard M. "Military Force in the Foreign Policy of the Eisenhower Presidency." *Political Science Quarterly* (Spring 1985), 100:97–116.

Scheer, Robert. *How the United States Got Involved in Vietnam.* Santa Barbara, Calif.: Center for the Study of Democratic Institutions, 1965.

Bibliography

Schlesinger, Arthur M. *The Bitter Heritage: Vietnam and American Democracy, 1941–1966.* Boston: Houghton Mifflin, 1967.

Schlesinger, Arthur M. *The Cycles of American History.* Boston: Houghton Mifflin, 1986.

—— *A Thousand Days: John F. Kennedy in the White House.* Boston: Houghton Mifflin, 1965.

Scigliano, Robert. *South Vietnam: Nation under Stress.* Boston: Houghton Mifflin, 1963.

Scigliano, Robert, and Guy H. Fox. *Technical Assistance in Vietnam: The Michigan State University Experience.* New York: Praeger, 1965.

Scribner, Charles R. "The Eisenhower and Johnson Administrations' Decision-making on Vietnamese Intervention: A Study of Contrasts." Ph.D. dissertation, University of California, Santa Barbara, 1980.

Shafer, D. Michael. *Deadly Paradigms: The Failure of U.S. Counterinsurgency Policy.* Princeton, N.J.: Princeton University Press, 1988.

Shaplen, Robert. *The Lost Revolution.* New York: Harper & Row, 1965.

Sheehan, Neil. *A Bright Shining Lie: John Paul Vann and America in Vietnam.* New York: Random House, 1988.

Smith, R. B. *An International History of the Vietnam War.* Vol. 1. *Revolution versus Containment, 1955–61.* New York: St. Martin's Press, 1983.

Spanier, John. *American Foreign Policy since World War II.* 11th ed. Washington, D.C.: CQ Press, 1988.

Spector, Ronald H. *The United States Army in Vietnam: Advice and Support: The Early Years, 1941–1960.* Washington, D.C.: GPO, 1983.

Sperlich, Peter W., and William L. Lunch. "American Public Opinion and the War in Vietnam." *Western Political Quarterly* (March 1979), 32:21–44.

Stevenson, Charles A. *The End of Nowhere: American Policy toward Laos since 1954.* Boston: Beacon Press, 1972.

Sullivan, Marianna P. *France's Vietnam Policy: A Study of French-American Relations.* Westport, Conn.: Greenwood Press, 1978.

Summers, Harry G., Jr. *On Strategy: A Critical Analysis of the Vietnam War.* Novato, Calif.: Presidio Press, 1982.

A Symposium on America's Stake in Vietnam. New York: American Friends of Vietnam, 1956.

Thompson, Kenneth W. "The Strengths and Weaknesses of Eisenhower's Leadership." In Richard A. Melanson and David Myers, eds., *Reevaluating Eisenhower: American Foreign Policy in the Fifties,* pp. 13–30. Urbana: University of Illinois Press, 1987.

Thompson, W. Scott, and Donaldson D. Frizzell, eds. *The Lessons of Vietnam.* New York: Crane, Russak, 1977.

Thorne, Christopher. "Indochina and Anglo-American Relations, 1942–1945." *Pacific Historical Review* (February 1976), 45:73–96.

Toulouse, Mark G. *The Transformation of John Foster Dulles: From Prophet of Realism to Priest of Nationalism.* Macon, Ga.: Mercer University Press, 1985.

Tran Van Don. *Our Endless War: Inside Vietnam*. San Rafael, Calif.: Presidio Press, 1978.

Ulam, Adam B. *The Rivals: America and Russia since World War II*. New York: Viking Press, 1971.

United States Department of Defense. *The Pentagon Papers: The Defense Department History of United States Decision Making on Vietnam*. Senator Gravel edition. 4 vols. Boston: Beacon Press, 1971.

United States Department of State. *Bulletin*. Washington, D.C.: GPO, 1953–61.

—— *Foreign Relations of the United States, 1950*. Vol. 1. *National Security Affairs; Foreign Economic Policy*. Washington, D.C.: GPO, 1977. (*Foreign Relations of the United States* will be hereafter abbreviated and cited in the notes as *FRUS*.)

—— *FRUS, 1952–1954*. Vol. 12. *East Asia and the Pacific*. Washington, D.C.: GPO, 1984.

—— *FRUS, 1952–1954*. Vol. 13. *Indochina*. Washington, D.C.: GPO, 1982.

—— *FRUS, 1952–1954*. Vol. 16. *The Geneva Conference*. Washington, D.C.: GPO, 1981.

—— *FRUS, 1955–1957*. Vol. 1. *Vietnam*. Washington, D.C.: GPO, 1985.

—— *FRUS, 1955–1957*. Vol. 9. *Foreign Economic Policy; Foreign Information Programs*. Washington, D.C.: GPO, 1987.

—— *FRUS, 1958–1960*. Vol. 1. *Vietnam*. Washington, D.C.: GPO, 1986.

—— *FRUS, 1961–1963*. Vol. 1. *Vietnam, 1961*. Washington, D.C.: GPO, 1988.

—— *A Threat to the Peace: North Viet-Nam's Effort to Conquer South Viet-Nam*. Washington, D.C.: GPO, 1961.

United States House of Representatives. Committee on Armed Services. *United States-Vietnam Relations, 1945–1967: Study Prepared by the Department of Defense*. 12 vols. Washington, D.C.: GPO, 1971.

United States President. *Public Papers of the Presidents of the United States: Dwight D. Eisenhower, 1953–59*. 7 vols. Washington, D.C.: GPO, 1958–60.

—— *Public Papers of the Presidents of the United States: Lyndon B. Johnson, 1965*. Washington, D.C.: GPO, 1966.

United States Senate. Committee on Foreign Relations. *Executive Sessions of the Senate Foreign Relations Committee (Historical Series)*. Vol. 5. 83d Cong., 1st sess., 1953. Washington, D.C.: GPO, 1977.

—— *Executive Sessions of the Senate Foreign Relations Committee (Historical Series)*. Vol. 6. 83d Cong., 2d sess., 1954. Washington, D.C.: GPO, 1977.

—— *Executive Sessions of the Senate Foreign Relations Committee (Historical Series)*. Vol. 8. 84th Cong., 2d sess., 1956. Washington, D.C.: GPO, 1978.

—— *Report on Indochina: Report of Senator Mike Mansfield on a Study Mission to Vietnam, Cambodia, Laos, October 15, 1954*. Washington, D.C.: GPO, 1954.

—— *Vietnam, Cambodia, and Laos: Report by Senator Mike Mansfield, October 6, 1955*. Washington, D.C.: GPO, 1955.

Bibliography

—— *The Vietnam Hearings*. New York: Random House, 1966.

von der Mehden, Fred R. *South-East Asia, 1930–1970: The Legacy of Colonialism and Nationalism*. New York: Norton, 1974.

Warner, Denis. *The Last Confucian*. New York: Macmillan, 1963.

Warner, Geoffrey. "Britain and the Crisis over Dien Bien Phu, April 1954: The Failure of United Action." In Lawrence S. Kaplan, Denise Artaud, and Mark R. Rubin, eds., *Dien Bien Phu and the Crisis of Franco-American Relations, 1954–1955*, pp. 55–77. Wilmington, Del.: Scholarly Resources, 1990.

Weigley, Russell F. *The American Way of War: A History of United States Military Strategy and Policy*. Bloomington: Indiana University Press, 1977.

—— *History of the United States Army*. Enlarged edition. Bloomington: Indiana University Press, 1984.

Williams, William A., Thomas McCormick, Lloyd Gardner, and Walter LaFeber, eds. *America in Vietnam: A Documentary History*. New York: Norton, 1985.

Wise, David, and Thomas B. Ross. *The Invisible Government*. New York: Random House, 1964.

INDEX

Index

Index

Index

Index